D'Nealian® Handwriting

K

Teacher's Edition

Author
Donald Neal Thurber

Editorial Offices: Glenview, Illinois • New York, New York
Sales Offices: Reading, Massachusetts • Atlanta, Georgia
Glenview, Illinois • Carrollton, Texas • Menlo Park, California

1-800-552-2259
http://www.sf.aw.com

Author

Donald Neal Thurber
Former Principal and Curriculum Director
Gibraltar School System
Rockwood, Michigan

Educational Consultants

Mimi Brodsky Chenfeld
Creative Movement
Columbus, Ohio

Joan Eich
Special Needs and Learning Styles
Teacher Consultant
Ottawa, Illinois

Anthony D. Fredericks, Ed.D.
Home-School Involvement
Assistant Professor
York College
York, Pennsylvania

Dale R. Jordan Ph.D.
Director, Jones Learning Center
University of the Ozarks
Clarksville, Arkansas

Ngoc-Diep T. Nguyen, Ph.D.
Cultural Diversity
Illinois Resource Center
Des Plaines, Illinois

Barbara Troolin, Ph.D.
Special Populations
Manager for the Office of
Compliance/Equal Opportunities
Department of Education
St. Paul, Minnesota

Betty J. C. Wright
Introducing D'Nealian® Handwriting
Teacher, Bodine Elementary School
Oklahoma City, Oklahoma

Sharon Hughes and Cheryl Williams
Writing Centers
Teachers, Meadow Glens Elementary School
Naperville, Illinois

We thank:
The students of Meadow Glens Elementary School in Naperville, Illinois, for their contributions to the Writing Center photos and projects.
The staff and children of Days of Creation Arts Programs, Columbus, Ohio, for their part in *Ready, Eager, and Waiting.*

Illustrations
Marika Hahn 40, 42, 45, 48, 49, 50, 55, 57, 61, 64, 65, 67, 68, 69, 72, 79, 84, 87, 91, 95, 100, 107, 109, 110, 119, 129, 134, 136, 139, 142, 143, 145, 148, 153, 156, 161, 163, 165; **Joe Rogers** 10, 19, 31, 32, 33, 34, 43, 47, 51, 52, 54, 58, 60, 70, 71, 73, 74, 76, 78, 80, 81, 82, 85, 86, 89, 94, 104, 111, 114, 120, 126, 127, 132, 133, 137, 138, 140, 144, 146, 147, 149, 150, 151, 154, 155, 158, 159, 162, 164, 166, 167; **Phyllis Tarlow** 12, 16, 17, 27, 38; **Jack Wallen** 93, 98, 102, 103, 105, 108, 112, 115, 116, 117, 123, 124, 125, 128

Photographs
Unless otherwise credited, all photographs are the property of Addison Wesley Educational Publishers Inc.

Bill Connelly T35–T36; **Phyllis Fredericks** T27, 5A; **Larry Hamill** T29–T31; **Allen Zak** for Days of Creation, T57–T74, 101A

ISBN: 0-673-59219-7

789ARK

Reader Consultants

Joyce Alexander
Bellerive Elementary School
St. Louis, Missouri

Jurodell Brown-Banks
Foerster Elementary School
Houston, Texas

Sr. June Canoles, S.N.D.
Cupertino, California

June Chikasuye
Instructional Materials Director
San Lorenzo Unified School District
San Lorenzo, California

Donna Drake
Summit Drive Elementary School
Greenville, South Carolina

Donna Eicher
Stanwood School
New Stanton, Pennsylvania

Rick Guiterrez
Harmony Hills Elementary School
San Antonio, Texas

Sherry Kent
Fairfield Intermediate School
Fairfield, Texas

Sharon Lewis
Mary Orr Intermediate School
Mansfield, Texas

Joyce Massey
Sycamore Elementary School
Fort Worth, Texas

Donald McIlvaine
Bovard Elementary School
Greensburg, Pennsylvania

Debby Pegram
Piney Grove School
Kernerville, North Carolina

Sheila Rojas
Curriculum Coordinator
Washoe County School District
Reno, Nevada

Shirley Smallwood
Bishop Elementary School
Fort Worth, Texas

Charlene Taite
Hainerberg Elementary School
(Department of Defense)
Wiesbaden, Germany

Mercedes Torres
Mary Fogerty Elementary School
Providence, Rhode Island

Judy Underhill
Oak Grove Middle School
Clearwater, Florida

Lois Vogel
David Turnham Elementary School
Dale, Indiana

Eleanor Weatherby
North Waco Elementary School
Waco, Texas

Teacher Contributors

The following teachers contributed activities to the Activity Banks in the D'Nealian® Teacher's Edition. We acknowledge them with gratitude.

Karen Anderson
Monrovia, Indiana
Debbi Anderson
Maple Grove, Minnesota
Larissa Antaramian
Glenview, Illinois
Roslyn Arneson
Lake Norden, South Dakota
Janice G. Barel
Utica, Michigan
Alyson Bass
Lake Jackson, Texas
Diann Bates
Roeland Park, Kansas
Susan Bell
Sharon, Wisconsin
Jane P. Bergman
Scandia, Minnesota
Patricia J. Berryman
Fresno, California
Shirley Black
Shawnee, Kansas
James J. Bolton
Danville, Illinois
Eileen Brothers
Albany, New York
Roxann Brown
Mullen, Nebraska
Joyce Brownsberger
Louisville, Ohio
Elizabeth Purvis Bruguiere
Massies Mill, Virginia
Pam Buffett
Evanston, Illinois
Audrey Burkhalter
Kokomo, Indiana
Patricia A. Burnaford
East Detroit, Michigan
R. Sue Buttrick
South Jacksonville, Illinois
Marci Cain
Lost Springs, Kansas
Paula Cannon
Ocala, Florida
Nancy Caton
Woodridge, Illinois
Sheryl Chenault
Dallas, Texas
Betty Collett
Fort Smith, Arkansas
Linda Coltrane
McCune, Kansas
Jane Connor
Edgerton, Wisconsin
Carol Conover
Wayne, Pennsylvania
Kim Cornelius
Martinsville, Texas
Raleen Cox
Olathe, Kansas
Laura Craig
Battle Creek, Michigan
Jean Cross
Chanute, Kansas
Miriam Cyprus
Colorado Springs, Colorado
Colleen Dannenhauer
Ewing, Missouri
Etta L. Davenport
Old Town, Maine
Marjorie Davis
Chanute, Kansas
Evangelina Reyna De La Rosa
Lyford, Texas
Mary Lou Dohrwardt
Jackson, Wisconsin
Denise Downhour
Cottage Grove, Minnesota
Marian Edson
Scarsdale, New York
Aida A. Edstrom
Maplewood, Minnesota
Gina Elfstrom
Pasadena, Texas
Suzanna Elguea
El Paso, Texas
Jayne Embree
Franklinville, North Carolina
Lorraine Fabian
Graytown, Ohio
Roberta Feddersen
Napa, California
Carol Ferry
Glenshaw, Pennsylvania
Janet Fiandt
Goshen, Indiana
Diane Fioretti
Burlington, Connecticut
Lora Fisher
Mt. Hope, Kansas
Brenda M. Fisher
Zachary, Louisiana

Vickie Foreman
San Angelo, Texas
Judi Forsee
Clarksville, Indiana
Lynn Fortman
Lucas, Ohio
Carolyn Garvaglia
Niagara, Wisconsin
Marjorie Gaskill
Volborg, Montana
Bonnie L. Gaynor
Franklin, New Jersey
Janis A. Giblin
Oak Creek, Wisconsin
Cathy Gillit
Abilene, Texas
Marly Glaw
Marietta, Georgia
Ann Godorhazy
Columbus, Ohio
Carol Goetz
Waterloo, Iowa
Kathy Graves
Bovina, Texas
Josephine Gregory
Fairfield, North Dakota
Barbara Gribben
Florence, Colorado
Anita Griffin
Lancaster, Texas
Darlene Gustafson
Glendale Heights, Illinois
Carol Hahn
San Angelo, Texas
Margaret W. Haney
Plain City, Ohio
Barbara J. Hansmeier
Jacksonville, Illinois
Donna Hartman
Ambler, Pennsylvania
Leann Hartman
Quapaw, Oklahoma
Susan Haskell
Forked River, New Jersey
Mary G. Heine
West Bend, Wisconsin
Pam Herrmann
Alamosa, Colorado
Lori Herron
San Angelo, Texas
Carole Hickins
Waterloo, Iowa
Nancy Hill
Pea Ridge, Arkansas
Paula Horton
Chancellor, South Dakota
Penny Huempfner
Cadott, Wisconsin
Jane M. Iken
Milbank, South Dakota
Teri Ingram
Topeka, Kansas
Elizabeth Jack
Vacaville, California
Roberta Jelniker
Frisco, Colorado
Dana Lee Johnson
Chesterfield, Missouri

Marilou Johnson
Lock Haven, Pennsylvania
Janet Johnson
Findlay, Ohio
Linda G. Johnson
Evanston, Illinois
Carolyn Jones
Richardson, Texas
Janice Kane
St. Helena, California
Joan Kendzior
Medinah, Illinois
Karla Kensey
Hilliard, Ohio
Mary Ellen Kessler
Trenton, New Jersey
Kathy Kettman
Waukegan, Illinois
Audrey E. Kithcart
Kingston, New York
Maureen Knoernschild
Whitefish Bay, Wisconsin
Marilyn Knudson
Englewood, Colorado
Linda Kotula
Perrysburg, Ohio
Judy Kralik
Woodridge, Illinois
Diane Lane
Hilliard, Ohio
Cyrie Fagan Lange
Thetford, Vermont
Belinda Lavender
San Antonio, Texas
Melissa Leftwich
Crested Butte, Colorado
Monica Lehnen
Evart, Michigan
Vonda Lichtenfelt
Fraser, Michigan
Juel Liebke
Sierra Vista, Arizona
Rosemary Logan
Las Vegas, Nevada
Rosemary Lohndorf
Boulder, Colorado
Elizabeth Luck
Disputanta, Virginia
Nancy R. Martin
Omaha, Nebraska
Mary L. May
Moro, Illinois
Janice McCauley
New Albany, Indiana
Marion J. McCreary
King of Prussia, Pennsylvania
Marshall McKee
Belleville, Illinois
Cam Miller
Black Hawk, South Dakota
Priscilla Miller
Harper Woods, Michigan
Connie Moeller
Grand Island, Nebraska
Fran Moore
Lake Forest, Illinois
Carol A. Morris
East Prairie, Missouri

Joyce Morrison
Martinsville, Texas
DeMetrice Muhammad
Chicago, Illinois
Betty Neal
Sandy, Utah
Penny L. New
Galena, Kansas
Barbara Norman
Bakersfield, California
Anne K. O'Brien
Denver, Colorado
Jean Omolecki
Ottawa, Illinois
Linda Paavola
Lake Geneva, Wisconsin
Janette Peacock
Maryland Heights, Missouri
Chris Perry
Lapeer, Michigan
Cynthia A. Phillips
Colbert, Georgia
Sheridan Pierson
Onamia, Minnesota
Sandra Pollock
Skokie, Illinois
Lea Rae Porta
Lowry City, Missouri
Sarah Puett
Houston, Texas
Joanna Ransom
Amherst, New York
Ann Renner
Eden Prairie, Minnesota
Cindy Renzelman
Graymont, Illinois
Sandy Rissler
Reelsville, Indiana
Karen Ruple
Wyoming, Michigan
Marilyn Sams
San Angelo, Texas
Melody Searle
Olathe, Colorado
Mary Seipkes
Wadena, Minnesota
Anita Skop
Brooklyn, New York
Ingeborg Smith
Rockford, Michigan
Sue Smith
Edmund, Oklahoma
Ellen Smyser
Granger, Iowa
Barbara Snowberger
Lehighton, Pennsylvania
Carol A. Solberg
Blair, Wisconsin
Mary Louise Sonnenburg
Stockton, California
Jo Ann M. Spear
Weldon, Iowa
Terri Steffes
Columbia, Missouri
Cheryl Stelter
W. Charleston, Vermont
Ann Stowell
Gunnison, Colorado

Kathleen V. Sullivan
Pembroke, Massachusetts
Sandy Szymkowiak
Toledo, Ohio
Geraldine Taft
Loa, Utah
Sharon Talasek
West Columbia, Texas
Karen Tebbenhoff
Arnold, Missouri
Victoria D. Therrien
Auburn, New Hampshire
Janet Thomas-Perkins
Scarsdale, New York
Cindy Trantham
Richardson, Texas
Delphine Tremback
Chicago, Illinois
Ann Underwood
Jeffersonville, Indiana
Marge Uricchio
Bradford Woods, Pennsylvania
Ruth Van Matre
Delphi, Indiana
Beverly M. Vest
McKinney, Texas
Helen Villarreal
San Antonio, Texas
Mary Lee Vitton
Omaha, Nebraska
Lois R. Vogel
Dale, Indiana
Kimberly Wachenheim
Chandler, Arizona
Dona Wallen
Clark, South Dakota
Janie Walters
Sublette, Kansas
Raanne Wavra
East Grand Forks, Minnesota
Alyce J. Wehrenberg
La Crosse, Wisconsin
Suzann Westermann
San Antonio, Texas
Tess Wickett
Ames, Nebraska
Mary Jo Williams
Hamlet, Indiana
Amy Wolf
Hilliard, Ohio
Pam Yeary
Orlando, Florida

Contents

D'Nealian® Handwriting

- **Solid Foundation for Legibility**
- **Transition Easy As 1-2-3**
- **Resources to Meet All Needs**

Scott Foresman-Addison Wesley

D'Nealian® Handwriting

S F A W

3

Grades K–6

D'Nealian® Handwriting—A Better Way!

D'Nealian® Handwriting, the innovative, continuous-stroke method of teaching children to write, was introduced by Scott Foresman in 1978. Since that time, teachers in classrooms around the world have confirmed our research—the D'Nealian method is an effective way to teach handwriting! The D'Nealian style is what makes the difference.

Continuous stroke means fewer pencil lifts than ball-and-stick so there are fewer chances for mistakes.

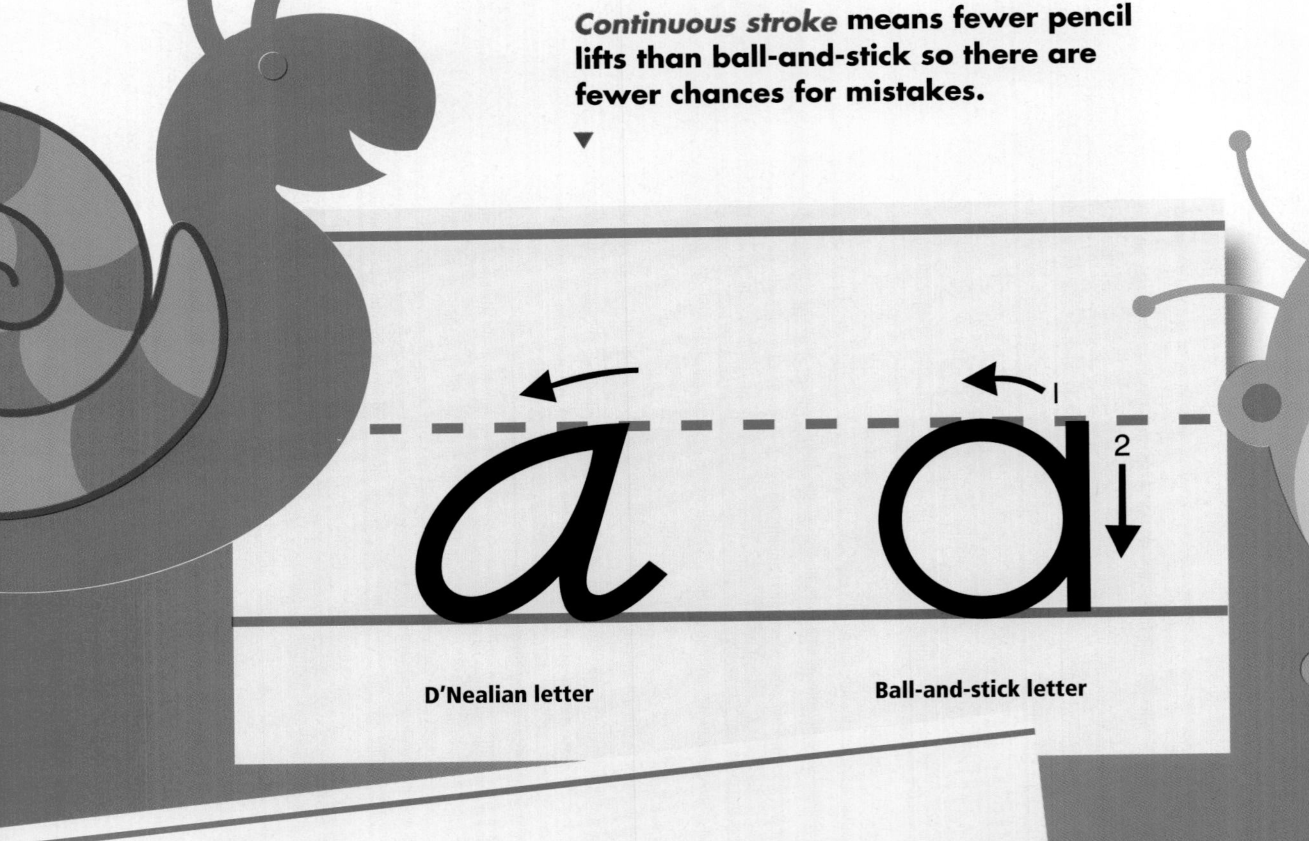

wagon

Same letters. Simple connections.

Slanted D'Nealian manuscript uses most of the same basic letter forms as cursive handwriting. Add a few simple connecting strokes, and children easily progress from manuscript to cursive. Ball-and-stick manuscript forces children to go back to square zero and learn a different alphabet for cursive.

Letters formed with the same basic letter strokes **are taught in sequence, so children can write words right away!**

▼

dad

D'Nealian exercise — kids write real words!

_ a _

Fill-in-the-blank exercise found in other programs.

MEET A TRUE ORIGINAL

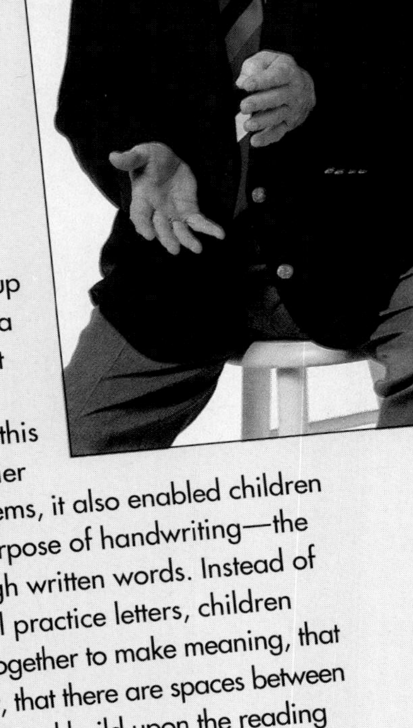

The original continuous-stroke handwriting program began as one person's drive to make handwriting easier for kids.

As a first-grade teacher, Donald Neal Thurber saw the frustration kids faced with the ball-and-stick method. (Even the person who introduced the method eventually branded it "ill-advised.") Don also noted the difficulty of learning one alphabet for manuscript, only to have to start over to learn another for cursive, and he decided to step back from the traditional way of teaching handwriting and figure out how to do it better. He came up with a simple but ingenious idea: a slanted manuscript in which most letters are formed with a single, continuous stroke. Not only did this make learning handwriting easier and solve many legibility problems, it also enabled children to achieve more rapidly the purpose of handwriting—the communication of ideas through written words. Instead of turning out pages of individual practice letters, children quickly learned that letters go together to make meaning, that words develop from left to right, that there are spaces between words—concepts that reinforce and build upon the reading and writing lessons that are so important for first graders to learn. As the frustrations of learning handwriting were replaced by the joys of success, D'Nealian students developed the handwriting fluency that contributes to the ease with which children mature as readers and writers.

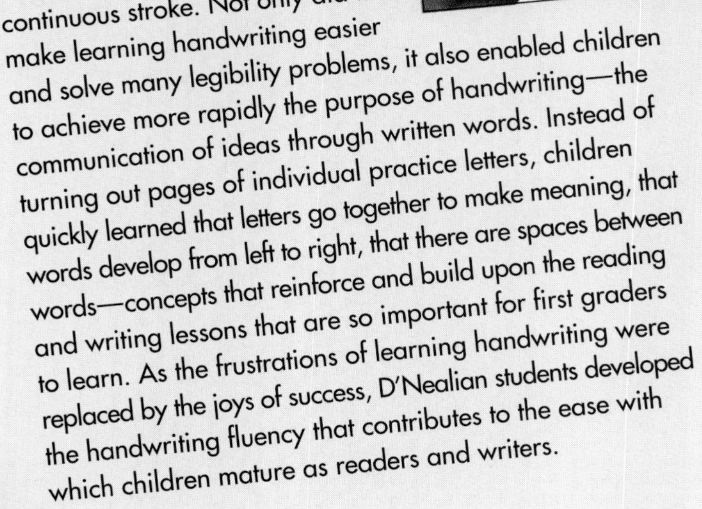

Read more about Donald Neal Thurber's ideas on pages T20-T21.

A Solid Foundation for Legibility

D'Nealian® Handwriting is designed to help students form clear, readable letters right from the start.

You need to space letters and words.
Letters in a word should not be too close.
too close
Letters in a word should not be too far apart.
t o o f a r
Leave more space between words.
just fine
30 Letter and Word Spacing

◀ ***Readiness*** **in Grade One lays the groundwork for letter formation by introducing the concepts of shape, size, slant, spacing, and line.**

Clear letter models guide letter formation.

Printed words help students see how print and handwriting compare.

door
dog

▶ ***Lessons*** **focus on letter formation and provide plenty of practice opportunities.**

d d d d

My Words

add
add

dad
dad

34 Writing d
Children trace and write the letter **d** and the words **add** and **dad**.

Grade 1

Starting dot tells students "where to start."

Immediate practice in complete words encourages writing.

Red baseline guides young hands and eyes.

Personal word list links reading, writing, and spelling.

Letter models help left-handers.

Ever widening practice opportunities ensure students' success in writing legibly.

Practice

a d o g c e s

◀ ***Practice*** **presents similar letters in sequence.**

Review **expands practice of similar- stroke letters to the context of real words.** ▼

Review

dog dog

dogs dogs

cage cage

cages cages

goose goose

geese geese

seed seed

seeds seeds

Evaluation

Remember: Close the letters **a, d, o,** and **g.**

dad dad

cage cage

a goose a goose

good dogs good dogs

Check Your Handwriting
Did you close the letters **a, d, o,** and **g?**

Yes No

42 Evaluation
Children trace and write words and phrases with the letters a, d, o, g, c, e, and s.

Pages from Grade 1

◀ ***Assessment,*** **including self-evaluation, leads both teacher and student to examine the features of each letter's formation that are crucial to legibility.**

Transition Is Easy As 1-2-3

D'Nealian® makes the transition from manuscript to cursive as easy as 1-2-3. Writing legibly in cursive feels rhythmic, familiar, and easy. That's the beauty of D'Nealian® Handwriting.

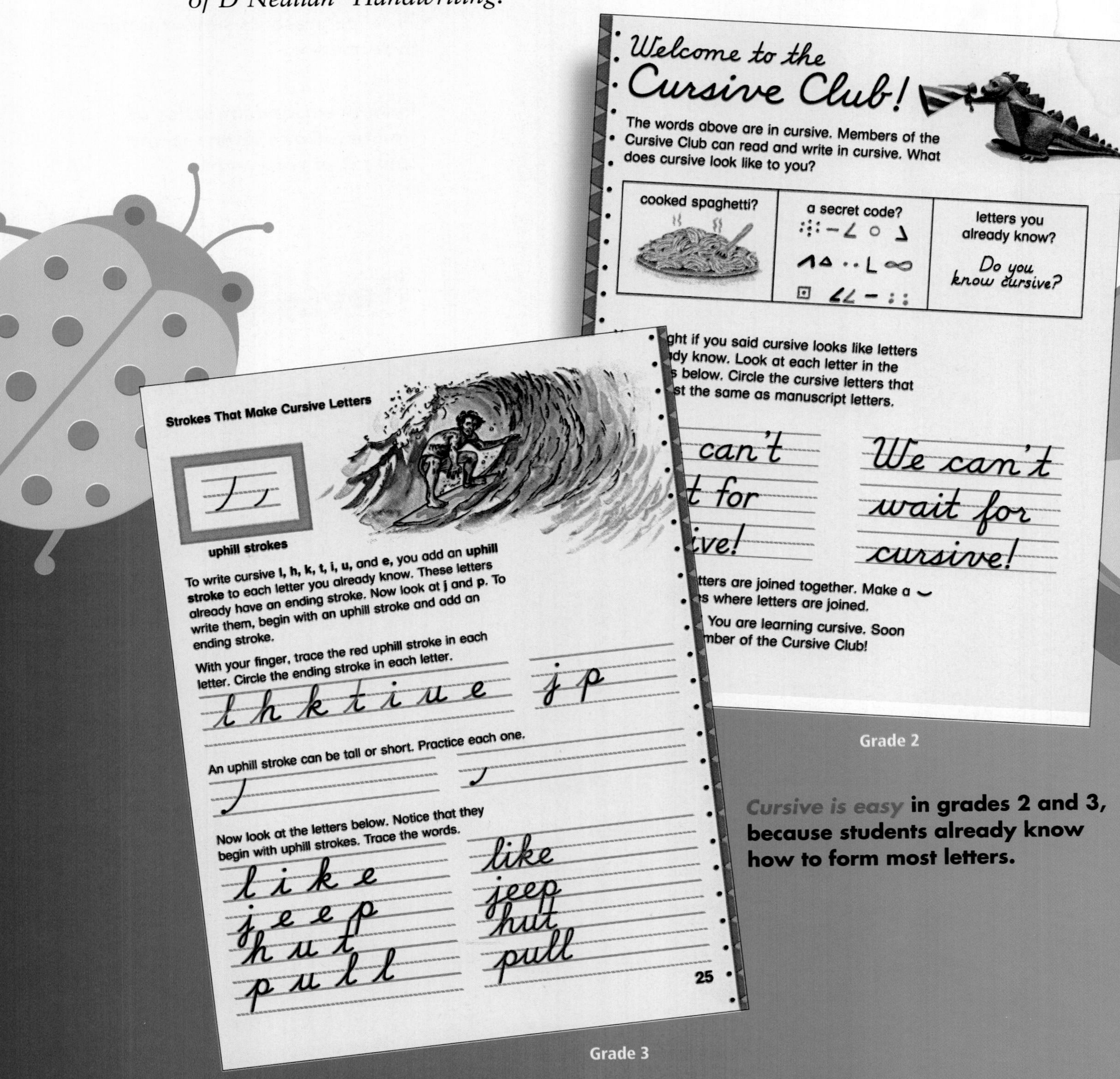

Grade 2

Grade 3

Cursive is easy in grades 2 and 3, because students already know how to form most letters.

From manuscript to cursive

Uphill stroke

Overhill stroke

Sidestroke

Three simple strokes connect most letters.

Easy-to-Use Teacher's Edition

▶
Core Teaching Plan **helps you deliver basic handwriting instruction quickly and easily.**

▶
Activity Bank **offers motivating, hands-on activities to choose from to meet the needs of your students. See page T15 for topics.**

Objectives
Traces and writes the lower-case letter **d**.
Writes words with the letter **d**.

Prepare
Introduce children to the letter:
- Say it.
- Read the letter description and write the letter.
- Air trace the letter and write it on the chalkboard for children to copy.

Teach
Using the pupils' page, have children:
- finger trace the large model **d**;
- trace and write the letter using the starting dots;
- write words with the letter **d**.

Follow Up
Self-Evaluation Have children check their work by asking themselves:
- Do my **d's** curve down to the bottom line?
- Do my **d's** curve up right to the beginning?

Additional Resource
Manuscript Alpha Touch letter **d**

Description
Middle start; around down, touch, up high, down, and a monkey tail.

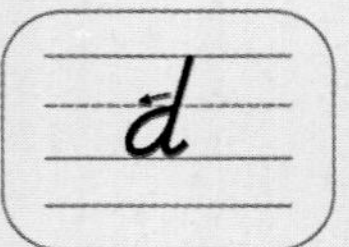

ACTIVITY BANK

Spacing Cue (Eye-Hand Coordination, Letter Spacing) A wonderful idea I've used with my first-graders is to have them fold their writing paper in half three times. This makes eight writing spaces or columns across each line. Then I have children find their "best" letter and draw a heart around it.
Mary L. May
Midway School
Moro, IL

Letter Search (Visual Discrimination, Likenesses and Differences) Give each child a crayon and several pages from a children's magazine or newspaper. Challenge children to search the pages to find and circle all the lower-case letter **d's**. Continue the activity until one child has circled twenty letters and is declared the winner.

Phonics Corner
Associate the letter **d** with the sound heard at the beginning of *dog* and *door*. Use the couplet to stress /d/.

My **dog** sits by the **door** each **day**,
And waits for me to come home and play.

Have children act out things that dogs do that begin with /d/ such as dig, duck, dive, and play dead.

34

Grade 1 Teacher's Edition

Teacher-generated and teacher-tested activities

Phonics connection in every letter lesson

ACTIVITY BANK

A wealth of activities helps you easily accommodate students' learning styles and abilities and your own unique teaching style.

- Creative Projects
- Learning Modalities
- Critical Thinking
- Small Groups
- Special Needs
- Practical Applications
- Attention Deficit Disorder
- Immature Learners
- Legibility
- Gifted and Talented
- Letter Practice
- Transition
- Students At-Risk
- Multilingual
- Cross-Curricular Activities
- Research
- Early Literacy

MEET:

Ngoc-Diep T. Nguyen, Ph.D.
Teacher Educator; Consultant

In the past few years, multicultural education has become a popular discussion topic in many schools. We, as classroom teachers, are encouraged to consider culture as an important factor that affects teaching and learning both inside and outside the school. We are asked to celebrate cultural diversity in our classrooms. We are challenged to become more culturally sensitive.

There are four basic principles that operate in a classroom where cultural diversity is celebrated:
1. Respectful treatment of all people.
2. Appreciation of diversity.
3. Consideration of a human experience from multiple perspectives.
4. Willingness to make decisions through compromise.

Strategies that will help children appreciate cultural diversity include:
1. Creating a classroom environment that is accepting of cultural differences.

Since culture i immense field, unrealistic to exp know everything a all groups of peo It is realistic to ex yourself and you students to be open learning about oth people and to using another as resource

2. Clearing up cross-cultural miscom nication as it occurs.
3. Teaching students many points of view of the same phenomenon and encouraging them to state their own perspectives.
4. Incorporating activities from a variet of resources, including the home and community.

[Highlights from the article on page T26 of this teacher's edition.]

Teacher to Teacher

Q. *Is it important to correct the pencil grip that some of my pupils are using?*

A. Pupils can develop unusual ways of holding their pencils. Attention to the grip now will help prepare pupils for a lifetime of writing. The grip taught in the Position for Writing lessons in Unit 1 provides for comfort and control. This in turn helps prevent tiring and loss of legibility as speed and length of writing time increases.

Q. *Should my pupils be able to read cursive handwriting before I teach them to write it?*

A. Most pupils have seen and read a great deal of cursive by the time they begin learning to write it. Lessons that preview cursive also will help make the transition.

There are certain things, however, that you can do in the classroom to ensure that pupils can read cursive before writing it:
- Write an occasional sentence in cursive on the board.
- Show spelling words in both writing styles.
- Vary the writing style you use for bulletin-board headings.

Q. *Some of my pupils' parents are concerned because D'Nealian® Handwriting doesn't look like the manuscript they wrote. What can I say?*

A. Most parents respond favorably when they see that the connection between D'Nealian manuscript and cursive forms leads to an earlier and easier transition to cursive writing.

▲

Professional articles **throughout the Teacher's Edition provide in-service-in-a-book for D'Nealian teachers.**

Do-It-Yourself D'Nealian®

The handy, zippered portfolio is packed with resources to add flexibility to your teaching.

- D'Nealian® Font software
- Practice and Review Masters
- Teacher's Idea Book

▶ PLUS

- Colorful posters
- Writing prompt transparencies
- Alphabet wall charts
- Teaching transparencies
- Alphabet stickers
- D'Nealian ruler
- Write-on/wipe-off cards

Practice and Review Masters **have two exercises for every letter—one formative and one for practicing the letter in writing. In Grades 4 and 5, students practice connecting letters before using them in writing.**

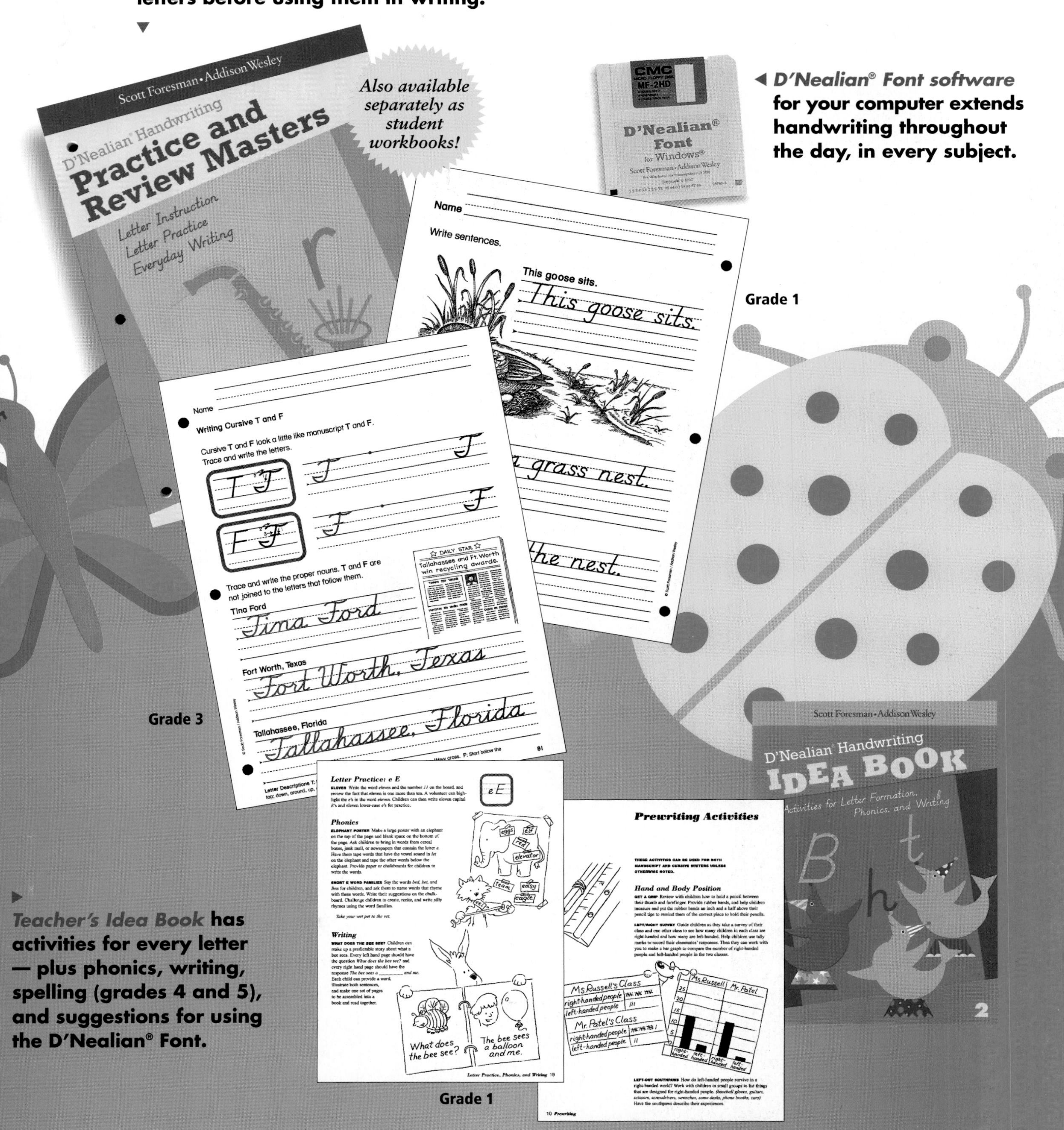

D'Nealian® Font software **for your computer extends handwriting throughout the day, in every subject.**

Grade 1

Grade 3

Teacher's Idea Book **has activities for every letter — plus phonics, writing, spelling (grades 4 and 5), and suggestions for using the D'Nealian® Font.**

Grade 1

Grade 2

A Variety of Resources Ensures Success

▸ BIG BOOKS

Big Book of Letters
Class Big Books
Kindergarten Big Books

▸ PRACTICE

Practice and Review Masters
Practice and Review Workbooks
Reteaching Books
Home/School Connection
Teaching Transparencies
D'Nealian® Journal

▸ HANDS-ON LEARNING

- Manuscript Flash Cards
- Alpha-Touch Letters
- Vinyl Mat
- Practice Slate
- Desk Tapes
- Lauri® Alphabet
- Handwriting Re-Write Cards
- Alphabet/Number Cards

▸ ADDITIONAL TEACHING AIDS

- Above-the-Chalkboard Alphabet (in English and Spanish)
- Alphabet Wall Chart
- Alphabet Stickers
- Handwriting Paper
- Pencils
- Rulers
- Handwriting Research and Information Book
- Handwriting Video

Talking with:

Donald Neal Thurber

Q *How did the D'Nealian® Handwriting Program develop?*

A I guess it began with an idea that something was wrong with the way other teachers and I were teaching handwriting. The first clue came when I was teaching first grade, about 1960. It occurred to me that I was spending all this time trying to get students to write manuscript straight up and down, but later a teacher would have them writing slanted cursive. Then in 1961, I learned about ITA, the Initial Teaching Alphabet. In ITA, some of the letters are printed with a continuous stroke. I realized that there was a nice rhythm to forming those letters, and, of course, the traditional circles-and-sticks method lacked rhythm.

I didn't do anything about these ideas until 1965, when I met a teacher who encouraged me to make notes on everything I found about handwriting, and then, when the ideas synthesized in my head, to begin writing. I did that, and in 1968, I published my first pamphlet on a new method of handwriting. As for the name, D'Nealian simply is based on my first and middle names—Donald Neal.

Once I published that first pamphlet, I started going around, persuading people to try my method. I did a lot of work dealing with one teacher here, another one there. I figured if I could get one teacher to try the D'Nealian method, and he or she liked it and was successful with it, then the teacher next door might decide to try it, then it might spread to the rest of the building, then to the rest of the district, then to neighboring districts, and so on. That's how it worked.

Q *What is D'Nealian® Handwriting?*

A It's a program in which the inconsistencies and illogic of most traditional handwriting methods are eliminated. It involves a unique, lower-case manuscript alphabet that is very easy to write and that leads into cursive writing with virtually no trouble at all. Most letter forms are the basic forms of corresponding cursive letters. Also, most letters are formed with one continuous stroke, so that rhythm, an essential ingredient in cursive writing, is built in from the beginning. The manuscript letters are slanted as cursive letters are. As a result, when the time comes to learn cursive, the basic patterns are already there; the manuscript that has been learned is not unlearned but, rather, built upon. This saves a lot of teaching and learning time and effort.

It's a program in which the inconsistencies and illogic of most traditional handwriting methods are eliminated.

Another aspect of D'Nealian® Handwriting is that it does not require use of oversized primary pencils and large writing lines at the early stages. Some young children may do better with very large pencils, but not all. So I recommend that teachers make writing instruments of various sizes and fairly small writing-line size available to children from the very beginning. Flexibility is what's important.

Q *How does the D'Nealian® Program handle legibility?*

A One of the most important points about the program is that it stresses legibility but recognizes the fact that writing is an individual product and that no two people write alike. One child's writing may be larger than another's; one may tend to write letters closer together than another; one may slant to the right while another slants to the left; one may make more circular parts while others may make more oval shapes. If teachers look for consistent slant, size, and spacing in each child's writing, legibility will develop. Yet, the D'Nealian® Program does have model letters—with a certain slant—for children to imitate, does suggest writing-line sizes, and does recommend a certain spacing.

Children entering school are highly motivated to learn to write, and this method builds on that motivation by treating handwriting as the individual effort that it is.

Q *What makes D'Nealian® Handwriting more individualistic than other programs?*

A Models are given because children need something to start with. For example, I recommend a "normal" slant (a right slant of about fifteen to twenty degrees) based on a study of thousands of children's papers. The point is that this method doesn't insist that all children follow someone else's slant precisely. As long as they're consistent, students can write vertically, slant to the right, or slant to the left. Look for legibility, period. That's why the program does not include any kind of transparent overlays for children to place over their own writing for evaluation.

Children entering school are highly motivated to learn to write, and this method builds on that motivation by treating handwriting as the individual effort that it is. Children compete against themselves, trying to improve their own legibility, rather than compete against an artificial standard. Children are happier and do better work in this kind of learning situation. The D'Nealian method does not frustrate them by demanding the impossible. The result is what I hear over and over from teachers using the method: "The pupils like to write now."

Q *Are letters taught in alphabetical order?*

A No. Letters are taught according to similarity of formation. Alphabetical order is important, but who says when it has to be learned? With D'Nealian® Handwriting, children learn a couple of vowels and a couple of consonants almost right away. They can make some words, some phrases. As they learn more letters, they make more words. After they've learned how to make all the letters, alphabetical order will come.

Q *What are the advantages of having children begin to write words almost right away?*

A Well, there's the matter of motivation. It's not important to children to write whole pages of individual letters. Handwriting is much more meaningful to children when they can take home a paper with words on it and say, "Look, this says 'dog.'" Also, writing words helps teach letter and word spacing and helps establish the concept of left-to-right. And if you have students writing whole words very early, you're developing the idea that letters go together to make sentences, which can be read. I want letters to make sense to children; I want them to know that letters do something, that they're not just isolated things to construct for drill perfection.

Q *Do teachers need any special preparation for teaching D'Nealian® Handwriting?*

A Not really. Mainly, the teacher needs to understand the philosophy of it. There's been no problem with teachers learning how to write the lower-case manuscript alphabet, which is the aspect of D'Nealian® Handwriting that's most different from traditional methods. They pick it up right away. The helps provided in the teacher's editions will be enough.

Advantages

OF D'NEALIAN® HANDWRITING

Continuous Skill Progression

Scott, Foresman *D'Nealian® Handwriting* is a simplified method of teaching handwriting. It replaces discontinuous skill progression with a logical program of *continuous skill progression.* From the very beginning of their handwriting instruction, children learn the basic letter forms, size, slant, rhythm, and spacing that they will need for all the writing they will ever do.

The D'Nealian method motivates children by helping them write early, using an adult-like alphabet. They write words beginning in *Book 1*. It thrills children to know they are writing much as adults and older brothers and sisters write.

Letter Forms

Most D'Nealian lower-case manuscript letters provide the basic forms for the corresponding cursive letters. Each letter that is not dotted or crossed is made with a continuous stroke. This means that a beginning writer needs to find the starting place on the paper only once for each letter. By contrast,

a b c d e f g h i j k l m
n o p q r s t u v w x y z

D'Nealian® Manuscript

a b c d e f g h i j
k l m n o p q r
s t u v w x y z

D'Nealian® Cursive

letters made with circles and straight lines require from two to four pencil lifts each.

The transition from flowing lower-case D'Nealian manuscript to cursive is so easy it comes naturally to many children. All manuscript letters but **f, r, s, v,** and **z** become cursive letters with the addition of simple joining strokes, the most important of which are the uphill and the overhill strokes.

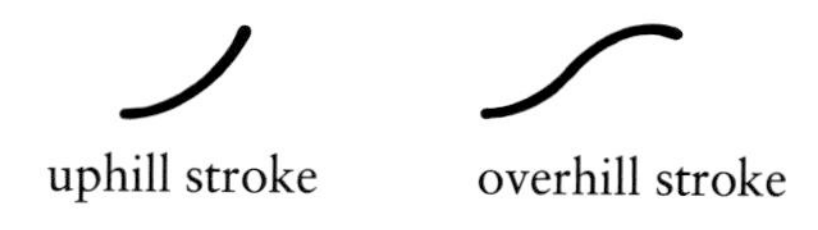

uphill stroke overhill stroke

D'Nealian® Handwriting further simplifies writing by using the same numbers and punctuation marks in both manuscript and cursive.

Slant

A child who can learn the vertical alignment used in ball and stick alphabets can just as easily be taught to slant. D'Nealian® Handwriting teaches children from the start to slant their letters and so eliminates the need to learn a new alignment when the child begins cursive.

Size

At kindergarten, children use three-quarter-inch ruled paper with a dotted middle line and red base line. In first grade, they move into one-half-inch ruled paper with a dotted middle line and red base line, which they use through third grade. At fourth grade, a change to standard ruled notebook paper is recommended and typical adult size is taught from fourth through eighth grade.

Teaching and learning of size have been simplified. In D'Nealian manuscript there are only three heights for letters: tall, small, and letters with descenders. Tall letters extend from the top line to the bottom line. Small letters extend only from the middle line to the bottom line. Letters with descenders extend half a line down from the bottom line. The letters **t** and **d** are full tall letters. They do not fall short of the top line. Thus the D'Nealian method eliminates two difficult "exceptions."

tall letters and all capital letters

small letters

descender letters

Spacing

Another component of D'Nealian® Handwriting's continuous skill progression is its handling of spacing. Like word formation and slant, spacing is taught from the very beginning in both manuscript and cursive. As soon as children learn two letters in manuscript (**a** and **d**), they trace three words (**a, add,** and **dad**). When pupils have had two groups of letters at grade one (**a, d, o, g,** and **c, e, s**), they write phrases (*a goose* and *good dogs*), moving smoothly into correct word spacing. When the transition to cursive is made, D'Nealian® Handwriting introduces correct spacing as early as possible.

Rhythm

Because most letters are made with one continuous stroke, children using the D'Nealian lower-case manuscript alphabet establish from the beginning a smooth, rhythmic flow. Young children are spared the ordeal of putting parts together to form letters. Furthermore, because the transition to cursive involves little more than adding strokes to letters children already have learned to make, the rhythm stays with the child.

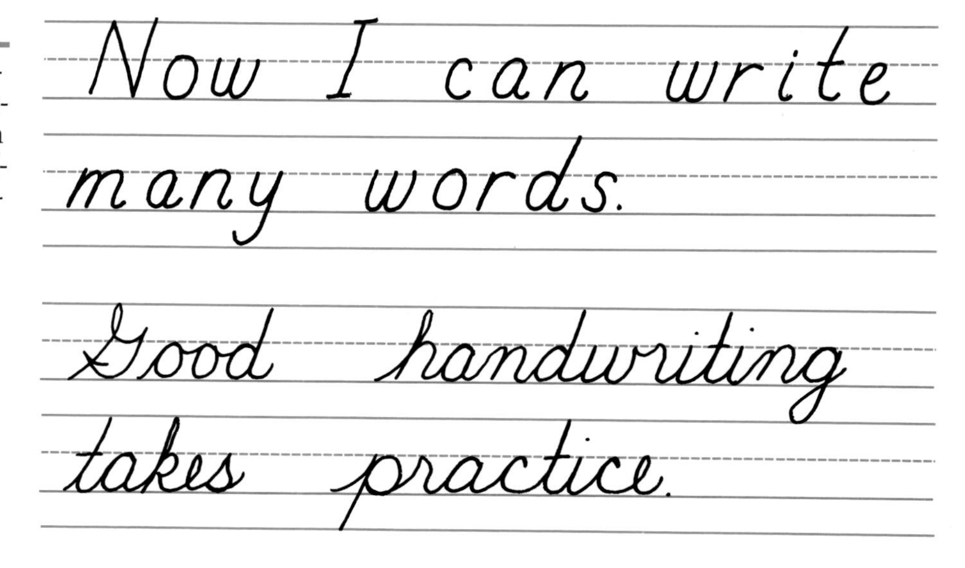

Flexible Evaluation of Handwriting

D'Nealian® Handwriting gives teachers and children flexibility in dealing with individual differences in handwriting, one of the more individual skills one learns. It is encouraging for children to be praised for writing legibly, even though their writing may deviate from a perfect model.

In D'Nealian® Handwriting, legibility is the primary standard for evaluation and is based on flexible but standard criteria for letter form, slant, size, and proportion. The examples on the right give an idea of acceptable and unacceptable variations in students' personal styles of handwriting.

Standards for letter form enable the letter to be distinguished clearly from other letters. In the letter **a**, for example, the round part of the letter must be open, the letter must close at the top, and the ending stroke must align with the bottom of the letter. D'Nealian manuscript letters are presented with a slight right-hand slant. Some children, however, will naturally print vertically or with a slight left-hand (backhand) slant. A consistent slant that does not interfere with legibility is acceptable.

The D'Nealian® Program also allows flexibility within a range of reasonable and practical sizes. Again, the key is legibility. At higher levels, children are given specific practice in letter proportion. For example, a tall letter, such as **l**, should be twice the height of a small letter, such as **e** or **i**. •

These **a**'s are acceptable in the D'Nealian® Program.

a a a a a

These **a**'s could be confused with **u**, **d**, **o**, and **q**, respectively.

a a a a

These slants are acceptable.

grandmother
grandmother
grandmother

These slants are not acceptable.

grandmother

Hints FOR HANDWRITING INSTRUCTION

Special Helps

In kindergarten and grade one, begin handwriting instruction by giving each child a D'Nealian model of his or her name. This may be on heavy paper or cardboard that can be propped up on a child's desk for reference.

Set up a handwriting center in your classroom. You may have the following items on hand:

- paper and pencils in different sizes, textures, and colors
- magazines and newspapers for cutting out letters and pictures
- a picture file with a picture for each capital and lower-case letter (people's names may be used for capital letters)
- a small chalkboard
- paste or white glue and things for gluing, such as fabric scraps, macaroni, glitter, buttons, and string
- a sandbox or container of sand in which pupils can finger trace letters
- brushes of various sizes, which children can dip in water, for writing letters and numbers on the chalkboard

For further information about writing centers and suggestions for activities that extend writing, see the Unit Opener pages in this teacher's edition.

A paraprofessional or teacher's aide can be of particular help. While you demonstrate from the front of the class, this second person can walk among children to check handwriting—especially direction of the stroke.

If there are left-handed children in the class, learn to write left-handed at the chalkboard. This will help left-handed children visualize how a letter is formed "their way."

From the beginning, encourage children to cross out the incorrect letters instead of erasing them. Young children tend to erase long and hard and are disappointed when their work is messy or has holes in it. By simply crossing out letters, pupils have neater papers and can see the mistakes they made.

Occasionally return illegible or messy papers to pupils for recopying to reinforce the need for legibility and neatness in all handwriting that others are to read. This is equally important for work in content areas other than handwriting.

Some children will try to do cursive writing in first grade. If children are so motivated (and you think they can handle it), they should be taught the correct way to make the transition. It is important not to let children experiment too much without guidance because they may form bad habits.

The transition is easy for most letters. An uphill stroke is added at the beginning of these letters:

e h i k
l t u

A beginning uphill stroke and a sidestroke or ending stroke are added to these letters:

b j p w

An overhill stroke is added at the beginning of these letters:

a c d m
n x y

A beginning overhill stroke and a sidestroke or ending stroke are added to these letters:

g o q

These letters must be taught:

Letters that end like **h** naturally join letters that begin like **a.** Be careful to work with children on joinings for sidestroke letters. These involve changes in the beginning stroke of the letter that follows the sidestroke letter:

on br
vi wh

Most children making the transition at first grade will not be ready to learn cursive capitals. There is no harm in letting them use manuscript capital letters for a while.

Paper

The following paper sizes are recommended in the D'Nealian® Program:

Kindergarten
3/4" with red base line, dotted midline, descender line

Books 1 and 2
1/2" with red base line, dotted midline, descender line

Book 3
1/2" with red base line, dotted midline, descender line for manuscript writing only; for cursive writing, 1/2" with blue base line, dotted midline, no descender line

Books 4–8
1/3" notebook paper, no midline or descender line

A few children may show a strong preference for paper of a different size. As long as a different size does not interfere with the legibility or ease of writing, a child may be permitted to use a size different from that used by others in the class.

Pencils

It is recommended that medium-soft pencils be used well into middle grades. By fifth or sixth grade, children may begin using pens.

The size pencil a child uses should be left to his or her preference. A variety of sizes should be available in the classroom, but most children, even beginning writers, will be comfortable with a standard-sized pencil, the type found in most homes.

One way for children to hold a pencil is to grasp it lightly between the thumb and index finger, usually about an inch above the pencil point.

An alternate grip, currently under study at the University of Michigan, is the new D'Nealian® Handwriting grip. This newly refined grip is accomplished by placing the pencil between the index and middle fingers, resting on the web of the hand. It is then grasped with the thumb, index and middle fingers about an inch from the point. The thumb gently holds the pencil in place against the other two fingers. The hand rests on the heel of the hand and slides on the tips and nails of the fourth and fifth fingers. This provides a firm structure that doesn't require much finger-tip pressure to hold the writing tool. Often a child who holds the pencil too tightly also grasps it too close to the point. A simple remedy is to wrap a rubber band around the pencil an inch above the point. The child should hold the pencil above the rubber band.

Position

The posture of children learning handwriting should be the same good posture essential to healthy body growth. Children should sit tall, with both feet on the floor and arms relaxed on a table or desk.

Paper should be positioned at a slant for both manuscript and cursive writing. The slant of the paper should approximately parallel the writing arm. For left-handed children, the paper should slant from the right at the top to the left at the bottom. The right-handed child should slant the paper from the left at the top to the right at the bottom.

Photos in the front of the pupil books for kindergarten through grade three illustrate correct posture and paper position.

Pupils new to D'Nealian® Handwriting

Children will transfer into your class from schools where D'Nealian® Handwriting is not taught. It is inconsistent with D'Nealian philosophy, which emphasizes legibility and individuality, to insist that a child doing superior work with another method be forced to change to D'Nealian style. On the other hand, most children who are doing poor or mediocre work with another method should be strongly encouraged to learn D'Nealian® Handwriting. Its simplicity is particularly useful for children having difficulty with other methods.

If young transfer students maintain their old method of manuscript writing instead of learning D'Nealian manuscript, they will need extra help making the transition to cursive, which in the D'Nealian® Program is taught at grade two. These children most likely will not have established the form, size, slant, and rhythm necessary for cursive writing.

CELEBRATING

Cultural Diversity

By Ngoc-Diep T. Nguyen, Ph.D.

The simple realization that there are other points of view is the beginning of wisdom. Understanding what they are is a great step. The final test is understanding why they are held. **Charles Campbell** *The New Outlook*

In the past few years, multicultural education has become a popular topic of discussion in many schools. We, as classroom teachers, are encouraged to consider culture as an important factor that affects teaching and learning inside and outside of schools. We are asked to celebrate cultural diversity in our classrooms and challenged to become more culturally sensitive. The following principles and strategies may prove useful.

Guiding Principles

Four basic principles operate where cultural diversity is celebrated:

1. Respectful treatment of all people. Both teachers and students understand that although one may disagree with a person or an opinion, one will always speak to and about other people with respect.

2. Appreciation of diversity. There is fostered in the classroom an attitude that differences are not merely tolerated, but are appreciated. Students and teachers look to each other's respective experiences as resources for learning and problem solving.

3. Consideration of a human experience through multiple perspectives. Students are encouraged to consider many perspectives on the same topic of study in order to be better informed. Parallel with this is respect for perspectives that may be contrary to their own.

4. Willingness to make decisions through compromise. A person who is culturally sensitive is one who is more willing to share decisions and make compromises. Students are taught the skills of collaboration and conflict resolution as part of the class curriculum.

Classroom Strategies

Here are some suggestions for teachers who wish to help their students celebrate cultural diversity:

1. Create a classroom environment that is accepting of cultural differences. Encourage students to learn about and share in each other's cultural backgrounds. At the same time, set clear ground rules that everyone must follow. One of these is that one must speak with respect to and about those who are different.

2. Cross-cultural miscommunication sometimes happens. When it does, heed the advice of social linguist, John Gumperz:

- Check your everyday assumptions.
- Clearly state to students your own assumptions about activities.
- Ask explicit, not general, questions.
- When appropriate, talk openly with students about discrimination.
- Listen carefully until your students finish. Sometimes the most important message is at the end.

3. Since a major skill in cross-cultural awareness is the ability to accept alternative perspectives, it is important that students be taught many points of view of the same phenomenon. Students should be encouraged to state their own perspectives, and these should be affirmed, even if seemingly contrary to the popular view.

4. One of the biggest problems with taking a proactive approach to celebrating cultural diversity is the seeming lack of resources. Such books as Tiedt and Tiedt's *Multicultural Teaching: A Handbook of Activities, Information, and Resources* and James Banks's *Teaching Ethnic Studies* offer practical assistance.

A final word of advice. Since culture is an immense field, it is unrealistic to expect to know everything about all groups of people. It is realistic to expect yourself and your students to be open to learning about other people and to using one another's knowledge as resources.

Ngoc-Diep T. Nguyen is a teacher educator and a consultant at the Illinois Resource Center, Des Plaines, Illinois. She also conducts research in second-language learning and cultural adaptation. She is co-author, with Louisa Finnberg, of the Multicultural/Multilingual activities that appear in the Activity Banks of each teacher's edition.

D'NEALIAN INSIGHT

INVOLVING PARENTS

BY
ANTHONY D. FREDERICKS, Ed.D.

Anthony D. Fredericks is an Assistant Professor of Education at York College, York, PA, where he teaches methods courses. He is the author of 15 books and over 200 professional articles. He currently writes columns for *Teaching PreK–8* and *Reading Today.*

Parents are a tremendous resource and asset for the classroom. Research, as well as casual observation, has demonstrated that when parents are invited to become active participants in the dynamics of the classroom, students are motivated to learn and their achievements escalate.

The success of your outreach efforts will be based on several important factors. These have been shown to be essential ingredients in any successful and effective effort of parental involvement. Consider them as necessary elements for your home-school activities.

Shared Workload Parents need to be told, and certainly need to understand, that participation in their child's education will have a direct effect on the child's academic achievement.

Empowerment Many parents feel disassociated from the school because they have not been given any decision-making power in terms of their children's education. It is vitally important to provide parents with a sense of "ownership"—to ask for their advice, solicit their input, and let them make purposeful decisions.

Constant Communication Research has demonstrated that regular and frequent communication from school can do more to ensure parental involvement than any other single factor. Whether that communication takes the form of newsletters, phone calls, memos, or notes, it is essential that it be sustained and continuous.

Continuous Participation Successful parent participation is built on a foundation of long-term commitment. Working to include all parents in the affairs of the classroom for the entire school year demonstrates the value you place on parental involvement.

You may wish to consider some of the following activities as part of your outreach efforts. Plan to tailor them to the needs and dynamics of your own classroom.

- Work with colleagues to produce a regular parent newsletter to answer parents' concerns about education. A brief "Dear Abby" format may be appealing.
- Call two parents each week to share good news about their children's progress.

> "Parents need to be told, and certainly need to understand, that participation in their child's education will have a direct effect on the child's academic achievement."

- Set up a "Family of the Week" bulletin board in your classroom. Invite members of the family to help arrange pictures, memorabilia, and labels.
- Establish a "Coffee Klatsch" or a "Brown-Bag Lunch" once a month to discuss common concerns with parents.
- Invite parents into your classroom to share their interests, backgrounds, or hobbies.
- Have students prepare a calendar of upcoming events in the classroom. Duplicate it and send it home.
- Invite parents who speak languages other than English to teach songs or rhymes in that language to small groups of children or to the entire class.
- Work with your students to prepare an informational packet for the parents of new students assigned to your classroom. Include such information as daily schedules, dates of special events, and names of volunteers who help out during the year.
- Involve parents in a "Homework Council" designed to establish homework standards and expectations.

The participation of parents within and throughout your curriculum can be a valuable component of students' scholastic growth. Taking advantage of parents as partners in the educational process is certainly one of your most important responsibilities.

[Editor's Note: ScottForesman produces a D'Nealian Home/School Connection for teachers of grades K–3. These may be ordered through the Scott-Foresman catalog.]

Telling Parents About D'Nealian® Handwriting:

One Teacher's Words

by Betty J. C. Wright

Betty J. C. Wright is a teacher in the Bodine Elementary School in Oklahoma City, Oklahoma. She was Oklahoma City Teacher of the Year in 1989–1990 and is a winner of the 1991 Presidential Award for Excellence in Education.

When parents are new to a school that uses D'Nealian® Handwriting or when a school has recently adopted the program, there are bound to be questions. Here is how one teacher answers them.

Writing is a natural form of expression, and, indeed, young children have a unique way of expressing themselves. The walls and furniture in homes often tell the story of their special form of written expression. Parents quickly learn that a child with an unattended crayon, marker, or pencil, can be hazardous to the house.

Then suddenly one day, sometime between the toddler and kindergarten age, that fascinating and intriguing tool that was a no-no for so long is taken off the shelf and placed into long-awaited hands. First attempts at forming letters are enthusiastically shared with anyone who is willing to notice. Refrigerators in homes across the country serve as showcases for Tommy's "special brand of writing." From that point on, the child's world is filled with the joy of communicating via paper and pencil.

With so much excitement and emphasis on handwriting in the early years, it's quite natural for parents to expect schools to keep that joy of writing alive and provide their children with the basic letter forms and skills that will be required throughout life.

For the past five years, the D'Nealian® Handwriting method has been taught in my school. The children are relaxed and excited about their handwriting. Teachers from grade level to grade level have a consistent method of teaching, and this consistency provides for continuous progress. Parents are proud of their children's success and take pride in showing off their children's writing. Teachers take pride in leading their children through the program and are very pleased with the results.

Kindergarten and first-year children are introduced to the D'Nealian basic letter forms, size, slants, rhythm, and spacing right from the beginning. Most D'Nealian letters are formed with one continuous stroke. The flexibility allowed for individual style in D'Nealian® Handwriting lends itself perfectly to the individual rate of fine motor development in each child. Children glow with excitement when they are finally able to put these mysterious letters together to form words.

D'Nealian workbooks are convenient, provide plenty of practice, and are adaptable for whole-group instruction or individual seat work. Provisions for the child with special needs are included in the Activity Banks that appear with each lesson in the teacher's edition. The program has a Reading and Writing strand that calls for children to write in response to literary selections. Pupils are given many opportunities to apply their handwriting skills to real-life writing tasks.

The transition from D'Nealian manuscript to cursive is easier and less stressful to children than in traditional handwriting programs. D'Nealian letters are slanted from the beginning, and the basic rhythm of forming the letters is securely established by the time children are introduced to cursive writing. Most of the manuscript and cursive letters are the same size and shape. Connecting strokes and letters flow easily as children make the move from manuscript to cursive writing.

D'Nealian® Handwriting, with its graceful lines and beautiful form, keeps children interested in maintaining their handwriting style as they grow older. Young children love the sophisticated appearance of the D'Nealian letters and often refer to it as "grown-up" writing. Many children compare D'Nealian® Handwriting to calligraphy.

Thirty years ago, a man by the name of Donald Neal Thurber dreamed of an easy-to-write handwriting program that would produce legible, motivated writers. In 1978, that dream became a reality when ScottForesman published his program for the first time.

Today, teachers all across the nation are working to instill that dream in the hearts and minds of their children. We play a vital role in giving the world confident, legible writers.

Creative Movement

BY MIMI BRODSKY CHENFELD

Movement is our first means of expression and communication. Unless children are taught to be cautious or to repress their feelings, their movement and play combine language, improvisation, problem solving, imagination, and physical coordination.

Daily doses of friendly reassurance are very important. I always begin by greeting and welcoming children into a safe, warm environment. We share simple welcome rituals using songs, poems, and gestures from many sources. Simply waving to everyone in the group is a simple welcoming ceremony.

We share simple welcome rituals.

Warming up is an enjoyable, positive experience. As we shake our muscles, wiggle, jiggle, twist, clap, kick, and stretch, we practice listening skills, following directions, demonstrating comprehension, paying attention, expanding vocabularies and learning cooperation. I encourage children to add their own interpretations to every warm-up. My music is eclectic, from Bach to folk to pop to rock. If we're studying the circus, we use circusy music and do circus warm-ups like juggling, walking on tiptoes, and marching.

Warm-ups, or exercise times, during the school day are healthy, pleasant breaks for you and the children. They're important ends in themselves, as well as steps on the way to more challenging activities. If we don't invite children to stretch and shake out their muscles for a few minutes as part of every day, then how can we expect them to be ready to participate in a

Warming up is an enjoyable, positive experience.

Invite children to stretch and shake out their muscles.

Sometimes the best choreography is right in the words themselves.

We talk about that race long ago . . . .

major movement activity? They need to know that movement is part of their daily schedule, as natural as snack time or story time.

Beyond daily exercise breaks and warm-ups, we move to numbers, letters, words, colors, directions, instructions, pictures, poems, and our own names. When you look for movement possibilities in whatever you're doing, you'll see how easy it is and how delighted children are to "show off" ideas with body shapes and action patterns. For example, use a story like "Goldilocks and the Three Bears." When the Bear family walks in the woods, Baby Bear has a little walk, Mama Bear has a medium-sized walk, and Papa Bear—well you know what great, big steps he takes! What about the way the bears might run if they want to get home in a hurry? They certainly don't run like children, do they?

The bears no doubt left notes at home that said, "Baby Bear's chair. Don't touch!" in Baby-Bear writing. Mama Bear's note is probably in medium-sized writing, and, well, let children demonstrate the BIG letters Papa Bear might write!

It's fun to explore all the possibilities. Try the Three Billy Goats Gruff trip-trapping over the bridge. Little Billy Goat trip-traps with small bouncy feet, Medium Billy Goat trip-traps with medium rhythms, and Big Billy Goat Gruff traps with HUGE trip-trapping footwork. Children love to explore different levels of movement, especially from small to big.

You don't have to look far. Sometimes the best choreography is right in the words themselves. "Hickory, Dickory, Dock" will inspire children to show up-and-down movement. They just *do* what the rhyme says.

One day you might decide to play with that old fable, "The Tortoise and the Hare." But make it a surprise! Try not to do things in ordinary ways. No matter how exciting an idea, it can always be deadened by dullness. The first day that we play with this fable, we talk about that race long ago, when the two finalists were Cheetah and Hare. Any fast rhythms will do to help children feel the exciting segments of the race. Believe it or not, Hare wins! So then, of course, everyone laughs when old, slowpoke Tortoise challenges Champion Hare to a race across the lake.

The race is on! Try fast music for Hare's hopping movement and slow

Children are delighted to "show off" ideas with body shapes and action patterns.

. . . smug old Hare thinks that Tortoise will never catch up and stretches out in the sun for a nice snooze.

music for Tortoise's crawl. Believe it or not, children *love* to crawl. Keep changing the music—fast/slow; fast/slow.

Of course we all know that smug old Hare thinks that Tortoise will never catch up and stretches out in the sun for a nice snooze.

But while Hare is sleeping, Tortoise keeps going. Unbelievable as it may seem, Tortoise is the winner! Yaaay! We jump and clap for joy! I turn my fist into a microphone and myself into a newspaper reporter and interview the winner.

"Tortoise, can you explain how you won when you're the slower animal?"

"I never gave up! I never stopped!"

Children have wonderful responses. They'll tell you the important lessons! Give them all a chance to make a news statement from either Tortoise or Hare or both. It's easy to talk about how many things we were slow in learning, and because we kept practicing, we improved, just as we did when we were learning to walk, ride bikes, run, jump, read, and write.

They race to the table of markers and paper, heads filled with ideas.

After children talk, improvise, move, laugh, dance to an idea, written language and visual images come so easily. They will race to the table of markers and paper, heads filled with ideas.

We never choose parts. Together, we celebrate ideas and interpret them in our own ways, but within the group. We close in on favorite scenes or choose those aspects of a story or theme that lend themselves to imaginative movement interpretation.

When children feel safe from criticism, from embarrassment, when they learn in playful, encouraging, loving climates, they will always move. They are ready to be moved by being welcomed into the exciting world of creative education.•

Mimi Brodsky Chenfeld is an author, teacher, consultant, lover of children, and a pioneer in the field of creative movement. Her books, *Teaching Language Arts Creatively, 1987* and *Creative Activities for Young Children, 1983* (Harcourt Brace Jovanovich), are widely used. Her favorite proverb is "All of my children are prodigies."

SUCCESS

for all students in the classroom

BY BARBARA TROOLIN, Ph.D.

Barbara Troolin is an educational administrator and consultant. She is currently Manager for the Office of Monitoring and Compliance/ Equal Education Opportunities, Department of Education, St. Paul, Minnesota.

Although the concept of inclusion and committing to success for all students is challenging, it requires us, at the same time, to develop a closer working relationship with students. Providing an environment in which all students can succeed is one of the most rewarding experiences of our profession.

How can teachers increase the chance that all students can succeed in the classroom? School staff and administrators, community members, parents, students, and others must believe that a positive school climate, flexible and relevant curriculum, needed instructional supports, and a spirit of collaboration will make a difference in student learning.

Key elements to the success of a program of inclusion are:

Values in Education

At the core of all we do is the student. If we believe that all students can learn, and that we can make that happen, we will be surrounded by opportunities for success.

Support

A spirit of collaboration and teamwork among administration, school boards, and the community can set the stage for improving educational programs and creating an environment in which all students can be successful.

Instructional Planning Teams

To address each student's instructional needs, involve a variety of people who know the child. The focus should be on instructional challenge, not the student's deficits.

Parent and Student Involvement

Parents and children must be seen as essential and valued members for planning instruction. One of the most important factors overall for the success of all students in the classroom is parent involvement. Encourage parents to ask about schoolwork and comment on their children's progress.

Supports Within Reach

Instead of students leaving the classroom to get supports, such as technology and specialized staff, consideration should be given to providing supports within the classroom environment.

Individualized Learning

If we hold high expectations for achievement by all students, we must be aware of their individual needs. For example, in handwriting, students should spend time on legibility issues they need to work on, not skills they have already mastered.

Active Participation of Students

Although learning styles may differ from student to student, it is hard to argue about how important it is to have students actively engaged in learning. For example, writing a thank-you note or making a poster are ways to engage students in meaningful handwriting tasks.

Flexible Grouping

Because students are at different levels of achievement in different areas of the curriculum, and all instruction can't be individualized for every child in every subject, grouping is a common strategy for instruction. Changing the membership of groups, changing staff, and having students teach students are ways in which groupings can be kept effective.

Information and Resources

Teachers need to read, visit, engage in discussions, share experiences, try new ideas, and identify their own and collective needs in order to access information and services available to them. We encourage you to find out about grants, foundations, and community and state resources that can help you create the best conditions for every child in your classroom.•

RECOGNIZING

Classroom Problems

BY

DALE JORDAN, Ph.D.

> "Recognizing problems is the first step in easing teacher and student frustration."

No teacher can diagnose and remediate all problems encountered in his or her classroom. However, recognizing major clues to a child's limitations can help the teacher modify daily expectations.

Any of five problems may become apparent during handwriting instruction. They are immaturity for learning, poor visual control for close work, and three forms of learning disability, poor visual memory, poor auditory memory, and dysgraphia—poor control of the muscles used in handwriting. Any of these problems can cause immense frustration both for the child and for the teacher. If not addressed, they can lead to a vicious cycle for the child, who will not experience the success that helps motivate children to learn. Recognizing the problems is the first step in easing teacher and student frustration.

Immaturity for learning

Problems resulting from immaturity include short attention span and poor listening comprehension. Children whose central nervous systems are not yet fully developed not only have trouble paying attention to the teacher, but also may misunderstand what they actually hear. Missing the essential parts of oral messages, they do not know what the teacher expects them to do. They neither follow group discussions nor get the point of stories read to the class.

Conversely, there are recognizable signs of maturity. A child who is ready for handwriting can:

- control pencil, crayons, scissors, staying within lines
- button and zip clothing
- remember a series of instructions
- keep full attention until the task is finished
- match corners when folding paper
- copy simple shapes successfully
- confidently choose which hand to use

Poor visual control for close work

Although the reason isn't known, the number of farsighted children is increasing. These children have poor vision for sustained close work in school. Yet the traditional vision test, the Snellen eye chart, in essence assesses a child's ability to see the chalkboard twenty feet away, but not what is on his or her desk eighteen inches away.

During close work, farsighted children become restless, lose the place, and stray from the line. A child's handwriting may indicate poor visual control for close work. Pupils with poor vision for paper-and-pencil work often

- cannot put a finger on a given place on the page
- write too large for the work space
- space unevenly, leaving wide gaps or jamming letters together
- complain of headache during sustained close work
- begin to squint soon after starting to copy from the chalkboard
- lean very close to their papers
- continuously change posture while writing (lean sideways, lean back)
- cannot sustain quality; writing deteriorates as work continues

Learning disability

Learning disability is a general term used to identify a learner who cannot conserve standard form. Children who cannot remember what they have seen are unable to conserve visual form. Children who cannot remember what they have heard are unable to conserve auditory form. Children who cannot repeat movements of their bodies may lack conservation of tactile or kinesthetic form.

Poor visual memory

Successful learners can create and store mental pictures of what is seen. The learning disabled child seldom possesses ability to accurately recall what has been seen.

Poor visual memory brings with it confused directionality. Affected children do not develop the left-to-right and top-to-bottom awareness that are essential to learning in all areas, not the least of which is handwriting. Problems resulting from lack of directional awareness range from reversed letters to working backwards. Children who work backwards are said to have *mirror-image* (or simply *mirror*) orientation. (Some, but not all, children outgrow this orientation.) If the teacher displays the letter **d,** the child may perceive **b.** If the teacher presents the word *saw,* the child reads *was*. Asked to put his or her finger on the top left corner of the page, the mirror child touches the opposite side. Children with poor visual memory may

- confuse left/right, over/under
- have difficulty learning information in sequence (alphabet, phone numbers)
- reverse or rotate letters and symbols such as **b** and **d, d** and **q, 7** and **L**
- transpose letters and numbers (*was* for *saw,* **31** for **13**)
- whisper the previous terms while writing items in a sequence
- confuse similarity and difference

Poor auditory memory

Pupils with poor auditory memory typically fully understand only 20%–30% of what they hear, although they can, in fact, hear sound. A breakdown occurs at the point where what is heard passes into memory. The child cannot retrieve meanings for words he or she hears, cannot understand the overall meaning of an idea expressed orally, and cannot retain a sequence. A sequence the child can follow while listening may immediately scramble when the child tries to "play it back." The child may pretend to have understood what the teacher has said, may turn to classmates for what to do, may do nothing, or may panic or rebel and so create a disturbance.

Although a pupil with poor auditory memory may be able to write the correct spellings of many words, he or she lacks the *auditory-to-motor* proficiency needed to connect quickly what has just been heard with what was learned previously, and then to write accurately what was said. The deficiency becomes particularly problematic when the teacher uses spelling words in dictated sentences. Actually, all writing, whether from dictation or from one's own inner voice, is difficult for children with poor auditory memory. Children with poor auditory memory characteristically:

- cannot complete writing-from-dictation tasks in the allotted time
- constantly erase and try again until "it looks right"
- cannot follow a sequence of oral directions
- frequently transpose vowel-consonant combinations (*brid* for *bird*)
- bluff or try to pick up clues from other students

Dysgraphia

Dysgraphia—lack of control of the muscles used in handwriting—may or may not be associated with poor visual and/or auditory memory. The syndrome involves a short-circuiting both of directionality and of mental images as pencil touches paper.

Evidence of dysgraphia includes backward handstrokes, circular symbols—**o**'s and **0**'s—made by moving the pencil in a clockwise direction, and smudging and irregularity resulting from heavy pressure. The child puts out painstaking effort to make symbols merely legible. His or her cursive handwriting can be seen as a series of isolated elements strung together.

A dysgraphic child has problems with figure-ground control, which limit the child's ability to keep consistent spacing, both horizontally between successive words and vertically. The child has trouble numbering every other line on a sheet of paper. Dysgraphic students should not be pushed to write quickly. Symptoms of dysgraphia include:

- backward handstrokes (e.g., reversed circles)
- labored writing with heavy pressure
- lack of control in numbering lines
- much erasing and repetition of mistakes

While no teacher can solve all of these learning problems, knowing reasons for various behaviors can cue the teacher to reduce pressure and modify expectations. Children with the symptoms described above should be referred to appropriate specialists for further evaluation.•

Dale R. Jordan, Ph.D. is currently the director of the Jones Learning Center at the University of the Ozarks in Clarksville, Arkansas. He has taught and has been an administrator at both the elementary and college level. Dr. Jordan formerly was Director of Diagnosis at the Jordan Diagnostic Center in Oklahoma City, Oklahoma.

CAPITALIZING ON MODALITY STRENGTHS

by Joan Eich

Joan Eich is a teacher consultant in the Ottawa, Illinois, elementary schools. Her work is in the area of academic and behavioral concerns. Ms. Eich is the author of the Special Needs activities that appear in the Activity Banks of each teacher's edition.

As teachers we know that all children can learn, but that they do not all learn the same way. We, as teachers, want to know how to help make learning efficient, effective, and enjoyable for each child.

The academic task of handwriting requires basic motor and memory skills. Because a child's rate of learning and ability to recall information is influenced by many factors, it is important to identify the most efficient sensory input channel and memory channel for each child and to encourage their use. The four input and memory channels are: visual (seeing), auditory (hearing), kinesthetic (doing), and tactile (touching).

Each child enters school with an established style of learning. Whichever sensory channel is the most efficient for the child to receive, implant, retrieve, and express information is called his or her modality strength.

Modality-based instruction leads to successful teaching because it capitalizes on the child's capabilities. It is most important to match the child's learning strength when introducing and practicing a basic skill. For this reason, Activity Banks at the end of each lesson in this book offer activities that address handwriting practice through a variety of modalities.

Suggestions in the Activity Banks are intended for four kinds of learners:

1. **The visual learner** Visual learners remember best what they see or can visualize. Therefore, the best instructional and practice methods include:
   - copying from models
   - watching and analyzing visual stimuli
   - responding to visual aids such as pictures, posters, illustrations, symbols, or signs
   - creating mental pictures
   - facilitating neurological imprints of information and focusing a child's attention by such procedures as using brilliant colors to highlight letters

   Cue words that will help visual learners focus their attention include "Watch," "Eyes up here," "Look carefully," "Picture in your mind...." Visual learners think in terms of images.

   For handwriting activities, it is essential that these children implant a good visual image of the letters. Visual learners benefit from:
   - highlighting, coloring, tracing, and copying letters before they write them
   - associating pictures with letters
   - closing their eyes to form a mental picture of the letter
   - observing word configurations
   - using the visual after-image technique (for example, stare intently at a model of lights arranged in the form of a letter for fifteen seconds, close their eyes, and see an after-image on the inside of their eyelids)
2. **The auditory learner** Auditory learners remember best by what they hear and say. Therefore, the best methods of instruction and practice include:
   - repeating what they hear
   - describing
   - discussing
   - listening to music; singing songs
   - listening to and repeating stories and rhymes

- making sound/symbol associations
- making and listening to tapes and records
- dramatizing and role-playing

Auditory learners are able to focus and sustain their attention to verbal directions. Simply cue them by saying, "Listen." They may, however, have more difficulty than other children with letter form, space, slant, and letter size. Auditory learners think in terms of sound.

For handwriting activities, it is important that these children listen carefully to stroke descriptions and sound/symbol associations in order to remember the letters. Auditory learners respond to:

- using mnemonic devices such as sentence associations, rhymes, songs, stories, and initial letter associations
- saying and hearing letter stroke descriptions
- responding to oral directions and games that involve listening and reacting

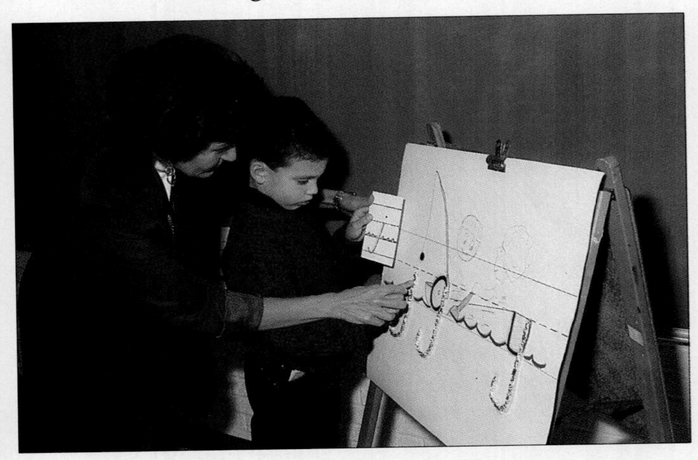

3. **The kinesthetic learner** The kinesthetic learner remembers best what is experienced through muscle movement. Therefore, the best instructional and practice strategies involve:
   - manipulating objects in various hands-on activities
   - dramatizing, miming, pantomiming, and gesturing
   - role-playing
   - participating in active games

Kinesthetic learners are active and often have short attention spans. Therefore, provide short, dispersed practice sessions. Demonstrate what you want them to do because they typically experience great difficulty following oral, sequential instruction and directions. Cue their attention by saying, "Watch!" "Now it's your turn." Kinesthetic learners think in terms of action.

For handwriting activities, it is essential that these children practice the letter strokes by using first their large and then small muscles to facilitate motor memory. Kinesthetic learners will be responsive to:

- air tracing letters
- manipulating large three-dimensional letters
- using action words and associations
- playing games that involve movement
- following large letter pathways on the chalkboard with a variety of writing instruments
- using warm-up and relaxation finger exercises to relieve the tension created by tight pencil grip and intense writing pressure

4. **The tactile learner** Tactile learners remember best by touching, feeling, and manipulating. Therefore, the best methods of instruction and practice include:
   - finger tracing
   - manipulating
   - project-based activities
   - games involving motion and physical contact

Tactile learners also tend to have short attention spans and therefore require short, dispersed practice sessions. Demonstrate your instructions. Cue their attention by saying, "Watch carefully!" "Now it's your turn." When they are writing, tactile learners have difficulty adjusting the size of their letters. Due to excessive pencil pressure, they tend to have messy papers with heavy lines and smudges. Tactile learners think in terms of touch.

For handwriting activities, it is essential that these children actually touch with their fingertips the shape of letters and strokes. This can be accomplished by having them handle three-dimensional letters and textured letters before attempting to form them. Tactile learners benefit from:

- finger tracing textured letters, using all of their fingers or at least the index finger and second finger together
- closing their eyes for greater concentration as they fingertrace
- practicing back writing and palm writing
- making their own textured letters from arts and crafts materials
- tracing and retracing letter models many times
- playing active games and using action words

In the general school population approximately 40% of the students are visual learners, 30% are auditory learners, and 30% are kinesthetic/tactile learners. Young children, students-at-risk, and underachievers are almost exclusively kinesthetic and tactile learners.

[Editor's Note: The Activity Banks that accompany each lesson in the teacher's editions often contain special needs activities. The chart on page T37 identifies the children with special needs, their characteristics, and strategies that work best in teaching them.]

Category	Characteristics	Teaching Method
Immature Learners	• Difficulty following directions • Short attention span • Underdeveloped fine motor control • Delayed concept formation • Mixed handedness • Typically kinesthetic/tactile learners • Include the "slow" learners	• Need to experience learning through hands-on activities
Students-at-Risk	• Unmotivated and underachieving	• Use a multimodality approach • Stress kinesthetic/tactile modes, coupled with highly motivating activities of practical value • Provide ample praise and positive consequences for good work
Children with Attention Deficit Disorders	• Difficulty focusing and sustaining attention to a task • Highly distractible, impulsive, and disorganized • Usually kinesthetic/tactile learners with secondary modality strengths	• Use a multimodality approach along with a variety of attending cues, strategies, and devices
Children with Kinesthetic Tactile Deficits	• Unable to receive, process, store, retrieve, and/or express information effectively by means of kinesthetic or tactile modes • Often reverse strokes, use excessive pencil pressure, have a poor pencil grip, exhibit inconsistency in letter size, form, slant, and spacing • Have poor eye-hand coordination and lack fine motor control	• Keep writing volume minimal and periods of practice short • Stress the child's stronger sensory modes in order to compensate for any neurological kinesthetic/tactile interference
Children with Visual Deficits	• Difficulty receiving, processing, storing, recalling, and/or expressing information by the visual mode • Difficulty with visual sequencing and discriminating size and form visually • Difficulty determining directionality, including letter and word reversals • Problem recognizing spatial relationships and figure-ground • Difficulty fixating, scanning, tracking, and converging on print • Inability to copy examples correctly	• Bypass visual stimuli as much as possible • Learning and practice activities should use the child's other stronger perceptual modes in order to compensate for neurological visual interference
Children with Auditory Deficits	• Difficulty receiving, processing, storing, recalling, and/or expressing information by the auditory mode • Inability to follow verbal directions or recognize sound/symbol relationships • Poor auditory sequencing and discrimination	• Bypass auditory stimuli when possible • Learning and practice activities should use child's stronger perceptual modes to compensate for neurological auditory interference **Allow children to:** • Experience letter formation and handwriting concepts • Engage large muscles (arms) before using small muscles (fingers) • Practice letters on vertical plane first (chalkboard), then on slanted plane (easel), and finally on desktop • Use letter models to trace and copy • Use templates to control strokes, then proceed to textured models • Use large letters, gradually reducing size

Manuscript Lower-case

a Start at the middle line; curve down left to the bottom line; curve up right to the beginning, and close; retrace down, and swing up.
[Middle start; around down, close up, down, and a monkey tail.]

b Start at the top line; slant down to the bottom line; curve up right to the middle line; curve left, and close.
[Top start; slant down, around, up, and a tummy.]

c Start a little below the middle line; curve up left to the middle line; curve down left to the bottom line; curve up right, and stop.
[Start below the middle; curve up, around, down, up, and stop.]

d Start at the middle line; curve down left to the bottom line; curve up right to the beginning; touch, and keep going up to the top line; retrace down, and swing up.
[Middle start; around down, touch, up high, down, and a monkey tail.]

e Start between the middle line and the bottom line; curve up right to the middle line; curve down left; touch, and keep going down to the bottom line; curve up right, and stop.
[Start between the middle and bottom; curve up, around, touch, down, up, and stop.]

f Start a little below the top line; curve up left to the top line; slant down to the bottom line. Make a crossbar on the middle line.
[Start below the top; curve up, around, and slant down. Cross.]

g Start at the middle line; curve down left to the bottom line; curve up right to the beginning, and close; retrace down to halfway below the bottom line, and hook left.
[Middle start; around down, close up, down under water, and a fishhook.]

h Start at the top line; slant down to the bottom line; retrace up halfway; make a hill to the right, and swing up.
[Top start; slant down, up over the hill, and a monkey tail.]

i Start at the middle line; slant down to the bottom line, and swing up. Make a dot above the letter.
[Middle start; slant down, and a monkey tail. Add a dot.]

j Start at the middle line; slant down to halfway below the bottom line, and hook left. Make a dot above the letter.
[Middle start; slant down under water, and a fishhook. Add a dot.]

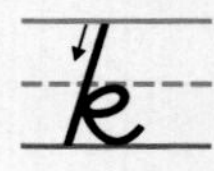

Start at the top line; slant down to the bottom line; retrace up halfway; curve right; make a small loop left, and close; slant down right to the bottom line, and swing up.
[Top start; slant down, up into a little tummy, and a monkey tail.]

l Start at the top line; slant down to the bottom line, and swing up.
[Top start; slant down, and a monkey tail.]

m Start at the middle line; slant down to the bottom line; retrace up, and make a hill to the right; retrace up; make another hill to the right, and swing up.
[Middle start; slant down, up over the hill, up over the hill again, and a monkey tail.]

n Start at the middle line; slant down to the bottom line; retrace up; make a hill to the right, and swing up.
[Middle start; slant down, up over the hill, and a monkey tail.]

o Start at the middle line; curve down left to the bottom line; curve up right to the beginning, and close.
[Middle start; around down, and close up.]

p Start at the middle line; slant down to halfway below the bottom line; retrace up; curve down right to the bottom line; curve left, and close.
[Middle start; slant down under water, up, around, and a tummy.]

q Start at the middle line; curve down left to the bottom line; curve up right to the beginning, and close; retrace down to halfway below the bottom line, and hook right.
[Middle start; around down, close up, down under water, and a backwards fishhook.]

r Start at the middle line; slant down to the bottom line; retrace up; curve right, and stop.
[Middle start; slant down, up, and a roof.]

s Start a little below the middle line; curve up left to the middle line and down left halfway; curve down right to the bottom line; curve up left, and stop.
[Start below the middle; curve up, around, down, and a snake tail.]

t Start at the top line; slant down to the bottom line, and swing up. Make a crossbar on the middle line.
[Top start; slant down, and a monkey tail. Cross.]

u Start at the middle line; slant down to the bottom line, and curve right; slant up to the middle line; retrace down, and swing up.
[Middle start; down, around, up, down, and a monkey tail.]

v Start at the middle line; slant down right to the bottom line; slant up right to the middle line.
[Middle start; slant down right, and slant up right.]

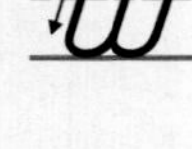

Start at the middle line; slant down to the bottom line, and curve right; slant up to the middle line; retrace down, and curve right; slant up to the middle line.
[Middle start; down, around, up, and down, around, up again.]

x Start at the middle line; slant down right to the bottom line, and swing up. Cross through the letter with a slant down left.
[Middle start; slant down right, and a monkey tail. Cross down left.]

y Start at the middle line; slant down to the bottom line, and curve right; slant up to the middle line; retrace down to halfway below the bottom line, and hook left.
[Middle start; down, around, up, down under water, and a fishhook.]

z Start at the middle line; make a bar to the right; slant down left to the bottom line; make a bar to the right.
[Middle start; over right, slant down left, and over right.]

Manuscript Capital

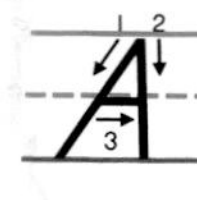

Start at the top line; slant down left to the bottom line. Start again at the same point; slant down right to the bottom line. Make a crossbar in the middle line.
[Top start; slant down left. Same start; slant down right. Middle bar across.]

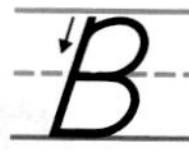

Start at the top line; slant down to the bottom line; retrace up; curve down right to the middle line; curve left, and close; curve down right to the bottom line; curve left, and close.
[Top start; slant down, up, around halfway, close, around again, and close.]

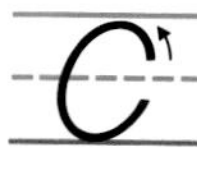

Start a little below the top line; curve up left to the top line; curve down left to the bottom line; curve up right, and stop.
[Start below the top; curve up, around, down, up, and stop.]

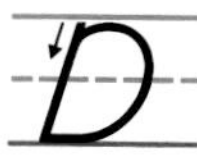

Start at the top line; slant down to the bottom line; retrace up; curve down right to the bottom line; curve left, and close.
[Top start; slant down, up, around, and close.]

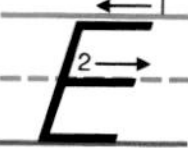

Start at the top line; make a bar to the left; slant down to the bottom line; make a bar to the right. Make a bar to the right on the middle line.
[Top start; over left, slant down, and over right. Middle bar across.]

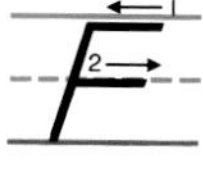

Start at the top line; make a bar to the left; slant down to the bottom line. Make a bar to the right on the middle line.
[Top start; over left, and slant down. Middle bar across.]

Start a little below the top line; curve up left to the top line; curve down left to the bottom line; curve up right to the middle line; make a bar to the left.
[Start below the top, curve up, around, down, up, and over left.]

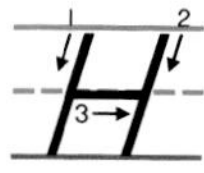

Start at the top line; slant down to the bottom line. Start again at the top line, to the right of the first start; slant down to the bottom line. Make a crossbar on the middle line.
[Top start; slant down. Another top start, to the right; slant down. Middle bar across.]

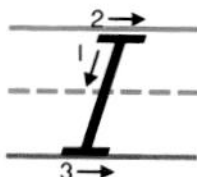

Start at the top line; slant down to the bottom line. Make a small crossbar at the top line, and another at the bottom line.
[Top start; slant down. Cross the top and the bottom line.]

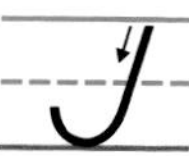

Start at the top line; slant down to the bottom line; curve up left, and stop.
[Top start; slant down, and curve up left.]

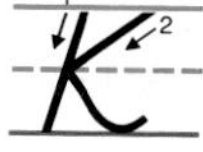

Start at the top line; slant down to the bottom line. Start again at the top line, to the right of the first start; slant down left to the middle line, and touch; slant down right to the bottom line, and swing up.
[Top start; slant down. Another top start, to the right; slant down left, touch, slant down right, and a monkey tail.]

Start at the top line; slant down to the bottom line; make a bar to the right.
[Top start; slant down, and over right.]

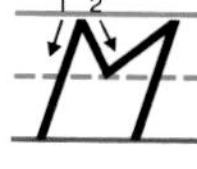

Start at the top line; slant down to the bottom line. Start again at the same point; slant down right to the middle line; slant up right to the top line; slant down to the bottom line.
[Top start; slant down. Same start; slant down right halfway, slant up right, and slant down.]

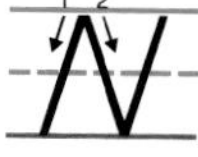

Start at the top line; slant down to the bottom line. Start again at the same point; slant down right to the bottom line; slant up to the top line.
[Top start; slant down. Same start; slant down right, and slant up.]

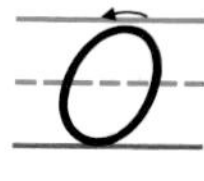

Start at the top line; curve down left to the bottom line; curve up right to the beginning, and close.
[Top start; around down, and close up.]

Start at the top line; slant down to the bottom line; retrace up; curve down right to the middle line; curve left, and close.
[Top start; slant down, up, around halfway, and close.]

Start at the top line; curve down left to the bottom line; curve up right to the beginning, and close. Cross through the bottom line of the letter with a curve down right.
[Top start; around down, and close up. Cross with a curve down right.]

Start at the top line; slant down to the bottom line; retrace up; curve down right to the middle line; curve left, and close; slant down right to the bottom line, and swing up.
[Top start; slant down, up, around halfway, close, slant down right, and a monkey tail.]

Start a little below the top line; curve up left to the top line and down left to the middle line; curve down right to the bottom line; curve up left, and stop.
[Start below the top; curve up, around, down, and a snake tail.]

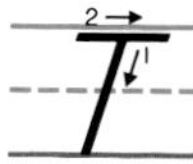

Start at the top line; slant down to the bottom line. Make a crossbar at the top line.
[Top start; slant down. Cross the top.]

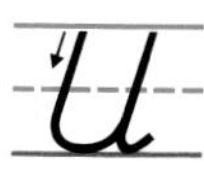

Start at the top line; slant down to the bottom line; and curve right; slant up to the top line; retrace down, and swing up.
[Top start; down, around, up, down, and a monkey tail.]

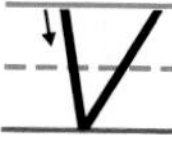

Start at the top line; slant down right to the bottom line; slant up right to the top line.
[Top start; slant down right, and slant up right.]

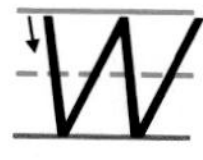

Start at the top line; slant down right to the bottom line; slant up right to the top line; slant down right to the bottom line; slant up right to the top line.
[Top start; slant down right, slant up right, slant down right, and slant up right again.]

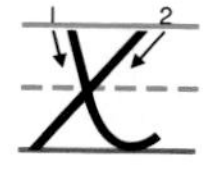

Start at the top line; slant down right to the bottom line; and swing up. Cross through the letter with a slant down left.
[Top start; slant down right, and a monkey tail. Cross down left.]

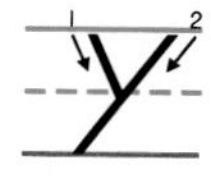

Start at the top line; slant down right to the middle line. Start again at the top line, to the right of the first start; slant down left to the middle line; touch, and keep going down to the bottom line.
[Top start; slant down right halfway. Another top start, to the right; slant down left, and touch on the way.]

Start at the top line; make a bar to the right; slant down left to the bottom line; make a bar to the right.
[Top start; over right, slant down left, and over right.]

Letter Descriptions

Cursive Lower-case

a Go overhill; retrace halfway; curve down to the bottom line; curve up right to the middle line, and close; retrace down, and swing up.
[Overhill; back, around down, close up, down, and up.]

b Go uphill to the top line; loop left down to the bottom line; curve up right to the middle line; curve left; and sidestroke right.
[Uphill high; loop down, around, up, and sidestroke.]

c Go overhill; retrace halfway; curve down to the bottom line, and swing up.
[Overhill; back, around, down, and up.]

d Go overhill; retrace halfway; curve down to the bottom line; curve up right to the middle line; touch, and keep going up to the top line; retrace down, and swing up.
[Overhill; back, around down, touch, up high, down, and up.]

e Go uphill to the middle line; loop left down to the bottom line; and swing up.
[Uphill; loop down, through, and up.]

f Go uphill to the top line; loop left down to halfway below the bottom line; loop right up to the bottom line; close; and swing up.
[Uphill high; loop down under water, loop up right, touch, and up.]

g Go overhill; retrace halfway; curve down to the bottom line; curve up right to the middle line, and close; retrace down to halfway below the bottom line; and loop left up through the bottom line.
[Overhill; back, around down, close up, down under water, loop up left, and through.]

h Go uphill to the top line; loop left down to the bottom line; retrace up halfway; make a hill to the right, and swing up.
[Uphill high, loop down, up over the hill, and up.]

i Go uphill to the middle line; retrace down, and swing up. Make a dot above the letter.
[Uphill; down, and up. Add a dot.]

j Go uphill to the middle line; retrace down to halfway below the bottom line; and loop left up through the bottom line. Make a dot above the letter.
[Uphill; down under water, loop up left, and through. Add a dot.]

k Go uphill to the top line; loop left down to the bottom line; retrace up halfway; curve right; make a small loop left, and close; slant down right to the bottom line, and swing up.
[Uphill high; loop down, up into a little tummy, slant down right, and up.]

l Go uphill to the top line; loop left down to the bottom line, and swing up.
[Uphill high; loop down, and up.]

m Go overhill; slant down to the bottom line; retrace up, and make a hill to the right; retrace up; make another hill to the right, and swing up.
[Overhill; down, up over the hill, up over the hill again, and up.]

n Go overhill; slant down to the bottom line; retrace up; make a hill to the right, and swing up.
[Overhill; down, up over the hill, and up.]

o Go overhill; retrace halfway; curve down to the bottom line; curve up right to the middle line; close; and sidestroke right.
[Overhill; back, around down, close up, and sidestroke.]

p Go uphill to the middle line; retrace down to halfway below the bottom line; retrace up; curve down right to the bottom line; curve left; close; and swing up.
[Uphill; down under water, up, around into a tummy, and up.]

q Go overhill; retrace halfway; curve down to the bottom line; curve up right to the middle line, and close; retrace down to halfway below the bottom line; loop right up to the bottom line; close; and swing up.
[Overhill; back, around down, close up, down under water, loop up right, touch, and up.]

r Go uphill to the middle line; sidestroke right; slant down to the bottom line, and swing up.
[Uphill; sidestroke, down, and up.]

s Go uphill to the middle line; slant down to the bottom line; curve left, and close; retrace to the bottom line, and swing up.
[Uphill; down, around, close, and up.]

t Go uphill to the top line; retrace down, and swing up. Make a crossbar on the middle line.
[Uphill high; down, and up. Cross.]

u Go uphill to the middle line; retrace down, and curve right; slant up to the middle line; retrace down, and swing up.
[Uphill; down, around, up, down, and up.]

v Go overhill; slant down to the bottom line, and curve right; slant up to the middle line; and sidestroke right.
[Overhill; down, around, up and sidestroke.]

w Go uphill to the middle line; retrace down, and curve right; slant up to the middle line; retrace down, and curve right; slant up to the middle line; and sidestroke right.
[Uphill; down, around, up, down, around, up again, and sidestroke.]

x Go overhill; slant down right to the bottom line, and swing up. Cross through the letter with a slant down left.
[Overhill; slant down right, and up. Cross down left.]

y Go overhill; slant down to the bottom line, and curve right; slant up to the middle line; retrace down to halfway below the middle line; and loop left up through the bottom line.
[Overhill; down, around, up, down under water, loop up left, and through.]

z Go overhill; curve down right to the bottom line; curve down right again to halfway below the bottom line; and loop left up through the bottom line.
[Overhill; around down, around again, and down under water, loop up left, and through.]

Cursive Capital

Start at the top line; curve down left to the bottom line; curve up right to the beginning, and close; retrace down, and swing up.
[Top start; around down, close up, down, and up.]

Start at the top line; slant down to the bottom line; retrace up; curve down right to the middle line; curve down right again to the bottom line; curve up left; touch; sidestroke right, and stop.
[Top start; down, up, around halfway, around again, touch, sidestroke, and stop.]

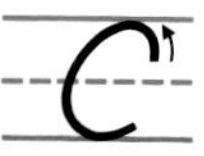

Start a little below the top line; curve up left to the top line; curve down left to the bottom line; and curve up right.
[Start below the top; curve up, around, down, and up.]

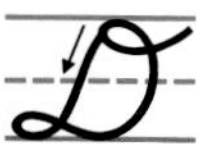

Start at the top line; slant down to the bottom line; curve left, and loop right; curve up right to the beginning; close; loop right, swing up, and stop.
[Top start; down, loop right, curve up, around, close, loop right, through, and stop.]

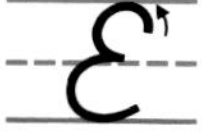

Start a little below the top line; curve up left to the top line; curve down left to the middle line; curve down left again to the bottom line; and curve up right.
[Start below the the top; curve up, around to the middle, around again to the bottom line, and up.]

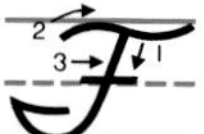

Start a little below the top line; slant down to the bottom line; and curve up left; sidestroke right. Make an overhill-underhill crossbar at the top line; and a straight crossbar on the middle line.
[Start below the top; down, around, up, and sidestroke. Wavy cross and a straight cross.]

Start at the bottom line; go uphill to the top line; loop left down to the middle line, and swing up; slant down to the bottom line; curve up left, across the uphill; sidestroke right, and stop.
[Bottom start; uphill high, loop through the middle, up, curve down, around, through the uphill, sidestroke, and stop.]

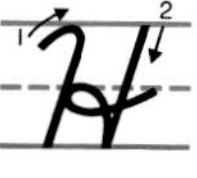

Start a little below the top line; curve up right to the top line; slant down to the bottom line. Start again at the top line, to the right of the first start; slant down to the bottom line; retrace up halfway; curve left, touch, loop right, swing up, and stop.
[Start below the top; make a cane. Top start, to the right; down, up, left, touch, loop right, through, and stop.]

Start a little below the middle line; sidestroke left; curve down right to the bottom line; go uphill to the top line; loop left down to the bottom line, and swing up.
[Start below the middle; sidestroke left, curve down, around, uphill high, loop down, and up.]

Start at the bottom line; curve up left to the top line; loop right down to halfway below the bottom line; loop up left, and through.
[Bottom start; curve up, around, touch on the way down under water, loop up left, and through.]

Start a little below the top line; curve up right to the top line; slant down to the bottom line. Start again at the top line, to the right of the first start; slant down left to the middle line, and touch; slant down right to the bottom line, and swing up.
[Start below the top; make a cane. Top start, to the right; slant down left, touch, slant down right, and up.]

Start a little below the top line; curve up right to the top line; loop left, and keep going down to the bottom line; curve left; loop right, and swing up.
[Start below the top; uphill; loop down, loop right, and up.]

Start a little below the top line; curve up right to the top line; slant down to the bottom line; retrace up, and make a hill to the right; retrace up; make another hill to the right, and swing up.
[Start below the top; make a cane, up over the hill, up over the hill again, and up.]

Start a little below the top line; curve up right to the top line; slant down to the bottom line; retrace up; make a hill to the right, and swing up.
[Start below the top; make a cane, up over the hill, and up.]

Start at the top line; curve down left to the bottom line; curve up right to the beginning, and close; loop right, swing up, and stop.
[Top start; around down, close up, loop right, through, and stop.]

Start at the top line; slant down to the bottom line; retrace up; curve down right to the middle line; curve left, and close.
[Top start; down, up, around halfway, and close.]

Start a little below the top line; curve up right to the top line; curve down right to the bottom line; loop right, and swing up.
[Start below the top; curve up, around, down, loop right, and up.]
For an alternative way of writing cursive *Q*, see the stroke description for manuscript *Q* on page T39.

Start at the top line; slant down to the bottom line; retrace up; curve down right to the middle line; curve left, and close; slant down right to the bottom line, and swing up.
[Top start; down, up, around halfway, close, slant down right, and up.]

Start at the bottom line; go uphill to the top line; loop left down to the middle line; curve down right to the bottom line; curve up left, across the uphill; sidestroke right, and stop.
[Bottom start; uphill high, loop through the middle, curve down, around, through the uphill, sidestroke, and stop.]

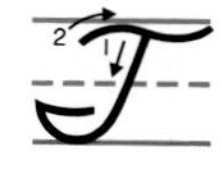

Start a little below the top line; slant down to the bottom line, and curve up left; sidestroke right. Make an overhill-underhill crossbar at the top line.
[Start below the top; down, around, up, and sidestroke. Wavy cross.]

Start a little below the top line; curve up right to the top line, slant down to the bottom line, and curve right; slant up to the top line; retrace down, and swing up.
[Start below the top; make a cane, around, up, down, and up.]

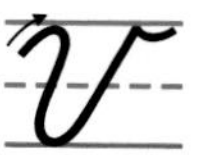

Start a little below the top line; curve up right to the top line; slant down to the bottom line, and curve right; slant up right to the top line; sidestroke right, and stop.
[Start below the top; make a cane, around, slant up right, sidestroke, and stop.]

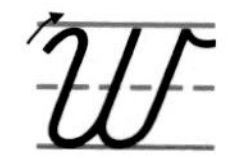

Start a little below the top line; curve up right to the top line; slant down to the bottom line, and curve right; slant up to the top line; retrace down, and curve right; slant up to the top line; sidestroke right, and stop.
[Start below the top; make a cane, around, up, down, around, up again, sidestroke, and stop.]

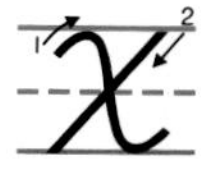

Start a little below the top line; curve up right to the top line; slant down right to the bottom line, and swing up. Cross through the letter with a slant down left.
[Start below the top; curve up, slant down right, and up. Cross down left.]

Start a little below the top line; curve up right to the top line; slant down to the bottom line, and curve right; slant up to the top line; retrace down to halfway below the bottom line; loop up left, and through.
[Start below the top; make a cane, around, up, down under water, loop up left, and through.]

Start a little below the top line; curve up right to the top line; curve down right to the bottom line; curve down right again to halfway below the bottom line; loop up left, and through.
[Start below the top; curve up, around, down, around again, and down under water, loop up left, and through.]

Numbers

Start at the top line; slant down to the bottom line.
[Top start; slant down.]

Start a little below the top line; curve up right to the top line; curve down right to the middle line; slant down left to the bottom line; make a bar to the right.
[Start below the top; curve up, around, slant down left, and over right.]

Start a little below the top line; curve up right to the top line; curve down right to the middle line; curve down right again to the bottom line; curve up left, and stop.
[Start below the top; curve up, around halfway; around again, up, and stop.]

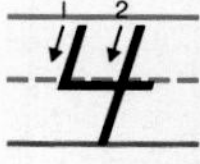

Start at the top line; slant down to the middle line; make a bar to the right. Start again at the top line, to the right of of the first start; slant down through the bar to the bottom line.
[Top start; down halfway; over right. Another top start, to the right; slant down, and through.]

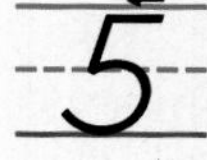

Start at the top line; make a bar to the left; slant down to the middle line; curve down right to the bottom line; curve up left, and stop.
[Top start; over left; slant down halfway; curve around, down, up, and stop.]

Start at the top line; slant down left to the middle line; curve down left to the bottom line; curve up right to the middle line; curve left, and close.
[Top start; slant down, and curve around; up; and close.]

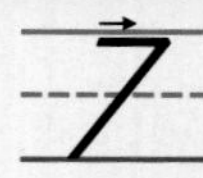

Start at the top line; make a bar to the right; slant down left to the bottom line.
[Top start; over right; slant down left.]

Start a little below the top line; curve up left to the top line and down left to the middle line; curve down right to the bottom line; curve up left; slant up right, through the middle line, to the beginning, and touch.
[Start below the top; curve up, around, down; a snake tail; slant up right; through; and touch.]

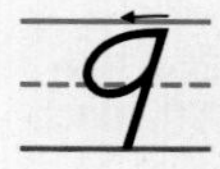

Start at the top line; curve down left to the middle line; curve up right to the beginning, and close; slant down to the bottom line.
[Top start; curve down, around, close; slant down.]

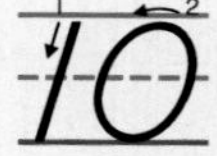

Start at the top line; slant down to the bottom line. Start again at the top line, to the right of the first start; curve down left to the bottom line; curve up right to the top line; and close.
[Top start; slant down. Another top start to the right; curve left and down, around, and close.]

Descripciones de las letras de

molde minúsculas

Empieza en el medio. Traza una curva hasta abajo, curva hacia la derecha, sube y cierra. Baja por la misma línea y termina con una colita.

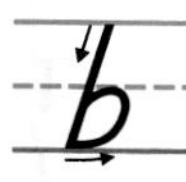

Empieza arriba. Traza una línea inclinada hasta abajo, traza una curva hacia la derecha y arriba, y forma una barriguita.

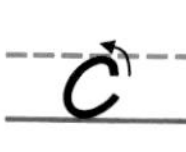

Empieza debajo de la línea del medio. Traza una curva hacia arriba, sigue la curva hacia la izquierda y abajo, sube un poquito.

Empieza en el medio. Traza una curva hacia la izquierda y abajo, sube hasta el principio, sigue hasta arriba, baja por la misma línea y termina con una colita.

Empieza entre las líneas del medio y abajo. Traza una curva hacia arriba, curva hacia la izquierda y abajo, toca, baja y sube un poquito.

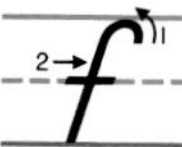

Empieza debajo de la línea de arriba. Traza una curva hacia arriba. Sigue y baja con una línea inclinada hasta abajo. Traza una pequeña línea horizontal en el medio.

Empieza en el medio. Traza una curva hacia la izquierda hasta la línea de abajo, curva hacia la derecha, sube y cierra. Vuelve por la misma línea hacia abajo hasta debajo del agua y termina con un gancho hacia la izquierda.

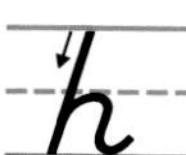

Empieza arriba. Traza una línea inclinada hasta abajo. Sube por la misma línea hasta el medio. Curva a la derecha, baja y termina con una colita.

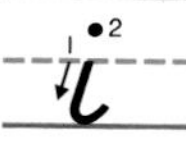

Empieza en el medio. Traza una línea inclinada hasta abajo y termina con una colita. Añade un punto arriba.

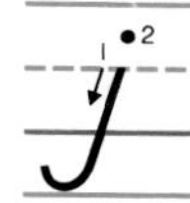

Empieza en el medio. Traza una línea inclinada hasta debajo del agua y termina con un anzuelo hacia la izquierda. Añade un punto arriba.

Empieza arriba. Traza una línea inclinada hasta abajo, sube por la misma línea hasta la mitad, forma una barriguita y termina con una colita.

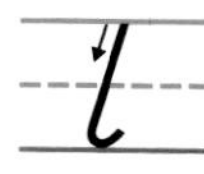

Empieza arriba. Traza una línea inclinada hasta abajo y termina con una colita.

Empieza en el medio. Traza una línea inclinada hasta abajo, vuelve por la misma línea, curva hacia la derecha, baja vuelve y curva otra vez hacia la derecha, baja y termina con una colita.

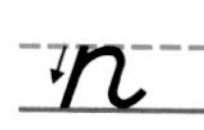

Empieza en el medio. Traza una línea inclinada hasta abajo, vuelve por la misma línea, curva hacia la derecha, baja y termina con una colita.

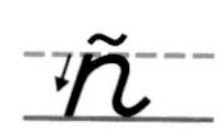

Repite la letra n. Traza arriba un sombrerito de línea ondulada.

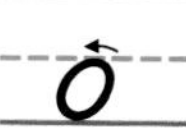

Empieza en el medio. Curva hacia la izquierda y abajo, y cierra en redondo hacia la derecha.

Empieza en el medio. Traza una línea inclinada hasta debajo del agua. Vuelve por la misma línea hasta arriba, curva y forma una barriguita.

Empieza en el medio. Traza una curva hacia la izquierda y abajo, curva hacia arriba y cierra. Vuelve por la misma línea hasta debajo del agua y termina con un gancho a la derecha.

Empieza en el medio. Traza una línea inclinada hasta abajo. Sube por la misma línea, curva a la derecha y para.

Empieza debajo de la línea del medio. Curva hacia la izquierda y arriba, sigue la curva hacia abajo un poco, curva hacia la derecha y termina con una colita hacia la izquierda.

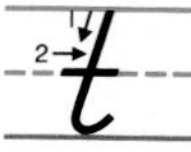

Empieza arriba. Traza una línea inclinada hasta abajo y termina con una colita. Traza una raya corta horizontal en el medio.

Empieza en el medio. Traza una línea inclinada hasta abajo, curva, sube inclinando hasta el medio, baja por la misma línea y termina con una colita.

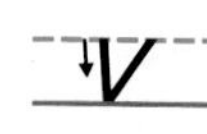

Empieza en el medio. Traza una línea inclinada hacia abajo y la derecha, y sube inclinando hacia la derecha hasta la línea del medio.

Empieza en el medio. Traza una línea inclinada hacia la derecha y sube inclinando hacia la derecha hasta la línea del medio y repite.

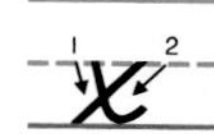

Empieza en el medio. Traza una línea inclinada hacia la derecha y abajo, y termina con una colita. Traza una línea cruzada de derecha a izquierda.

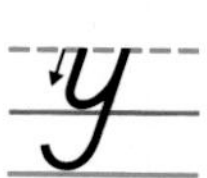

Empieza en el medio. Traza una línea inclinada hasta abajo, curva a la derecha y sube. Baja por la misma línea hasta debajo del agua y termina con un gancho a la izquierda.

Empieza en el medio. Traza una línea corta hacia la derecha, baja inclinando hacia la izquierda y abajo, y termina con una línea corta horizontal hacia la derecha.

Descripciones de las letras de

molde mayúsculas

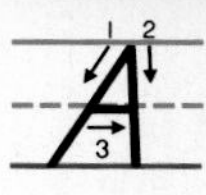
Empieza arriba. Traza una línea inclinada hacia la izquierda y abajo. Empieza otra vez en el mismo punto y baja hacia la derecha hasta abajo. Traza una línea horizontal en el medio.

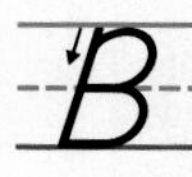
Empieza arriba. Traza una línea inclinada hasta abajo. Vuelve por la misma línea hacia arriba, curva en redondo hacia la derecha y toca en el medio. Curva otra vez en redondo hacia la derecha y cierra abajo.

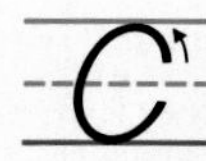
Empieza debajo de la línea. Curva hasta arriba, y curva en redondo hacia la izquierda y hasta abajo. Curva un poquito hacia arriba y para.

Empieza arriba. Traza una línea inclinada hasta abajo. Vuelve por la misma línea hasta arriba. Curva en redondo hacia la derecha y abajo, y cierra.

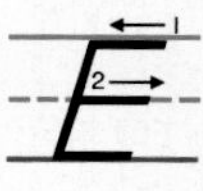
Empieza arriba. Traza una línea corta hacia la izquierda, baja inclinado hasta abajo. Traza una línea corta hacia la derecha. Traza una línea corta en el medio.

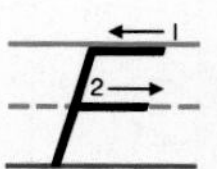
Empieza arriba. Traza una línea corta hacia la izquierda, baja inclinado hasta abajo. Traza una línea corta en el medio.

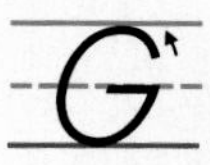
Empieza debajo de la línea. Curva hasta arriba y curva en redondo hacia la izquierda y hasta abajo. Curva un poquito hacia arriba y traza una línea corta hacia la izquierda.

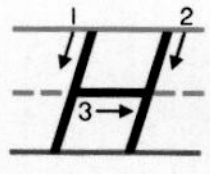
Empieza arriba. Traza una línea inclinada hasta abajo. Empieza otra vez arriba a la derecha y traza otra línea inclinada hasta abajo. Une con una línea corta horizontal en el medio.

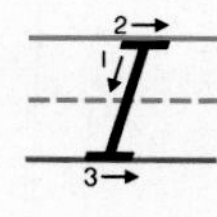
Empieza arriba. Traza una línea inclinada hasta abajo. Una línea corta arriba y otra línea corta abajo.

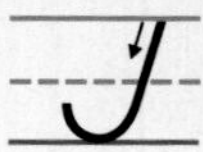
Empieza arriba. Traza una línea inclinada hasta abajo. Curva hacia la izquierda.

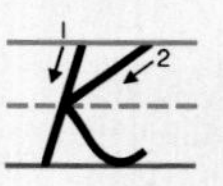
Empieza arriba. Traza una línea inclinada hasta abajo. Empieza otra vez arriba a la derecha. Traza una línea inclinada hacia la izquierda y al medio. Sigue inclinado a la derecha hasta abajo y termina con una colita.

Empieza arriba. Traza una línea inclinada hasta abajo y sigue con una línea corta horizontal hacia la derecha.

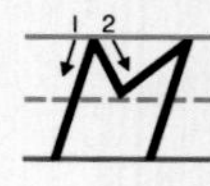
Empieza arriba. Traza una línea inclinada hasta abajo. Empieza otra vez en el mismo punto hacia la derecha hasta el medio. Vuelve arriba hacia la derecha y sigue con una línea inclinada hasta abajo.

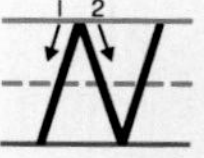
Empieza arriba. Traza una línea inclinada hasta abajo. En el mismo comienzo traza una línea inclinada hacia la derecha y abajo. Traza una línea inclinada hasta la línea de arriba.

Repite la "N". Traza un sombrerito de línea ondulada encima de la letra.

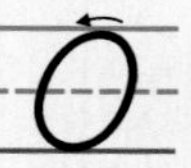
Empieza arriba. Traza una curva hacia la izquierda y abajo, sube en redondo y cierra.

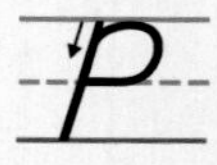
Empieza arriba. Traza una línea inclinada hacia abajo, sube por la misma línea, traza una curva hacia la derecha hasta el medio, curva hacia la izquierda y cierra.

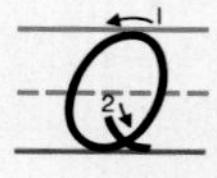
Empieza arriba. Traza una curva hacia la izquierda y abajo, sube en redondo y cierra. Traza una raya que cruce el fondo de la letra, con curva hacia abajo y a la derecha.

Empieza arriba. Traza una línea inclinada hacia abajo, sube por la misma línea, traza una curva hacia la derecha hasta el medio. Curva hacia la izquierda y cierra. Traza una línea inclinada hacia la derecha y abajo, y termina con un rabito.

Empieza debajo de la línea de arriba. Traza una curva hacia la izquierda y arriba. Curva y baja hasta el medio y termina con una cola de serpiente hasta la línea de abajo.

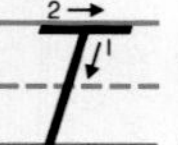
Empieza arriba. Traza una línea inclinada hacia abajo. Traza una raya horizontal atravesada arriba.

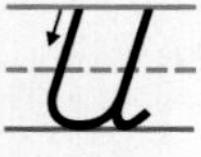
Empieza arriba. Baja, una curva a la derecha. Sube, baja por la misma línea y termina con un rabito.

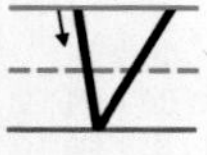
Empieza arriba. Traza una línea inclinada hacia la derecha y abajo. Sube con línea inclinada hacia la derecha y arriba.

Empieza arriba. Traza una línea inclinada hacia la derecha y abajo. Traza una línea inclinada hacia la derecha y arriba. Baja con una línea inclinada hacia la derecha y sube otra vez inclinando hacia la derecha.

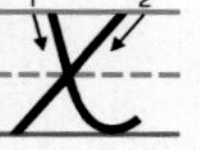
Empieza arriba. Traza una línea inclinada hacia la derecha y abajo y termina con un rabito. Cruza con una línea hacia la izquierda y abajo.

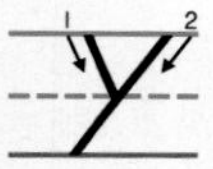
Empieza arriba. Traza una línea inclinada hacia la derecha y abajo hasta el medio. Empieza otra vez a la derecha de la línea y traza otra línea inclinada hacia la izquierda. Toca en el medio y sigue hasta abajo.

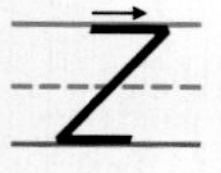
Empieza arriba. Traza una línea recta hacia la derecha. Traza una línea inclinada hacia la izquierda y abajo, y termina con una línea recta hacia la derecha.

Descripciones de las letras

cursivas minúsculas

a Sube la cuesta hasta el medio, vuelve hacia atrás, traza una curva hacia abajo, sube y cierra, baja por la misma línea y sube un poquito.

b Sube la cuesta hasta arriba, traza un lazo hacia la izquierda y abajo, haz una curva y sube. Termina con una corta raya.

c Sube la cuesta hasta el medio, vuelve en curva hacia atrás hasta la línea. Haz una curva y sube un poquito.

d Sube la cuesta hasta el medio, vuelve hacia atrás en la misma línea, traza una curva hacia abajo, toca, sube hasta arriba, baja y sube un poquito.

e Sube la cuesta, traza un lazo, hacia la izquierda y abajo, y sube un poquito.

f Sube la cuesta hasta arriba, traza un lazo hacia la izquierda y abajo hasta debajo del agua. Traza un lazo hacia la derecha y arriba, toca y sube un poquito.

g Sube la cuesta hasta el medio, vuelve hacia atrás, traza una curva hacia abajo, sube y cierra. Vuelve por la misma línea hasta debajo del agua, traza un lazo hacia la izquierda y arriba, y atraviesa un poco la línea.

h Sube la cuesta hasta arriba, traza un lazo hacia la izquierda y abajo, sube la cuesta, baja y sube un poquito.

i Sube la cuesta hasta el medio, baja y sube un poquito. Añade un punto arriba.

j Sube la cuesta hasta el medio, baja hasta debajo del agua, traza un lazo hacia la izquierda y arriba, y atraviesa la línea. Añade un punto arriba.

k Sube la cuesta hasta arriba, traza un lazo hacia la izquierda y abajo, sube y haz una barriguita. Traza una línea inclinada hacia abajo y a la derecha y sube un poquito.

l Sube la cuesta hasta arriba, traza un lazo hacia la izquierda y abajo y sube un poquito.

m Sube la cuesta hasta el medio, baja, sube la cuesta, baja, sube otra vez más y baja, y sube un poquito.

n Sube la cuesta hasta el medio, baja, y sube la cuesta otra vez y baja, y sube un poquito.

ñ Repite la "n." Traza un sombrerito de línea ondulada encima de la letra.

o Sube la cuesta hasta el medio, vuelve hacia atrás, traza una curva hacia abajo, sube y cierra en redondo. Termina con corta raya horizontal.

p Sube la cuesta, traza una línea hasta debajo del agua, vuelve a subir, haz una barriguita y sube un poquito.

q Suba la cuesta hasta el medio, vuelve hacia atrás, traza una curva hacia abajo, sube y cierra, vuelve por la misma línea hasta debajo del agua. Haz un lazo hacia la derecha y arriba, toca y sube un poquito.

r Sube la cuesta. Traza una pequeña línea inclinada hacia abajo, baja y sube un poquito.

s Sube la cuesta. Baja, curva hacia la izquierda, cierra abajo y sube un poquito.

t Sube la cuesta hasta arriba, baja por la misma línea y sube un poquito. Cruza con raya corta en el medio.

u Sube la cuesta, baja, curva a la derecha, sube, baja por la misma línea y sube un poquito.

v Sube la cuesta hasta el medio, curva y baja, curva y sube. Termina con raya corta horizontal.

w Sube la cuesta, baja, curva y sube. Baja otra vez, curva y sube. Termina con raya corta horizontal.

x Sube la cuesta hasta el medio, curva y baja inclinado hacia la derecha y abajo. Sube un poquito. Cruza en el medio con raya hacia la izquierda y abajo.

y Sube la cuesta hasta el medio, curva y baja, curva y sube. Vuelve hasta debajo del agua, traza un lazo hacia izquierda y arriba.

z Sube la cuesta hasta el medio, curva hacia la derecha y abajo, toca la línea, curva hasta debajo del agua. Traza un lazo hacia la izquierda y arriba, y atraviesa la línea.

Descripciones de las letras

cursivas mayúsculas

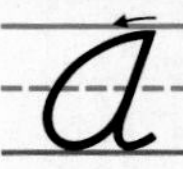

Empieza arriba, traza una curva hacia la izquierda y abajo, sube y cierra, baja por la misma línea y sube un poquito.

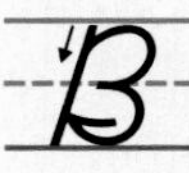

Empieza arriba, baja con un trazo inclinado, sube por el mismo trazo, curva hasta el medio, curva otra vez y toca. Raya horizontal y para.

Empieza debajo de la línea de arriba, traza una curva hacia arriba, curva hasta abajo y sube un poquito.

Empieza arriba, baja con trazo inclinado, curva a la izquierda, traza un lazo hacia la derecha, curva hacia arriba y cierra, traza un lazo hacia la derecha, atraviesa y para.

Empieza debajo de la línea de arriba, traza una curva hacia arriba, curva hacia la izquierda hasta el medio, curva otra vez hasta abajo y sube un poquito.

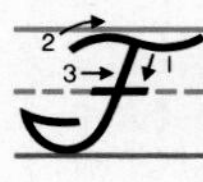

Empieza debajo de la línea de arriba, baja inclinado. Sube y traza una raya horizontal pequeña. Traza línea atravesada horizontal ondeada y línea atravesada horizontal recta.

Empieza abajo, sube la cuesta con una curva hasta arriba, traza un lazo y atraviesa por el medio, sube, traza una curva hacia abajo, curva, atraviesa la cuesta. Raya horizontal y para.

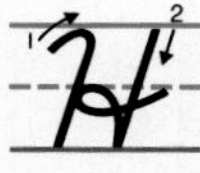

Empieza debajo de la línea de arriba, traza un bastón hasta la línea de abajo. Empieza otra vez arriba, a la derecha, baja y sube hacia la izquierda hasta el medio, curva y toca, traza un lazo hacia derecha, atraviesa y para.

Empieza debajo de la línea del medio con una raya horizontal hacia la izquierda, traza una curva hacia abajo, curva y sube la cuesta hasta arriba, traza un lazo hacia la izquierda y abajo, y sube un poquito.

Empieza abajo, traza una curva hacia arriba, curva y toca al pasar hacia abajo hasta debajo del agua, traza un lazo hacia la izquierda y arriba, y atraviesa un poquito.

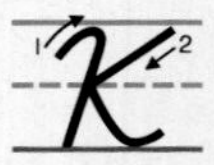

Empieza debajo de la línea de arriba, traza un bastón hasta abajo. Empieza otra vez arriba a la derecha, traza una línea inclinada hacia la izquierda y al medio toca, traza una línea inclinada hacia la derecha y abajo, sube un poquito.

Empieza debajo de la línea de arriba, sube la cuesta, traza un lazo hacia la izquierda y abajo, traza un lazo hacia la derecha y sube un poquito.

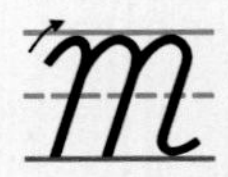

Empieza debajo de la línea de arriba, traza un bastón hasta abajo, sube por la misma línea, curva y baja. Sube, curva y baja otra vez y sube un poquito.

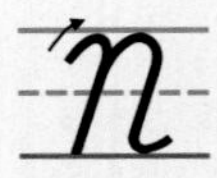

Empieza debajo de la línea de arriba, traza un bastón hasta abajo, sube por la misma línea, curva y baja otra vez y sube un poquito.

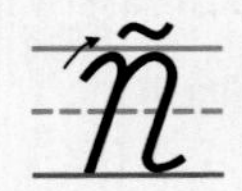

Repite la "N". Traza un sombrerito de línea ondulada encima de la letra.

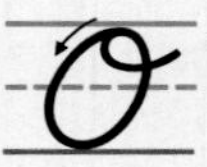

Empieza arriba, traza una curva hacia abajo, sube en redondo y cierra. Traza un lazo hacia la derecha, atraviesa y sube un poquito.

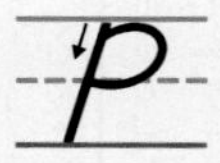

Empieza arriba, baja y sube por la misma línea, traza una curva hacia la derecha hasta el medio y cierra.

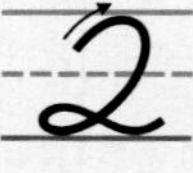

Empieza debajo de la línea de arriba, traza una curva hacia la derecha y arriba, curva hacia la izquierda y baja, traza un lazo hacia la derecha y sube un poquito.

Para escribir de una manera alternativa la letra *Q* cursiva, véase la descripción de trazos para la letra *Q* de molde en la página T39.

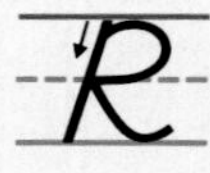

Empieza arriba, baja y sube por la misma línea, traza una curva hacia la derecha hasta el medio y cierra, traza una línea inclinada hacia la derecha y abajo y sube un poquito.

Empieza abajo, sube la cuesta hasta arriba, traza un lazo hacia la izquierda a través de la línea del medio, traza una curva hacia abajo, curva y atraviesa la primera línea, haz una raya horizontal y para.

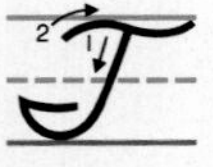

Empieza debajo de la línea de arriba, baja, curva y sube. Raya horizontal. Linea atravesada horizontal y ondeada.

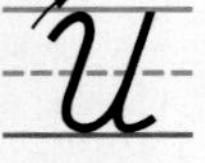

Empieza debajo de la línea de arriba, traza un bastón, curva y sube, baja por la misma línea y sube un poquito.

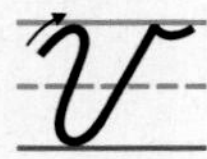

Empieza debajo de la línea de arriba, traza un bastón hacia abajo y curva. Traza una línea inclinada hacia la derecha y arriba. Raya horizontal y para.

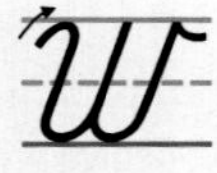

Empieza debajo de la línea de arriba, traza un bastón hacia abajo. Curva y sube, baja por la misma línea, curva y sube otra vez. Raya horizontal y para.

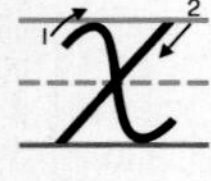

Empieza debajo de la línea de arriba, traza una curva hacia arriba, sigue con línea inclinada hacia abajo y a la derecha. Sube un poquito, traza una línea atravesada hacia la izquierda y abajo.

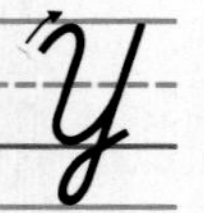

Empieza debajo de la línea de arriba, traza un bastón hasta abajo. Sube, baja por la misma línea hasta debajo del agua, traza un lazo hacia la izquierda y arriba y atraviesa un poquito.

Empieza debajo de la línea arriba, traza una curva hacia la derecha y arriba. Sigue la curva y baja, curva otra vez hacia la derecha y baja hasta debajo del agua. Traza un lazo hacia la izquierda y arriba y atraviesa un poquito la línea de abajo.

Descripciones de

los números

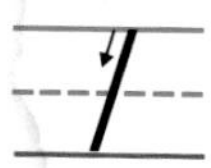

Empieza arriba, traza una línea inclinada hasta la línea de abajo.

Empieza debajo de la línea de arriba, traza una curva hacia arriba y curva a la derecha, baja con línea inclinada hacia abajo e izquierda y sigue con línea recta hacia la derecha.

Empieza debajo de la línea de arriba, traza una curva hacia arriba y continúa por la derecha hasta el medio, curva otra vez, hasta abajo y sube un poquito.

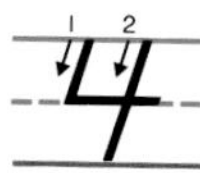

Empieza arriba, baja hasta el medio, traza una línea recta hacia la derecha. Empieza de nuevo arriba a la derecha con una línea inclinada hasta abajo y atraviesa la línea.

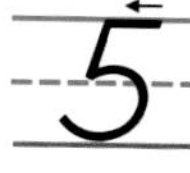

Empieza arriba, traza una línea hacia la izquierda, baja inclinando hasta el medio, curva hacia la derecha y sube un poquito.

Empieza arriba, traza una línea inclinada hacia abajo y termina con una curva hacia arriba, y cierra.

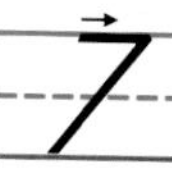

Empieza arriba, traza una línea hacia la derecha, baja con una línea inclinada hacia abajo y la izquierda.

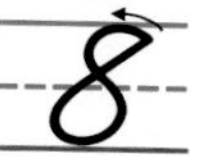

Empieza debajo de la línea de arriba. Traza una curva hacia arriba, y baja. Haz una curva al revés de la otra y cierra con una línea inclinada hasta arriba y a la derecha pasando por el medio de las curvas.

Empieza arriba, traza una curva hacia la izquierda abajo hasta la mitad, cierra con una línea inclinada hacia abajo.

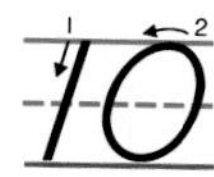

Empieza arriba, traza una línea inclinada hasta abajo. Empieza otra vez arriba al lado del otro y curva a la izquierda y abajo, y sigue la curva hasta arriba y cierra en redondo.

Spanish Glossary

above	encima
across	a través, en medio, horizontal
add a dot	añade un punto
again	otra vez, de nuevo
a little	un poquito
another	otro, otra
around	traza una curva
back	atrás
backwards	hacia atrás, al revés
bar across	raya horizontal
below	debajo
bottom	abajo, bajo
close/close up	cierra
cross	raya o línea horizontal, a través, atraviesa, cruza
cross the top	raya o línea arriba
cross through	cruza, atraviesa
curve	curva, traza una curva
down	abajo, bajo, baja
fishhook	anzuelo
overhill	sube la cuesta hasta el medio
uphill	sube la cuesta
halfway	hasta la mitad
high	alto, alta, hasta arriba
into a (little) tummy	en una barriguita
keep going	sigue
left	izquierda
letter	letra
loop	lazo
make a cane	traza un bastón
middle bar	raya horizontal en el medio
middle	medio
middle start	empieza en el medio
monkey tail	colita
over right	a la derecha, hacia la derecha
over left	a la izquierda, hacia la izquierda
over the hill	sube la cuesta
right	derecha
roof	techo
same start	mismo comienzo
side stroke	raya horizontal
slant	inclinado, inclinada
snake tail	cola de serpiente
start	empieza
start below the middle	empieza debajo de la línea del medio
start below the top	empieza debajo de la línea de arriba
stop	para
straight cross	línea horizontal recta
the top and the bottom	arriba y abajo
through	a través
to the	al, a la
top line	línea de arriba
top start	empieza arriba
touch	toca
touch on the way	toca al pasar
tummy (little)	barriguita
up	arriba, sube
under water	debajo del agua
wavy cross	línea horizontal ondeada
with a curve	con una curva

Scope and Sequence Chart

KEY:

RB Reteaching Book

Preparing for handwriting

	Kindergarten	Book 1
Eye-Hand coordination	17-18	15-16
Fine motor coordination	19-20	17-18
Left-to-right progression	15-16	19-20
Letter discrimination	40,102	21-24
Likenesses and differences	9-10	9-10
Number discrimination	22	25-26
Print awareness	163-164	32, 86
Shape	9-10	
Spatial relationships	11-14	11-14
above-below beside	13	
around		12
over-under	14	14
left and right	7, 8, 16	
top-bottom	12	
top-middle-bottom	12	12
up-down	11	11
Visual discrimination	9-10, 22, 40, 102	9-10, 21-26

Learning handwriting

Letters

Manuscript

	Kdgn	Book 1	Book 2	Book 3	Book 4	Book 5	Book 6	Book 7	Book 8
a	41-42, 55	33, 40, 41	12-13, 18, 19	13, 20, 21	6	6	6	6, 9	9, 25, 31
A	131-132, 145	111,118,119 RB 57	12-13, 18, 19	13, 20, 21	7	7	7	5, 8	6, 8, 23, 31, 39, 43
b	59-60, 69	44, 50, 51 RB 15	22-23, 26, 27 RB 10	15, 20, 21 RB 9	6	6	6	6, 9	9, 25, 31
B	133-134, 145	112, 118, 119 RB 59	22-23, 26, 27 RB10	15, 20, 21 RB 9	7	7	7	5, 8	8, 31, 39
c	49-50, 56	37, 40, 41 RB 7	14-15, 18, 19	14, 20, 21	6	6	6	6, 9	9, 25, 31
C	103-104, 113	93, 98, 99	14-15, 18, 19	14, 20, 21	7	7	7	5, 8	6, 8, 23, 31, 39, 43
d	43-44, 55	34, 40, 41	12-13, 18, 19 RB 5	13, 20, 21	6	6	6	6, 9	9, 25, 31
D	135-136, 145	113, 118, 119 RB 61	12-13, 18, 19 RB 5	13, 20, 21	7	7	7	5, 8	6, 8, 23, 31, 39, 43
e	51-52, 56	38, 40, 41 RB 9	16-17, 18, 19 RB 7	14, 20, 21 RB 6	6	6	6	6, 9	9, 25, 31

	Kdgn	Book 1	Book 2	Book 3	Book 4	Book 5	Book 6	Book 7	Book 8
E	147-148, 161	121, 128, 129 RB 69	16-17, 18, 19 RB 7	14, 20, 21 RB 6	7	7	7	5, 8	6, 8, 23, 31, 39, 43
f	57-58, 69	43, 50, 51 RB 13	22-23, 26, 27 RB 9	15, 20, 21 RB 8	6	6	6	6, 9	9
F	149-150, 161	122, 128, 129 RB 71	22-23, 26, 27 RB 9	15, 20, 21 RB 8	7	7	7	5, 8	6, 8, 23, 31,39
g	47-48, 55	36, 40, 41 RB 5	14-15,18,19 RB 6	13, 20, 21 RB 5	6	6	6	6, 9	9, 31
G	105-106, 113	94, 98, 99 RB 41	14-15, 18, 19 RB 6	13, 20, 21 RB 5	7	7	7	5, 8	6, 8, 23, 31, 39, 43
h	65-66, 70	47, 50, 51 RB 17	24-25, 26, 27 RB 11	16, 20, 21 RB 10	6	6	6	6, 9	9, 25, 31
H	125-126, 130	106, 108, 109 RB 53	24-25, 26, 27 RB 11	16, 20, 21 RB 10	7	7	7	5, 8	6, 23, 31 43
i	71-72, 89	53, 62, 63	30-31, 38, 39 RB 13	17, 20, 21	6	6	6	6, 9	9, 25, 31
I	115-116, 129	101, 108, 109 RB 47	30-31, 38, 39 RB 13	17, 20, 21	7	7	7	5, 8	6, 8, 23, 31, 39, 43
j	79-80, 89	57, 62, 63 RB 25	34-35, 38, 39 RB 17	18, 20, 21 RB 14	6	6	6	6	9
J	121-122, 129	104, 108, 109 RB 51	34-35, 38, 39 RB 17	18, 20, 21 RB 14	7	7	7	5, 8	8, 31, 39, 43
k	67-68, 70	48, 50, 51 RB 19	24-25, 26, 27 RB 12	16, 20, 21 RB 11	6	6	6	9	9, 31
K	127-128, 130	107, 108, 109 RB 55	24-25, 26, 27 RB 12	16, 20, 21 RB 11	7	7	7	5, 8	8, 23, 31, 39, 43
l	61-62, 69	45, 50, 51	22-23, 26, 27	15, 20, 21	6	6	6	6, 9	9, 25, 31
L	117-118, 129	102, 108, 109 RB 49	22-23, 26, 27	15, 20, 21	7	7	7	5, 8	6, 8, 23, 39, 43
m	85-86, 90	60, 62, 63 RB 31	36-37, 38, 39 RB 20	18, 20, 21 RB 17	6	6	6	6, 9	9, 25, 31
M	137-138, 145	114, 118, 119 RB 63	36-37, 38, 39 RB 20	18, 20, 21 RB 17	7	7	7	5, 8	6, 8, 23, 31, 39, 43
n	83-84, 90	59, 62, 63 RB 29	36-37, 38, 39 RB 19	18, 20, 21 RB 16	6	6	6	6, 9	9, 25, 31
N	139-140, 146	115, 118, 119 RB 65	36-37, 38, 39 RB 19	18, 20, 21 RB 16	7	7	7	5, 8	6, 8, 23, 31, 39, 43
o	45-46, 55, 90	35, 40, 41	12-13, 18, 19	13, 20, 21	6	6	6	6, 9	9, 25, 31
O	107-108, 113	95, 98, 99	12-13, 18, 19	13, 20, 21	7	7	7	5, 8	6, 8, 23, 31, 39, 43

	Kdgn	Book 1	Book 2	Book 3	Book 4	Book 5	Book 6	Book 7	Book 8
p	87-88, 90	61, 62, 63 RB 33	36-37, 38, 39	18, 20, 21	6	6	6	6, 9	9, 25
P	141-142, 146	116, 118, 119	36-37, 38, 39	18, 20, 21	7	7	7	5, 8	8, 23, 31, 39, 43
q	91-92, 99	65, 70, 71 RB 35	42-43, 48, 49 RB 21	19, 20, 21 RB 18	6	6	6	6	9, 25
Q	109-110, 114	96, 98, 99 RB 43	42-43, 48, 49 RB 21	19, 20, 21 RB 18	7	7	7	8	31
r	81-82, 90	58, 62, 63 RB 27	34-35, 38, 39 RB 18	18, 20, 21 RB 15	6	6	6	6, 9	9, 25, 31
R	143-144, 146	117, 118, 119 RB 67	34-35, 38, 39 RB 18	18, 20, 21 RB 15	7	7	7	5, 8	6, 8, 23, 31 39, 43
s	53-54, 56	39, 40, 41 RB 11	16-17, 18, 19 RB 8	14, 20, 21 RB 7	6	6	6	6, 9	9, 25, 31
S	111-112, 114	97, 98, 99 RB 45	16-17, 18, 19 RB 8	14, 20, 21 RB 7	7	7	7	5, 8	6, 8, 23, 31, 39, 43
t	63-64, 70	46, 50, 51	24-25, 26, 27	16, 20, 21	6	6	6	6, 9	9, 25, 31
T	119-120, 129	103, 108, 109	24-25, 26, 27	16, 20, 21	7	7	7	5, 8	6, 8, 23, 31, 34, 43
u	73-74, 89	54, 62, 63	30-31, 38, 39 RB 14	17, 20, 21	6	6	6	6, 9	9, 25, 31
U	123-124, 130	105, 108, 109	30-32, 38, 39 RB 14	17, 20, 21	7	7	7	5, 8	6, 8, 23, 39, 43
v	93-94, 99	66, 70, 71	42-43, 48, 49	19, 20, 21	6	6	6	6	9, 25
V	153-154, 161	124, 128, 129	42-43, 48, 49	19, 20, 21	7	7	7	5, 8	6, 31, 39, 43
w	75-76, 89	55, 62, 63 RB 21	32-33, 38, 39 RB 15	17, 20, 21 RB 12	6	6	6	6, 9	9, 31
W	155-156, 161	125, 128, 129 RB 75	32-33, 38, 39 RB 15	17, 20, 21 RB 12	7	7	7	8	6, 8, 23, 31, 39, 43
x	97-98, 99	68, 70, 71 RB 39	44-45, 48, 49 RB 23	19, 20, 21 RB 20	6	6	6	6, 9	9
X	157-158, 161	126, 128, 129 RB 77	44-45, 48, 49 RB 23	19, 20, 21 RB 20	7	7	7	8	6, 39, 43
y	77-78, 89	56, 62, 63 RB 23	32-33, 38, 39 RB 16	17, 20, 21 RB 13	6	6	6	6, 9	9, 25, 31
Y	159-160, 161	127, 128, 129 RB 79	32-33, 38, 39 RB 16	17, 20, 21 RB 13	7	7	7	8	6, 8, 23, 31, 39
z	95-96, 99	67, 70, 71 RB 37	44-45, 48, 49 RB 22	19, 20, 21 RB 19	6	6	6	6	9, 31
Z	151-152, 161	123, 128, 129 RB 73	44-45, 48, 49 RB 22	19, 20, 21 RB 19	7	7	7	5, 8	6, 31

	Kdgn	Book 1	Book 2	Book 3	Book 4	Book 5	Book 6	Book 7	Book 8
a-z	100	76		20	6	6	6	6, 9	9, 25, 31
A-Z	165-166	131		20	7	7	7	5, 8	6, 8, 23, 31, 39, 43
Numbers	24, 26, 28-30, 32, 34, 36-38	78-81	46-47	12	8	8	8	12, 16, 30, 32, 33, 42, 43	9, 14, 18, 20, 27, 30, 34, 35, 38, 40, 44
Number Words		78-81		71, 72, 76					
Measurements					66	66-67	66		9, 28, 34
Ordinal Numbers					68	68-69	68		
Time				71	62	62	62	32, 33, 42	44
Maintaining Manuscript				41, 51, 58-59, 76, 98, 122-123	6-7, 34-35 76, 90	6-7, 34-35	6-7, 34-35		
Transition			41, 54-55, 58	10, 24, 25-28					
Cursive									
a			69, 74, 75	42, 48, 49 RB 27	26, 29, 30	26, 29, 30	26, 29, 30	11, 28, 29, 32	32, 47
A			94, 96, 97	80, 84, 85 RB 42	26, 29, 30	26, 29, 30	26, 29, 30	10, 31	15
b			79, 80, 81 RB 37	52, 54, 55 RB 36	37, 39, 40	37, 39, 40	37, 39, 40	11, 32	12, 26, 28, 32
B			109, 112, 113 RB 54	104, 106, 107 RB 53	37, 39, 40	37, 39, 40	37, 39, ,40	10, 31	15
c			71, 74, 75 RB 28	42, 48, 49	26, 29, 30	26, 29, 30	26, 29, 30	11, 29	32, 47
C			94, 96, 97 RB 43	80, 84, 85	26, 29, 30	26, 29, 30	26, 29, 30	10, 31	11, 15
d			70, 74, 75	42, 48, 49 RB 28	26, 29, 30	26, 29, 30	26, 29, 30	11, 28, 29, 32	32, 47
D			118, 122, 123 RB 61	114, 118, 119 RB 61	26, 29, 30	26, 29, 30	26, 29, 30	10, 31	15
e			64, 66, 67 RB 26	34, 38, 39	14, 15, 16	14, 15, 16	14, 15, 16	11, 28, 29, 32	26, 32
E			95, 96, 97 RB 44	82, 84, 85	14, 15, 16	14, 15, 16	14, 15, 16	10, 31	15
f			86, 88, 89 RB 42	64, 68, 69 RB 41	49, 51, 52	49, 51, 52	49, 51, 52	11, 29, 32	26, 28, 32
F			108, 112, 113 RB 53	102, 105, 106 RB 52	49, 51, 52	49, 51, 52	49, 51, 52	10, 31	11
g			72, 74, 75 RB 32	46, 48, 49 RB 31	28, 29, 30	28, 29, 30	28, 29, 30	11, 32	47

	Kdgn	Book 1	Book 2	Book 3	Book 4	Book 5	Book 6	Book 7	Book 8
G			115, 122, 123 RB 56	112, 118, 119 RB 56	28, 29, 30	28, 29, 30	28, 29, 30	10, 31	15
h			61, 66, 67 RB 24	32, 38, 39 RB 21	12, 15, 16	12, 15, 16	12, 15, 16	11, 28, 29, 32	26
H			100, 104, 105 RB 45	88, 94, 95 RB 44	12, 15, 16	12, 15, 16	12, 15, 16	10, 31	15
i			63, 66, 67	34,38, 39 RB 24	13, 15, 16	13, 15, 16	13, 15, 16	11, 28, 29, 32	26, 32
I			116, 122, 123 RB 58	112, 118, 119 RB 58	13, 15, 16	13, 15, 16	13, 15, 16	10, 31	
j			65, 66, 67 RB 27	36, 38, 39	14, 15, 16	14, 15, 16	14, 15, 16	11, 29	26
J			119, 122, 123 RB 62	116, 118, 119 RB 62	14, 15, 16	14, 15, 16	14, 15, 16	10, 31	15
k			62, 66, 67 RB 25	32, 38, 39 RB 22	12, 15, 16	12, 15, 16	12, 15, 16	11, 29, 32	26
K			100, 104, 105 RB 46	88, 94, 95 RB 45	12, 15, 16	12, 15, 16	12, 15, 16	10, 31	15
l			61, 66, 67	32, 38, 39	12, 15, 16	12, 15, 16	12, 15, 16	11, 29, 32	22, 26, 32
L			120, 122, 123 RB 64	116, 118, 119 RB 64	12, 15, 16	12, 15, 16	12, 15, 16	10, 31	15
m			71, 74, 75 RB 30	44, 48, 49 RB 30	27, 29, 30	27, 29, 30	27, 29, 30	11, 29	47
M			101, 104, 105 RB 48	90, 94, 95 RB 47	27, 29, 30	27, 29, 30	27, 29, 30	10, 31	11, 15
n			71, 74, 75 RB 29	44, 48, 49 RB 29	27, 29, 30	27, 29, 30	27, 29, 30	11, 28, 29, 32	32, 47
N			101, 104, 105 RB 47	90, 94, 95 RB 46	27, 29, 30	27, 29, 30	27, 29, 30	10, 31	11
o			78, 80, 81 RB 35	52, 54, 55 RB 34	37, 39, 40	37, 39, 40	37, 39, 40	11, 28, 29, 32	12, 28, 32, 47
O			95, 96, 97	82, 84, 85 RB 43	37, 39, 40	37, 39, 40	37, 39, 40	10, 31	15
p			65, 66, 67	36, 38, 39 RB 26	14, 15, 16	14, 15, 16	14, 15, 16	11, 29	26
P			110, 112, 113	104, 106, 107 RB 54	14, 15, 16	14, 15, 16	14, 15, 16	10, 31	
q			73, 74, 75 RB 34	46, 48, 49 RB 33	28, 29, 30	28, 29, 30	28, 29, 30	11	47

	Kdgn	Book 1	Book 2	Book 3	Book 4	Book 5	Book 6	Book 7	Book 8
Q			117, 122, 123 RB 59	114, 118, 119 RB 59	28, 29, 30	28, 29, 30	28, 29, 30	10, 31	
r			85, 88, 89 RB 41	62, 68, 69 RB 40	49, 51, 52	49, 51, 52	49, 51, 52	11, 28, 29, 32	26, 28
R			110, 112, 113 RB 55	104, 106, 107 RB 55	49, 51, 52	49, 51, 52	49, 51, 52	10, 31	11, 15
s			84, 88, 89 RB 40	62, 68, 69 RB 39	49, 51, 52	49, 51, 52	49, 51, 52	11, 28, 29	26, 28
S			115, 122, 123 RB 57	112, 118, 119 RB 57	49, 51, 52	49, 51, 52	49, 51, 52	10, 31	11, 15
t			62, 66, 67	32, 38, 39 RB 23	13, 15, 16	13, 15, 16	13, 15, 16	11, 28, 29, 32	26, 32
T			108, 112, 113 RB 52	102, 106, 107 RB 51	13, 15, 16	108, 112, 113	13, 15, 16	10, 31	15
u			63, 66, 67	34, 38, 39 RB 25	13, 15, 16	13, 15, 16	13, 15, 16	11, 32	26, 32
U			102, 104, 105	90, 94, 95 RB 48	13, 15, 16	13, 15, 16	13, 15, 16	10, 31	
v			83, 88, 89 RB 38	60, 68, 69 RB 37	48, 51, 52	48, 51, 52	48, 51, 52	11, 32	12, 28, 47
V			102, 104, 105 RB 49	92, 94, 95	48, 51, 52	48, 51, 52	48, 51, 52	10, 31	
w			78, 80, 81 RB 36	52, 54, 55 RB 35	37, 39, 40	37, 39, 40	37, 39, 40	11, 29	12, 26, 28
W			103, 104, 105 RB 50	92, 94, 95 RB 49	37, 39, 40	37, 39, 40	37, 39, 40	10, 31	15
x			72, 74, 75 RB 31	44, 48, 49	27, 29, 30	27, 29, 30	27, 29, 30	11	47
X			120, 122 , 123 RB 63	116, 118, 119 RB 63	27, 29, 30	27, 29, 30	27, 29, 30	10, 31	
y			73, 74, 75 RB 33	46, 48, 49 RB 32	28, 29, 30	28, 29, 30	28, 29, 30	11	47
Y			103, 104, 105 RB 51	92, 94, 95 RB 50	28, 29, 30	28, 29, 30	28, 29, 30	10, 31	15
z			83, 88, 89 RB 39	60, 68, 69 RB 38	48, 51, 52	48, 51, 52	48, 51, 52	11	28, 47
Z			117, 122, 123 RB 60	114, 118, 119 RB 60	48, 51, 52	48, 51, 52	48, 51, 52	10, 31	
a-z			61-90	32-40, 42-50, 52, 57, 60-70				11, 28, 29, 32	12, 22, 26, 28, 32, 47
A-Z			94-120	80-97, 102-121				10, 31	11, 15

	Kdgn	Book 1	Book 2	Book 3	Book 4	Book 5	Book 6	Book 7	Book 8
Joining Strokes			41, 54, 55, 58	25-28, 66-67					
Beginning			55-57	25-28					
Ending			55, 56	25-26					
Overhill			56, 69, 70-73, 83	26, 28, 42, 44, 46					47
Sidestroke			57, 82, 83 87	27-28, 52, 60, 66-67	38, 50	38, 50	38, 50	20, 22, 27	12, 28, 40, 42, 45
v, z, s, r, f			83-86, 88, 89	27, 60-70	48, 49, 51, 52	48, 49, 51, 52	48, 49, 51-53		
Uphill			55, 61-65, 78-79, 84-86	25, 28, 32, 34, 36					26
Legibility								4, 7, 23, 25, 30, 31, 45, 47	
Adjusting handwriting			21, 92, 111	23, 41, 51, 58, 110 122-123, 124	9, 34, 35, 60, 63, 65, 81, 87, 90	9-10, 33-36, 43, 63, 65, 81, 88, 90-91	9, 34-36, 63, 65 88-90		
adult proportion					32-33, 63, 67	32, 33, 88, 91	18, 32, 33,		
size			21, 92, 111	23, 41, 51, 57, 58, 122-123	32, 34, 65, 87, 90,	9, 10, 34, 63, 65, 90		12, 13, 30, 39, 40, 43	9, 11, 14, 18, 20, 24, 30, 35, 37, 38, 39, 44
without writing lines			21, 99	23, 51, 58, 98,110, 122-123, 124	9, 10, 32, 34, 64, 65, 83	9, 35, 36		32	9, 35
Letter size and form		27-28, 87-88	8, 60, 91	8, 23, 30, 78, 110, 122	18, 32-33, 42-43	18, 32-33, 42-43	18, 32-33, 42-43	13, 21, 22, 25, 28, 31, 38, 46, 47	13, 19, 22, 26, 28, 32
Letter slant		29, 72, 89, 130	9, 40, 77, 91, 129	9, 22, 31, 79, 109, 111	19, 54-55	19, 73-74	19, 73-74	25, 33	33
Letter, word, and sentence spacing		30, 90	10, 50, 77, 91	9, 31, 87, 97, 109, 124	19, 73-74	19, 73-74	19, 73-74	13, 17, 25	
Speed and legibility; timed writing					22, 44, 56, 75, 84, 92	22, 44, 56, 75, 84, 92	22, 44, 56, 75, 84, 92	25, 41	16, 41
Common-stroke letter groups									
Manuscript									
capitals									
C, G, O, Q, S	103-114	93-100							
I, L, T, J, U, H, K	115-130	101-110							
A, B, D, M, N, P, R	131-146	111-120							
E, F, Z, V, W, X, Y	147-162	121-130							
lower case									
a, d, o, g, c, e, s	41-56	33-42	12-20						
f, b, l, t, h, k	57-70	43-52	22-28						
i, u, w, y, j, r, n, m, p	71-90	53-64	30-40						
q, v, z, x	91-99	65-72	42-45,48-50						

	Kdgn	Book 1	Book 2	Book 3	Book 4	Book 5	Book 6	Book 7	Book 8
Capital and lower-case manuscript									
aA, dD, oO, gG, cC, eE, sS			12-17	13-14					
fF, bB, lL, tT, hH, kK			22-25	15-16					
iI, uU, wW, yY, jJ, rR, nN, mM, pP			30-37	17-18					
qQ, vV, xX			42-45	19					
Evaluating handwriting	29, 37, 55 69, 89, 99 113, 129, 145, 161	40, 42, 50, 52, 62, 64, 70, 72, 82, 84, 98, 100, 108, 110, 118, 120, 128, 130, 143	18, 20, 26, 28, 38, 40 48, 50, 53, 66, 68, 74, 76, 80, 82, 88, 90, 96, 98, 104, 106, 112, 114, 122, 124, 127	20, 22, 38, 40, 48, 50, 54, 56, 68, 70, 75, 84, 86, 94, 96, 101, 106, 108, 118, 120, 127	15, 17, 25, 29, 31, 39, 41, 47, 51, 53, 59, 95	15, 17, 25, 29, 31, 39, 41, 47, 51, 53, 59, 95	15, 17, 29, 31, 39, 41, 47, 51, 53, 59, 95	4, 7, 12, 13 23, 25, 30, 31, 39, 40, 43, 45, 47	9, 11, 14, 18, 20, 24, 30, 35, 37, 38, 39, 40

Everyday Handwriting

	Kdgn	Book 1	Book 2	Book 3	Book 4	Book 5	Book 6	Book 7	Book 8
Abbreviations				51, 98, 111	62-67, 80, 82	35, 64, 66-67, 82-83	64, 66-67, 82		
Address Book						65			
Addresses			99, 112	51, 98	64, 65	64, 65	64	33, 43	20, 30, 35
Announcements					76	76	76, 92		
Assignment notebook					22, 83	83	83		
Authors				59					
Autograph book				124					
Awards					60		60		
Birthday					35	83			
Bookplate					9		9		
Books					42, 86, 87	87			
Business card					34	36			
Business letter						91			7, 35
Calligraphy					70-71	70-71	70-71		
Charts				122-123			81		
Comic strips							36		
Dates			112	111	82	82	82		
Days		133-134			82		82		
Diagrams								39	25
Directions		139	29		92	84	56	46	27
Envelopes			99	98		35	64		
Forms		132		41	32, 63, 83	34	34-35	12, 30, 43	14, 20, 30, 37, 38
Games									6, 40, 46
Instructions					71		10		
Invitations		137	111			10			
Job application						34	34		
Jokes		140							
Journals					46,55,78-79	78-79	78-79	32	
Labels			21						
Letter designs					36, 85				
Library reservation card							35		

	Kdgn	Book 1	Book 2	Book 3	Book 4	Book 5	Book 6	Book 7	Book 8
License plates							85		
Limericks							89		
Lists			92	12, 57	66, 69, 78, 87	86	44, 69, 87		
Measurements					66,67	66-67	66		
Membership cards						72			
Messages					10, 44, 75	92	75		
Get Well						76			
Telephone				110	75		75		
Months		135-136			82		82		
Name cards					32				
Note taking					56, 84	22, 75	84, 91		
Paragraph							80		
Place cards						60			
Poetry					88-89	87, 88, 89	72, 88	7, 23	13, 22
Postcards				51	65	9	65		
Posters				58	90		90		
Proper nouns			13, 107	80, 121	80	81	69		
Puzzles					35			5, 35	8, 23, 29, 43
Recipes					67		67		
Riddles					72	85		4, 7	5
Schedules				23	63	63	22, 63		
Signs					81	90		42	
Thank-you note		138	121	97	91				
Time				71	62	62	62		
Titles (book)				59	86, 87	80, 86	86		

Language Arts

	Kdgn	Book 1	Book 2	Book 3	Book 4	Book 5	Book 6	Book 7	Book 8
Reading and Writing pages		73-75, 141-143	51-53, 125-127	73-75, 99-101, 125-127	23-25, 45-47, 57-59, 93-95	23-25, 45-47, 57-59, 93-95	23-25, 45-47, 57-59, 93-95	7, 23, 45	
Proofreading		75, 143	53, 127	75, 101, 127	20-21, 25 47, 59, 95	20-21, 25 47, 59, 95	20-26, 47, 59, 95	26	17
Capitalization		92, 133-136, 140	13, 31, 45, 99, 105, 107 116	80, 82, 88, 90, 92, 98, 102, 104, 106, 112, 121	80, 82	81, 82-83, 87, 88-89	21, 69, 82, 86, 88-89	7, 10, 12, 13, 14, 15, 16, 23, 28, 30, 31, 32, 33, 34, 36, 39, 40, 42, 43, 45	6, 9, 11, 12, 13, 14, 15, 16, 17, 18, 20, 22, 27, 30, 31, 34, 35, 36, 38, 40
Punctuation		92, 140	13, 23, 25, 45, 99, 105	59, 80, 109, 111	8, 42, 62, 77, 80, 82, 86, 87, 88	54, 62, 66, 77, 80, 81, 86, 87, 91	8, 21, 54, 62, 66, 77, 86, 87	4, 7, 9, 13 14, 15, 18 19, 23, 24, 26, 28, 29, 32, 33, 36, 38, 40, 41, 42, 43, 46	4, 5, 9, 13, 15, 16, 17, 21, 22, 26, 31, 35, 36, 42, 44

Ready, Eager, and Waiting

BY MIMI BRODSKY CHENFELD

Ready or not, here they come! Children come in so many varieties! Most of them are excited, anticipating the great adventure of "real school." They are chatterboxes, busybodies, movers and shakers, daredevils—action-packed children curious about, in and out of, everything. They're eager to learn, to master new skills, to discover and use their amazing powers. They're verbs personified. These are "hands on" children.

Others have been taught to sit still, be quiet, wait for instructions. They've taken oaths of silence and have cloistered their own diminished spirits. Too many have already named themselves failures and are afraid even to try. These are "hands off" children.

But, ready or not, here they are! What is in store for them as they enter our lives?

Will their days be dictated by tightly structured schedules, passive seat work, minimal social interaction, rare opportunities for playful activities? Will skills be taught through isolated drills? Will the hands of the clock crawl from moment to moment? Or will they be invited into warm, safe communities of learning with days enriched by relevant, active, engaging activities? Will their wonder and curiosity be strengthened, their spontaneity, humor, and self-esteem encouraged as they constantly discover relationships, make connections, find meanings? Will the hands of the clock dance around the hours?

It's up to us.

Like it or not, our power to engage children, to discourage or affirm, is formidable. With a flick of an eye, we can pierce the fragile lining of a child's spirit. With a smile, we add a stitch to that lining.

We are the role models. When we think and behave in closed, narrow, rigid systems, we pass on that stunted attitude to our students.

When we are open and flexible in our approach, that freer spirit will warm the weather of our rooms.

Keep in mind that we humans are originals with our own combinations of styles. We all learn in our own way and at our own pace. No single material or methodology works equally effectively with every individual. That awareness is a mandate for creating exciting environments that offer wide arrays of learning opportunities so that all of our students are caught in the excitement of education.

Mimi Brodsky Chenfeld is an author, teacher, consultant, lover of children and a pioneer in the field of creative movement. Her books, *Teaching Language Arts Creatively* and *Creative Activities for Young Children* (Harcourt, Brace, Jovanovich), are widely used. Her favorite proverb is "All of my children are prodigies."

The following pages contain clusters of suggestions, possibilities, brain-storming notes from my journal to yours. These are not lists of formulas or strategies. The ideas overflow and overlap. Let them trigger your own

creative process. Play with them, rearrange them, substitute, or add your own interpretations. *And don't forget to make room for the energies and input of your students.* They will surprise you with their imaginative offerings. All of the ideas celebrating these delightful themes are healthy and good in themselves for any occasion and purpose. As with all ideas, time is the only limitation.

Countless teachers and children have taught me and shared with me. I am especially grateful to the following people for their generous outpouring of ideas that contributed so richly to the following section:

Mary C. Byrne, teacher at Montrose School, Bexley, Ohio; **Marilyn Cohen,** teacher at Bet Shraga Hebrew Academy, Albany, New York; **JoAnn Holtrey,** Barnett Recreation Center, Columbus, Ohio; **Barbara Kienzle,** teacher at Hamilton Alternative School, Columbus, Ohio; **Nancy Moorman,** Early Childhood consultant with the Institute of Personal Power, Bay City, Michigan; **Sharon Mueller,** teacher at Hamilton South, Lockbourne, Ohio; **Dr. Gerald Nehman,** Director of the Environmental Institute for Technical Transfer, University of Texas, Arlington, Texas; **Marilyn Nelson,** teacher at Moler School, Columbus, Ohio; **Linda O'Brien,** teacher at Forest Park Elementary School, Columbus, Ohio; **Janis Pechenik,** teacher at Green Meadows School, East Greenbush, New York; **Barbara Selinger,** teacher at Washington School, East Orange, New Jersey; **Rose Stough,** teacher at Moler School, Columbus, Ohio; **Leslie Zak,** the staff and children at Days of Creation Arts Program, Columbus, Ohio

Contents

Here I Am!

Our favorite topic! Our very own selves!
Our names!

■ We celebrate our names on tags, charts, T-shirts, and posters. We love the letters in our names. Children look for the letters in their names everywhere: in magazines and newspapers, on billboards and license plates, even in nature shapes, such as twigs, nests, and branches of trees. Trace, cut, color, and shape letters in snow, in clay, in mud, in sand, and in the air.

■ The sounds of our names are music to our ears. How we love to hear our names called out in syllables. Play instruments or let bodies move to the rhythm of names. Keep the beat; clap the syllables. Make cheers and chants for names. For example, Ben ja min: **hop, hop, hop** or Kev in: **stamp, clap.**

■ What do we see when we look in the mirror? Our colors, our hair, our loose teeth, our tallest selves, our funniest faces, our proudest postures. Create self-portraits drawn or painted on paper plates or bags in oval shapes with old-fashioned frames. Then create a display with "Our faces on the wall are the fairest of them all."

■ Marilyn Cohen's students love to try to match their classmates' recent pictures to their baby photos. What a challenge! She brainstorms with her class by asking: *What kinds of things did you do when you were babies?* The answers begin with crawl, cry, reach and go on and on. The children pretend to be babies, improvising babies' movements. Then she asks: *What can you do now? Children might suggest jump, twist, leap, run.*

Have your students add their favorite combinations of activities and demonstrate them. Chart the ideas or make stories and pictures about them. For example: *Jamila tiptoes, does jumping jacks, and sit-ups. Antonio skips and jogs.*

■ We like to do so many things. We have hobbies. Let's pantomime things we like to do and see who can guess what they are. Carla may pantomime *swimming*. Mario might pantomime *playing the piano*. Now the whole class can show the movements of Carla's hobby and of Mario's.

■ Body shapes are fascinating. Children lie on paper on the floor, trace their shapes, cut them out, and fill them with colors, words, buttons, even pictures of themselves. Then the shapes hang from a clothesline or cover the walls of the room.

Outside, on sunny days, shapes are shadows. Invite children to race or dance with their shadows and write shadow poems, songs, and stories.

■ Books about ourselves tell the way we look, feel, think, and move. They name our favorite places, people, games, food, weather, colors, toys, seasons, and activities. Barbara Selinger's class tapes shiny aluminum foil on their covers to look like mirrors.

■ Even though our kindergarten students are very young, they have a knapsack full of memories and history. Highlight some of those events and experiences by creating clothesline time lines. Begin by writing birth dates on sentence strips and clipping them to the line. Follow with other events that children identify as important to them. Every child's time line will be different, as we are all unique individuals. Ask children to act out some of the themes on the time lines.

■ If some of us are shy or need extra encouragement, remember the beautiful Zimbabwe proverb, *If you can walk, you can dance. If you can talk, you can sing.*

My Five Senses

Welcome to the world of seeing, hearing, tasting, smelling, and touching—our windows to the world, bringing us immediate impressions that enrich the quality of our daily lives. By developing these amazing powers, we become more perceptive, appreciative people.

■ Eyes are like cameras. It's fun to focus on objects in the room, point to them, and name them. Write the words they suggest on charts or the chalkboard and label them with titles such as **Everything We See** or **We See So Many Things.** The titles could be written on a drawn picture of an eye.

Pictures add life to words. Movement adds more life to the ideas. Invite children to interpret words they named through body movement. They might, for example, be rag dolls by hanging limp and shaking loose, or they could be toy planes by spreading their arms to form airplane wings.

■ Suggest, *Let's use our color film and take "eye pictures"* of the colors around us. Ask questions such as, *What colors are you wearing today? Who else is wearing those colors? What else in the room is the same color?*

Then, with "close-up zoom lenses," have children look carefully at small objects. How much can be seen in a mitten, a scarf, or a paperweight?

Make time for children to sketch their observations and add words to describe the experience.

■ With their eyes closed, have children listen very carefully and tell what sounds they hear. They might suggest footsteps, pencils scratching, or a clock ticking.

Encourage them to imitate the sounds of animals, people, nature, and machines.

Let each child have a turn hiding behind a screen and making a familiar sound for the others to guess. After the sounds are identified, have children try interpreting sounds through body movements.

■ Fill mystery jars with different scents. Marilyn Cohen includes duplicate scents so that children are challenged to match similar contents like coffee or cinnamon or mint. When the smelling and matching game is over, her class draws symbols and labels on the jars.

■ Barbara Selinger says, *Kids love anything you put in a bag!* With eyes closed or blindfolded, Barbara's students excitedly reach their hands into mystery containers and describe the hidden objects. Their vocabularies expand as they use vivid sensory words like *soft, hard, smooth, or prickly.*

■ Using our senses isn't a once-a-year activity. We take those incredible powers with us wherever we go and in whatever we do. As we develop awareness, we magically turn the ordinary into the extraordinary.

Celebrating this ongoing theme gives us important opportunities to talk with our students about the courage and determination of those who do not have the use of one or more of their senses. Sign language and Braille fascinate children. Community resource people competent in these areas are waiting to be invited into your classroom.

People I Love

Our children come to us from a diverse mix of family settings. Statistics describing the state of families in our country make us reel, prod us to renew our vows to help our young students find close, warm relationships in the greater family of our classes and schools.

Extra sensitivity and respect are absolute requirements in exploring this theme. If we use only traditional terms like mother and father, we're excluding those children who aren't able to claim such relationships—those children who live with other relatives, stepparents, or foster parents.

Think inclusively. Our vocabulary reflects our thoughtfulness. It's easy, for example, to change the word *mother* or *father* to the *grown-up who lives in your house.* May the children always find from us respect and understanding for the lives they share.

■ *The questions Who lives with you? and What other people are in your family?* elicit many answers and demonstrate that most families include people of different sizes and ages from newborns to octogenarians. Value every contribution. Put the names and relationships from children's responses on a chart, board, or wall. This gathering itself is comforting as it reassures children that they're not alone in the world.

■ Children enjoy creating family portraits using any media they choose. Add names to the pictures. Discuss the people depicted, emphasizing that babies are smaller than older children or adults. Have children show those contrasts in body movement and shapes. This perception of size and shape discrimination carries through many ideas and themes.

■ Family trees, posted on a bulletin board, can become a forest. Encourage children to draw and write a name for members of their family, covering every leaf in the display.

■ Extend the naming and recording of family members to those relatives, friends, and neighbors with whom children feel close. Vocabularies, geographies, and relationships combine and expand when suggestions such as *Aunt Mattie in Boston, Mr. Jefferson two doors down,* and *Jethro in West Virginia* are added to the ever-growing population. Use maps and globes to locate places mentioned. Then ask children to show how those people might talk, act, or do things.

■ What do we enjoy doing with these favorite family members and neighborhood friends? Children will have many responses ready from *taking walks* to *celebrating holidays.* Ask children to describe their favorite activities, act them out, and draw pictures of them. As children share experiences meaningful to them, their own lives are affirmed and their classmates' lives are enriched.

■ *What do we especially love about these people?* is the kind of question that inspires numerous ideas, such as *I love Grandma Olivia because she sings to me* or *I like to watch Mr. Howard do magic tricks.* Those answers are a great source for showing, telling, pantomiming, and singing.

■ In safe, loving environments, children freely express themselves as they talk about friends. Ask what friends like to do together and what makes a good friend. List suggestions on a chart or the chalkboard, going beyond activities. Include the ideas of caring about each other and helping each other.

■ Experiment with whole-group and small-group activities that encourage cohesiveness.

1. Invite children to show the special ways friends greet each other: giving high fives, shaking hands, and putting an arm around someone's shoulder, for example.
2. Give classroom friends time to paint and read together as well as share responsibility for taking care of toys, pets, plants, and other things in the room.
3. Play partner games. Children can pick tags that feature one–half of an image and then find the classmate with the matching half. Animals, plants, colors, numbers, shapes, and letters are excellent images for matching. When the partners find each other, encourage them to paint or draw portraits of each other.
4. Improvise songs that you know, inserting names of your students. Watch their eyes light up as you greet each child by name with *Josh is my sunshine, my only sunshine. He makes me happy when skies are gray....*

■ Here is the beginning of meaningful multicultural education as young children share their own experiences and learn about those of others. Invite some of those "outside" people your children love to visit your classroom. One of Janis Pechenik's kindergarten students, Jeremy, brought his grandmother to class to share with his friends. She arrived in a wheelchair!

■ Many of our young children are lonely. Regularly repeating and expanding the activities suggested in this section will help them feel part of a group of loving people.

Where We Live

Our children live in an immense variety of shelters from mansions to abandoned automobiles, from condominiums to houseboats. Many of our students dwell in family homes going back generations. Others are constantly on the move, caught in America's mobility track, the world of the migrant worker, or that of the homeless. Sensitivity is the key to all of our communication. As we talk together, let's be as expansive as possible, making a place for every experience. Let's keep our promises to the children that they will always find safety and love in the shelter of our class and in the community of our rooms.

■ After talking about different kinds of houses, use the children's suggestions to inspire ideas for models, paintings, or block structures representing their own homes or any home they decide to make. A variation of this activity is to design a large house with many window spaces and encourage children to paste, tape, or draw their faces in the spaces.

■ Some children already know their addresses. Gather all the street names and numbers for a huge class address book with illustrations and symbols added for extra color and interest. Young students are very proud when they find their names and are motivated to learn whatever words and numbers are attached to those names.

■ Brainstorm ideas about the things we do in our homes. Your chart or the chalkboard will soon fill with activities such as: wash dishes, sweep floors, set tables, make beds, cook, go to sleep, dust, play. Each of those household activities is fine subject matter for movement, pantomime, song, and story. Encourage children by saying: *Show us how you wash dishes. What's the movement?* or *Let's all sweep to a cheery song.* Afterwards, children can draw their favorite activity on a square and add their squares to an outline of a house. You'll probably come up with a patchwork quilt, of sorts, in the shape of a house.

■ Is there room in your room for children to play their favorite game — house?

■ Barbara Kienzle and her students take walks around the neighborhood, noting and collecting information about the surrounding community. When they return, they construct a three-dimensional rendering using blocks, boxes, scraps, and other materials. Maps are checked to be sure no ponds, playgrounds, or bridges have been left out. Barbara's students never tire of playing with their neighborhood.

■ A wall map can be started on a spread of white paper tacked to a bulletin board. Tape or draw a central location like the school or a public park. Children continue the development of the community by adding streets, houses, trees, signs, and stores.

■ Challenge children to name all the kinds of vehicles they have seen on roads and in traffic. Let each child choose a favorite and become that vehicle. Designate a traffic lane through, around, or across the room or outdoors around a field or playground. Then ask children to move as buses, cars, trucks, or whatever they choose to be, zooming along the highway until you signal them to stop. Your signals could be red and green or stop and go.

■ Look beyond to shelters around the world such as igloos, tepees, mud huts, log cabins. Find music to fit the different cultures as children learn about other ways in which basic needs are met. Stories, dances, customs of those cultures warm the walls of the places where people live.

Places to Go

Two words guaranteed to excite young children are "Let's go!" As they take their ever-expanding powers into an ever-expanding world, understandings, skills, knowledge, and confidence increase.

■ Ask children to tell the special places they like to go. Write their suggestions on charts with picture symbols added to each idea. Because children love to sign their names to everything, invite them to write their signatures or letters by the places they would most like to visit. Plan your field trips based on the most popular places.

■ Transportation is one of children's favorite themes. Here is a natural place to connect that lively subject. Ask: *How do we get where we're going?* Children will gladly show the movement of walking, skipping, running, skating, biking, traveling by train, car, boat, or plane. Any lively music is perfect for accompaniment. Songs about ways of going places are fun to sing, make up, and play.

■ Sometimes the best field trips happen in our own rooms before we ever leave our buildings! Questions, ideas, games, songs, art projects reveal information about those places adding rich dimensions to the experience. By the time the class actually makes the trip, it has a wealth of knowledge. When children return from the trip, their enthusiasm continues.

A delightful project, prior to any trip, is to prepare tickets of admission to the place or event. Tickets can be different sizes and colors, illustrated with words, numbers, and images.

■ What do firefighters do? Pretending they're firefighters alerted into action, children can slide down the poles on their jungle gyms. Children love to be fire engines zooming around the playground, making siren noises. Encourage everyone to explore ways to show fire with their bodies. Waving arms and shaking fingers and hands will surely emerge from the patterns. Give children a chance to be all parts of the story, taking turns being the firefighter, the fire engine, and the fire itself. Watch your firefighters screech to a stop, pull out heavy hoses, and aim at the fire. Sound effects don't even need to be suggested; they come naturally. Watch the fiery arms of the flames slowly stop as the fire goes out. Making firefighter hats, building stations, and painting fire engines are favorite follow-ups.

■ Create a post office with a P.O. box for everyone. Children can write notes, cards, and letters to classmates. They can make their own stamps to put on the letters.

■ Children enjoy filling a knapsack with letters and delivering them. They'll also gladly become airplanes when a letter needs to be sent air mail.

■ Wherever we go, we take our imagination, curiosity, and sense of adventure with us. Try to make space in your room for playing store, restaurant, fire station, and library.

What People Do

The human family is woven with interdependence. As young children look around, they see people who help them in special ways. We can encourage them to develop respect and appreciation for all varieties of occupations, to see the dignity in all work.

■ Ask: *Who are the people around us who help us?* On a chart or the chalkboard write children's suggestions, such as *secretaries, bus drivers, custodians, crossing guards.* Whenever possible, personalize the categories by including names of the individuals.

Then ask: *What do these people do, and how do they help us?* Ask children to show their ideas. They might pantomime typing, driving, sweeping, and stopping traffic. They'll also enjoy making objects they identify with different jobs.

Children's interpretations of what people do are delightfully original and full of surprises.

■ When Janis Pechenik invites community and school helpers to visit her class, she asks them to bring in an object from their work to show and give to the children. The school nurse brought in enough hair nets for every student. Following the visit, their play took on an exciting dimension as Janis's class of nurses, their heads protected by hair nets, took temperatures and pulses.

■ Barbara Kienzle's students discuss questions they want to ask people about their jobs. They interview the people, finding out specific and interesting information, which is then transformed into books, games, stories, and songs.

■ When Mary C. Byrne's students spend time exploring the different kinds of work people do, Mary takes the opportunity to help them think in nonsexist ways. Men are nurses. Women are police officers. This enlightened thinking is demonstrated in their play.

■ After talking to a librarian who read stories to them, a group of kindergartners played story hour, taking turns being the storyteller and pretending to "read" books to puppets, dolls, and classmates. They sang stories, used felt board and cutouts, and wore storytelling aprons with pockets full of ideas.

■ Encourage children to express appreciation to some of the school and community helpers you've talked about. Letters and pictures, cards and poems are excellent "Thank-you" projects. Children delight in presenting special gifts of original wishes, cheers, songs, or dances to those who help them.

Feeling Good

This theme is basic. Healthy, happy children with positive attitudes toward themselves and others are free to develop skills, imagination, and competencies; free to be successful learners and kind citizens. This theme is ongoing, never to be confined to a one-time slot or calendar page.

■ Our bodies need exercising every day. Compile a selection of music especially for warm-up exercises. Young students love to move to anything from rhythms representing the cultures of the world, to songs they sing as they move, to drumbeats, hand claps, or favorite popular hits. Add their suggestions.

Tap children's large exercise vocabularies. They may suggest *jumping jacks, hopping, clapping, stretching, bending, touching toes, swaying,* or *sit-ups.* The words themselves spark ideas for drawings, magazine cutouts, or designs of the movements that can be turned into bright, action-filled displays.

■ We need exercise breaks whenever our energy sags or needs channeling. Schedule exercise times as part of your daily program. Include exercise leaders as classroom helpers, giving children turns to choose and lead the patterns. Those few moments will yield immediate enjoyment and success.

■ Connect exercise and movement patterns to every theme. Circus exercises could include clowns juggling and acrobats walking tightropes.

Stories are rich with exercise possibilities. Challenge children to choreograph some warm-up exercises for Winnie the Pooh or plan some flying exercises for Peter Pan.

■ Marilyn Cohen's students brainstorm ideas for "What makes us feel good?" Their many suggestions are the raw material for pictures, stories, boards, charts, puppet shows, songs, and pantomime games.

Another dimension of that activity is to gather information from children under the heading, *When we feel good we. . . .* Ideas may include: *jump for joy, clap, cheer, shout, hug, walk tall.*

■ We feel good when we learn in loving environments. Nancy Moorman's students enjoy making "warm, fuzzy" clotheslines. The children decorate clothespins featuring their names and self-portraits or original designs. Friendly notes and pictures are continuously slipped into the clothespins so that children have ongoing gifts from each other. Naturally *someone* will make sure that no clothespin is empty, that every child's pin holds gifts.

■ We feel good when we're welcomed into our class every morning. Mary Byrne's children share greeting and words of welcome from any language they know. Add gestures to the multicultural salutations. Make up new songs together that include the welcome words, the children's names, and the movement. Keep improvising and expanding. You'll never "wear out your welcome!"

Bodies and Brains

Unless they have been scarred by harsh or abusive experiences, most young children are fascinated by and proud of their bodies and their brains. As we mainstream children with special needs, we learn that positive encouragement of what we can do, rather than despairing over what we can't do, increases accomplishments and multiplies success stories. When all of our children learn to respect, appreciate, and care for their bodies and brains, greater self-esteem and self-confidence are nurtured and regard for others is strengthened.

■ Bodies and brains go together. Instincts, thoughts, feelings, memories, facts, language, coordination, perception are all miraculously working fulltime for us, stamping us as unique individuals.

Because our brains send instructions through our bodies, we learn to play instruments, to ride bikes, to roller–skate, to eat with utensils, to build with blocks, to paint pictures, to wash our faces—the list goes on and on. Also, brains and bodies are good learners. Remember how hard it was when we first learned how to set a table or tie a shoe? Those skills became easier after much practice. Our bodies and brains are so smart that the more we practice things like letters and numbers, writing and cutting, the easier they'll get. Let's stop as often as possible to celebrate achievements.

Linda O'Brien and her students mark accomplishments on huge charts that ask: *How Are We Growing?* The chart features contributions shared and demonstrated by every child. Everyone is proud of Ebony, who learned to "speak on the soapbox" and of Allissia, who now writes her **b**'s and **d**'s.

■ Barbara Kienzle's children know that when they're gathered on the rug, their favorite place in the room, many delightful activities are enjoyed. One of their favorites is playing "Simon Says" featuring special body parts: finger dances, nose dances, elbow dances. Sometimes Simon sends one movement through different parts of the body, perhaps a wiggle to the fingers or a flap to the arms. Any lively music will keep the rhythm going.

■ Adding and combining ideas to body and brain exercises is exhilarating. When our students are doing exercises and dancing, it's fun to challenge them to "add another movement" or "add jump" or "add clapping hands." The human body's possibilities for variation staggers the imagination. Children feel successful as they explore the wondrous ways their bodies coordinate, balance, shift, and stretch.

■ Nancy Moorman's class makes photo albums featuring their year of growing. Janis Pechenik's children make books about themselves that celebrate their accomplishments, the high points of their year. We always have reasons to celebrate. Even the smallest success is worthy of praise.

Eating Right

When people talk about the basics of life, food is usually first on the survival list. It definitely ranks high on the interest and vocabulary scale of young children. Ironically, within the borders of our fertile land, many children have eating habits that are damaging to their health; many have serious food disorders; and many are hungry. Our youngest students are ready to form good eating patterns, learn about nutrition, develop appreciation and respect for nourishing food, and feel compassion for those people who know hunger as a regular part of life.

■ Barbara Selinger and her students talk about the four food groups. Using four large boxes, Barbara asks the children to help decorate and label the boxes, one for each food group. From magazines, children cut out pictures of food to fit the different groups. When the boxes are full of many examples, Barbara's class prepares a "buffet dinner." With paper plates, they move around the room, stopping at each of the four boxes, choosing one item from each of the boxes, and pasting it on their plates. Set on tables or taped to bulletin boards, the plates make delightful art exhibits as well as resource materials for continued activities.

■ When children snack on healthy foods like apples, carrots, and raisins, they can "feel" their muscles growing. They'll show you how fast they can run, how high they can jump, how "over" they can bend. Just ask them!

■ Nancy Moorman's students take turns being dieticians and deciding which nutritious snacks to enjoy for snack time. They fill in calendar days with pictures and symbols for those snacks. They help prepare and serve the food at snack time.

■ Teachers like Barbara Kienzle, Marilyn Cohen, and Janis Pechenik are cooking all the time. Barbara uses cookbooks and stories like Maurice Sendak's *Chicken Soup with Rice*. What could be tastier than warm chicken soup with rice on a cold winter day, along with Sendak's story to be shared and enjoyed? Janis Pechenik gathers recipes for every letter of the alphabet. From A to Z her students find nutritious food to cook. Marilyn Cohen's children celebrate food from different cultures. The people of the world have astonishing varieties of delicious and unusual nutritious foods that are fun to make and eat. As children cook, they count, measure, mix, sort, pour, scoop, cut and peel. Let's not leave out other ingredients of the activity, such as expanding understanding and appreciation of food and its values and respect for the process of preparing food.

■ Food is a special part of almost every holiday, occasion, ceremony, and celebration. Plan a multicultural festival featuring the different backgrounds of your students or the cultures most fascinating to them through story, song, or pictures. Make tacos for Cinco de Mayo, cornbread for a Native American harvest pow wow, egg rolls for Chinese New Year, or sweet potato pie for the African American unity holiday of Kwanza. Expand the festival to include songs, stories, dances, and games.

■ When children are asked to help others, they respond with enthusiasm. Collect food for community shelters. Invite your students to organize the contributions any way they want to. Even our youngest students are ready to learn about compassion and responsibility.

Pick a Pet

If you took a survey of favorite topics in children's lives, you'd probably find pets near the top of the list. Pets have ways of bringing out the best in children—caring, responsibility, respect, and affection. Sometimes children who don't relate to any other person respond to a family or class pet. Even the youngest students have extensive information. Just ask them. They'll tell you.

■ Ask: *What pets live in your house or your neighborhood?* Catch the words as they pour out. Be sure to include room on charts for children who do not own pets but can name their favorite ones. Combine students' names, pet names, and pictures of pets.

■ Barbara Selinger's students spend lively hours gathering descriptive words for pets like *furry* or *fast* or *jumpy* and matching them with pets that have those characteristics. Those characteristics can also be shown in movement. Barbara's children draw their pet pictures on oak tag, cut them out, mount them on sticks, and make Pet Puppets. Any lively music will get a Pet Puppet Parade going. Give the puppets a rest and invite children to turn themselves into their favorite pets and show their special movement.

■ With toys, boxes, tubes, and discarded objects, Barbara Kienzle's students build shelters and imaginative toys for their pets to live in and play with.

■ Marilyn Cohen's class turns into a pet shop featuring children's stuffed animals brought in for the occasion. They play pet store, have pet shows, and even gather pet facts into colorful graphs.

■ Don't forget: healthy pets need their exercise!Children love to make up exercises and warm-ups for pets. (Fish exercises are very different from gerbil gymnastics.)

■ Barbara Kienzle encourages delightful silliness and imaginative playfulness when she challenges her students with questions such as: *What if we had an elephant for a pet?* or *How about a dinosaur for a pet?* Invite your students to show, tell, pantomime, and draw the results.

■ Everyone loves Mary's little lamb. Sharon Mueller turned herself into Mary and skipped around the room with her kindergartners following behind her singing the nursery rhyme. When they got to "school," she turned on rock-and-roll music, and she and her students tried to make the children in the rhyme "laugh and play." Then she turned herself into an authority figure, stopping the music and somewhat sternly reminding the group that *This is against the rule—to have these lambs in school.* Sharon (Mary) skipped the lambs around the room and back "home."

■ The children wanted to repeat this again and again. While they rested, they made up variations of the verse, giving every child the chance to make up a new pet. They sang the original verses, acted them out, and turned them into a terrific book. Two entries were *Misty had a little cat; its tail was long and white,* and *Shanika had a little giraffe; its neck was yellow and black.*

On the Farm

Even though most of them have known only urban environments, young children are still fascinated by the image of "farm." Maybe because farms take us back to the earth, to the wonders of growing things, to our relationships with nature, to the beauty of simplicity, and to a purposeful world that is easy to understand and respect.

■ Marilyn Cohen asks her class to think about different kinds of farms—horse farms, vegetable farms, flower farms, dairy farms. Each has its own particular arrangement with its own unique features. Many farms offer combinations of purposes.

■ Farms are rooted in weather and seasons. Seeing an apple orchard in the spring is a very different experience from seeing one in autumn. With farms we are reminded of the importance of keeping a harmony with nature. We plant and harvest at specific times. We need certain kinds of soil, land, water, and sunshine for crops to grow and for animals to feel healthy and happy. There's so much for children to talk about.

They already know a great deal about farms from picture books, nursery rhymes, and songs, and are eager to share that information and to sing it, show it, build it, dance it. Create a chart of children's questions and suggestions. Make room for their cut-out pictures of farm scenes. Always display their original illustrations and constructions.

■ Mary C. Byrne and her students enjoy talking about the "olden days," when many more people lived on farms and children had specific chores, helping in so many ways. Children always want to help and are eager to tackle meaningful jobs. They love responsibility. When Mary and her students talk about children of that period, they suggest all kinds of farm duties: *helping to feed, clean, and care for animals; tending gardens; watering flowers; picking fruits and vegetables; preparing food.* Children's ideas, along with their names, can be printed on charts or on the chalkboard. Each suggestion inspires movement, mime, music, dramatic or graphic interpretation. For example, *Let's show farm children milking cows/picking apples/brushing a horse,* or *Let's show the dance of seeds as they grow into different vegetables and fruits.*

■ Janis Pechenik's students love books about farm animals. One of their favorite nursery tales is "The Little Red Hen," which they enjoy improvising in movement and dialogue, using homemade props. As the Little Red Hen travels around the farm (classroom), asking all the other farm animals for help in baking bread, not only do the children see the sequence of interrelated steps in the process, they learn important lessons about cooperation. It's an especially delicious experience if the enactment of the story is followed by baking real bread and sharing it.

■ Expanding and improvising familiar songs such as "The Farmer in the Dell" and "Old MacDonald Had a Farm" are easy and natural activities. Don't stop at the prescribed verses. Can't Old MacDonald have a pig, a horse, a rabbit, or an owl? Why can't the Farmer in the Dell take a bull, a cow, a haystack, and an apple tree? Be inclusive. And, don't just sing it—lead children to do it.

■ Baby animals are favorite farm images. Children love the challenge of turning themselves into big horses with big gallops, then shaking out that movement and following it with the gallops of baby horses. Any bouncy rhythms will keep the movement lively. Try it with big and little ducks, cats, cows, pigs, or sheep. Add animal sounds. Mix and match. Let horses quack and cows gobble. Share the fun!

I Saw It at the Zoo

Dr. Gerald Nehman, working on environmental educational programs and activities to help raise the next generation of "stewards of the earth," considers the zoo an excellent resource for sharing important values and concepts with young children. Spurred by more enlightened and committed philosophies, many zoos in our country are moving toward providing lovely natural environments for healthy animals. Wooded areas, gardens, waterfalls, and streams brighten their landscapes.

■ Dr. Nehman encourages us to talk with children as we study pictures, read books, and visit zoos. Some points to raise with children are: *What is beautiful about the earth? about nature?* and *Imagine the variety of animals in the world. Let's learn about them.* As we discuss such ideas, children see the importance of having rich soil for growing food to feed the animals, clean water for drinking and for plants and animals to live.

■ Zoo animals from A to Z! Name them, write them, illustrate them, sculpt them, dance them, make sound effects for them, and create masks honoring them. Celebrate them in a Zoo Parade. Include animal puppets, stuffed animals, masks, costumes, and children showing animal movements. Any lively marching music will energize the parade.

■ When you invite children to experiment with categories, their responses will astonish you. They'll have so many ideas: *big* animals, *small* animals, *hopping* animals, *flying* animals, *climbing* animals, *swimming* animals, *slow* animals, *fast* animals, *cute* animals, *furry* animals. Prepare labels for the categories and post them all around the room. Ask children to think of, illustrate, name, and cut out pictures of animals that fit those descriptions. Multiply the fun by asking children to show the different categories in movement, accompanied by rhythm instruments and original songs.

■ Mary C. Byrne's students close in on animal tracks. They make designs of hooves, claws, and webbed feet leading to natural habitats, all constructed from discarded materials.

■ Barbara Kienzle and her children transform their entire room into a zoo. Adding images to a mural covering the walls of the room, they divide the space into sections of the zoo—reptile house, aviary, monkey jungle. Each area has its own constructions, pictures, and activities. Favorite songs such as Woody Guthrie's "I'm Goin to the Zoo, Zoo, Zoo" are sung and improvised. Sometimes Barbara even tapes a life-size representation of a baby elephant or giraffe to the wall. How children love measuring themselves against it, making up stories for it, sketching it, and singing about it.

■ Janis Pechenik's and Barbara Selinger's students delight in the challenge to create brand-new animals by combining names, features, and movements. With felt, colored paper, clay, pipe cleaners, and other materials, the children introduce their new imaginative animals. Have you ever met a *horsefish?* What about a *tigerbird?*

Things on Wheels / Machines at Work

Growing up in our high–tech, fast-paced society, is it any wonder that our young children are utterly fascinated by moving objects, curious about how things work, eager to get their busy hands on anything they can manipulate, and brimming with information about complicated technical subjects?

Visit a room where young children are learning in a variety of ways, with many choices offered, surrounded by interesting and diverse materials, and you'll find them working alone, with classmates, or in larger groups. Some willl be dressing up, trying on roles complete with props, dialogue, and body movement. Some will be painting, drawing, sculpting, or arranging. Others will be playing house, feeding dolls and friends while they answer telephones, or going to the store. Some children will be reading, writing, or listening to music. Still others will be busily hammering away, repairing real or imaginary objects.

And you can be sure that in every room where children are invited to decide their own activities and follow their own interests, groups of them will be driving some kind of vehicle while others will be bent over toy vehicles rolling along imaginatively constructed highways, streets, and bridges. In such classrooms where children are involved in active learning, wheels are always turning.

■ The rooms of Rose Stough and Marilyn Nelson are full of collections of "things"—hooks, buttons, old keys, locks, screws, hinges, broken clocks, parts of machines. Their students constantly enjoy working with the assortment of items, making collages, inventing, sorting, cataloging, comparing, and repairing.

Sometimes they have scavenger hunts to look for wheels in the rooms, in school, in books and magazines, and in the immediate outside environment. They find wheels on cars, bikes, trikes, trucks,

trains, skates, wagons, wheelbarrows, and lawnmowers.

They cut out pictures of wheels, paint and make colorful designs of wheels, and create books and murals featuring wheels.

Songs like "The Wheels on the Bus Go Round and Round" are easily improvised by adding such lyrics as: "The wheels on the trucks are very big," or "The wheels on the clocks go tick-tock-tick."

Marilyn's and Rose's students love books about machines like *Mike Mulligan and the Steam Shovel.* Double the enjoyment of the story with children's original illustrations and dramatic interpretations.

How can we get the motion of wheels in our bodies? Children will have no trouble shaping small wheels with their fingers and hands. Swinging and rotating arms overhead and alongside bodies easily catches the shape and energy of larger wheels. Celebrate the idea of wheels by doing cartwheels! And, don't somersaults express the movement of wheels in motion?

■ In Rose Stough's and Marilyn Nelson's rooms, children can be found building toy car racing tracks, using inclined planes and levers to raise and lower the tracks; discovering ramps; hammering nails into soft wood; driving screws into blocks of wood with pre-drilled holes; examining the mechanism of a broken clock; studying simple machines like eggbeaters, toy telephones, and pencil sharpeners. Children are always challenged to observe and understand how machines make work easier.

After Marilyn Cohen and her students visit a dairy farm, they return to enjoy many projects and activities. One of their favorites is to make butter. The children take turns vigorously shaking jars of heavy cream. It takes a long time and great effort to shake the cream into butter. While the children rest from their labors, Marilyn introduces an old-fashioned butter churn that children clearly see speeds up the process. Much easier! But, when Marilyn invites them to use an electric mixer to make their butter, their eyes widen with astonishment and appreciation. They gain immediate respect and understanding for the work of machines.

■ After gathering ideas and images of many different kinds of familiar machines such as electric drills, washers, dryers, clocks, and vacuum cleaners, young children delight in the challenge of, "Using our bodies, how can we show these machines at work?" With brilliant ingenuity and imagination, young children have worked together to choreograph car washes, clothes dryers, and clocks. Through spinning, jumping, tumbling, and vibrating, they convey the workings of machines they understand in movement. Invite them to have fun trying.

■ When children realize that each part of a machine has its own repetitive movement and function (and often its own sound) that contribute to the workings of the whole machine, they enjoy forming small groups and adding their own specific, repetitive, mechanical movement pattern to the others. Lamont's arms do a lifting gesture, up/down, up/down. He links that to Estella's finger wiggles. Jill adds her foot stomps. Tanika taps her head. Add sounds to the movement. Add more fun by suggesting, *Let's turn this machine to high or fast and watch Lamont, Estella, Jill, and Tanika speed up their lifting, wiggling, stomping, and tapping.* See what happens when you suggest, *Let's turn this machine to low or slow.* Use fast and slow music to accompany the mechanical movements of the original machines.

■ Mary C. Byrne sets the largest clear plastic storage bin she can find on a table and offers her students many opportunities to play and, as a byplay, to make important discoveries about how things work. When her bin is filled with sand, children roll wheels through it, dig in it, make little playgrounds on it, and build roads and bridges over it. When water fills her bin, the children see how wheels turn in liquids, making waves and churning energy.

■ When Mary's students take breaks from their "work choices" (that is, art centers, reading corners, games shelves, stuffed animal and doll houses, housekeeping and store areas), they learn about interesting machines in their room, like hinges. They observe hinges in action as they open and close doors and cabinets. When they discover that they even have hinges in their own bodies as they swing their arms and wave to their neighbors, their surprise changes to delight.

Everything hinges on joyful, successful ways of learning!

Blast Off!

Despite scientific discoveries to the contrary, most young children believe that they are at the center of the universe. The swirl of moon, stars, and sun revolves around their lives. When they wish upon stars, they often express private ownership: "That's my wishing star."

One night, a young friend walked from room to room in the house. A few minutes later, she ran excitedly to her mother announcing, "Mommy! There's a moon outside every window!"

Before we speed up our young children's acquisition of technical information about such concepts as space, let's help them keep the wonder of it all for as long as possible. Plato said that there is no other beginning of learning except wonder.

■ While admiring the flags of the nations of the world on a recent visit to the United Nations, I rediscovered the universal enchantment with such images as sun, moon, and stars. Variations of these symbols appear on the majority of the world's flags.

Together with our students, we begin a star search and a sun and moon search. Images are everywhere–on flags, stamps, jewelry, clothing, wrapping paper, boxes, cans, and packages lining the shelves of stores. These are favorite images that children love to cut, draw, or form from multitudes of materials, from glitter to fluorescent markers, to recycled aluminum foil or shiny gift paper. Our rooms can be transformed into planetariums, space stations, and observatories with mobiles, murals, and windowpanes; in shoe boxes, fast-food containers, or on clothespins hanging from clotheslines. In this setting, children become stargazers, astronomers, and astronauts.

■ It's fun to divide a wall into a night picture of Earth and sky. Let it be an ongoing project by encouraging children to continue adding ideas. Outlines of houses, trees, cars, people, mountains, and telephone poles can appear on Earth with stars, moon, and sun added to the sky. Even a spaceship or a space station might whirl around among the stars.

■ Sometimes the sun hides behind clouds. If we hide our faces behind peek-a-boo hands, we can tell stories about the sun hiding behind clouds. Slowly the clouds float away, and the sun begins to shine through. As children slowly open their hands to reveal their faces, we talk about how the sun brightens everything. Watch the faces of your students light up as bright as the sun. Ask: *How can we show the sun's rays warming everything?* Don't be surprised when children's arms stretch and sway as they spread the warmth to all corners of your room.

■ People have been wishing on stars for centuries! After children design their own stars, with help if needed, invite them to and draw their wishes on them. Hang them, tape them, display them around the room. As the wishes are shared and read, favorite lullabies provide excellent background music. Turn the wishes into original songs. Interpret the wishes in movement.

■ It takes strength and speed to travel through the sky to outer space. *Ask: Can we turn our bodies into rocket ships?* Have children crouch down on an imaginary launching pad. Then give these directions.

Ready to go!
Countdown: 10-9-8-7-6-5-4-3-2-1
Blast off!
Keep jumping. Higher. Higher. Higher.
Arms straight overhead.
We're almost there.
We made it!
Now we're ready for another adventure!

D'Nealian® Handwriting

K

Author
Donald Neal Thurber

Scott Foresman
Addison Wesley

Editorial Offices: Glenview, Illinois • New York, New York
Sales Offices: Reading, Massachusetts • Atlanta, Georgia
Glenview, Illinois • Carrollton, Texas • Menlo Park, California

1-800-552-2259
http://www.sf.aw.com

Acknowledgments

Illustrations
Liz Allen 11, 18, 22, 43, 51, 56, 81, 82, 87, 88, 97, 98, 113, 114, 129, 130; Nan Brooks 9, 10, 15, 20, 40, 77, 78, 83, 91, 92, 121, 122, 131, 132, 143, 144, 147, 148, 161, 162, 167; Randy Chewning 12; Rondi Collette 23, 24, 45, 46, 49, 50, 75, 76, 79, 80, 105, 106, 115, 116, 125, 126, 135, 136, 145, 146, 149, 150; Judith dufour-Love 109, 110, 117, 118, 137, 138, 153, 154; Creston Ely 41, 42, 71, 72, 155, 156; Lydia Halvorsen 123, 124, 127, 128; Linda Hawkins 46, 48, 62, 66, 76, 80, 92, 98, 132, 134, 142, 158; Gary Hoover 53, 54, 63, 64, 65, 74, 102, 120, 144, 163, 164; Ruth Linstromberg 25, 27, 31, 33, 35, 42 (crayons), 52, 54, 61, 62, 65, 66, 107, 108, 119, 120, 139, 140, 151, 152, 159, 160; Leonard Lubin 17; Yoshi Miyake 41; James Needham 89; Cheryl Kirk-Noll 47, 48; Stella Ormai 85, 86, 95, 96, 141, 142, 157, 158; Gary Phillips 59, 60, 67, 68, 73, 74, 93, 94; Judy Sakaguchi 19, 30, 37, 38; Bob Shein 16; Lena Shiffman 103, 104, 111, 112, 133, 134, 165, 166; Georgia Shola 44, 72, 86, 142; Susan Swan 84; Titus Tomescu 14, 27, 100, 165, 166; Darcy Whitehead 3, 4, 5, 13, 21, 26, 39, 57, 73, 81, 93, 101, 107, 111, 137

Photographs
Unless otherwise credited, all photographs are the property of Addison Wesley Educational Publishers Inc.
Camerique 98; H. Armstrong Roberts, Inc./Abernathy 90; H. Armstrong Roberts, Inc./P. Degginger 154; Image Bank/Garry Gay 52; Image Bank/Dag Sundberg 84; Image Bank/Anne Van Der Vaeren 11; Tom Stack/Richard Buzzelli 154; Superstock, Inc., 69; Superstock, Inc./Akira Matoba 55; Superstock, Inc./Steve Vidler 122; Tony Stone Worldwide/Lawrence Manning 96

ISBN: 0-673-59213-8

23456789WC0403020100099

Contents

MEET:

Anthony D. Fredericks, Ed.D.
Assistant Professor of Education
York College

Many parents feel disassociated from the school because they have not been given any decision-making powers in terms of their children's education. Yet, it is vitally important that parents be provided with positive opportunities to decide on directions and components of their children's academics. In so doing, teachers are providing parents with a sense of "ownership"—asking parents for their advice, soliciting their input, and letting them make purposeful decisions. Their support, then, will be continuous and strong.

Listed below are several activities you may wish to consider as part of your outreach efforts. Plan to tailor them to the needs and dynamics of your own classroom. But, above all, embellish them with a spirit of sincerity, a healthy dose of enthusiasm, and a determination that they succeed.

Parents need to understand that taking part in their child's education will have a direct effect on the child's academic achievement.

- Work with colleagues to produce a regular parent newsletter to answer parents' concerns about education. (A brief "Dear Abby" format may be appealing to adults of widely varied backgrounds.)
- Set up a "Family of the Week" bulletin board in your classroom. Invite members of the family to help arrange pictures, memorabilia, and labels.
- Establish a "Kaffee Klatsch" or a "Brown-Bag Lunch" once a month to discuss common concerns with parents.
- Invite parents who speak languages other than English to teach songs or rhymes in that language to small groups of children or to the entire class.
- Work with your students to prepare a packet for the parents of new students assigned to your classroom.

[Highlights from the article on page T27 of this teacher's edition.]

Teacher to Teacher

Q. *Must I change my charts and bulletin-board letters to D'Nealian® Handwriting?*

A. From the beginning, children should be exposed to many styles of print in the classroom. As reading skills improve, so should their understanding that letters are not always formed in the same way. Continue to use previously developed charts and displays, but write new charts in D'Nealian® Handwriting to provide models.

Q. *What does research say about when to begin formal handwriting instruction?*

A. Handwriting is a motor skill; therefore, it depends largely upon developmental factors such as eye-hand coordination, directionality, and the ability to match shapes and sizes, as well as the ability to control a writing instrument. As with any motor skill, not all children will be ready at the same time. Close observation will indicate readiness.

Q. *Aren't circle and stick forms of manuscript closer to book print, and wouldn't they make it easier for my pupils to learn to read?*

A. Neither research nor experience supports this theory. In fact, classroom experience with D'Nealian® Handwriting users indicates that D'Nealian® Handwriting promotes letter forms that are rhythmical and easy for pupils to master. Teachers report that children write more, providing for that all important reading-writing connection. Recent studies show a close correlation between the amount of writing attempted and reading achievement.

Activity Bank Guide Unit 1

An Activity Bank appears with each lesson. It offers suggestions that can enrich the lesson, tailor to specific needs, or provide additional practice. In Unit 1, activities in the following categories appear on pages given in parentheses.

Early Literacy
Follow the Leader (6)
Shake It Out (6)
Tuning Up (6)
Ready, Set, Go (7)
Pick a Spoon (7)
Right, Left Turn (8)
Stack Them High (8)

Half and Half (8)
Circle the Matches (9)
Signs of Spring (10)
Button, Button (10)
Match the Deck (10)
An Up and Down World (11)
Human Yoyos (11)
Puppet Play (12)
Choose Your Colors (12)
Step Up to the Ladder (12)

Primary Pilots (13)
Treasure Hunt (13)
Obstacle Course (14)
It's in the Book (14)
Helpful Hints (15)
Road Runners (15)
Capture the Sticks (16)
The Right Stuff (16)
Picture Puzzles (17)
Fairy-Tale Trail (17)
Animals on the Move (18)
Lacing Strips (18)
String Along with Me (18)
Clay Play (19)
Nest Place Mats (19)
Popcorn Puppies (20)
Animal Tracers (20)
Pipe-Cleaner Play (20)

Creative
Signs of Spring (10)
An Up and Down World (11)
Nest Place Mats (19)

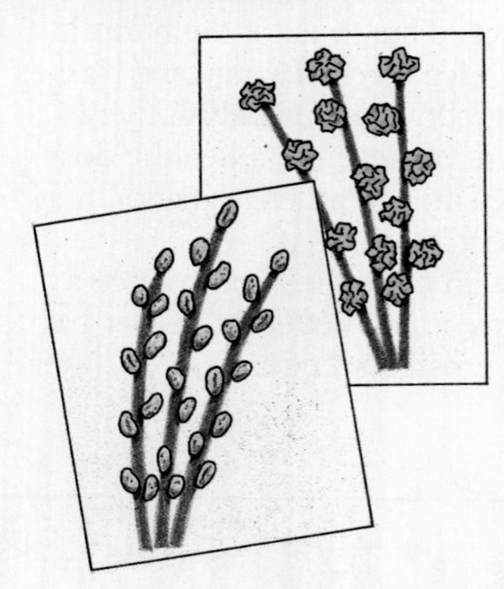

Critical Thinking
Choose Your Colors (12)

Learning Modalities
Auditory
Treasure Hunt (13)
Kinesthetic
Tuning Up (6)
Right, Left Turn (8)
Human Yoyos (11)
Puppet Play (12)
Primary Pilots (13)
It's in the Book (14)
The Right Stuff (16)
Fairy-Tale Trail (17)
Clay Play (19)
Tactile
Circle the Matches (9)
Animals on the Move (18)
Popcorn Puppies (20)
Pipe-Cleaner Play (20)
Visual
Follow the Leader (6)
Picture Puzzles (17)

Multicultural/Multilingual
Celebrating Us (9)
Over and Under We Go (14)
Hopping Birdies (16)

Small Groups
Half and Half (8)
Match the Deck (10)

Special Needs
Attention Deficit Disorder (9)(17)
Auditory Deficits (19)
Immature Learner (9)(11)(15) (17)

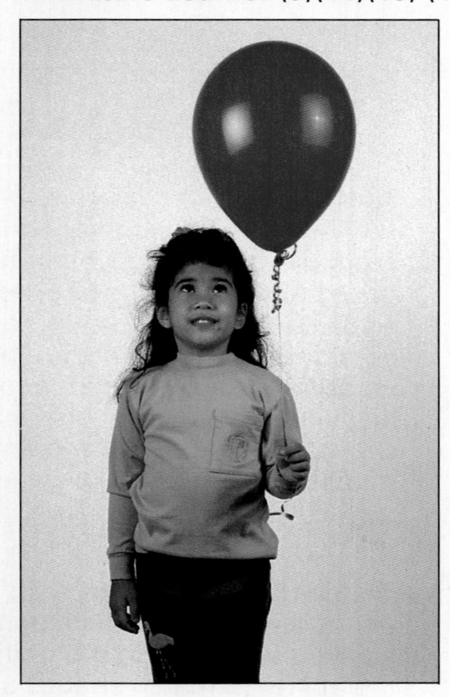

Unit Overview

Most of the children in your class have been scribbling and coloring for quite some time, and they are now ready for formal writing. Unit 1 is designed to help them prepare for the exciting world of D'Nealian® Handwriting.

The first thing children must learn is how to sit and hold their pencils properly. Once proper positioning is established, they work on important concepts such as *alike* and *different; up* and *down; above, beside,* and *below; top, middle,* and *bottom;* and *over* and *under.* The pencil and paper activities involving left-to-right progression, eye-hand and fine-motor coordination are essential preparation for the concentrated movement required in writing.

This is an exciting time for you and the children you teach. The colorful and imaginative activities presented in this book should inspire and encourage them, giving you all great satisfaction.

Bibliography

You may wish to obtain the following books to read aloud or provide for independent reading.

Dantzer-Rosenthal, Marya. *Some Things Are Different, Some Things Are the Same.* Morton Grove, Illinois: Albert Whitman & Company, 1986.

Haley, Bill. "Shake, Rattle, and Roll." *Bill Haley and the Comets' Greatest Hits,* MCAC 161E.

Hoban, Tana. *Over, Under, and Through.* New York: Macmillan, 1973.

Spier, Peter. *People.* Garden City, New York: Doubleday and Company, Inc., 1980.

Blueprint for a Writing Center

Setting up the Writing Center

As D'Nealian® Handwriting is being formally taught, children will increase their fine-motor control and fluency through purposeful writing. Interesting choices of independent activities, provided in the classroom Writing Center, will also lead children to regard writing as natural and pleasant.

Objective
Learns proper body position for good handwriting.

Prepare
Be sure each child has an appropriate desk or table, a chair, and a pencil.

To help children understand proper body position, have them put their feet far back under their chairs, then way out in front of them. Ask what happens to their bodies when their feet are in these positions. Explain that by putting both feet flat on the floor, they are helping to balance their bodies.

Teach (page 6)
Have children:
- look at and talk about the picture on the page;
- model the picture by sitting up straight with both feet on the floor;
- relax their arms on their desks.

Follow Up
Self-Evaluation Have children check their body position by asking themselves:
- Am I sitting up nice and straight?
- Are my feet flat on the floor?
- Do I feel relaxed?

Sitting Position for Writing

Left-handed

Right-handed

6 Sitting Position for Writing
Children position themselves comfortably for writing.

ACTIVITY BANK

Follow the Leader (Gross Motor, Visual) Play a game of "Follow the Leader" to help children stretch and loosen up their bodies. Start them off by standing on your tiptoes and lifting your arms above your head saying, *Reach for the sky.* Next, call on volunteers to show other exercises for classmates to mimic.

Shake It Out (Handwriting Position, Gross Motor) Play lively music, such as "Twist and Shout" or "Shake, Rattle, and Roll," and invite children to stand and shake their arms, hands, and bodies to the music. Next have them sit quietly and show how they can sit up, ready to write.

Tuning Up (Fine Motor, Kinesthetic) Since handwriting requires fine-motor muscles, we do exercises to "warm-up" our finger muscles. Before each handwriting lesson, have the class sing and demonstrate familiar finger plays, such as "Eensy, Weensy Spider."

Mary Louise Sonnenburg
Claudia Landeen School
Stockton, CA

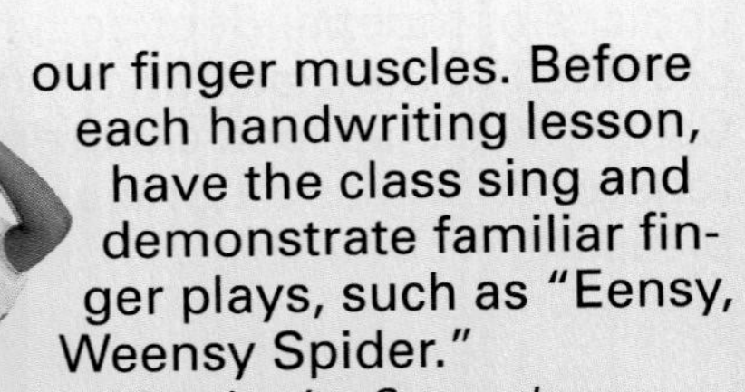

Right-handed Position for Writing

Right-handed Position for Writing 7

Children practice the proper position of their papers and pencils for good writing.

Objective

Learns proper positioning of paper and pencil for right-handed writing.

Prepare

In order for right-handed children to slant the paper correctly, have them pick up the paper by the upper right-hand corner and hold it straight out in front of them. The angle at which the paper hangs is close to the proper slant when it is placed on the desk.

Many children will have developed their own grip before coming to school. If the child seems comfortable with this grip and it is not too awkward, it is best not to try to change it.

Teach (page 7)

Have right-handed children:

- look at and talk about the pictures on the page;
- model the first picture with the paper slanted so that the left corner points toward the stomach;
- model the second picture by loosely grasping the pencil between thumb and first finger just above the slope caused by sharpening;
- relax their arms on their desks.

Follow Up

Self-Evaluation Have right-handed children check their paper and pencil position by asking themselves:

- Is my paper slanted properly?
- Am I holding my pencil correctly?
- Do I feel relaxed?

ACTIVITY BANK

Ready, Set, Go (Handwriting Position, Oral Language) Recite this rhyme to help children become aware of proper positioning for handwriting:

One, two,
Here's paper for you.
Three, four,
Feet flat on the floor.
Five, six,
Pick up your sticks (pencils).
Seven, eight,
Sit up straight.
Nine, ten,
Let's review again.

Karen Tebbenhoff
Sherwood Elementary
Arnold, MO

Pick a Spoon (Left and Right, Handwriting Position) To help children determine whether they are right- or left-handed, put a pile of plastic spoons on a table. Ask each child to tell the name of a food that must be eaten with a spoon. Then ask children to pick up a spoon and pretend to eat. Watch to see which hand they use to hold the spoon.

Objective
Learns proper positioning of paper and pencil for left-handed writing.

Prepare
In order for left-handed children to slant the paper correctly, have them pick up the paper by the upper left-hand corner and hold it straight out in front of them. The angle at which the paper hangs is close to the proper slant when it is placed on the desk.

Many children will have developed their own grip before coming to school. If the child seems comfortable with this grip and it is not too awkward, it is best not to try to change it.

Teach (page 8)
Have left-handed children:
• look at and talk about the pictures on the page;
• model the first picture with the paper slanted so that the right corner points toward the stomach;
• model the second picture by loosely grasping the pencil between thumb and first finger just above the slope caused by sharpening (left-handers should grasp the pencil a little higher than right-handers);
• relax their arms on their desks.

Follow Up
Self-Evaluation Have left-handed children check their paper and pencil position by asking themselves:
• Is my paper slanted properly?
• Am I holding my pencil correctly?
• Do I feel relaxed?

Left-handed Position for Writing

8 Left-handed Position for Writing

Children practice the proper position of their papers and pencils for good writing.

ACTIVITY BANK

Right, Left Turn (Left and Right, Kinesthetic) Set up an obstacle course in the classroom and have children pair off. Tell them they are going to pretend to be a remote-control car and the car's operator. Tell "operators" that they must tell "cars" when to turn left and right. After a time, have children switch roles.

Stack Them High (Gross Motor, Eye-Hand Coordination) Provide boxes of different shapes and sizes (from a large, deep box to a box that would hold jewelry). Ask children to stack the boxes, working from the largest on the bottom to the smallest on top.

Half and Half (Left and Right, Small Groups) Fold large pieces of paper in half lengthwise. Arrange children in groups of four and give each child paints and brushes. Assign two children in each group to paint only on the right side and the other two to paint only on the left side of the paper. When children have finished painting, ask them to exchange papers and paint on the side they have not yet painted on. Open up the papers and admire their work.

Circle the pictures.

Prewriting: Likenesses and Differences 9

Children circle the picture that matches the first one in each row.

Objective

Identifies objects that are alike.

Prepare

Let children work in groups of four.

- Have two children assume the same position while the other two assume positions that are different.
- Let classmates identify the two positions that are alike.

Teach (page 9)

Have children:

- identify the animals in the column at the left;
- identify the first row as pictures of birds;
- circle the bird that matches the one at the left;
- continue independently or as a group.

Follow Up

Self-Evaluation Have children check their own work by asking themselves:

- Did I circle one animal in each row?
- Is each of the animals I circled like the one in the box at the left?

ACTIVITY BANK

Special Needs (Attention Deficit Disorder, Immature Learners) Children who have trouble focusing on visual details should benefit from the following activity. Place three of the children's shoes, two of which match, in front of a shoe box. Have the children take turns putting the two matching shoes in the box. In the winter, you might want to substitute children's mittens, asking them to put on the matching pair.

Celebrating Us (Celebrating Cultural Diversity) Read and discuss the book *People* by Peter Spier with children. Most children find the eyes and noses pictured intriguing. Have them bring in photos or cut out magazine pictures of people. Let them work in groups to determine the similarities and differences in the eyes and noses. Have them compare their own eyes and noses.

Circle the Matches (Likenesses and Differences, Tactile) Place three objects, two of which match, in a sandbox or on a cookie sheet covered with salt. Children circle the matching objects.

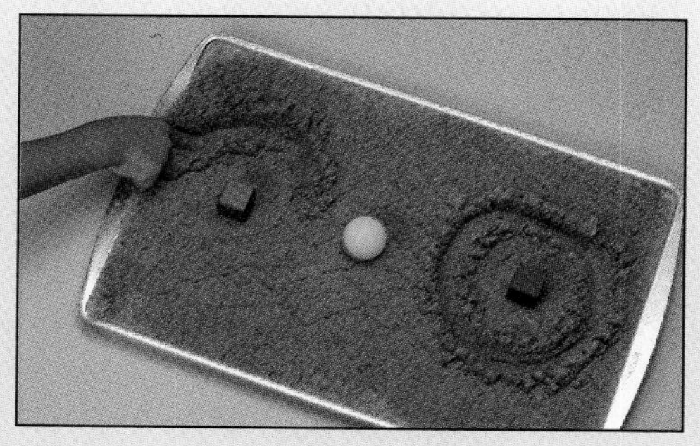

Objective
Identifies objects that are different.

Prepare
Put four objects in a paper bag, one of which is different from the others. Have children take turns reaching into the bag and pulling out the object that is different.

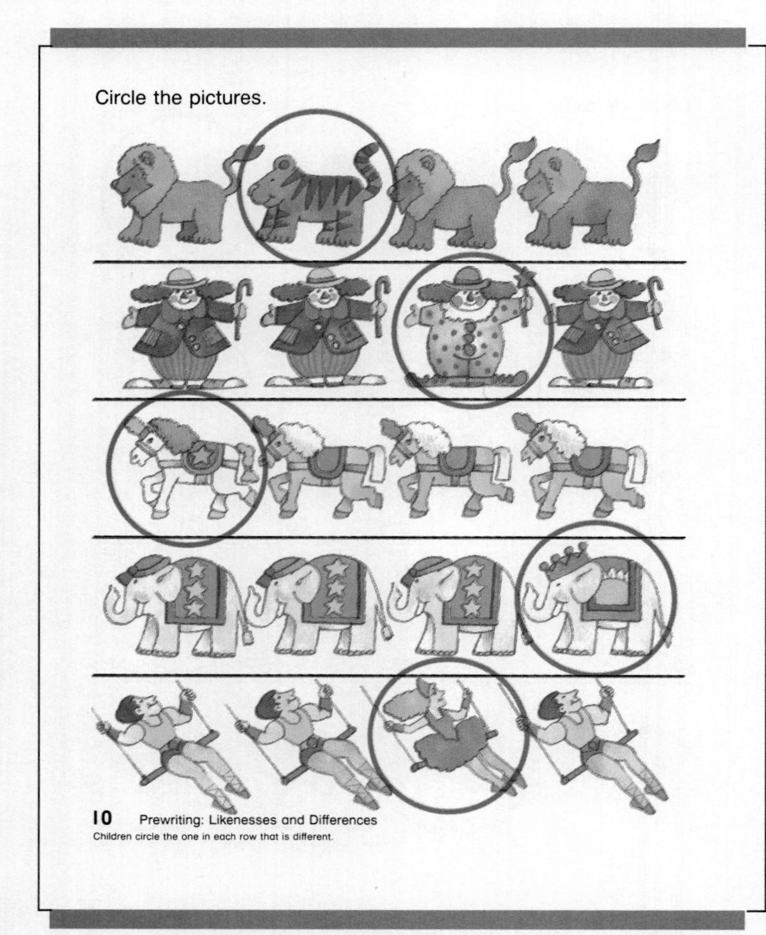

Circle the pictures.

10 Prewriting: Likenesses and Differences

Children circle the one in each row that is different.

Teach (page 10)
Have children:
- identify the various images on the page as circus performers;
- identify the first row as pictures of lions and tigers;
- circle the animal that is different;
- continue independently or as a group.

Follow Up
Self-Evaluation Have children check their own work by asking themselves:
- Did I circle one picture in each row?
- Is each picture I circled different from the others?

ACTIVITY BANK

Signs of Spring (Likenesses and Differences, Creative) To help my class become aware of spring growth, I bring in pussy willow and forsythia. We discuss their likenesses and differences and note their growth patterns. The children draw branches on paper. They glue puffed cereal down to make pussy-willow branches and crumpled yellow tissue paper to make forsythia branches.

Dana Lee Johnson
Highcroft Ridge School
Chesterfield, MO

Button, Button (Likenesses and Differences, Fine Motor) Give a box of assorted buttons or beads to individual children or to groups of two or three. Have them sort the items by color, size, or shape. Ask children to tell you how the items are alike or different.

Match the Deck (Likenesses and Differences, Small Groups) Use picture cards that contain pairs of the same object. Have children sit in a circle on a rug with the picture cards facedown in front of them. Taking turns, children turn over cards until they find two that are exactly the same. The one with the most matches wins.

Mark the picture.

Prewriting: Spatial Relationships 11

Children circle the birds that are **up** in the sky. They put an X on the birds that are **down** on the ground.

Objective
Demonstrates an understanding of **up** and **down.**

Prepare
Ask children what they can ride that goes up and down. Encourage suggestions such as elevator, escalator, airplane, or teeter-totter.

Let children demonstrate *up* and *down* by responding to these directions:

Put your hand up.
Put your leg up.
Put your hand down.
Put your leg down.
Stand up.
Sit down.

Teach (page 11)
Have children:
- tell what they see in the picture;
- circle the birds that are up in the sky;
- put an X on the birds that are down on the ground.

Follow Up
Self-Evaluation Have children check their own work by asking themselves:
- Did I circle all the birds that are *up?*
- Did I put an X on all the birds that are *down?*

ACTIVITY BANK

An Up and Down World (Spatial Relationships, Creative) Cover the top half of a bulletin board with blue paper and the bottom half with green paper. Children draw various things they would find in the sky or on the ground and tack them to the board.

Human Yoyos (Up and Down, Kinesthetic) Group children in pairs. Give each pair a long piece of string. Have each child in a pair hold one end of the string. Tell one child in each pair to be a yoyo. As this child moves down, have both children say *down.* Tell the child who is not the yoyo to pull the string, causing the partner to rise. Have both children say *up.* Let children take turns.

Special Needs (Immature Learners) Immature learners often understand spatial relationships best when the entire body gets involved. Have children hold the string of a helium balloon while singing this song (to the tune of "Mary Had a Little Lamb"):

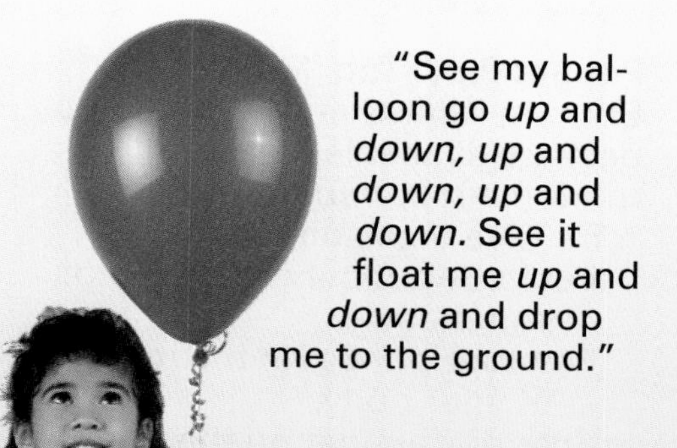

"See my balloon go *up* and *down, up* and *down, up* and *down.* See it float me *up* and *down* and drop me to the ground."

Objective
Demonstrates an understanding of **top, middle,** and **bottom.**

Prepare
Gather the class around a bookcase that has three shelves. Call on volunteers to choose items from the *top* shelf, the *bottom* shelf, and the *middle* shelf. Ask the class if they agree with the selections made.

Teach (page 12)
Have children:
- tell what they see in the picture;
- tell how many teddies are on the *top,* in the *middle,* and on the *bottom;*
- color the top teddy bear's shirt green, the middle bears' shirts red, and the bottom bears' shirts blue.

Follow Up
Self-Evaluation Have children check their own work by asking themselves:
- Are all the teddy bears' shirts colored?
- Is the top teddy bear wearing a green shirt?
- Are the middle teddy bears wearing red shirts?
- Are the bottom teddy bears wearing blue shirts?

ACTIVITY BANK

Puppet Play (Top, Middle, and Bottom; Kinesthetic) If hand puppets are available, use them to reinforce *top, middle,* and *bottom.* Give these directions:

Put your puppet on the top of your head.
Put your puppet in the middle of your body.
Put your puppet on the bottom of your foot.

Choose Your Colors (Top, Middle, and Bottom; Critical Thinking) Prepare a worksheet by drawing a large rectangle with the long side positioned vertically. Divide the rectangle into three equal boxes. Within these divisions, draw a square, a circle, and a triangle. Give directions for coloring the top, middle, and bottom shapes.

Step Up to the Ladder (Top, Middle, and Bottom; Gross Motor) Use a small stepladder and a collection of objects such as small stuffed animals to illustrate the concepts *top, middle,* and *bottom.* Have children sit around the ladder as you invite them to put objects on its steps by following directions that include the words *top, middle,* and *bottom.*

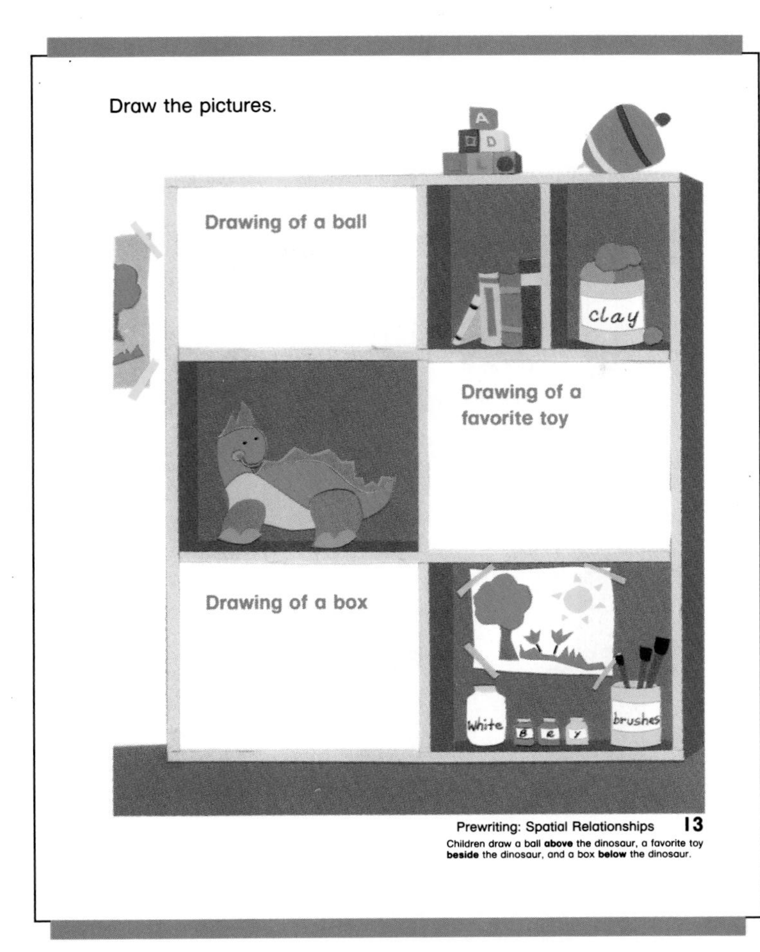
Draw the pictures.

Drawing of a ball

Drawing of a favorite toy

Drawing of a box

clay

White

brushes

Prewriting: Spatial Relationships 13

Children draw a ball **above** the dinosaur, a favorite toy **beside** the dinosaur, and a box **below** the dinosaur.

Objective

Demonstrates an understanding of **above, beside,** and **below.**

Prepare

Draw six large boxes, stacked two by two, on the chalkboard. In the middle box at the left draw a ball.

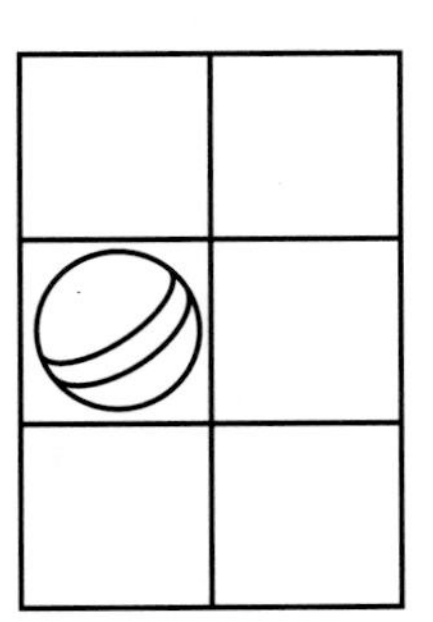

- Ask a volunteer to come to the board, draw something in one of the five empty boxes, and tell whether it is *above, beside,* or *below* the ball.
- Continue in this way, with volunteers calling on classmates to repeat the action.

Teach (page 13)

Have children:
- identify the picture of the bookcase and its contents;
- point to the dinosaur on the middle shelf at the left;
- draw a ball *above* the dinosaur;
- draw a favorite toy *beside* the dinosaur;
- draw a box *below* the dinosaur.

Follow Up

Self-Evaluation Have children check their own work by asking themselves:
- Did I draw in each of the empty spaces?
- Did I draw a ball above the dinosaur?
- Did I draw a toy beside the dinosaur?
- Did I draw a box below the dinosaur?

ACTIVITY BANK

Primary Pilots (Above, Beside, and Below; Kinesthetic) Have children make and then "pilot" paper airplanes by carrying them according to your instructions. Children might follow directions such as:

Pilot your plane above the sink.
Pilot your plane below the table.
Pilot your plane above a chair.
Land your plane beside me.

Remind your flying aces that they must keep a tight grip on their airplanes; unauthorized free-flying planes will be grounded.

Treasure Hunt (Above, Beside, and Below; Auditory) Hide an object somewhere in the room. Tell small groups of children to listen carefully as you tell them where to go to find the "treasure." Use as many words that indicate direction as possible. You might give instructions such as these:

Go straight to the windows.
Walk beside the big table.
Look below the piano.
Reach above the toy shelf.

■ Objective
Demonstrates an understanding of **over** and **under.**

■ Prepare
Use a flannelboard with pieces of felt that represent a bridge and various objects that might be found *over* or *under* a bridge.

Ask volunteers to come to the flannelboard and tell stories using the felt and the words *over* and *under.*

■ Teach (page 14)
Have children:
- tell what they see in the picture;
- draw a flag in the hands of the princess who is riding *over* the bridge;
- draw a ball in the hands of the knight who is riding *under* the bridge.

■ Follow Up
Self-Evaluation Have children check their own work by asking themselves:
- Did I draw a flag in the hands of the princess *above* the bridge?
- Did I draw a ball in the hands of the knight *below* the bridge?

Draw the pictures.

14 Prewriting: Spatial Relationships

Children draw a flag in the hands of the figure going **over** the bridge and a ball in the hands of the figure **under** the bridge.

ACTIVITY BANK

Obstacle Course (Over and Under, Oral Language) Use desks, tables, chairs, and other classroom furnishings to make an obstacle course in the room. Tell children that they will each have a turn moving through the course. Have children position themselves according to your directions as they maneuver the obstacles. As they go, have children verbalize what they are doing (*I am going under the table. I am stepping over the box.*)

It's in the Book (Over and Under, Kinesthetic) Read the book *Over, Under & Through* by Tana Hoban with children. Talk about the concepts and ask volunteers to demonstrate a few of them. Allow children to use props to demonstrate the concepts.

Over and Under We Go (Limited English Proficiency) Tie a rope between two chairs so that it is taut. Have children jump over or crawl under the rope as you say *over the rope* or *under the rope.* Try to also include the words for *rope, over,* and *under* in the language the children are most proficient in to help them along.

Objective

Demonstrates left-to-right progression.

Prepare

Tell children you want them to follow what you are doing with their eyes and that they should not move their heads.

- Slowly draw a line on the chalkboard from left to right.
- Watch to see whether children are moving only their eyes.
- Call on volunteers to repeat this activity, drawing the line a little faster each time.

Teach (page 15)

Have children:

- identify the scene as people heading toward their houses;
- point to the person on the bicycle;
- find the arrow and starting dot;
- finger trace a line to the dot at the right;
- draw a straight line from each starting dot to each ending dot on the page without lifting the pencil.

Follow Up

Self-Evaluation Have children check their own work by asking themselves:

- Did I draw a line from left to right in each path?
- Did I stay within the path from dot to dot?

ACTIVITY BANK

Helpful Hints (Left to Right, Fine Motor) My class uses a sand tray to practice left-to-right progression. We put two objects in the sand across from one another and draw a straight line from the one on the left to the one on the right.

Tess Wickett
Ames School
Ames, NE

Special Needs (Immature Learners) Involve arm muscles to help motor memory. Use a 2" dowel with a large dot on the end. Tie strings to a curtain ring on one end and to a lightweight airplane on the other. Hold the dowel at child's eye level and place the ring around it. Starting at the dot, the child pushes the plane from left to right, gliding it off the end and in for a landing.

Road Runners (Left to Right, Fine Motor) On sheets of construction paper, draw two horizontal lines 2" apart to represent a road. Give children these sheets, small pieces of paper, paste, and a tiny car. Have them pave a road for their cars by pasting the paper between the lines from left to right. Have them drive their cars left to right on their roads.

Objective
Demonstrates left-to-right progression.

Prepare
Have children name some household pets and the foods they eat.
• Draw these pets on the chalkboard.
• Draw the pets' food 6"or 7" to the right.
• Call on volunteers to draw a straight line from each pet to its food.

Teach (page 16)
Have children:
• identify the scene as one in which animals are heading toward their homes;
• point to the bird at the top;
• find the arrow and starting dot;
• finger trace a line to the dot at the right;
• draw a straight line from each starting dot to each ending dot on the page without lifting the pencil.

Follow Up
Self-Evaluation Have children check their own work by asking themselves:
• Did I draw a line from left to right in each path?
• Did I stay within the path from dot to dot?

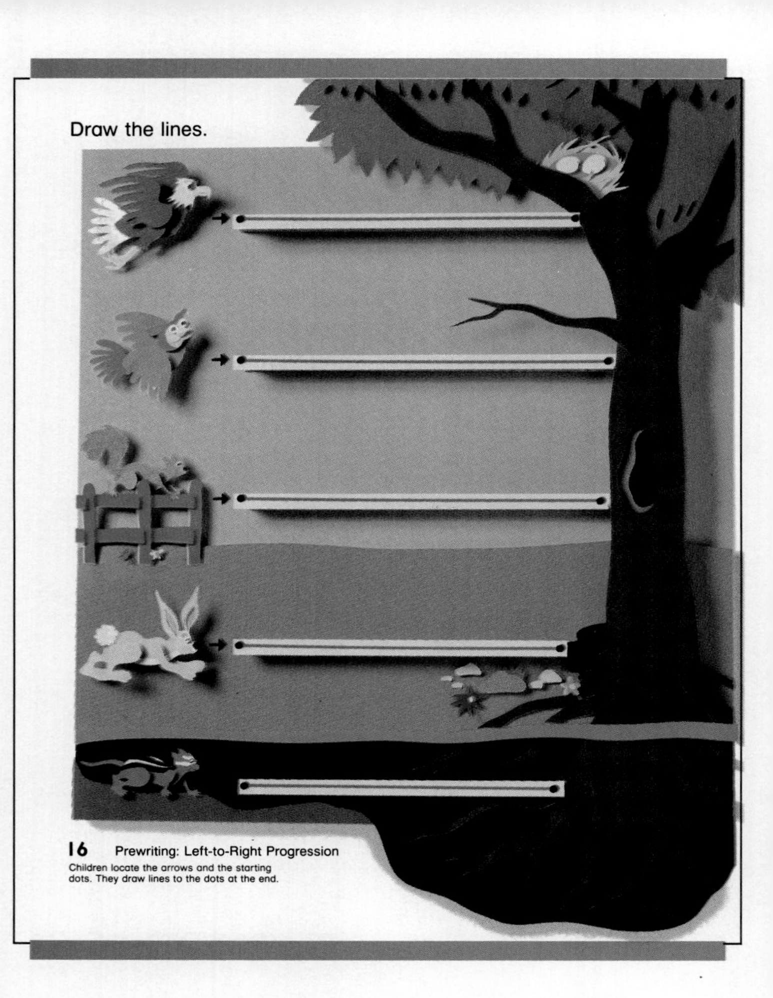

ACTIVITY BANK

Hopping Birdies (Limited English Proficiency) Give each child a picture of a bird. Tell children they must hop their bird left or right according to your directions. Say the word *bird* in their own language as well as in English.

Capture the Sticks (Left to Right, Gross Motor) On the chalkboard draw ten vertical lines 2" or 3" inches apart. Have children take turns using colored chalk to "capture the sticks" by drawing a horizontal line through the vertical lines. Make sure children draw from left to right.

The Right Stuff (Left and Right, Kinesthetic) Play "Go Right." Line children up behind you on the left side of an open area. Explain that you will give directions to move either left or right. They are to follow *only* those directions that tell them to move to the right. Give directions such as:

Hop to your right.
Tiptoe to the right.
March to your left.
Jump to the right.

After children become familiar with the game, have them take turns calling out directions.

Draw the lines.

FINISH

Prewriting: Eye-Hand Coordination 17

Children locate the arrows and the starting dots. They draw lines within the paths to the dots at the end.

Objective

Demonstrates eye-hand coordination.

Prepare

Draw curved lines on the chalkboard that simulate strokes children will use in handwriting. Invite children to come to the board and use the eraser to follow the line in a continuous stroke from left to right.

Teach (page 17)

Have children:

- identify the images as fairy tale characters going on a journey;
- point to the tortoise and the hare at top left;
- find the arrow and starting dot;
- finger trace a curved line to the dot at the finish line;
- draw a curved line from each starting dot to each ending dot on the page without lifting the pencil.

Follow Up

Self-Evaluation Have children check their own work by asking themselves:

- Did I draw a curved line in each path?
- Did I stay within the path from dot to dot?

ACTIVITY BANK

Picture Puzzles (Eye-Hand Coordination, Visual) Have children glue a picture onto construction paper. Draw puzzle-like lines through each picture and have children cut along the lines. Have children scramble the pieces, put them back together, then exchange them.

Special Needs (Attention Deficit Disorder, Immature Learners) Active learning works best with children who have attention deficit disorder. Invite children to "Take a Hike." Use colored chalk to draw large curved pathways on the classroom floor or on the playground, simulating those on page 17. Children walk the paths trying not to touch the sides.

Fairy-Tale Trail (Motor Development, Kinesthetic) Discuss the stories *The Tortoise and the Hare, Cinderella, Goldilocks,* and *The Three Billy Goats Gruff.* Talk about the fact that these characters are going from one place to another. Draw the characters at the start of large, curving paths on the chalkboard. Invite children to show how each would travel along the paths. Ask volunteers to draw a picture of each character's destination.

Objective
Demonstrates eye-hand coordination.

Prepare
On the chalkboard, draw three sets of wide vertical paths about two feet long, similar to those below. Include starting dots and direction arrows.
- Ask a volunteer to move a finger down the first path, without touching the sides or lifting the finger.
- After a number of children have finger traced this path, invite them to trace the other two paths.

Teach (page 18)
Have children:
- identify the images on the page as various baby animals heading down a path toward their parents;
- point to the baby beaver at top left;
- find the arrow and starting dot;
- finger trace a curved line to the dot near the parent beaver;
- draw lines downward from each starting dot to each ending dot without lifting the pencil.

Follow Up
Self-Evaluation Have children check their own work by asking themselves:
- Did I draw a line downward in each path?
- Did I stay within the path from dot to dot?

Draw the lines.

18 Prewriting: Eye-Hand Coordination

Children locate the arrows and the starting dots. They draw lines within the paths to the dots at the end.

ACTIVITY BANK

Animals on the Move (Fine Motor, Tactile) Provide modeling clay for each child. Ask children to make a baby animal and a grown-up animal of the same kind. Provide three paths similar to the ones on page 18 by cutting or marking heavy cardboard. Have children scoot their little animals from the top down to the grown-ups waiting at the bottom of each path.

Lacing Strips (Eye-Hand Coordination, Fine Motor) Cut several 4" x 12" strips of posterboard. On each strip, make a path of a different shape by punching holes at 1" intervals. Circle the starting hole in green and the last hole in red.

Starting with the green hole and finishing with the red, children use yarn to connect the holes and form the path.

String Along with Me (Eye-Hand Coordination, Fine Motor) Provide practice in small-muscle control by having children string beads, macaroni, or popcorn. Patterns could be: two beads, three macaroni, one popcorn, or one red bead, two green beads, one blue bead, and so on.

Trace the lines. Color the pictures.

Prewriting: Fine Motor Coordination 19

Children locate the arrows and the starting dots. They trace the gray lines and then color the picture.

Objective

Demonstrates fine motor coordination.

Prepare

Give each child a piece of paper with the outline of a young bird on it. Supply children with small feathers (or colored popcorn) and glue. Have children glue the feathers or popcorn on the bird using tweezers or their fingers.

Teach (page 19)

Have children:

- tell what they see in the four panels on the page;
- find the arrow and starting dot;
- finger trace the **O** shape in the first panel;
- pencil trace all the shapes on the page;
- color the picture.

Follow Up

Self-Evaluation Have children check their work by asking themselves:

- Did I trace all the shapes?
- Did I stay within the gray lines?

ACTIVITY BANK

Special Needs (Auditory Deficits) Help establish mental-image associations for letter strokes by emphasizing the visual. Provide tagboard with large models of these strokes incorporated into a picture:

Fishhook: aluminum-foil rope

Monkey Tail: brown fur fabric

Curves: bubble packing

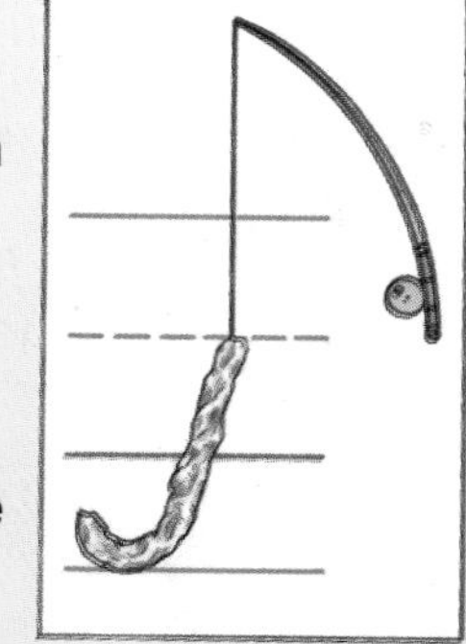

Children finger trace each of these strokes.

Clay Play (Kinesthetic, Eye-Hand Coordination) Have children use clay to roll out skinny "snakes." Children form a circle, a **v** shape, a **j** shape, and so on, tracing them with their fingers. If left to harden, the shapes can be painted and reused.

Marly Glaw
Shreiner School and Academy
Marietta, GA

Nest Place Mats (Fine Motor, Creative) Invite children to make place mats in the form of birds' nests. Pass out heavy brown paper. Prepare six 9" strips of heavy yellow paper and seven 6" strips of heavy orange paper.

Children paste yellow strips horizontally on the brown paper. Next they paste the orange strips vertically over the yellow. Then they cut their papers in an oval shape.

Objective
Demonstrates fine motor coordination.

Prepare
Put a picture of an animal under the acetate of an overhead projector, draw an animal on the chalkboard, or laminate an animal photograph. Arrange dots and trace lines over and below the animal as shown below. Have children:
- draw lines from top dot to bottom dot to "cage" the animal.
- trade places and erase the lines from dot to dot to "free" the animal.

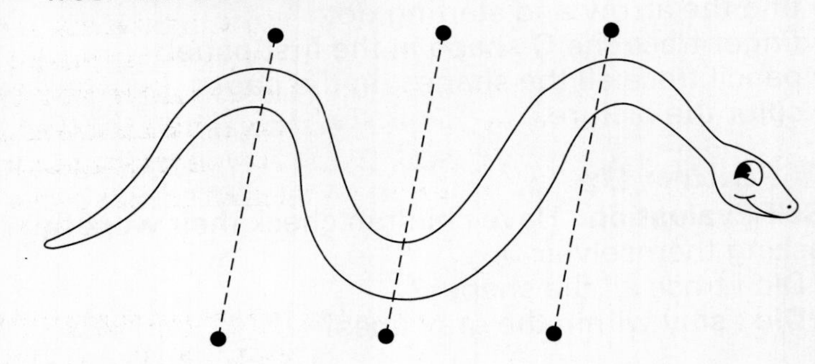

Teach (page 20)
Have children:
- tell what they see on the page;
- finger trace and pencil trace the missing strokes in each balloon.

Follow Up
Self-Evaluation Have children check their own work by asking themselves:
- Did I trace all the strokes?
- Did I stay within the gray lines?

ACTIVITY BANK

Popcorn Puppies (Tactile, Fine Motor) Give children a bowl of popcorn and sheets of paper containing the outline of a puppy. Have them glue popcorn on the inside of the body shape to represent fur, and then paint it. Let them eat the remaining popcorn upon completion of the task.

Animal Tracers (Fine Motor, Eye-Hand Coordination) Cut large pictures of animals from coloring books and paste them onto lightweight cardboard. Laminate them. Let children choose one or more, trace around them, and color them.

Pipe-Cleaner Play (Fine Motor, Tactile) My kindergarten children enjoy using pipe cleaners to form various strokes for D'Nealian letters. They enjoy creating curves, as used in the **r/R, s/S, c/C,** and **o/O,** and zigzags like those of the **z/Z.**

Lois R. Vogel
David Turnham Center
Dale, IN

MEET:

Ngoc-Diep T. Nguyen, Ph.D.
Teacher Educator, Consultant

In the past few years, multicultural education has become a popular discussion topic in many schools. We, as classroom teachers, are encouraged to consider culture as an important factor that affects teaching and learning both inside and outside the school. We are asked to celebrate cultural diversity in our classrooms. We are challenged to become more culturally sensitive.

There are four basic principles that operate in a classroom where cultural diversity is celebrated:
1. Respectful treatment of all people.
2. Appreciation of diversity.
3. Consideration of a human experience from multiple perspectives.
4. Willingness to make decisions through compromise.

Strategies that will help children appreciate cultural diversity include:
1. Creating a classroom environment that is accepting of cultural differences.
2. Clearing up cross-cultural miscommunication as it occurs.
3. Teaching students many points of view of the same phenomenon and encouraging them to state their own perspectives.
4. Incorporating activities from a variety of resources, including the home and community.

[Highlights from the article on page T26 of this teacher's edition.]

Since culture is an immense field, it is unrealistic to expect to know everything about all groups of people. It is realistic to expect yourself and your students to be open to learning about other people and to using one another as resources.

Teacher to Teacher

Q. *Are kindergartners and first graders ready to use regular pencils?*

A. Most children come to school having used regular pencils. However, during the pre-writing instruction period, pupils should experiment with different sizes and types of writing tools, including crayons. At this time the child can be encouraged to choose the instrument that fits his or her hand most comfortably.

Q. *Why does D'Nealian® Handwriting call for 3/4" paper at kindergarten and 1/2" paper at first grade?*

A. The fine-motor control of kindergarteners is best suited to 3/4" writing lines. These lines are a natural first step after first exploring letter formation on unlined paper.

By first grade, eye span and motor control are generally developed to the point where children are more comfortable with the 1/2" lines and smaller-sized letters.

Q. *Is it necessary to introduce the letters in the sequence that is used in the D'Nealian® Handwriting text?*

A. During the pre-writing period, you may show the D'Nealian form for any letter the child asks to see. At this stage you are not teaching for mastery. Later, however, when you begin formal instruction, the easiest, most efficient way to mastery is in the sequence used in the text. This is because manuscript letters are introduced in stroke groups, that is, all letters that use similar strokes are taught together to ensure easy mastery of all the letter forms.

Activity Bank Guide Unit 2

An Activity Bank appears with each lesson. It offers suggestions that can enrich the lesson, tailor it to specific needs, or provide additional practice. In Unit 2, activities in the following categories appear on pages given in parentheses.

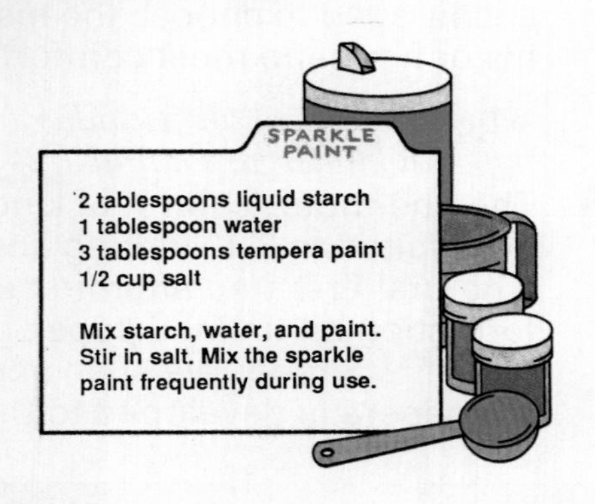

Unit Overview

Children love learning number concepts and writing numbers. In Unit 2, they will learn to write **1** through **10**, and to associate these numbers with countable objects. Before they begin writing, however, children will encounter an exciting "tracer page," full of strokes used in forming the number. These pages draw children in, inviting them to trace strokes and to color a picture.

Once they have practiced a particular number stroke, children will progress to writing the number on writing lines. As they write the number for the first time, they hear a description of how to write it. Pages on which children write their numbers are designed to encourage awareness of mathematics as well as actual number writing.

Two practice pages follow the numbers **1** through **5,** and two more complete the unit. On the second of these, children also employ simple computation.

Bibliography

You may wish to obtain the following books to read aloud or provide for independent reading.

Anno, Mitsumasa. *Anno's Counting Book*. New York: Thomas Y. Crowell Company, 1977.

Carle, Eric. *1, 2, 3 to the Zoo.* New York: Philomel Books, 1990.

Crews, Donald. *Ten Black Dots*. New York: Greenwillow Books, 1986.

Dunbar, Joyce. *Ten Little Mice*. New York: Harcourt Brace Jovanovich, 1990.

Extending Writing Through Activities

Have children develop a WANTED poster for a favorite story character. Pupils illustrate their character and give it an identification number, thereby practicing the handwriting skills they will learn in this unit. The poster is titled **WANTED by (child's name) for Making Reading Fun.**

Related writing activities include writing character phone numbers, making bingo cards, and designing counting cards (number and illustration of that amount).

Objective
Develops number discrimination.

Prepare
On the chalkboard or on a large sheet of paper, write a line of four numbers, one of which matches the first number. The numbers below are an example.

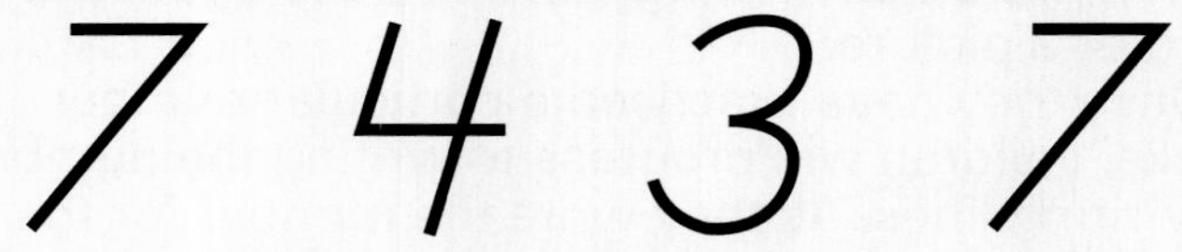

- Call on a volunteer to tell what the first number is.
- Have another child find the matching number and circle it.

Repeat using other numbers.

Teach (page 22)
Have children:
- identify the numbers on each shirt;
- circle the number in each row that matches the number on the shirt.

Follow Up
Self-Evaluation Have children check their own work by asking themselves:
- Did I circle a number in each row?
- Does the number I circled match the number on the shirt?

Additional Resource
Manuscript Alpha Touch numbers **1** through **10**

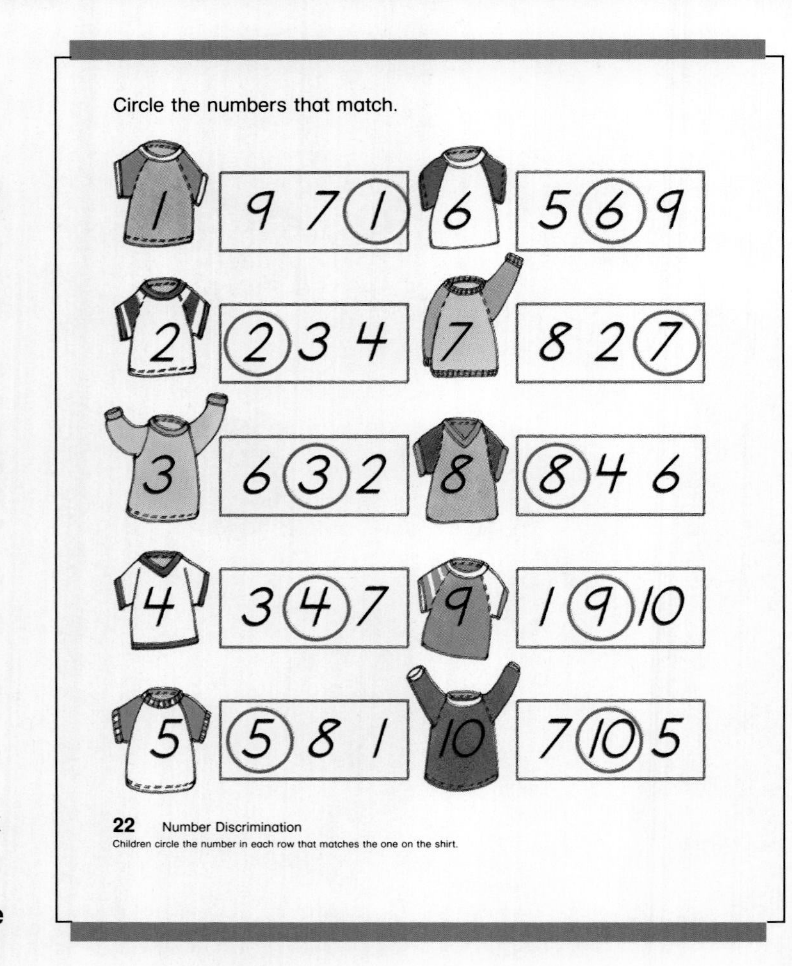
Circle the numbers that match.

Shirt	Numbers	Shirt	Numbers
1	9 7 (1)	6	5 (6) 9
2	(2) 3 4	7	8 2 (7)
3	6 (3) 2	8	(8) 4 6
4	3 (4) 7	9	1 (9) 10
5	(5) 8 1	10	7 (10) 5

22 Number Discrimination

Children circle the number in each row that matches the one on the shirt.

ACTIVITY BANK

Number Hop (Gross Motor, Number Recognition) Prepare a set of number cards from **1** to **10**. Play "Number Hop," a variation of "Simon Says." Have children line up in a row and move according to your directions and the number on the card you are holding up. For example, you might say, *Please take this many* (holding up the card with **3** on it) *giant steps forward.*

Shopping Spree (Number Recognition, Visual Discrimination) Give each child a newspaper page containing grocery prices in large type. Write a number from **1** to **10** at the top of each sheet. Have children find and circle that number as many times as they can.

Matching Numbers (Number Recognition, Print Awareness) Give each child a set of number cards from **1** to **10.** Hold up a card and ask children to hold up the card that matches yours. You may want to have children play this game in groups of two or three, deciding together which number to hold up and who will hold it.

Trace the lines. Color the picture.

Handwriting Strokes 23

Children locate the arrows and the starting dots. They trace the gray lines and then color the picture.

Objective

Traces the stroke used in writing the number **1**.

Prepare

Use the sand table to help children learn the stroke used in writing the number **1.** Sand in a large pan will also suffice. Place ice cream sticks one above the other at the correct angle to serve as dots for the **1** stroke. Have children draw lines from the top stick to the bottom stick with their fingers.

Teach (page 23)

Have children:

- tell what they see in the picture;
- find the first dot and arrow at top left;
- finger trace down the gray tracer line to the end dot;
- pencil trace all the lines from top to bottom;
- color the picture.

Follow Up

Self-Evaluation Have children check their own work by asking themselves:

- Did I trace all the strokes?
- Did I stay within the gray lines?

Additional Resource

Manuscript Alpha Touch number **1**

ACTIVITY BANK

Special Needs (Kinesthetic Deficits) Provide physical guides to help children with kinesthetic deficits memorize strokes. Glue five pencils to a piece of cardboard, being sure they are a "finger space" apart. Have children slide their fingers down between the pencils as they say, "Slant down!"

Wet Ones (Number Recognition, Gross Motor) My students love to write on the chalkboard with water and a paintbrush. Have them try to write ten strokes for number **1,** keeping slants consistent, before the first stroke dries.

Mary Lee Vitton
Mockingbird School
Omaha, NE

Puppets on Parade (Fine Motor, Eye-Hand Coordination) Make an outline of a puppet with its arms and legs akimbo on heavy paper for each child. Let children draw a face, color the body, and glue colorful yarn to the head. Help children cut out their puppets and punch a hole in the head and hands. Tie string through the holes and attach strings to an ice cream stick. Invite children to perform a puppet show.

Objective
Writes the number **1**.

Prepare
Hold up a puppet and have the puppet ask the children how many puppets they see.
- When children agree that there is one, have the puppet write the number **1** on the chalkboard.
- Have children stand like D'Nealian **1's.**
- Have children air trace **1** along with the puppet.

Teach (page 24)
Have children:
- tell what they see on the page;
- finger trace the model number **1** as you read the number description;
- pencil trace the two gray **1's,** starting at the dot;
- write **1's** using the starting dots.

Follow Up
Self-Evaluation Have children check their own work by asking themselves:
- Did I always start at the top?
- Did I slant all my **1's?**

Additional Resource
Manuscript Alpha Touch number **1**

Number Description
Top start; slant down.

ACTIVITY BANK

Textured 1's (Number Recognition, Tactile) Cut **1's** from sandpaper. Glue dried beans, unpopped corn, or cotton balls on cardboard to form **1's.** Have children finger trace them.

Talk About One (Critical Thinking, Oral Language) Ask children to name things in the classroom of which there are only one (a piano, clock, record player, rug, and so forth).

Number Books (Number Practice, Creative) Have children create number books, adding pages as they learn new numbers. Have them write the number **1** at the top of the first page, drawing a picture of one object to correspond with the number. Continue in the same manner with all the numbers through **10** as children learn them.

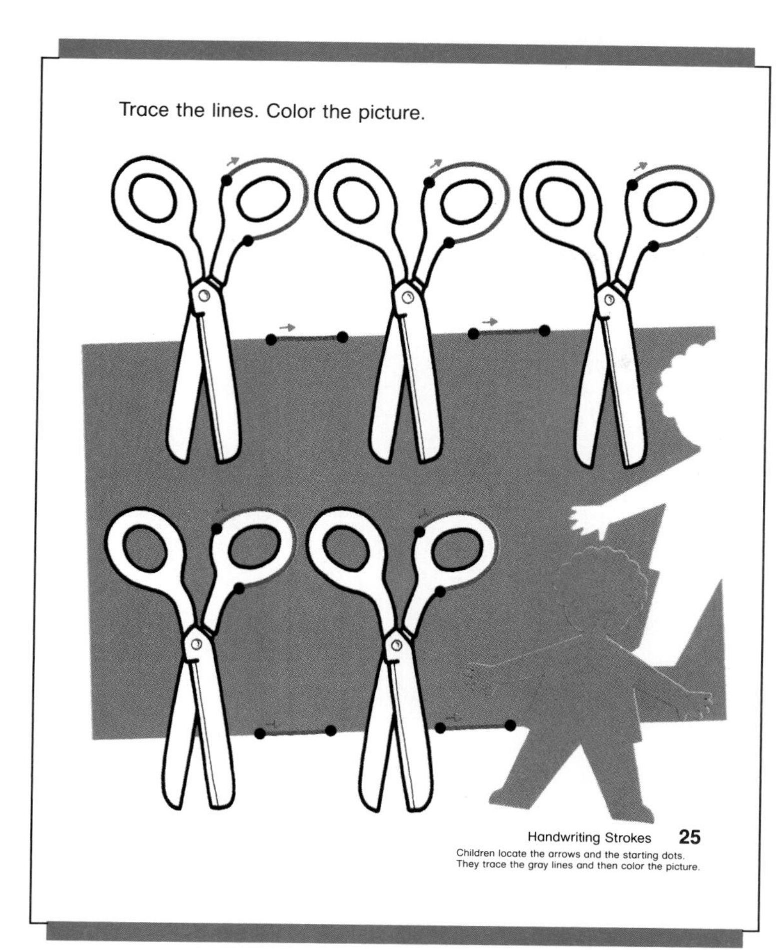
Trace the lines. Color the picture.

Handwriting Strokes 25

Children locate the arrows and the starting dots. They trace the gray lines and then color the picture.

Objective

Traces strokes used in writing the numbers **2** and **3**.

Prepare

On the chalkboard, draw the numbers **2** and **3** and point out the rounded parts. Pass out safety scissors and pieces of heavy white cardboard. Have children:

- feel the curve of the scissors handle with their fingers as you talk about the top curve of the **2** and **3**.
- feel the straight edge of the cardboard from left to right as you discuss the bottom stroke of **2**.

Teach (page 25)

Have children:

- identify the scissors and paper in the picture;
- find the first dot and arrow at top left;
- finger trace around the gray tracer line to the end dot;
- pencil trace all the curved lines from dot to dot;
- pencil trace all the straight lines from left to right;
- color the picture.

Follow Up

Self-Evaluation Have children check their own work by asking themselves:

- Did I move in the direction of the arrows?
- Did I stay within the gray lines?

Additional Resource

Manuscript Alpha Touch numbers **2** and **3**

ACTIVITY BANK

Skiing For 2 (Letter Recognition, Auditory) I invented little stories to coincide with the formation of the numbers. For example: *Number 2 is the skiing number. It goes* ***up*** *the slope,* ***down*** *the slope, and* ***off*** *the slope.* This easy method helps children remember proper formation. They love it!

Donna Hartman
Shady Grove Elementary
Ambler, PA

Special Needs (Visual Deficits) Children with visual deficits learn best by blocking sight. Tie one end of a jump rope to a chair and have the child twirl the other end in a clockwise motion to feel the direction of the stroke of **2** and **3** (guide the child's arm if necessary). Next, have the child trace a large tactile model of **2** and **3** while saying the following rhymes:

Two, two...around my ear.
Across down here.
Two, two.
Three, three...fly around like a bee. Fly again like a bee.
Three, three.

Here's My Heart (Fine Motor, Creative) Have children cut out half-heart shapes traced on folded construction paper. Children then draw or paste a picture of themselves in the center of the heart.

Objective
Writes the numbers **2** and **3**.

Prepare
Hold up two paper dolls and ask the children how many you are holding. Write the number **2** on the chalkboard. Do the same with three paper dolls and the number **3**. Have children:
- air trace **2** and **3** with you;
- come to the board to trace **2** and **3**.

Teach (page 26)
Have children:
- tell what they see in the picture;
- finger trace the model number **2** as you read the number description;
- pencil trace the two gray **2's,** starting at the dot;
- write **2's** using the starting dots.

Repeat the process for **3**.

Follow Up
Self-Evaluation Have children check their own work by asking themselves:
- Did I start at the starting dots?
- Did I write **2** and **3** within the writing lines?

Additional Resource
Manuscript Alpha Touch numbers **2** and **3**

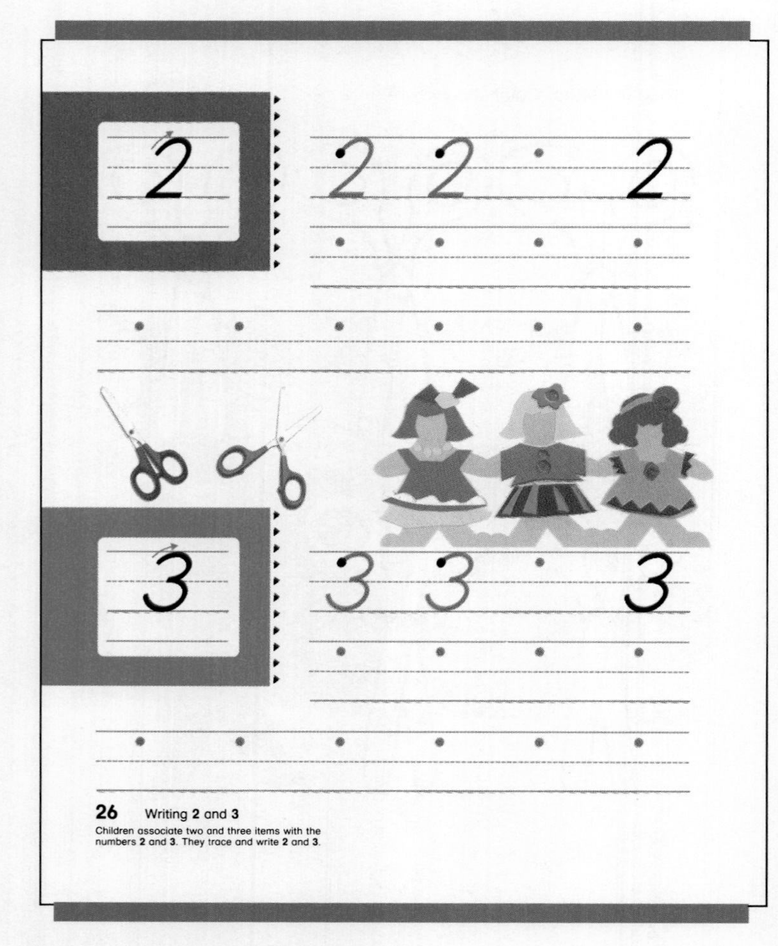

26 Writing 2 and 3

Children associate two and three items with the numbers 2 and 3. They trace and write 2 and 3.

Number Description
Start below the top; curve up, around; slant down left; and over right.

Start below the top; curve up, around halfway; around again, up, and stop.

ACTIVITY BANK

Fun with Three (Auditory, Oral Language) Many children will enjoy hearing and retelling stories, nursery rhymes, or songs in which the number **3** figures prominently. You may want to encourage memorization of some of these. The song "Three Blind Mice" is an easy one to start with, and the stories "The Three Little Pigs" and "The Three Billy Goats Gruff" are familiar favorites.

Count on Fruit (Number Practice, Critical Thinking) Draw one apple, two pears, and three bananas in three separate boxes on the chalkboard. Invite three volunteers to come up and write the numbers **1, 2,** and **3** beneath the appropriate pictures.

Make It Tactile! (Fine Motor, Tactile) My kindergarten class practices their numbers in a tactile fashion—by using a stick in dirt or sand, writing on the sidewalk with chalk, placing rocks or leaves in the shape of the number, and by fingerpainting. Writing is fun—so encourage children to have fun learning!

Colleen Dannenhauer
Ewing Elementary
Ewing, MO

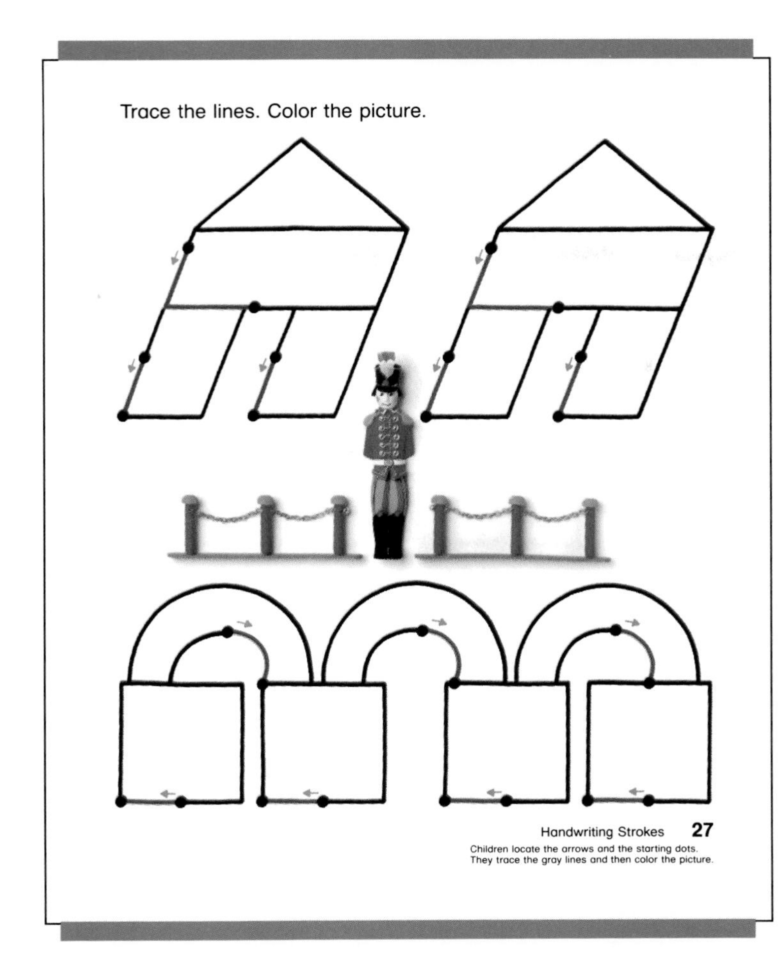

Objective

Traces strokes used in writing the numbers **4** and **5.**

Prepare

Make templates for the children shaped like the strokes below. Have children:

- finger trace and pencil trace the shapes;
- color the shapes.

You may want to have the children cut out the shapes they have made and paste them on heavier paper to create interesting designs.

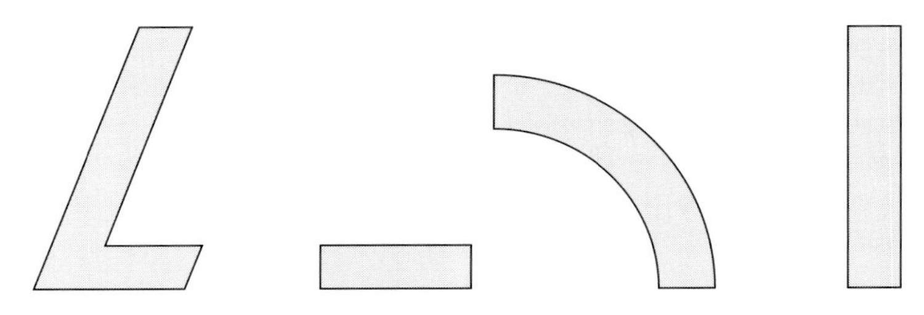

Teach (page 27)

Have children:

- tell what they see in the picture;
- find the first dot and arrow at top left;
- finger trace the gray tracer line down and over to the end dot;
- pencil trace all the lines from dot to dot;
- color the picture.

Follow Up

Self-Evaluation Have children check their own work by asking themselves:

- Did I start and end at the dots?
- Did I follow the direction of the arrows?

Additional Resource

Manuscript Alpha Touch numbers **4** and **5**

ACTIVITY BANK

Stand Up and Be Counted (Kinesthetic, Critical Thinking) Ask five volunteers to bring their chairs to the front of the room for a math game. Have children sit down. Tell them that you will hold up cards with numbers from **1** through **5** on them, and they must decide among themselves who will stand (or sit) to total the number. After three or four turns, call for new volunteers.

Sail Away (Eye-Hand Coordination, Fine Motor) Provide small boxes, wooden sticks, and prepared construction paper for children to make boats with masts. Paper should have a sail outline with a starting dot so children can trace it as they do the stroke for the number **4.** Have children cut out and paste the sails to the masts of their boats.

Salty Strokes (Fine Motor, Tactile) Put a thin layer of salt or sand in the top of a shirt or shoe box. Let children practice the strokes used in writing **1** through **5** on the scratchy surface.

Betty Collett
Beard Elementary
Fort Smith, AR

Objective
Writes the numbers **4** and **5**.

Prepare
Place four blocks on a table and ask children to count them. Write the number **4** on the chalkboard. Do the same with five blocks, writing **5** on the board. Have children:
- air trace **4** and **5** with you;
- come to the board to trace **4** and **5**.

Teach (page 28)
Have children:
- tell what they see in the picture;
- finger trace the model number **4** as you read the number description;
- pencil trace the two gray **4's,** starting at the dot;
- write **4's** using the starting dots.

Repeat the process for **5**.

Follow Up
Self-Evaluation Have children check their own work by asking themselves:
- Did I follow the arrows to make each **4** and **5**?
- Are all my numbers within the lines?

Additional Resource
Manuscript Alpha Touch numbers **4** and **5**

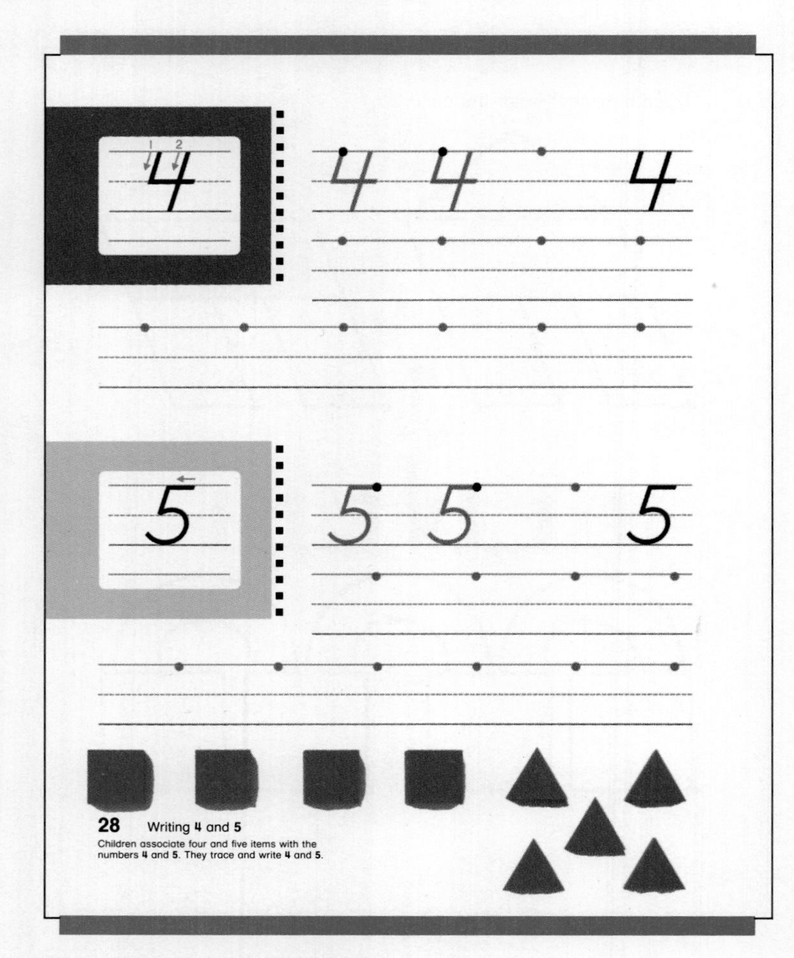

Number Description
Top start; down halfway; over right. Another top start, to the right; slant down, and through.

Top start; over left; slant down halfway; curve around, down, up, and stop.

ACTIVITY BANK

Going Shopping (Numbers, Kinesthetic) Put enough play grocery items around the room to allow groups of children to find up to five items. Give the leader of each group a large paper bag, and tell the class to "buy" four things at the grocery store. Ask volunteers to show the four items they bought. Ask others to count each item and write the number on a "sales slip" you have prepared. Repeat, varying the number.

Shape Up (Number Practice, Fine Motor) Draw a large triangle, square, and rectangle on a piece of paper and reproduce it for children. Have them trace each shape. Help them count the number of sides each shape has, and have them write that number inside the shape.

Number Match (Number Practice, Visual) Have children write each of the numbers **1** through **5** on 3" x 5" cards. Prepare the same cards for yourself. When you hold up a card, children should hold up the corresponding card. Children may practice this activity in small groups.

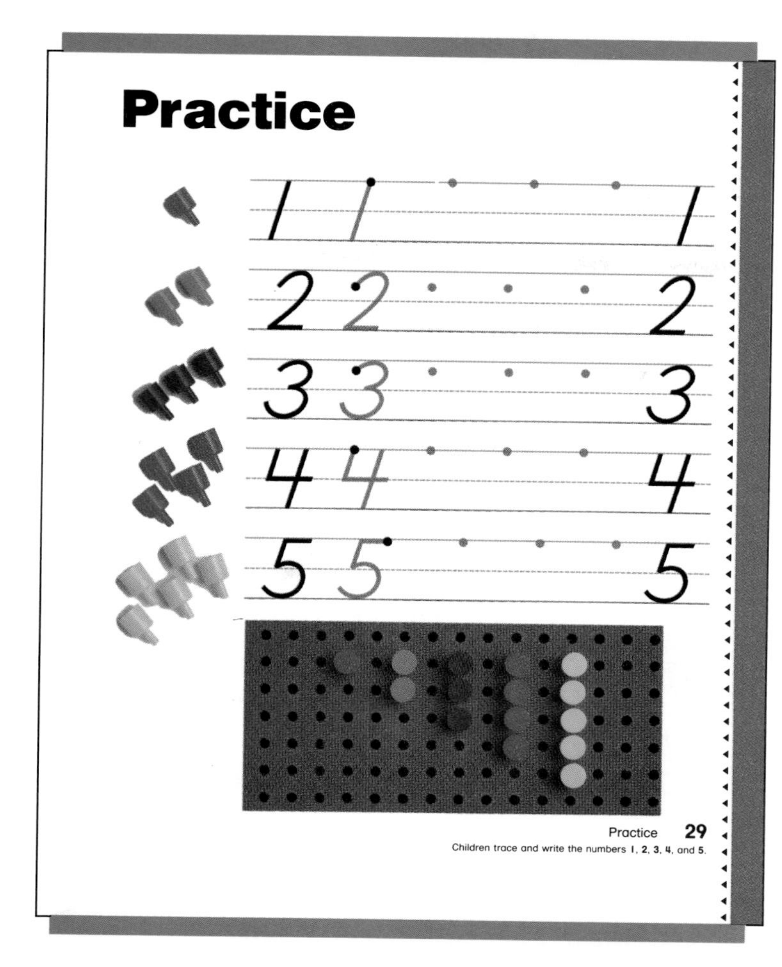

Practice

1 1 1

2 2 2

3 3 3

4 4 4

5 5 5

Practice 29

Children trace and write the numbers 1, 2, 3, 4, and 5.

Objective

Practices writing the numbers **1** through **5.**

Prepare

Wearing finger puppets on one hand, hold up various fingers and ask children to count them.

- Invite volunteers to wear the puppets and have them call on classmates to count the numbers.
- Have other volunteers write the numbers on the chalkboard.

Teach (page 29)

Have children:

- count the peg in the first row;
- finger trace the number **1;**
- trace and write **1** using the starting dots;
- continue in the same way with **2–5.**

Follow Up

Self-Evaluation Have children check their own work by asking themselves:

- Did I start each number at the starting dot?
- Do all my numbers slant the same way?

Additional Resource

Manuscript Alpha Touch numbers **1** through **5**

ACTIVITY BANK

Five-Part Melodies (Gross Motor, Kinesthetic) Pick out five different songs to play on the phonograph or tape recorder for the class. Have children air trace each of the numbers from **1** through **5** while each piece of music plays.

Human Chalkboards (Number Practice, Tactile) Ask children to pair off. Have one child write a number from **1** through **5** with his or her finger, using the other child's back as a chalkboard. The child being written on then writes that number on the chalkboard.

Mrs. Barbara Snowberger
Franklin Elementary
Lehighton, PA

Writing Numbers (Number Practice, Fine Motor) To provide practice in writing numbers, prepare a piece of heavy cardboard with an acetate overlay. On the cardboard, draw or paste groups of objects (such as blocks, dolls, and puppets) representing the numbers from **1** through **5.** Give each child an opportunity to count the objects in each group and write the numbers in crayon on the acetate.

Objective
Practices writing the numbers **1** through **5**.

Prepare
Pass out papers containing the large outline of a fish bowl.
- Ask children to draw and color from one to five fish in each bowl. They may decorate their drawings with sparkles and sequins if you'd like them to.
- Have each child hold up the finished drawing and ask classmates to tell the number of fish they see.
- Ask each artist to write that number below the fish.

Teach (page 30)
This page may be a bit more challenging for some of the children in your class. Have children:
- point to the **1** at the left and then look across to the fish bowl at the right;
- finger trace the number **1;**
- trace and write **1** using the starting dots;
- count the fish in the bowl and draw a fish if necessary to make a total of one;
- continue in this way, writing and drawing fish to total the number at the left.

Follow Up
Self-Evaluation Have children check their own work by asking themselves:
- Did I start each number at the starting dot?
- Are the number of fish in each bowl the same as the number at the left?

Additional Resource
Manuscript Alpha Touch numbers **1** through **5**

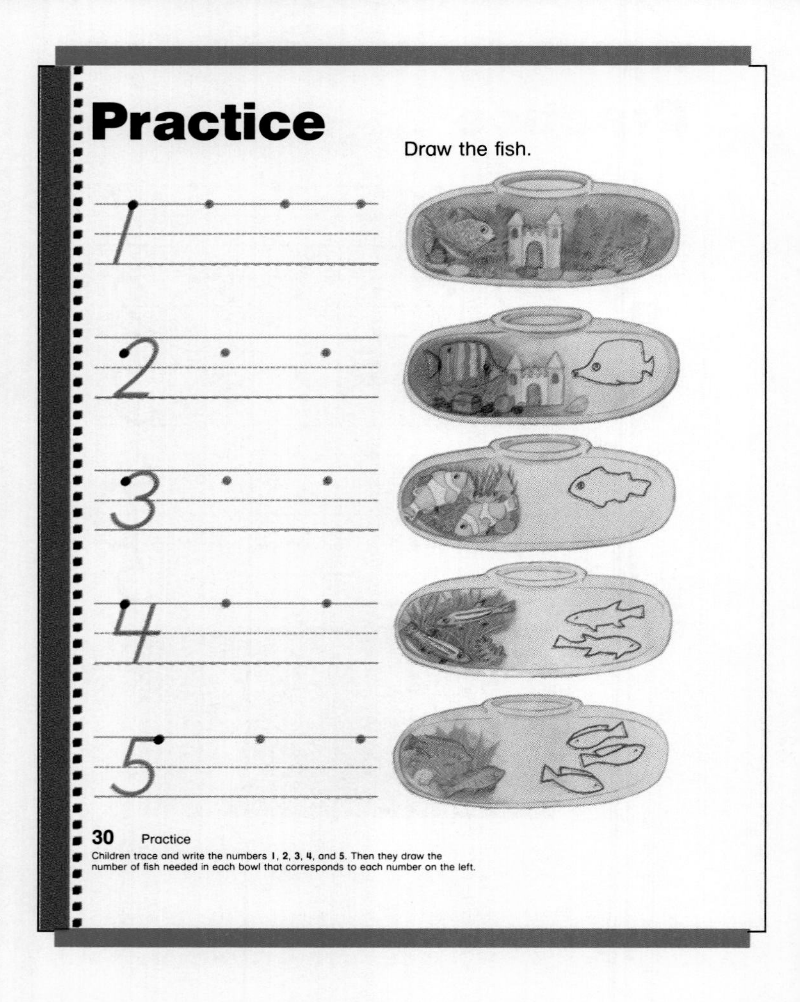
Practice

Draw the fish.

1

2

3

4

5

30 Practice

Children trace and write the numbers **1**, **2**, **3**, **4**, and **5**. Then they draw the number of fish needed in each bowl that corresponds to each number on the left.

ACTIVITY BANK

Clap for Numbers (Number Practice, Auditory) Write the numbers from **1** through **5** on the chalkboard. Tell children to listen carefully as you clap your hands from one to five times. They must write the number of claps on the chalkboard.

One Fish, Two Fish (Number Practice, Visual) Call five children to the chalkboard. Place from one to five fish on a flannelboard. Each child writes on the board the number of fish shown.

Following Directions (Number Recognition, Gifted) Have children write the numbers **1** through **5** in a vertical line on their papers. Then have them follow these directions:

Draw a line under the number that comes before **5**.

Draw a circle around the number that comes after **1**.

Draw an X on the number that comes between **2** and **4**.

Draw a triangle around the number that is one more than **4**.

Draw a square around the number that comes before **2**.

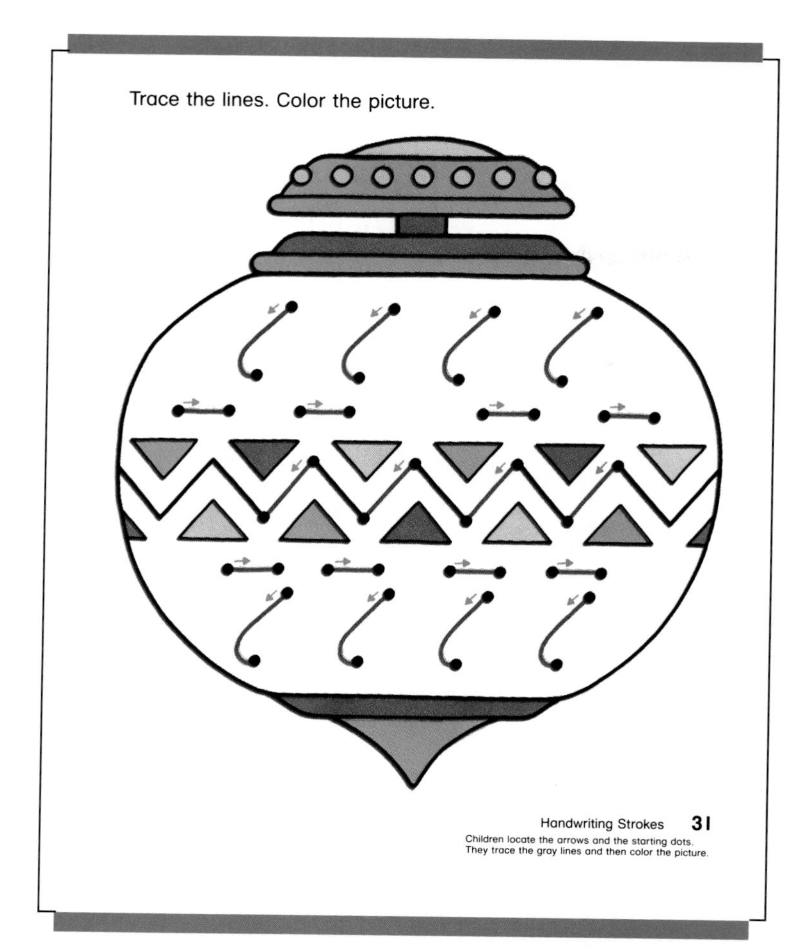

Objective

Traces strokes used in writing the numbers **6** and **7.**

Prepare

On the chalkboard, draw large numbers **6** and **7.** Invite children to find partners and arrange their bodies in the shape of a **6** or a **7.**

Teach (page 31)

Have children:

- tell what they see in the picture;
- find the first dot and arrow at top left;
- finger trace the gray tracer line;
- trace all the lines from dot to dot;
- color the picture.

Follow Up

Self-Evaluation Have children check their own work by asking themselves:

- Did I trace on the gray lines?
- Did I begin at the starting dot and follow the arrow?

Additional Resource

Manuscript Alpha Touch numbers **6** and **7**

ACTIVITY BANK

Five, Six, Pick up Sticks (Kinesthetic, Number Recognition) Recite the poem "One, Two, Buckle My Shoe." Ask for volunteers to act out verses. Next, ask children to play "Five, Six, Pick up Sticks." Put down seven sticks and call on different children to pick up the number of sticks you call out. A variation of this game is "Seven, Eight, Lay Them Straight," in which you ask children to put back a certain number of sticks.

Umbrella Art (Critical Thinking, Fine Motor) Draw an umbrella on a worksheet. Use dotted lines in the shape of the stroke used to make **6** for the handle. Write a different number from **1** through **7** on each umbrella. Have children trace the handle and draw raindrops to equal the number on the sheet.

A Number of Balloons (Number Recognition, Fine Motor) Give groups of children a helium balloon that has a **6** or a **7** written on it and a long string. Have children draw and cut out six or seven small objects, depending on the number on their balloons, and tape them to the strings. Hang balloons from the ceiling.

Objective
Writes the numbers **6** and **7**.

Prepare
Display six toys and ask children to count them. Write the number **6** on the chalkboard. Do the same with seven toys and the number **7**. Have children:
- air trace **6** and **7** with you;
- come to the board to trace **6** and **7**.

Teach (page 32)
Have children:
- tell what they see in the picture;
- finger trace the model number **6** as you read the number description;
- pencil trace the two gray **6's,** starting at the dot;
- write **6's** using the starting dots.

Repeat the process for **7**.

Follow Up
Self-Evaluation Have children check their own work by asking themselves:
- Did I close the curve of the **6**?
- Does each **7** touch the bottom line?

Additional Resource
Manuscript Alpha Touch numbers **6** and **7**

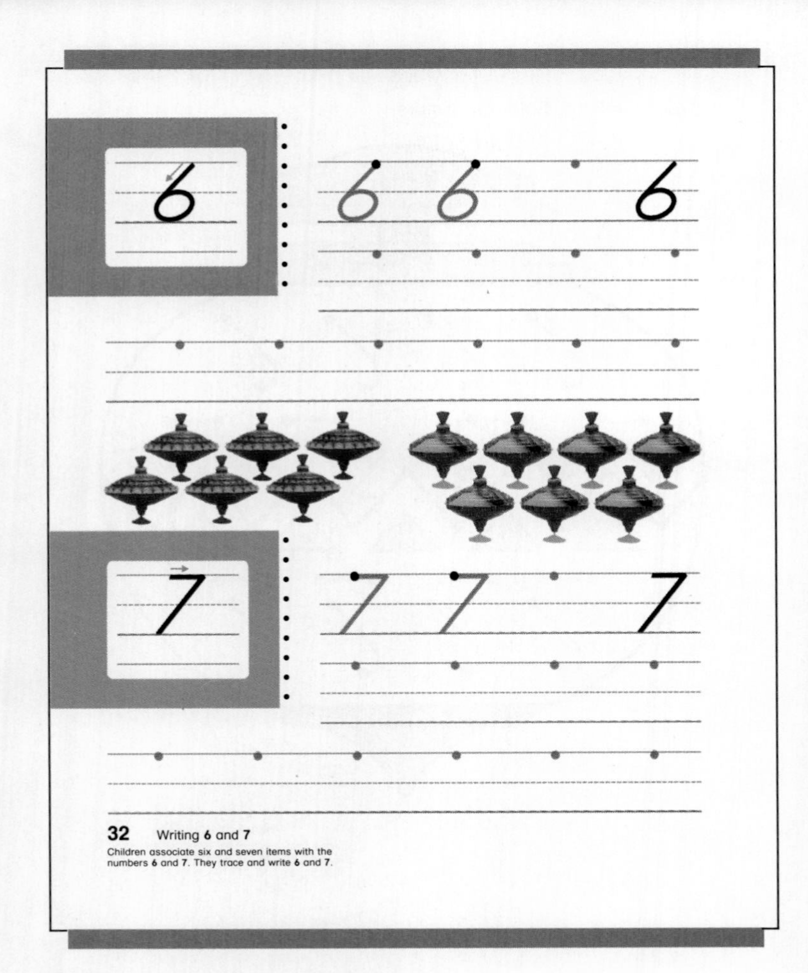

6 6 6 6

7 7 7 7

32 Writing 6 and 7

Children associate six and seven items with the numbers 6 and 7. They trace and write 6 and 7.

Number Description
Top start; slant down, and curve around; up; and close.

Top start; over right; slant down left.

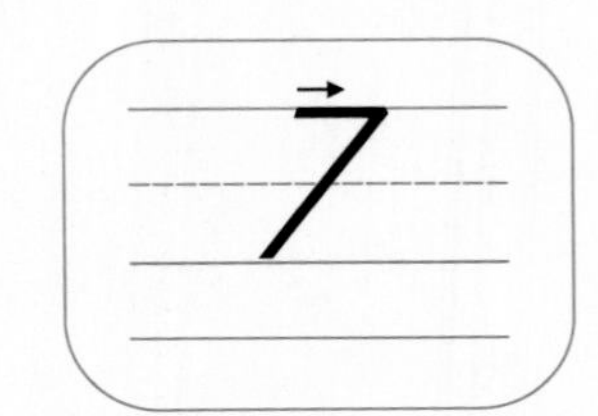

ACTIVITY BANK

Hidden Numbers (Critical Thinking, Gross Motor) Draw a simple picture on the chalkboard that contains the shape of the number **6**. Do the same with **7**. Children come to the board and use colored chalk to trace the number in each drawing.

Marly Glaw
Shreiner School and Academy
Marietta, GA

Calculate and Write (Left to Right, Number Practice) Prepare worksheets with groups of vertical lines up to seven. Have children draw one horizontal line along the bottom of each group of lines. Tell them to be sure their lines begin at the first vertical line and end at the last line in each group. Have children count the vertical lines in each group and write that number under the group.

Colorful Shapes (Number Recognition, Fine Motor) To reinforce familiarity with numbers, colors, and shapes, ask children to draw the following shapes with colorful markers:

one yellow circle
four blue dots
six green squares
seven red triangles

Have children discuss their drawings, then display them.

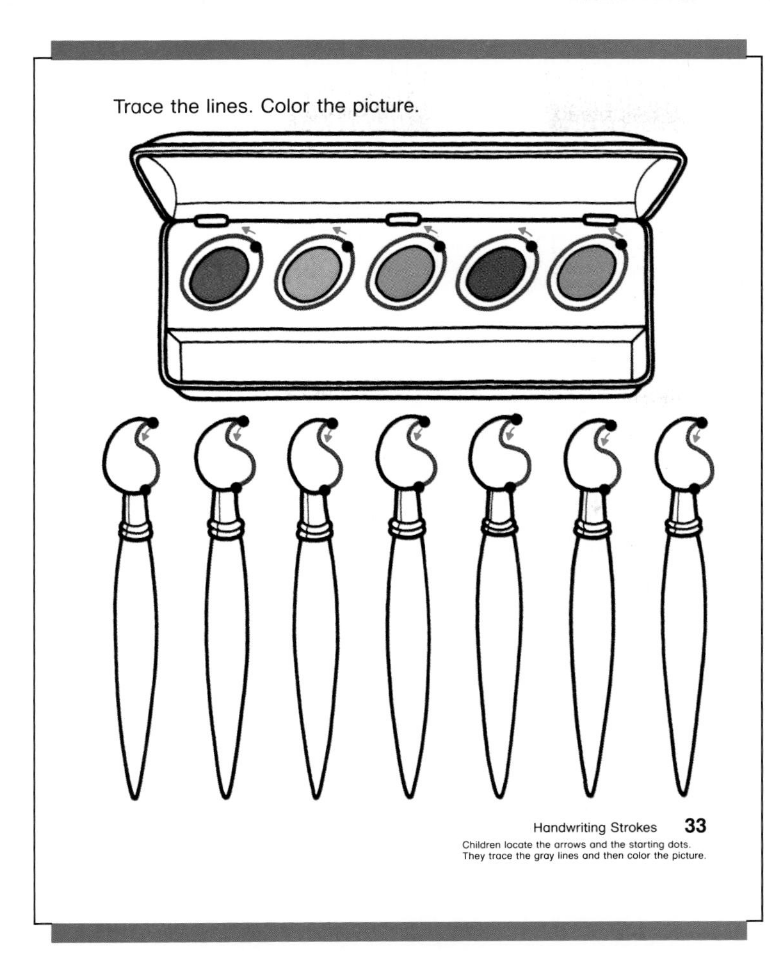

Objective

Traces strokes used in writing the numbers **8** and **9**.

Prepare

On the chalkboard, make several curved and oval lines like those below. Add arrows and starting dots. Have children dip paintbrushes in water and "paint" over the lines, following the arrows.

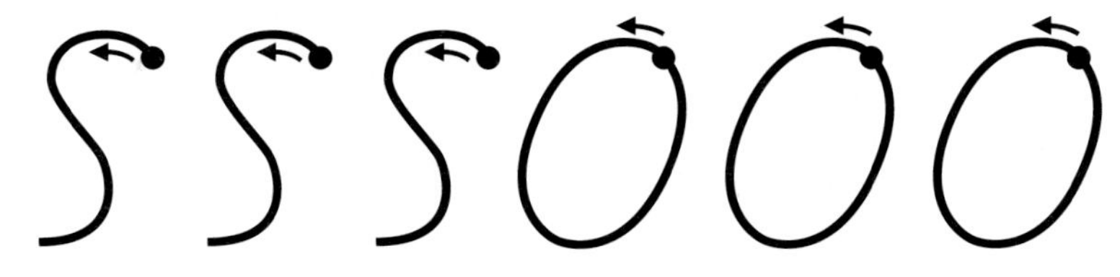

Teach (page 33)

Have children:

- tell what they see on the page;
- find the first dot and arrow at top left;
- finger trace around the gray tracer line;
- pencil trace all the oval and curved lines from dot to dot;
- color the picture.

Follow Up

Self-Evaluation Have children check their own work by asking themselves:

- Did I move in the direction of the arrows?
- Did I stay within the gray lines?

Additional Resource

Manuscript Alpha Touch numbers **8** and **9**

ACTIVITY BANK

I See Something (Visual, Auditory) Play "I See Something" with the class. Ask for a volunteer to start you off by looking around the classroom and thinking about the color of a certain object. For example, if the volunteer decides on the apple sitting on your desk, he or she should say, "I see something red." Children guess the object in turn, and the one who names it is next to be "it."

A Feel for Numbers (Number Recognition, Tactile) Glue sandpaper on pieces of 5" x 8" cardboard. Cut out D'Nealian numbers from **1** through **9.** Put them in a box or bucket. Have children take turns feeling a number, without looking, and telling what it is.

Vickie Foreman
Travis School
San Angelo, TX

Snake 'n' Eggs, Part One (Fine Motor, Number Recognition) Prepare a tracing worksheet. On the top half, draw eight snakes with bodies curved like the curve in **8.** On the lower half, draw nine eggs similar in shape to the stroke used in **9.** Have children trace the lines before coloring the snakes and eggs.

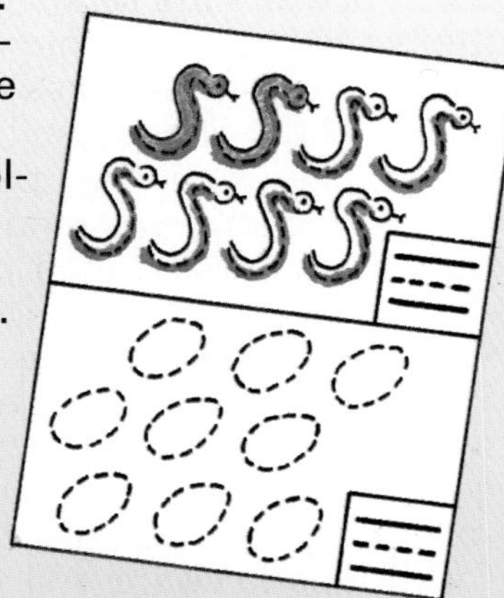

Objective
Writes the numbers **8** and **9**.

Prepare
Display eight paintbrushes and ask children to count them. Write **8** on the chalkboard. Do the same with nine paintbrushes and **9**. Have children:
- air trace **8** and **9** with you;
- come to the board to trace **8** and **9**.

Teach (page 34)
Have children:
- tell what they see in the picture;
- finger trace the model number **8** as you read the number description;
- pencil trace the two gray **8's**, starting at the dot;
- write **8's** using the starting dots.

Repeat the process for **9**.

Follow Up
Self-Evaluation Have children check their own work by asking themselves:
- Did I start at the starting dots?
- Is each **8** and **9** closed at the top?

Additional Resource
Manuscript Alpha Touch numbers **8** and **9**

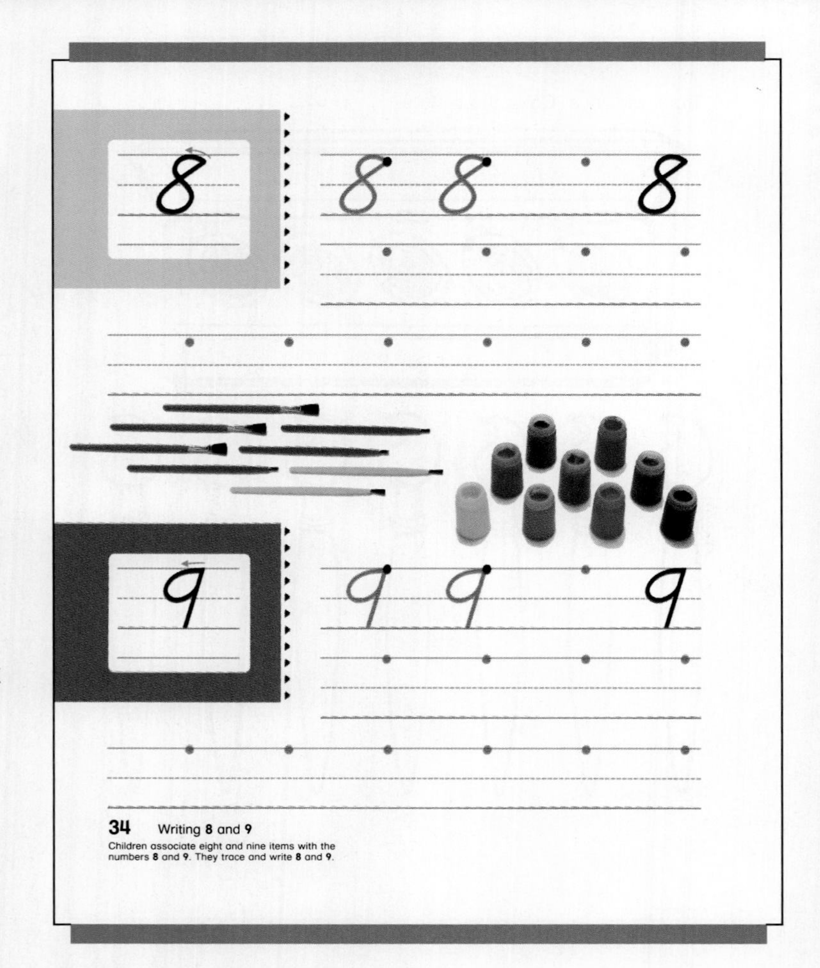
34 Writing 8 and 9
Children associate eight and nine items with the numbers 8 and 9. They trace and write 8 and 9.

Number Description
Start below the top; curve up, around, down; a snake tail; slant up right; through; and touch.

Top start; curve down, around, close; slant down.

ACTIVITY BANK

Snake 'n' Eggs, Part Two (Number Practice, Fine Motor) Return the worksheets on which children traced **8**-shaped strokes on the snake, and **9**-shaped strokes on the eggs. Ask children to count the snakes and eggs and write those numbers on their papers.

Paint Eight, Define Nine (Number Practice, Creative) Give each child a large piece of white paper. Have colorful paints, glue, glitter, rick-rack, stars, and so on, available for groups to share. Ask children to paint either the number **8** or **9** and then decorate it the way they think that number would like to look.

Special Needs (Auditory Deficits) Giving directions nonverbally can help children with auditory deficits be more successful. Give these children two 10" cardboard squares with the top, middle, and bottom lines highlighted to guide spacing. Add a starting arrow to each at the point where children write **8** or **9**. *Show* these children how to use "Sparkle Paint" (see recipe below) to write the numbers **8** and **9**.

SPARKLE PAINT

2 tablespoons liquid starch
1 tablespoon water
3 tablespoons tempera paint
1/2 cup salt

Mix starch, water, and paint. Stir in salt. Mix the sparkle paint frequently during use.

Trace the lines. Color the picture.

Finish

Start

Handwriting Strokes 35

Children locate the arrows and the starting dots. They trace the gray lines and then color the picture.

Objective

Traces a stroke used in writing the number **10.**

Prepare

On the chalkboard, draw a large D'Nealian **0.** Have children:

- search around the room for any objects that have this same shape;
- draw an **0** on paper and turn it into a happy face.

Teach (page 35)

Have children:

- identify the image on the page as a board game;
- find the first dot and arrow at top left;
- finger trace around the gray tracer line;
- pencil trace all the oval strokes from dot to dot;
- color the picture.

Follow Up

Self-Evaluation Have children check their own work by asking themselves:

- Did I write in the direction of the arrows?
- Did I stay within the gray lines?

Additional Resource

Manuscript Alpha Touch number **10**

ACTIVITY BANK

Play the Seashell Game (Critical Thinking, Number Recognition) Invite children to play the game on page 35 of their books. Have groups of four use a die or spinner with the numbers **1** through **6** on them. Tell them that they move forward as indicated by the die or spinner. If they land on the sun, they must sit in the shade of the umbrella until they throw or spin a **1.** The first to reach *Finish* wins.

Sorting to Ten (Number Recognition, Fine Motor) Write a different number from **1** through **10** on each section of several egg cartons. Have children work in groups to sort the correct number of small objects into each section.

Drawing by Numbers (Number Recognition, Fine Motor) Ask children to use crayons to draw the following on plain paper:

one yellow sun
two blue waves
four orange boats
six green trees
eight red seashells
ten brown grains of sand.

Ask children to make up a story to go with their drawings. Display their work in the classroom.

Objective
Writes the number **10**.

Prepare
Display ten seashells and ask children to count them. Write **10** on the chalkboard. Have children:
- air trace **10** with you;
- come to the board to trace **10**.

Teach (page 36)
Have children:
- tell what they see in the picture;
- finger trace the model number **10** as you read the number description;
- pencil trace the two gray **10's,** starting at the dot;
- write **10's** using the starting dots.

Follow Up
Self-Evaluation Have children check their own work by asking themselves:
- Did I leave enough space between each **10?**
- Do both parts of each **10** reach the top line?

Additional Resource
Manuscript Alpha Touch number **10**

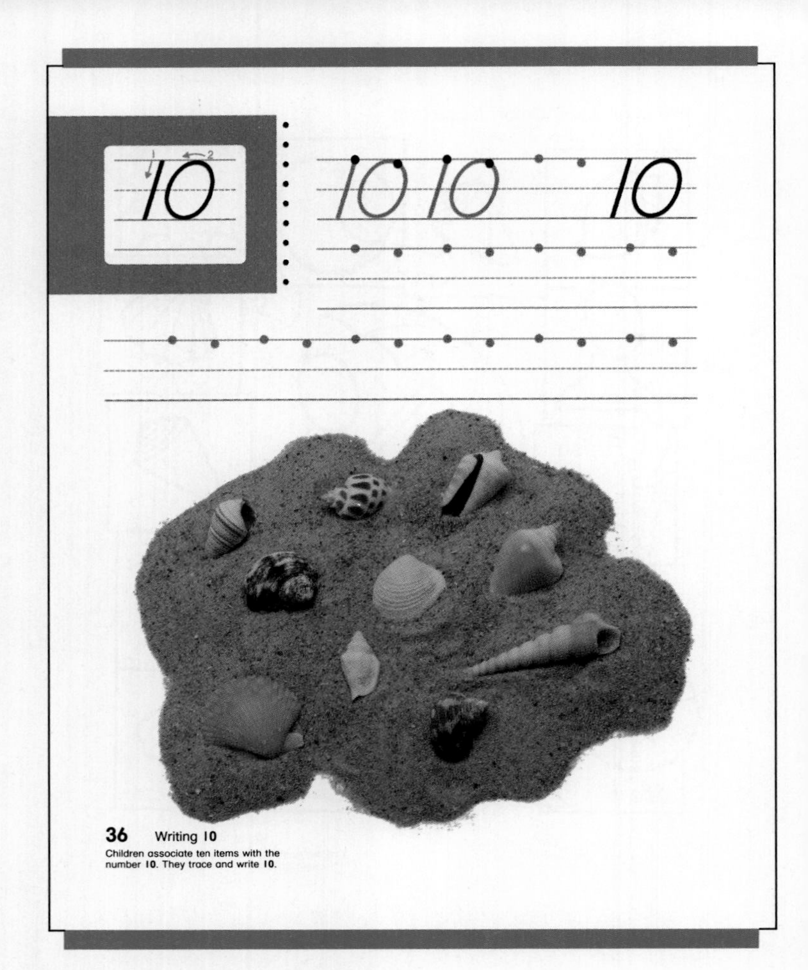

Number Description
Top start; slant down. Another top start to the right; curve left and down, around, and close.

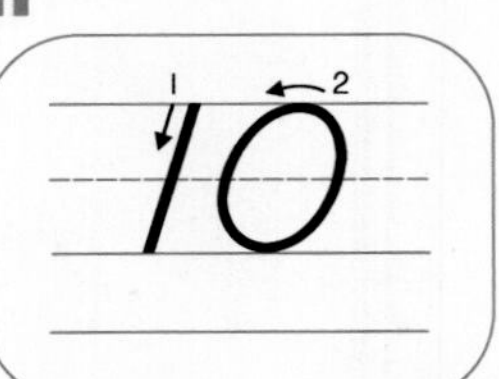

ACTIVITY BANK

A Shell Game (Number Practice, Critical Thinking) Display ten seashells on a table near the chalkboard. Ask a volunteer to come to the board and write a number from **1** to **10.** The writer calls on a classmate to come to the table and count out seashells equal to that number. When the class agrees that this is the correct amount, the game continues with other children.

Listen to the Beat (Auditory, Number Practice) Distribute paper with writing lines. Tell children to listen and count the number of sounds you make. Tap your foot from **1** to **10** times. Ask children to write the number of taps on their papers.

Count on Your Classmates (Number Practice, Visual) Call eleven children to the front of the room. Designate one of them "Number Writer" and the other ten "Numbers" Call seven children by name to stand up. Ask the class how many are left sitting. Have the Number Writer write that number on the board. Next have two more children stand and ask how many are now sitting. Number Writer writes that number. The game continues as you call on children to sit down.

Practice

6 6 6

7 7 7

8 8 8

9 9 9

10 10 10

Practice 37

Children trace and write the numbers 6, 7, 8, 9, and 10.

Objective
Practices writing the numbers **6** through **10.**

Prepare
Wearing finger puppets on both hands, hold up various fingers and ask children to count them.
Have children:
- call on classmates to count the numbers;
- write the numbers on the chalkboard.

Teach (page 37)
Have children:
- name the objects in each row;
- finger trace the number **6;**
- trace and write **6** using the starting dots;
- continue in the same way with **7–10.**

Follow Up
Self-Evaluation Have children check their own work by asking themselves:
- Did I start each number at the starting dot?
- Do all my numbers slant the same way?

Additional Resource
Manuscript Alpha Touch numbers **6** through **10**

ACTIVITY BANK

Clothespin Counting (Number Recognition, Fine Motor) Provide each child with ten clothespins and a shoe box. Tell children to clip eight clothespins to the sides of their boxes. Then have them add one more clothespin to make nine, then one more to make ten. Ask them to take away four clothespins and tell the number remaining. Continue in this way.

Write Your Number (Number Practice, Gross Motor) Make writing lines on the chalkboard. Have children count off to **10,** starting again until all have counted off. Have those who are **3's** come to the board and write **3.** Continue with all the numbers.

What's Missing? (Visual, Critical Thinking) Make large number cards from **6** through **10.** Give each number a different color, with a border around it to match. Place cards on the chalkboard ledge in numerical order. Tell children you are going to challenge their powers of memory. Have them close their eyes while you take away one of the cards. Volunteers should go to the board and write the missing number. For a real challenge, arrange the cards in random order.

Objective

Practices writing the numbers **6** through **10.**

Prepare

Pass out papers containing the large outline of an ant hill. Have children:

- draw from five to ten ants on each ant hill. You may want to have them decorate their drawings with sand;
- exchange papers and count the number of ants on their classmate's paper;
- write that number on the back of the drawing.

Teach (page 38)

This page may be a bit more challenging for some of the children in your class. Have children:

- point to the two butterflies at the left and then to the number **2** at the right;
- finger trace and pencil trace the number **2;**
- count the beetles in the next row and write the number **8** on the lines to the right;
- continue in this way, counting and writing all the numbers.

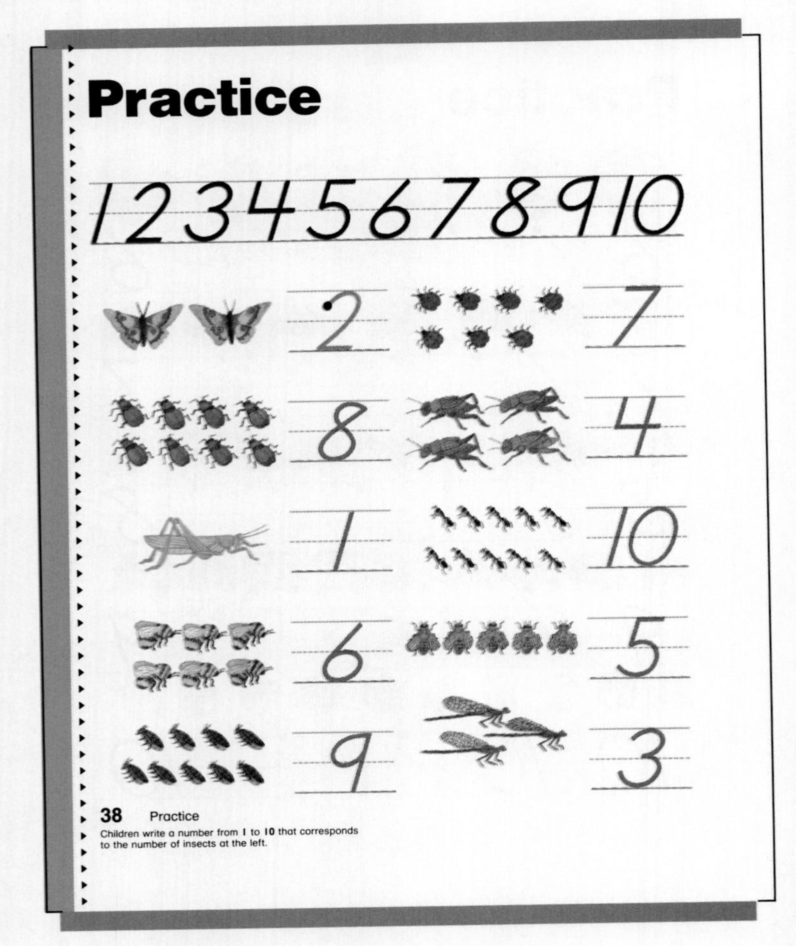

Practice

12345678910

2 7

8 4

1 10

6 5

9 3

38 Practice

Children write a number from **1** to **10** that corresponds to the number of insects at the left.

Follow Up

Self-Evaluation Have children check their own work by asking themselves:

- Did I write a number on each of the writing lines?
- Is the number I wrote the same as the number of insects?

Additional Resource

Manuscript Alpha Touch numbers **6** through **10**

ACTIVITY BANK

The Creature with Two Toes (Number Recognition, Creative) Have children draw a "Mystery Creature." Describe the creature and have them draw it. You might say, *It has a round body and a round head. It has three legs. Each foot has two toes. It has four arms, each with a paw. It has two eyes, one mouth, and ten ears.* Have children finish the pictures.

Special Needs (Attention Deficit Disorder) Children who have trouble paying attention need to feel totally involved. Invite them to be butterfly collectors. Have each child color a butterfly outline that you have prepared. Put these in a pile. Write **1** to **10** on the chalkboard and have a large cardboard magnifying glass with an acetate lens on hand. Call a number and have children, in turn, count out that many butterflies. Have children highlight the number on the board by placing the magnifying glass over it.

Let's Count My Way (Limited English Proficiency) Encourage children who speak a foreign tongue to demonstrate counting in their own language. Classmates can learn to identify these numbers by writing them on the chalkboard or on paper.

MEET:

Barbara Troolin, Ph.D.
Educational Administrator, Consultant

School staff and administrators, community members, parents, students, and others must believe that a positive school climate, flexible and relevant curriculum, instructional supports, and a spirit of collaboration will make a difference in student learning.

Certain elements are key to the success of a program of inclusion.

- Values—We must believe that all students can learn and that we can make that happen.
- Support—A spirit of collaboration and teamwork is essential.
- Planning Teams—To address each child's instructional needs, we must involve a variety of people who know the child.
- Parent and Child Involvement—Parents and children must be seen as essential and valued members for planning instruction.
- Supports Within Reach—Consideration should be given to providing supports in the classroom or other environments.

One of the most challenging issues facing educators today is the inclusion of students with a range of abilities in regular classrooms and other instructional settings and ensuring their success.

- Individual Learning—If we hold high expectations for achievement by all students, we must be aware of their individual needs.
- Active Participation—Keep students actively engaged in learning.
- Grouping—Keep groups flexible.
- Information and Resources—Read, visit, discuss, share information, and identify individual and collective needs.

(Highlights from the article on page T32 of this teacher's edition.)

Teacher to Teacher

Q. *Some workbooks I use in other subject areas present letters to trace or copy that are not D'Nealian letter forms. What should I do?*

A. Experienced D'Nealian teachers suggest that pupils be encouraged to read the letter form as it appears but to write the equivalent D'Nealian letter. The teacher may say, *We are going to write our way, the D'Nealian way.* If models are needed, the teacher can provide them on the board.

Q. *Is it important to correct the pencil grip some of my pupils are using?*

A. Kindergartners and first graders sometimes develop unusual ways of holding their writing instruments. Since it is almost impossible to change the grip later, attention to the grip now will help prepare the pupil for a lifetime of writing. The grip taught in the **Position for Writing** lessons in Unit 1 provides for comfort and control. This in turn helps prevent tiring and loss of legibility as speed and length of writing time increase.

An alternate grip now under study at the University of Michigan is the new D'Nealian® Handwriting grip. This grip involves placing the pencil between the index and middle finger, resting on the web of the hand.

Q. *Is it all right if all my pupils' handwriting does not look alike?*

A. In fact, it is unrealistic to expect that all pupils' handwriting will look alike. The goal of D'Nealian® Handwriting is legibility that allows for individuality of style. Pupils will be taught self-assessment skills that will help them improve legibility while developing their own styles.

Activity Bank Unit 3

An Activity Bank appears with each lesson. It offers suggestions that can enrich the lesson, tailor it to specific needs, or provide additional practice. In Unit 3, activities in the following categories appear on pages given in parentheses.

Early Literacy

Creative

Critical Thinking

Gifted and Talented

Learning Modalities: Auditory

Kinesthetic

Tactile

Visual

Legibility

Letter Practice

Multicultural/ Multilingual

Practical Applications

Small Groups

Special Needs

Unit Overview

In Unit 3, children are introduced to the lower-case D'Nealian alphabet in stroke groups. Each letter is presented in two pages. Children first encounter a large, inviting letter with two images whose names begin with the letter. They finger trace the letter while hearing a sentence that draws them into its shape and movement. Next, children relate the letter to an activity that involves coloring, drawing, circling, and other skills. They pencil trace the letter, write it, then trace a word containing the letter.

Each large letter is on a separate page, so that it can be torn out and rearranged alphabetically. After each stroke group, two practice pages are provided, featuring a word or words containing the letters learned. When children complete all the lower-case letters, they write them in alphabetical order.

Bibliography

You may wish to obtain the following books to read aloud or provide for independent reading.

Johnson, Crockett. *Harold and the Purple Crayon.* New York: Harper & Row, 1955.

Lionni, Leo. *The Alphabet Tree.* New York: Pantheon, 1968.

Martin, Jerome. *Mitten, Kitten.* New York: Simon and Schuster, Inc., 1991.

Morris, Ann. *Hats, Hats, Hats.* New York: Lothrop, Lee & Shepard Books, 1989.

Rogers, Fred. *Going to the Hospital.* New York: Putnam's Sons, 1988.

Extending Writing Through Activities

The trade book *Mitten, Kitten* by Jerome Martin can be used as a model for "Letter-Flip" pages. Using the letters as introduced in Unit 3, children write the beginning letters and illustrate the rhyming words. Pages can be saved and made into a book once all letters have been introduced.

Related writing activities include placing an apple cutout on the Writing Center Letter Tree and using invented spelling to label pictures cut from magazines.

Objective
Matches lower-case letters.

Prepare
On the chalkboard or on a large sheet of paper, write three lower-case letters, one of which matches the first letter. The letters below are an example.
- Call on a volunteer to tell what the first letter is.
- Have another child find the matching letter and circle it.

Repeat using other lower-case letters.

Teach (page 40)
Have children:
- identify the animals at the top of the page (help them understand that the giraffe represents *tall* letters, the dog represents *small* letters, and the cat represents *letters that fall*);
- identify the animal in each box and the type of letter each represents;
- circle the letter in each box that matches the letter on the animal.

Tall Letters
b d f h
k l t

Small Letters
a c e i m
n o r s u
v w x z

Letters That Fall
g j p q y

Circle the letters that match.

c p c | f f b
r s r | g q g
d d t | o a o

40 Lower-case Letter Discrimination

Children learn about tall letters, small letters, and descender letters. Then they circle the letter in each box that matches the one on the animal.

Follow Up
Self-Evaluation Have children check their own work by asking themselves:
- Did I circle a letter in each box?
- Does the letter I circled match the letter on the animal?

Additional Resource
Manuscript Alpha Touch letters **a** through **z**

ACTIVITY BANK

Follow the Trail (Critical Thinking, Visual) Play a tracking game with children. You will need a sand table or a large container of damp sand and a collection of objects to use for making tracks (a cup, fork, crayon, and so on). Have a volunteer make tracks using one of the objects. Other children then come to the sand and decide which object left the trail.

The abc Game (Letter Recognition, Kinesthetic) Make a set of lower-case letter cards. Distribute one or more of these cards to each child. Then sing "The Alphabet Song." As each child's letter is identified, the child should stand and hold up the card.

Warm Ups (Letter Practice, Fine Motor) As an alternative to having children go to the chalkboard to practice making letters, I devised a "warm-up sheet." After I demonstrate formation of a letter, students trace their warm-up letter repeatedly while I check for correct procedure. After the technique has been mastered, I pass out workbook pages.

Geraldine Taft
Loa Elementary School
Loa, UT

Objectives

Learns the shape of **a** by finger tracing a large model letter.
Writes the lower-case letter **a** and traces the word *a.*

Prepare

Talk to children about how strong ants are. Ask them to name some things they could lift if they were as strong as ants. Have children pretend to be ants carrying heavy burdens around the classroom.

Ask if an ant could fly an airplane. Let children talk about real and fanciful personalities.

Use the *D'Nealian® Handwriting Big Book* to preview the page.

Teach (page 41)

Have children:

- identify the lower-case letter **a;**
- find the ant at the starting arrow;
- finger trace the path from the ant to the apple while you say the following mnemonic sentence:
  The ant flies to the apple.
- air trace the letter **a.**

ACTIVITY BANK

Time to Grow 

a is for apple (Letter Practice, Fine Motor) Provide red, green, and yellow construction paper for tracing and cutting out large apples. Have children use a black crayon to write an **a** in the middle of each apple. All apples can be arranged on a bulletin board.

Pick an a (Letter Recognition, Gross Motor) Draw a large tree on the chalkboard. Next write various lower-case letters on the tree including **a.** Call on children to "pick" **a's** by circling them.

Phonics Corner

The sentence used to help children form the letter **a,**

The **ant** flies to the **apple.**

may also be used to work on sound-letter correspondence. Repeat the sentence and call on volunteers to tell you the words they hear that begin with /a/.

Teach (page 42)

Call attention to the picture at the top of the page. Have children:
- find and color each **a** in the apple puzzle red;
- tell what they see in the colored part of the puzzle.

Call attention to the lower half of the page. Have children:
- finger trace the boxed letter **a** as you read aloud the letter description;
- pencil trace the gray letters;
- write the letter **a** using the starting dots;
- trace the word *a*.

Follow Up

Self-Evaluation Have children check their own work by asking themselves:
- Did I start at the starting dots?
- Are my **a's** closed at the top?

Additional Resources

Manuscript Alpha Touch letter **a**
D'Nealian® Handwriting Big Book letter **a**

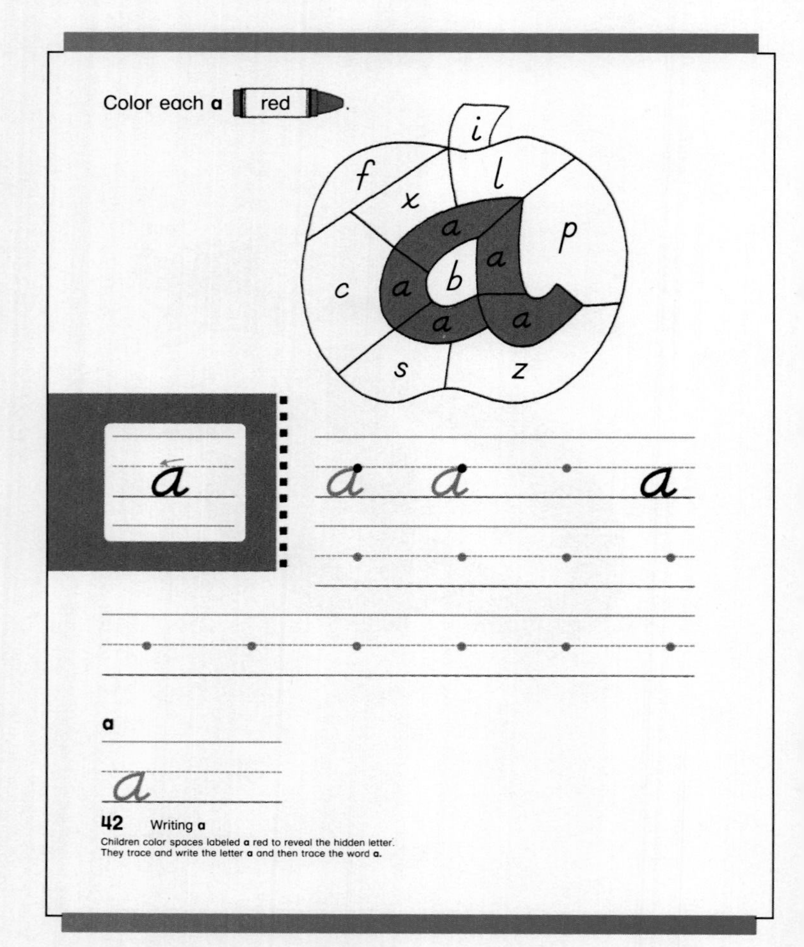

Letter Description

Middle start; around down, close up, down, and a monkey tail.

ACTIVITY BANK

Moving Write Along

Dramatic a's (Kinesthetic, Creative Thinking) Encourage children to act out the following:
picking apples from a tree
eating a big, juicy apple
piloting an airplane

Names of Sand (Letter Practice, Tactile) Write each child's name on a separate piece of construction paper. Have children trace their names with glue and shake sand over the letters for a "touch and feel" experiment. Children enjoy seeing their names written this way. As a variation of this activity, mix tempera paint into dry sand and spread on newspaper to dry.

Priscilla Miller
Beacon School
Harper Woods, MI

Letter Search (Letter Recognition, Print Awareness) Give each child pages containing large headline type from newspapers or magazines. Have them write a lower-case **a** at the top of each sheet. Ask them to circle the letter each time they find it.

Objectives

Learns the shape of **d** by finger tracing a large model letter.
Writes the lower-case letter **d** and traces a word with **d.**

Prepare

Talk to children about how dogs like to dig. Discuss the kinds of things a dog might bury. Write the words *dog* and *dig* on the chalkboard. Have children pretend to be dogs digging a hole in the ground.

Give one child a paper bone with a large D'Nealian **d** on it and ask the child to hide it in the classroom. Have the other children try to "dig up the bone." The one who finds it gets to hide it again.

Use the *D'Nealian® Handwriting Big Book* to preview the page.

Teach (page 43)

Have children:

- identify the lower-case letter **d;**
- find the dog at the starting arrow;
- finger trace the path from the dog to the doghouse while you say the following mnemonic sentence:
  The dog digs its way to the doghouse.
- air trace the letter **d.**

ACTIVITY BANK

Time to Grow 

Doghouse d (Fine Motor, Letter Practice) Have a plain doghouse with a large door on it at the writing center. Children cut around the door so that it will open. Then they write a **d** on plain paper. Help them glue the **d** behind the doghouse.

Artistic Alphabet (Gross Motor, Letter Practice) When introducing letters to my class, we pretend we are artists "painting" each letter on a big easel. The tops of our heads represent the top blue line. Our waist level is the dotted middle line. The floor is the bottom line. We "paint" letters this way.

Nancy Hill
Pea Ridge Elementary
Pea Ridge, AR

Phonics Corner

The sentence used to help children form the letter **d,**

The **dog digs** its way to the **doghouse.**

may also be used to work on sound-letter correspondence. Repeat the sentence and call on volunteers to tell you the words they hear that begin with /d/.

Teach (page 44)

Call attention to the pictures at the top of the page. Have children:

- identify the animals;
- listen as you read the words *dog, duck, alligator,* and *deer;*
- circle the words that begin with **d;**

Call attention to the lower half of the page. Have children:

- finger trace the boxed letter **d** as you read aloud the letter description;
- pencil trace the gray letters;
- write the letter **d** using the starting dots;
- trace the words *dad* and *add.*

Follow Up

Self-Evaluation Have children check their own work by asking themselves:

- Did I start at the starting dots?
- Do my **d's** stretch to the top line?

Additional Resources

Manuscript Alpha Touch letter **d**
D'Nealian® Handwriting Big Book letter **d**

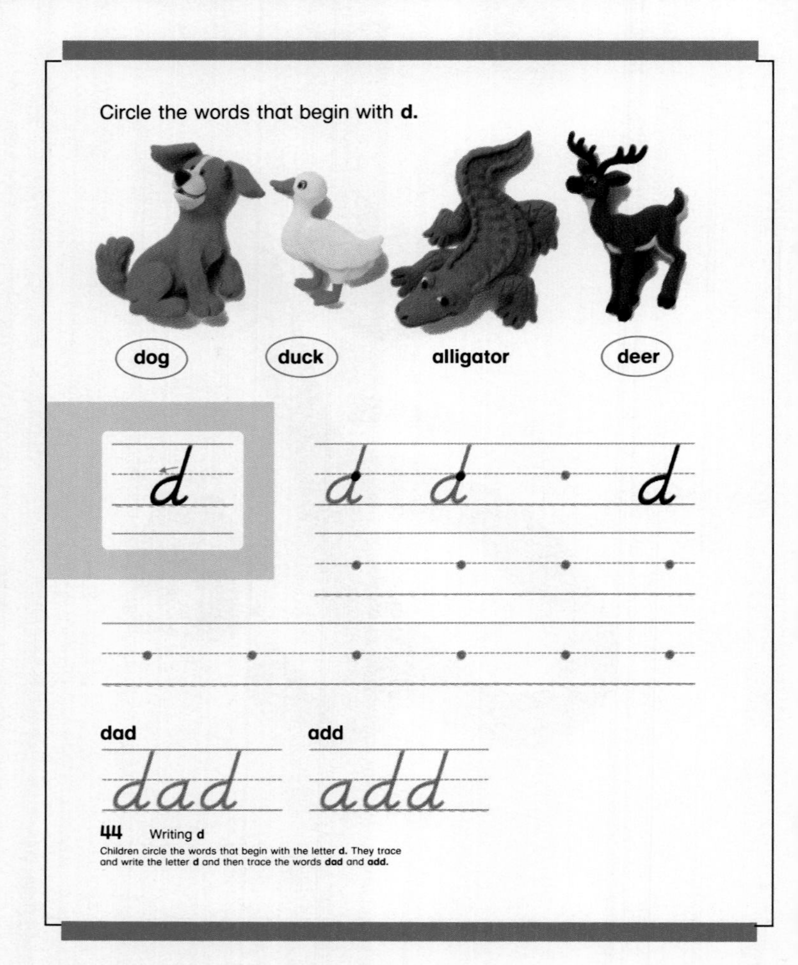
Circle the words that begin with **d**.

44 Writing d

Children circle the words that begin with the letter **d**. They trace and write the letter **d** and then trace the words **dad** and **add**.

Letter Description

Middle start; around down, touch, up high, down, and a monkey tail.

ACTIVITY BANK

Moving Write Along

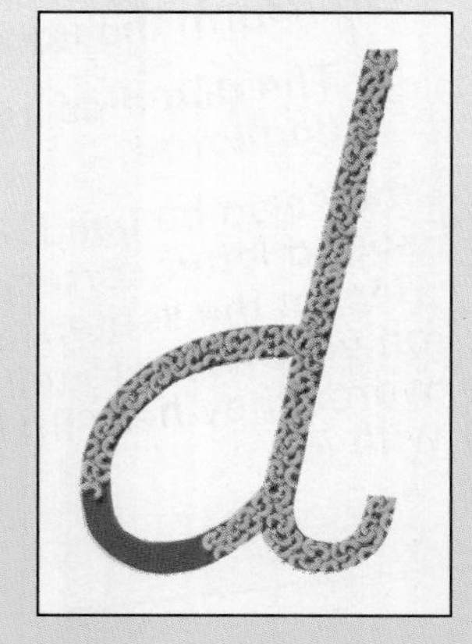

Decorating d (Fine Motor, Letter Recognition) Many of our activities revolve around letter sounds. I run off a letter on heavy paper. The children trace it and paste appropriate materials on it. For example, we put dinosaurs (shaped macaroni) on **d** and popcorn on **p**.

Janice G. Barel
Crissman Elementary
Utica, MI

Going to Grandma's (Oral Language, Phonics) Play this memory game. One child begins by saying, *I'm going to Grandma's, and I'm bringing a deer.* The next child must add another **d** word, for example, *I'm going to Grandma's, and I'm bringing a deer and a duck.* Players must repeat all previous **d** words before adding new ones.

Rhyming Game (Letter Practice, Fine Motor) Point out that the words *dad* and *add* rhyme. Invite children to compile a list of other words that rhyme with these two. Make a worksheet containing the letters below. Have children add a **d** in each blank. Read the words with them.

ba___ pa___ fa___
la___ sa___ ma___

Objectives

Learns the shape of **o** by finger tracing a large model letter.
Writes the lower-case letter **o** and traces a word with **o.**

Prepare

Have children play "Pass the Orange." Write the letter **o** on the chalkboard. Then write about 20 simple words, some of which have an **o** in them. Have children sit in a large circle. Play lively music as the children pass around a small, orange ball. When the music stops, the child holding the ball must go to the board and circle a word with the letter **o** in it.

Use the *D'Nealian® Handwriting Big Book* to preview the page.

Teach (page 45)

Have children:

- identify the lower-case letter **o;**
- find the octopus at the starting arrow;
- finger trace the path from the octopus to the otter while you say the following mnemonic sentence:
  The octopus plays an odd game with the otter.
- air trace the letter **o.**

ACTIVITY BANK

Time to Grow

Writing o (Letter Practice, Phonics) Write words that begin with **o** on the chalkboard and say them. Have children choose one of the words to illustrate at the writing center. Children should label their pictures with a large lower-case **o.**

Back to Back (Tactile, Fine Motor) Using one child's back as a chalkboard, have another child make a letter with his or her finger. The child being written on then writes the letter on paper.

Pam Buffett
St. Athanasius School
Evanston, IL

Phonics Corner

The sentence used to help children form the letter **o,**

The **octopus** plays an **odd** game with the **otter.**

may also be used to work on sound-letter correspondence. Repeat the sentence and call on volunteers to tell you the words they hear that begin with /o/.

Teach (page 46)

Call attention to the picture at the top of the page. Have children:

- identify the scene;
- trace the **o's** in the picture;
- color the picture.

Call attention to the lower half of the page. Have children:

- finger trace the boxed letter **o** as you read aloud the letter description;
- pencil trace the gray letters;
- write the letter **o** using the starting dots;
- trace the word *odd.*

Follow Up

Self-Evaluation Have children check their own work by asking themselves:

- Are my **o's** closed at the top?
- Do my **o's** slant the same way?

Additional Resources

Manuscript Alpha Touch letter **o**
D'Nealian® Handwriting Big Book letter **o**

Trace each **o.** Color the picture.

odd

46 Writing **o**

Children trace the **o's** and then color the picture. They trace and write the letter **o** and then trace the word **odd.**

Letter Description

Middle start; around down, and close up.

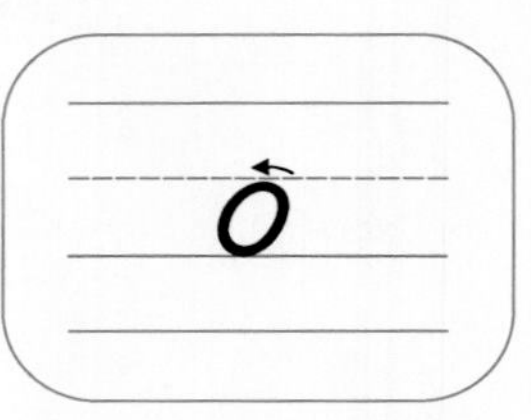

ACTIVITY BANK

Moving Write Along

Bag o' Letters (Tactile, Letter Practice) To practice letters, put 1/4 cup of finger paint inside a zip-lock bag. Squeeze out the air and seal. When laid on a table the bag becomes a slate. You can use a marker to make guidelines on the outside for writing.

Ruth Van Matre
Hillcrest Elementary
Delphi, IN

Clay-o (Fine Motor, Tactile) Give children clay. Tell them to roll it into a thin rope. Have them connect the ends to make an **o.** Encourage them to run their fingers around the **o.**

Finger Painting Letters (Letter Practice, Tactile) Cover a large table or children's desks with newspaper. Give each child a long piece of shelf paper or finger-painting paper. Sponge the paper with water and have children cover the paper with finger paint. Have them use their index fingers to make as many **o's** as they would like. Encourage them to turn their **o's** into octopuses.

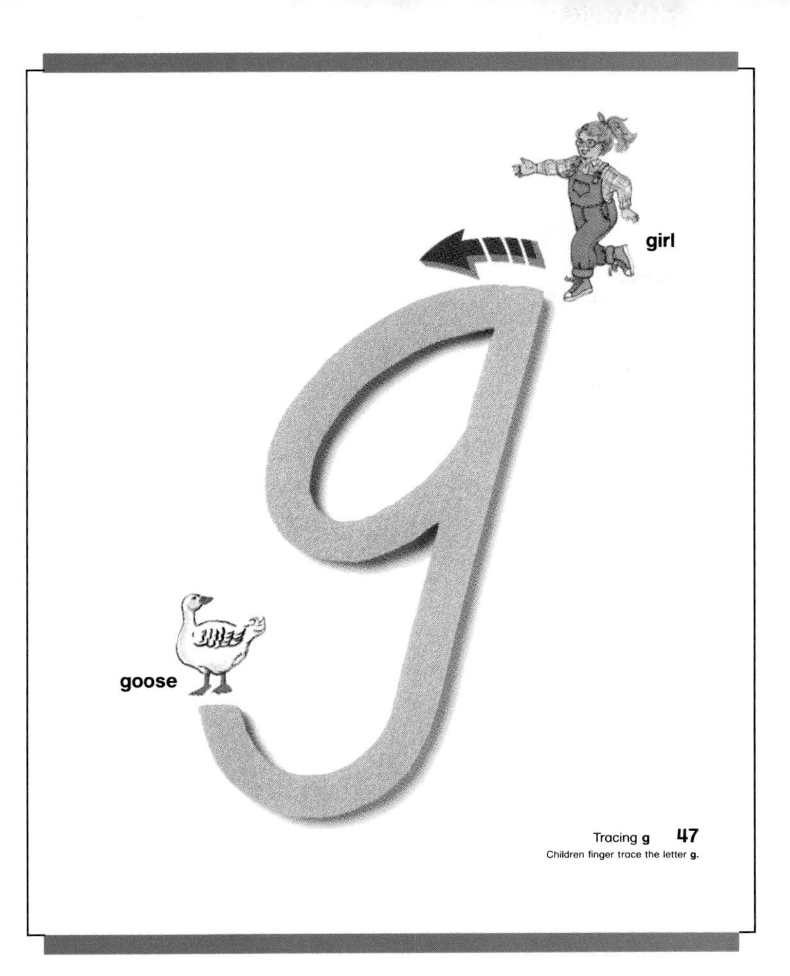

Objectives

Learns the shape of **g** by finger tracing a large model letter.
Writes the lower-case letter **g** and traces a word with **g.**

Prepare

Have children play "Go on a Goose Hunt." Make picture cards with the letters **a, d, o,** and **g** on them using sturdy cardboard. Above each letter paste a photograph or draw the image of an animal that represents the letter (ant, dog, octopus, and goose). Hide the cards around the classroom and have groups of children search for the **g** cards only.

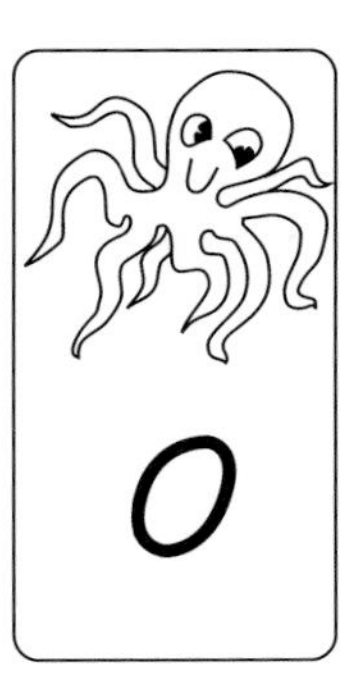

You might want to assign different groups to hunt for the other letters or ask groups to find one card for each letter.

Use the *D'Nealian® Handwriting Big Book* to preview the page.

Teach (page 47)

Have children:

- identify the lower-case letter **g;**
- find the girl at the starting arrow;
- finger trace the path from the girl to the goose while you say the following mnemonic sentence:
  Go with the girl to find her goose.
- air trace the letter **g.**

ACTIVITY BANK

Time to Grow

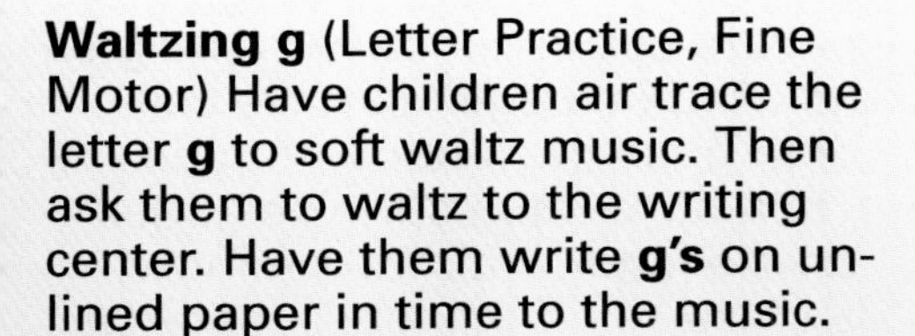

Waltzing g (Letter Practice, Fine Motor) Have children air trace the letter **g** to soft waltz music. Then ask them to waltz to the writing center. Have them write **g's** on unlined paper in time to the music.

Presto Chango (Critical Thinking, Gross Motor) Write a large letter of the alphabet on the chalkboard, a **g** for example. Choose someone to come up and use colored chalk to turn the letter into a picture. You might want to demonstrate how to do this for children.

Marly Glaw
Shreiner School and Academy
Marietta, GA

Phonics Corner

The sentence used to help children form the letter **g,**

Go with the **girl** to find her **goose.**

may also be used to work on sound-letter correspondence. Repeat the sentence and call on volunteers to tell you the words they hear that begin with /g/.

Teach (page 48)

Call attention to the picture at the top of the page. Have children:
- identify the girl and the goose;
- find and circle each hidden **g**.

Call attention to the lower half of the page. Have children:
- finger trace the boxed letter **g** as you read aloud the letter description;
- pencil trace the gray letters;
- write the letter **g** using the starting dots;
- trace the words *go* and *good.*

Follow Up

Self-Evaluation Have children check their own work by asking themselves:
- Are my **g's** closed at the top?
- Do my **g's** have their fishhooks?

Additional Resources

Manuscript Alpha Touch letter **g**
D'Nealian® Handwriting Big Book letter **g**

Circle each hidden **g.**

go

good

48 Writing g

Children find and circle the **g's** hidden in the picture. They trace and write the letter **g** and then trace the words **go** and **good.**

Letter Description

Middle start; around down, close up, down under water, and a fish-hook.

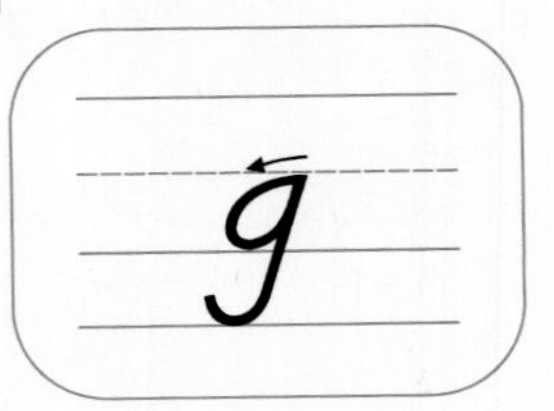

ACTIVITY BANK

Moving Write Along

Alphabet Sandwich (Letter Practice, Fine Motor) I teach my students that the writing lines are like a sandwich: The top line is the top slice of bread; the dotted line is the peanut butter and jelly; and the bottom line is the bottom slice of bread. Letters must be written within the sandwich, unless they are fishhook letters such as **g, j, q,** or **y,** which are like lettuce hanging out of the sandwich.

Marilyn Knudson
Alice Terry Elementary
Englewood, CO

Glittering Geese (Fine Motor, Tactile) Reproduce and enlarge the picture of the goose with the **g** on its wing on page 48. Have children trace the letter with glue. Then have them sprinkle glitter on the letter, wait for a minute, and shake off the loose material. Children may want to color the goose also. Completed geese might be lined up on the bulletin board and then used for tactile learning later.

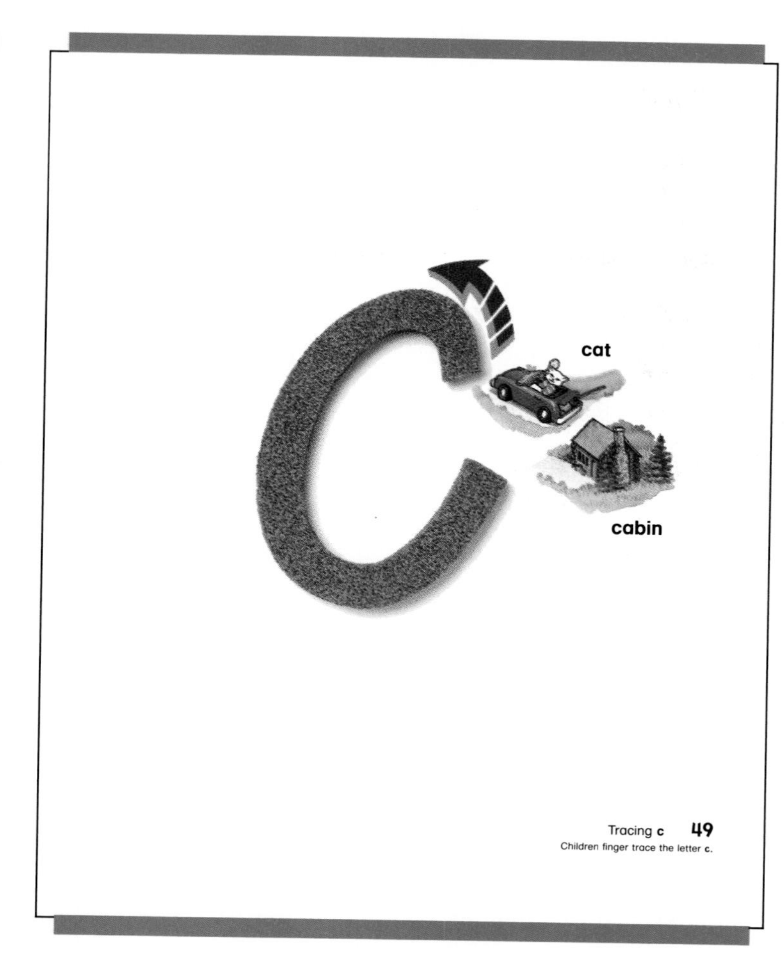

Objectives

Learns the shape of **c** by finger tracing a large model letter.
Writes the lower-case letter **c** and traces a word with **c**.

Prepare

Have an "Alphabet Race." Place five large letters **(a, d, o, g,** and **c)** on the floor. Have children stand in five rows across the room from the letters. Set up an obstacle course between the children and the letters. Ask children to pretend they are in racing cars. Call out children's names and the letter to which each should race. They may race one another or drive one at a time.

Use the *D'Nealian® Handwriting Big Book* to preview the page.

Teach (page 49)

Have children:

- identify the lower-case letter **c**;
- find the cat at the starting arrow;
- finger trace the path from the cat to the cabin while you say the following mnemonic sentence:
  The cat drives around the curve to the cabin.
- air trace the letter **c**.

ACTIVITY BANK

Time to Grow

c the Codfish (Letter Practice, Fine Motor) Distribute a simple outline of a large codfish. At the writing center, children make scales for the fish by writing **c's** all over it. They glue the fish to blue paper.

Clockwork c (Letter Practice, Fine Motor) I teach **c** using the concept of a clock. Draw circles on the chalkboard, marking 12:00 and 2:00 in each. Show how to begin at 2:00, go up to 12:00, and around to write **c**. Give children a ditto with "**c** circles" marked with 12:00 and 2:00. Next just mark 2:00. Finally they write **c** alone.

Barbara Norman
North Beardsley School
Bakersfield, CA

Phonics Corner

The sentence used to help children form the letter **c**,

The **cat** drives around the **curve** to the **cabin.**

may also be used to work on sound-letter correspondence. Repeat the sentence and call on volunteers to tell you the words they hear that begin with /k/.

Teach (page 50)

Call attention to the maze at the top of the page. Have children:

- identify the images on the page;
- identify the letters at the end of each path;
- finger trace the path from the cat to the **c;**
- draw a line from the cat to the **c.**

Call attention to the lower half of the page. Have children:

- finger trace the boxed letter **c** as you read aloud the letter description;
- pencil trace the gray letters;
- write the letter **c** using the starting dots;
- trace the words *cod* and *cocoa.*

Follow Up

Self-Evaluation Have children check their own work by asking themselves:

- Did I start at the starting dots?
- Do my **c's** slant the same way?

Additional Resources

Manuscript Alpha Touch letter **c**
D'Nealian® Handwriting Big Book letter **c**

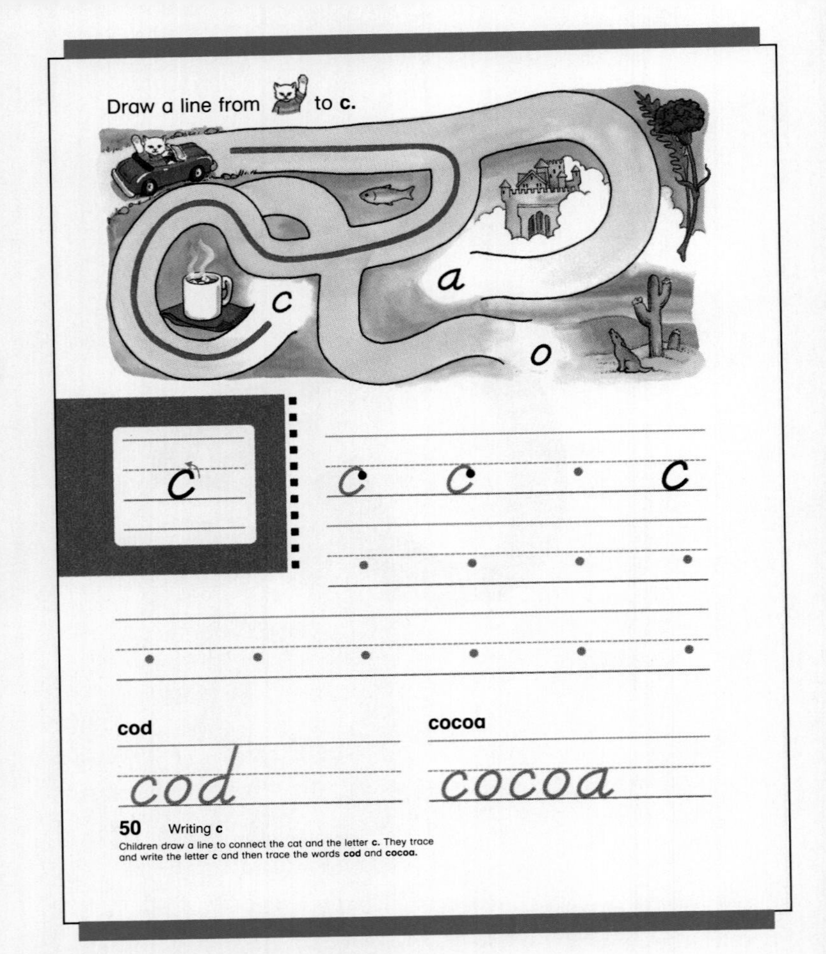
Draw a line from [cat] to **c.**

c a o

c c c c

cod cocoa

cod cocoa

50 Writing c

Children draw a line to connect the cat and the letter **c.** They trace and write the letter **c** and then trace the words **cod** and **cocoa.**

Letter Description

Start below the middle; curve up, around, down, up, and stop.

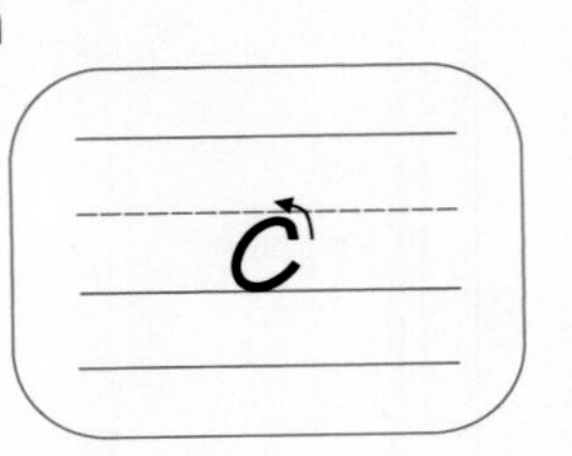

ACTIVITY BANK

Moving Write Along

Round the Bend (Fine Motor, Creative Thinking) Draw a very large lower-case **c** on paper. Give children toy cars and tell them the car will travel around the **c.** Tell them to draw a place the car would like to go to at the end of the **c.** After they have finished their drawings, have children "drive" their cars to the destinations they have drawn.

Big Is Beautiful (Letter Practice, Fine Motor) Make an overhead transparency of each letter as children learn them. Have a volunteer trace the letter so others can see on a large scale how each is formed. The big screen keeps their attention, and children love tracing on the transparencies.

Nancy Caton
Edgewood School
Woodridge, IL

Dot the c (Tactile, Fine Motor) Give each child a lower-case **c** cut out of posterboard. Supply white glue and have them make small dots all over the letter. When the glue dries, encourage them to feel the **c** with their fingers.

Objectives

Learns the shape of **e** by finger tracing a large model letter.
Writes the lower-case letter **e** and traces a word with **e**.

Prepare

Bring a dozen eggs to class and talk about various aspects of the egg: where it comes from, what kind of animal produces it, how it helps us, and so on. Following are some possibilities for working with eggs:

- Let volunteers break a few of the eggs into a bowl and tell what they see.
- If you have a kitchen in your classroom, you might want to make scrambled, hard-boiled, fried, or poached eggs with the children.
- Color eggs with food coloring or an egg-dyeing kit.
- Play "Spoon and Egg Race." Divide the children into four groups. Two groups line up on one side of the room and face the two groups on the other side. Each child holds a spoon. Put a hard-boiled egg in the spoons of the first children in two rows. These children run to the row across from them and pass off the egg to a classmate's spoon without using their other hand. They continue racing until all children have carried an egg.

Use the *D'Nealian® Handwriting Big Book* to preview the page.

Teach (page 51)

Have children:

- identify the lower-case letter **e;**
- find the elephant and the starting arrow;
- finger trace the path from the elephant to the eggs while you say the following mnemonic sentence:

  Will the elephant enjoy eggs for lunch?
- air trace the letter **e.**

ACTIVITY BANK

Time to Grow

What's in the Egg? (Fine Motor, Letter Practice) At the writing center, have a large egg-shaped piece of paper available. Have children write the letter **e** below the line you have drawn across the middle of the egg. Children cut the egg along this line. Help them insert a brad to hold the halves together. Have them make a drawing to glue to the back of the bottom half. Open the egg for a surprise!

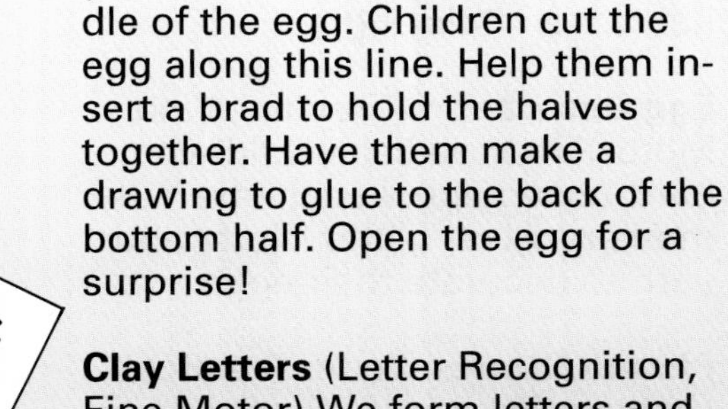

Clay Letters (Letter Recognition, Fine Motor) We form letters and words with clay. Some **e** words might be *egg, elephant,* and *end.*

Helen Villarreal
Antonio Olivares Elementary
San Antonio, TX

Phonics Corner

The sentence used to help children form the letter **e,**

Will the **elephant enjoy eggs** for lunch?

may also be used to work on sound-letter correspondence. Repeat the sentence and call on volunteers to tell you the words they hear that begin with /e/.

Teach (page 52)

Call attention to the picture at the top of the page. Have children:
- identify the letters on the eggs in the picture;
- color the eggs with an **e** on them.

Call attention to the lower half of the page. Have children:
- finger trace the boxed letter **e** as you read aloud the letter description;
- pencil trace the gray letters;
- write the letter **e** using the starting dots;
- trace the word *egg.*

Follow Up

Self-Evaluation Have children check their own work by asking themselves:
- Are all my **e's** the same size?
- Do my **e's** reach the middle line?

Additional Resources

Manuscript Alpha Touch letter **e**
D'Nealian® Handwriting Big Book letter **e**

Color eggs marked **e.**

egg

52 Writing e

Children color the eggs in the picture that have an **e** on them. They trace and write the letter **e** and then trace the word **egg.**

Letter Description

Start between the middle and bottom; curve up, around, touch, down, up, and stop.

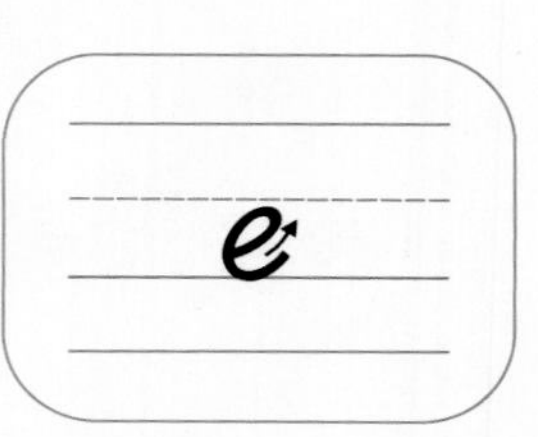

ACTIVITY BANK

Moving Write Along

Hatch an Egg (Letter Recognition, Visual) Draw a large egg on the chalkboard. Inside the egg, write several **e's** along with other letters learned. Tell children that the egg will not hatch until all the letters are gone, and they can help.

Call individuals to the board, point to a letter, and ask its name. Have them erase it with their index finger using the same stroke they use to trace the letter. When all letters have been erased, ask what they think might hatch from this egg.

Egg Decorating (Creative, Fine Motor) Provide each child with a hard-boiled egg. Let children use markers, glue, glitter, cloth, and yarn to decorate their eggs.

Picture Stories (Letter Practice, Creative) As a teacher of D'Nealian® Handwriting, I use this activity: We cut a picture out of a magazine and then write a story about the picture. My students love handwriting. We once cut out a picture of a pair of eyes and wrote about them.

Rosemary Logan
Robert E. Lake Elementary School
Las Vegas, NV

Objectives

Learns the shape of **s** by finger tracing a large model letter.
Writes the lower-case letter **s** and traces a word with **s.**

Prepare

Write the letter **s** on the chalkboard.
- Have the children say the sound of **s** in their most sibilant manner.
- Ask volunteers to pantomime words for doing things that begin with the **s** sound. You may want to whisper such suggestions as *sailing,* eating *soup, sipping,* being *silly, sleeping,* etc.

Next, draw a large **s** on the classroom floor.
- Invite children to walk the **s.**
- Invite children to race their toy cars along the **s.**

Use the *D'Nealian® Handwriting Big Book* to preview the page.

Teach (page 53)

Have children:
- identify the lower-case letter **s;**
- find the sailboat at the starting arrow;
- finger trace the path from the sailboat to the sun while you say the following mnemonic sentence:

  The sailboat sails to meet the sun.
- air trace the letter **s.**

ACTIVITY BANK

Time to Grow 

Sandy s (Letter Practice, Tactile) At a sand table or sandbox, have children pretend they are at the beach. Ask them to take turns writing lower-case **s** in the sand. At the writing center, have them write **s** on unlined paper, then trace the **s** with the tip of a glue bottle. Ask them to sift sand over the glue to make a tactile **s.**

Crafty Letters (Eye-Hand Coordination, Tactile) Have available thick yarn in assorted colors. Let children choose a color and create their own letter **s.** Distribute construction paper and have children paste a colorful yarn **s** on the paper.

Phonics Corner

The sentence used to help children form the letter **s,**

The **sailboat sails** to meet the **sun.**

may also be used to work on sound-letter correspondence. Repeat the sentence and call on volunteers to tell you the words they hear that begin with /s/.

Teach (page 54)

Call attention to the picture at the top of the page. Have children:

- identify the various letters;
- find and color each **s** blue;
- identify the resulting picture as a sailboat;
- color the rest of the picture in other colors.

Call attention to the lower half of the page. Have children:

- finger trace the boxed letter **s** as you read aloud the letter description;
- pencil trace the gray letters;
- write the letter **s** using the starting dots;
- trace the word *sea.*

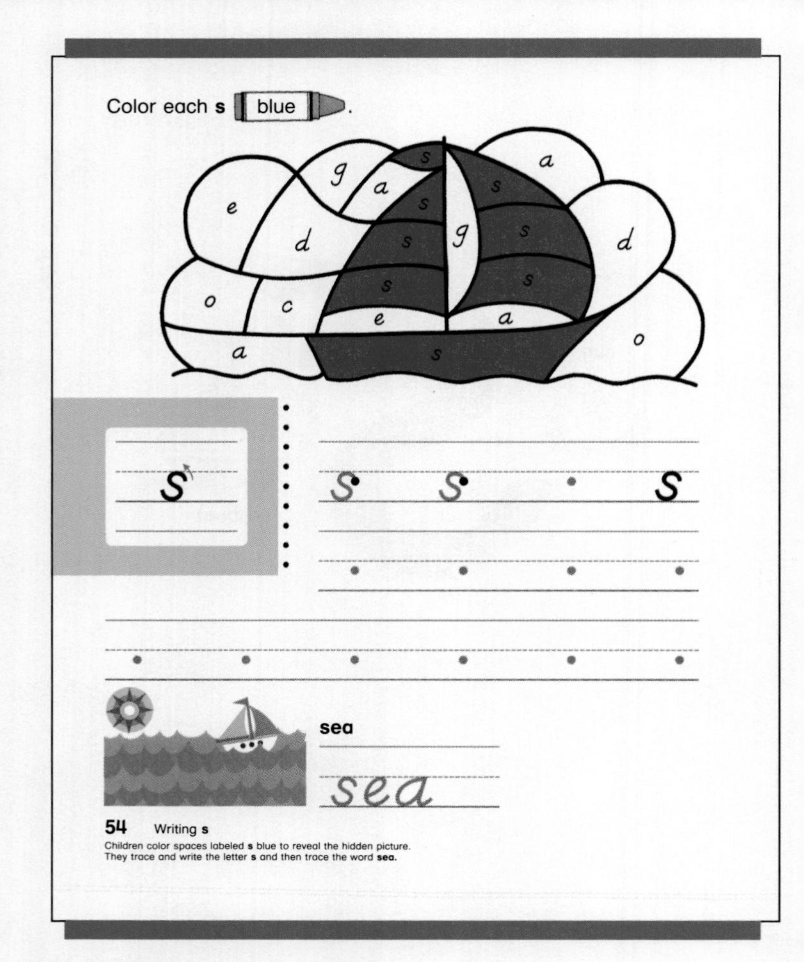

Follow Up

Self-Evaluation Have children check their own work by asking themselves:

- Did I start at the starting dots?
- Do my **s's** curve from the middle to the bottom line?

Additional Resources

Manuscript Alpha Touch letter **s**

D'Nealian® Handwriting Big Book letter **s**

Letter Description

Start below the middle; curve up, around, down, and a snake tail.

ACTIVITY BANK

Moving Write Along

Sail Away (Fine Motor, Gifted) Draw a simple outline of a sailboat along with four cut-out triangular shapes that will fit into the boat's sail. Pass out the boat picture and the shapes. Have children cut out the boat and paste the shapes in the proper position. Invite them to color the hull and then write **s's** on it.

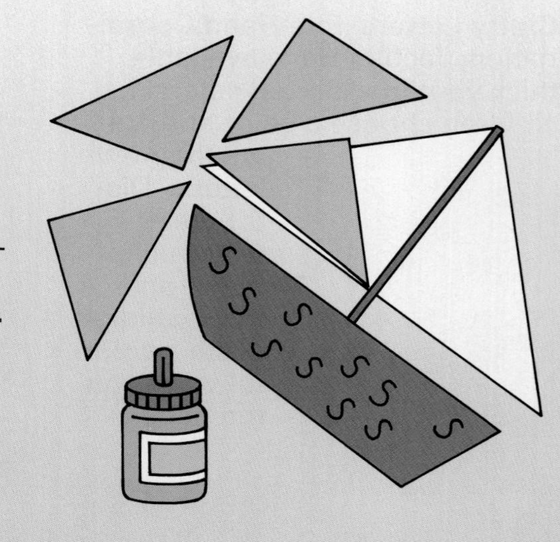

Rainbow Writing (Letter Practice, Fine Motor) I draw lines and letters on the chalkboard, putting dots where the letters start and arrows to show the direction of the strokes. The children enjoy using colored chalk to trace these letters when other work is finished. Sometimes two or three children trace after one another, using different-colored chalk. The children call these their "rainbow" letters.

Lora Fisher
Mt. Hope Grade School
Mt. Hope, KS

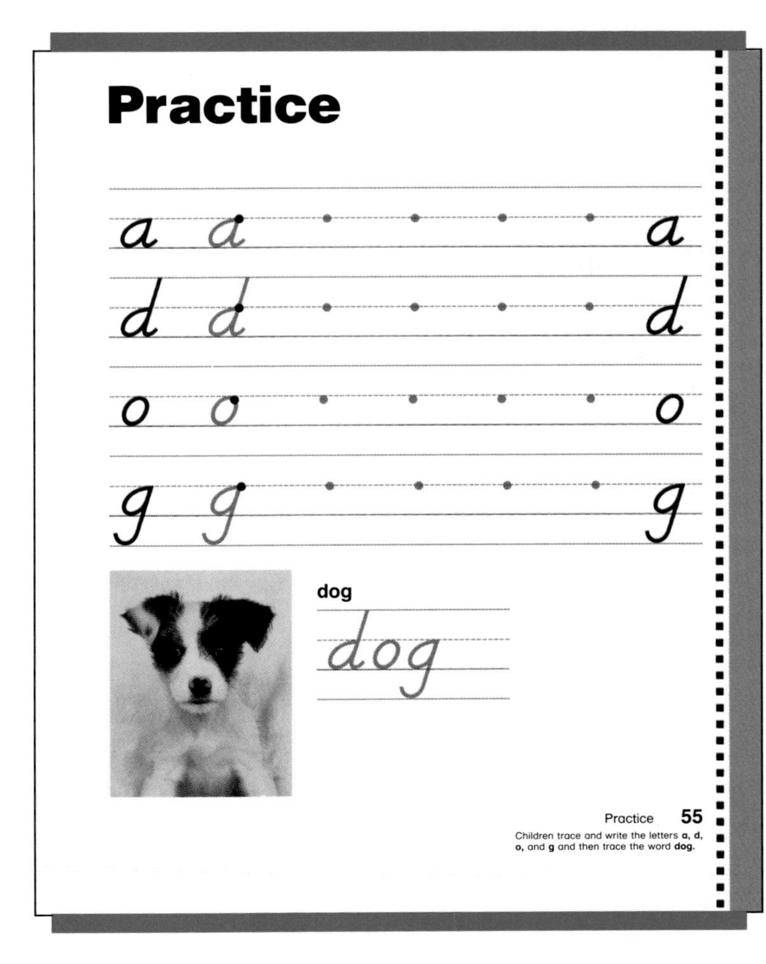
Practice

a a a

d d d

o o o

g g g

dog

dog

Practice 55

Children trace and write the letters **a, d, o,** and **g** and then trace the word **dog.**

Objectives
Practices writing the lower-case letters **a, d, o,** and **g.** Traces the word *dog.*

Prepare
Play "Toss the Beanbag" with the children using the letters **a, d, o,** and **g.** Tape a tick-tack-toe grid on the floor or draw one with chalk. Put each of the letters in the spaces as show below.

g	a	o
d	o	g
g	d	a

- Children throw the beanbags and identify the letters upon which the beanbags land.
- Children request a certain letter, and the thrower tries to land on that letter.

Teach (page 55)
Have children:
- identify the lower-case letters **a, d, o,** and **g;**
- pencil trace the gray letters;
- write each letter using the starting dots;
- trace the word *dog.*

Follow Up
Self-Evaluation Have children check their own work by asking themselves:
- Did I start all my letters at the starting dots?
- Are all my letters closed properly?

Additional Resources
Manuscript Alpha Touch letters **a,d, o,** and **g**
D'Nealian® Handwriting Big Book letters **a,d, o,** and **g**

ACTIVITY BANK

Collar Your Dog (Creative, Letter Practice) Using crayons and strips of colored paper, children can make dog collars. Have them write several **d's** on the collar. You may want them to draw or cut out a dog around whose neck they can attach their collar.

Name That Letter (Tactile, Letter Recognition) Cut out the letters **a, d, o,** and **g** from heavy sandpaper. Put these letters in a bag. Have a volunteer reach in the bag, feel a letter, identify it, and show it to the class for confirmation. Next, have the child write the letter on the chalkboard or overhead projector.

Pass the g (Kinesthetic, Letter Practice) Play some lively music. Have children sit in a circle and pass a large cardboard **g.** When the music stops, the child holding the **g** leaves the circle and writes a **g** on the chalkboard. The game continues until all children have written a **g.**

Objectives
Practices writing the lower-case letters **c, e,** and **s.** Traces the words *cages* and *geese.*

Prepare
Have children play "Alphabet Lotto" in groups of three, using the letters **a, d, o, g, c, e,** and **s.** Use index cards on which you or the children have written each of the target letters. Each letter should be written on two separate cards. Each group:
- shuffles the cards, places two of them face up, and deals the rest;
- takes turns matching one of the upturned cards to one in their hands or placing a card face up on the table;

The player with the most pairs at the end of the game wins.

Teach (page 56)
Have children:
- identify the lower-case letters **c, e,** and **s;**
- pencil trace the gray letters;
- write each letter using the starting dots;
- trace the words *cages* and *geese.*

Follow Up
Self-Evaluation Have children check their own work by asking themselves:
- Do all my letters slant the same way?
- Do all my letters touch the middle line?

Additional Resources
Manuscript Alpha Touch letters **c, e,** and **s**
D'Nealian® Handwriting Big Book letters **c, e,** and **s**

ACTIVITY BANK

Goose Feathers (Letter Practice, Fine Motor) Draw an outline of a goose. Make copies for children. Have them make feathers by writing **s's** on the goose. Have them color and cut out the goose and glue it to yellow paper.

Ornamental Letters (Tactile, Creative) Have children roll out clay "snakes." They can then form an **a, d, o g, c, e,** and **s,** running their fingers over each. If left to harden, the letters can be painted and decorated to make ornaments. The **o** becomes a holiday wreath, the **g** a Halloween ghost, and the **s** a birthday snake.

Marly Glaw
Shreiner School and Academy
Marietta, GA

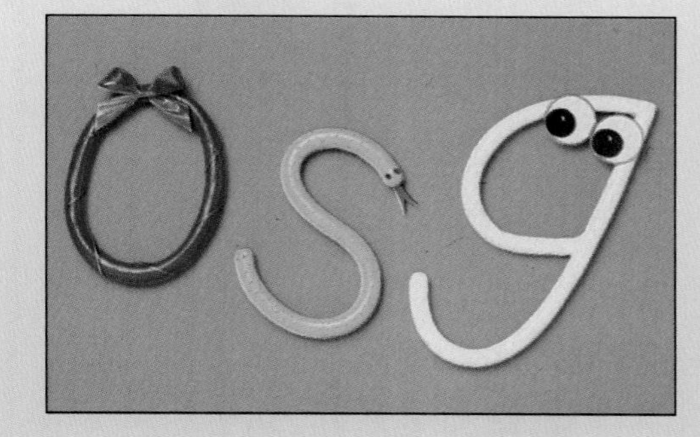

Special Needs (Immature Learners) Immature children enjoy hands-on activities. On pieces of large cardboard, make a write-on line and a D'Nealian letter. Cover both sides with clear acetate. Give children dough (see recipe) to roll into ropes, placing one on a letter. Turn the card over and have them make the letter without a model.

Peanut Butter Dough
1 cup each corn syrup and peanut butter
1 1/2 to 2 cups powdered milk
Mix all ingredients together.

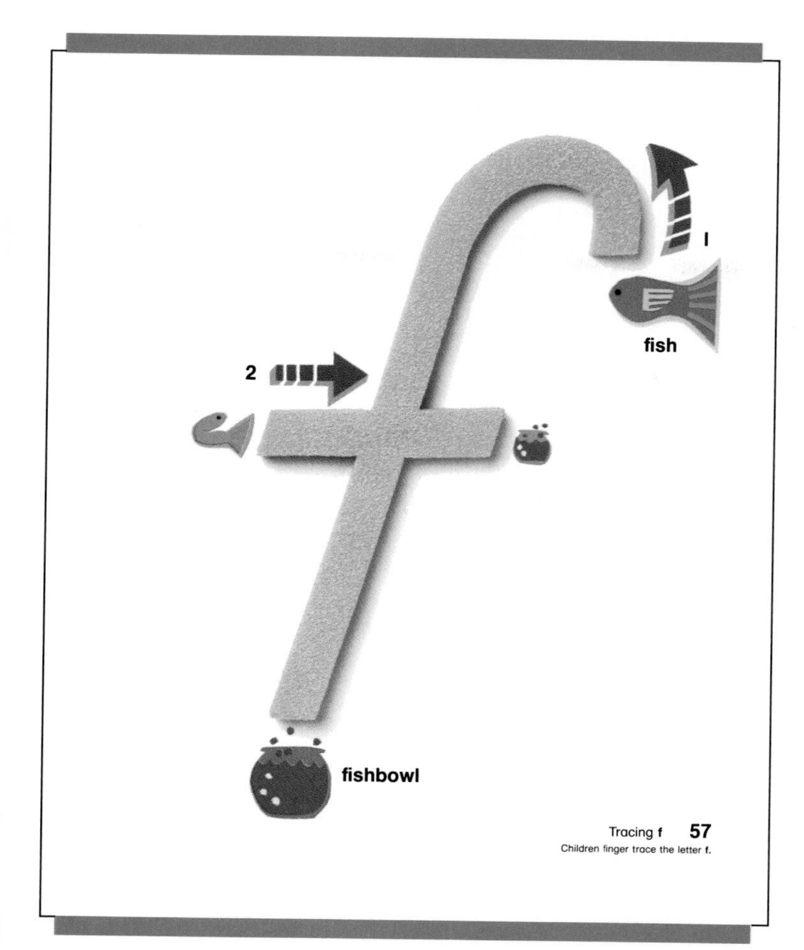

Objectives

Learns the shape of **f** by finger tracing a large model letter.
Writes the lower-case letter **f** and traces a word with **f.**

Prepare

Bring pictures of various kinds of fish to class or investigate the fish tank in your classroom if you have one.

- Talk about how gills help fish breathe in water.
- Talk about the importance of keeping the water clean in a fish's environment.
- Ask for volunteers to tell about how they care for pet fish.
- Discuss the fact that fish swim together in groups called schools.
- Invite children to swim around the room in schools of their own, making funny fish faces.

Use the *D'Nealian® Handwriting Big Book* to preview the page.

Teach (page 57)

Have children:

- identify the lower-case letter **f;**
- find the large fish at the starting arrow;
- finger trace the paths from each fish to its fishbowl while you say the following mnemonic sentences:

  First, the large fish swims down to its fishbowl. Then, the small fish swims across to its fishbowl.
- air trace the letter **f.**

ACTIVITY BANK

Time to Grow 

Fishy f (Creative, Fine Motor) Have children write lower-case **f** in pencil on unlined paper at the writing center. Ask children to use crayons to make their **f** into a fish.

Print Awareness (Letter Recognition, Visual) Invite children to look at labels, posters, signs, and so forth, in the room and point to the various **f's** they find. Encourage children to compare these **f's.**

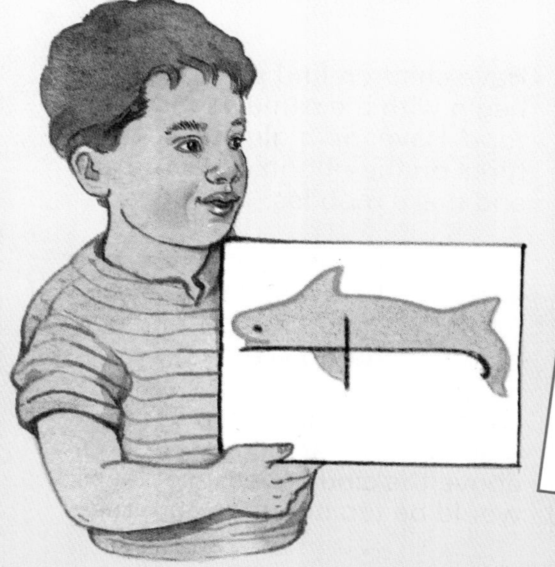

Phonics Corner

The sentence used to help children form the letter **f,**

First, the large **fish** swims down to its **fishbowl.** Then, the small **fish** swims across to its **fishbowl.**

may also be used to work on sound-letter correspondence. Repeat the sentence and call on volunteers to tell you the words that begin with /f/.

Teach (page 58)

Call attention to the photograph and words at the top of the page. Have children:

- identify the various food in the photograph;
- look at the large word *food* as you read it;
- find and circle the word that matches the word *food.*

Call attention to the lower half of the page. Have children:

- finger trace the boxed letter **f** as you read aloud the letter description;
- pencil trace the gray letters;
- write the letter **f** using the starting dots;
- trace the word *food.*

Follow Up

Self-Evaluation Have children check their own work by asking themselves:

- Did I cross all my **f's?**
- Do my **f's** slant the same way?

Additional Resources

Manuscript Alpha Touch letter **f**
D'Nealian® Handwriting Big Book letter **f**

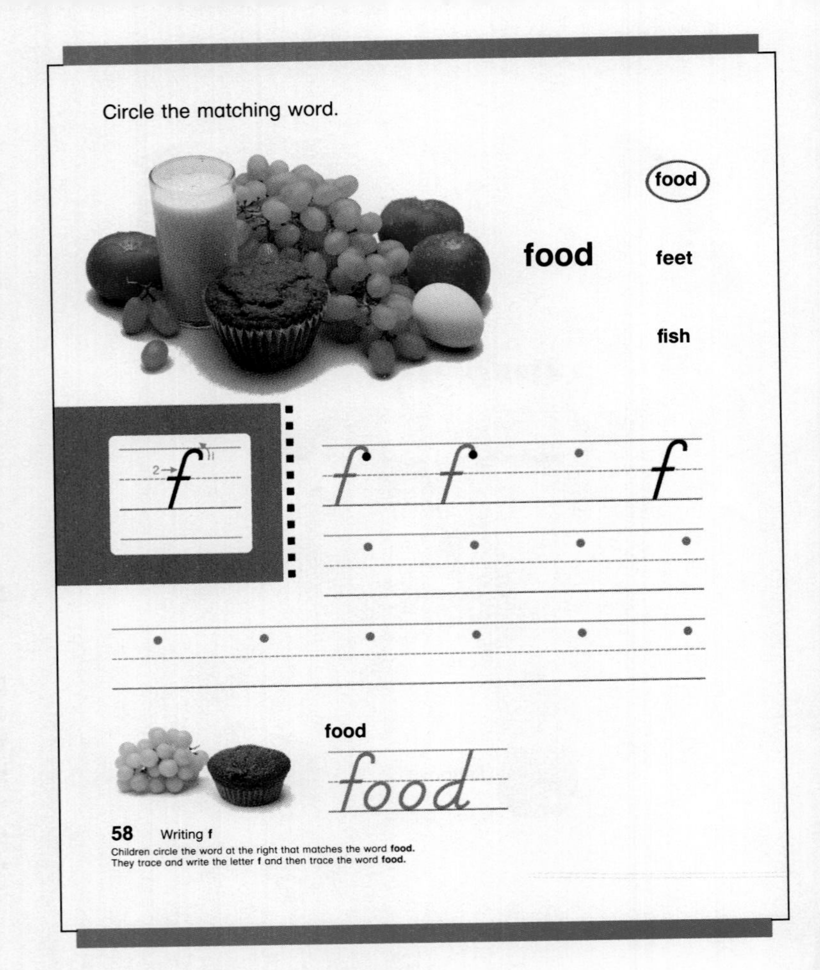

Letter Description

Start below the top; curve up, around, and slant down. Cross.

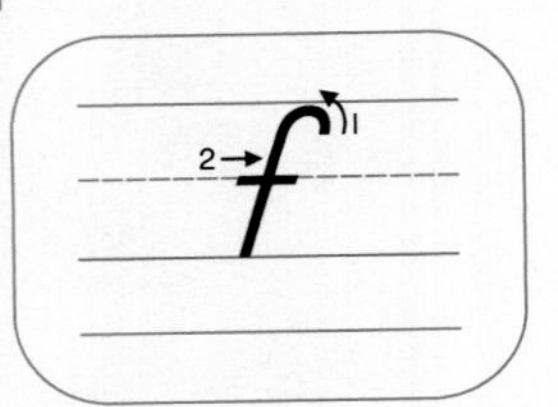

ACTIVITY BANK

Moving Write Along

Mobile Meal (Phonics, Creative) Provide each child with a white paper plate. Have children draw a favorite food on their plates. Attach ribbon to the bottom of each.

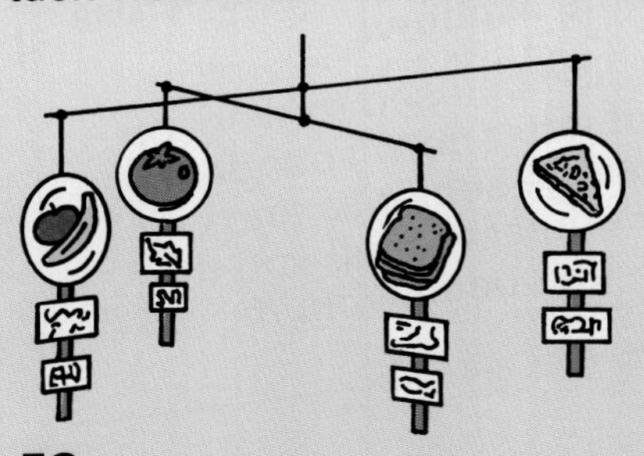

Have children find pictures that begin with the same sound as *food.* Have them glue these pictures on the ribbon. Attach string and make mobiles.

Letter Tales (Visual, Auditory) For extra fun, I draw and tell a story for each letter. It helps children remember letter placement. The letter **f,** for example, always stretches its head to the clouds to reach the sun. It never goes above the clouds because the sun would be too hot. It never goes below the grass as it is planted firmly in the ground.

Betty Neal
Waterford School
Sandy, UT

Foodfest (Celebrating Cultural Diversity) Have children bring in cans or boxes of food and discuss where the food is grown, whether they have ever tried it, and how it tastes. This foodfest could be expanded to include dishes (with recipes) from willing parents. Invite families to partake of the feast.

Objectives

Learns the shape of **b** by finger tracing a large model letter.
Writes the lower-case letter **b** and traces a word with **b**.

Prepare

Play "Alphabet Ball" with the children. Have them stand in two rows facing each other. All the children in one row have a large, bouncy ball. Children in turn bounce the ball across to their partners as you slowly sing "The Alphabet Song" together. Balls should be bounced at the sound of *a, b, c,* and so on. When all balls have been bounced, the partners bounce them back as you sing again.

Use the *D'Nealian® Handwriting Big Book* to preview the page.

Teach (page 59)

Have children:

- identify the lower-case letter **b;**
- find the boy at the starting arrow;
- finger trace the path from the boy to the ball while you say the following mnemonic sentence:
  The boy bounces the big ball.
- air trace the letter **b.**

ACTIVITY BANK

Time to Grow

b Ball (Fine Motor, Letter Practice) Have children write a **b** on colored paper at the writing center. Give them a cardboard circle. Ask them to place the circle over the **b** and trace the circle. They cut out the circle, cut it into three pieces, and then put it back together.

Make Your b-e-d (Letter Practice, Visual) Here's a trick to help students write **b** and **d:** Hold the fists inward with the thumbs pointing straight up. The left hand is the head of the bed (**b**) and the right is the foot of the bed (**d**). Write these letters as they look when made with thumbs and fists.

Pam Yeary
Pershing Elementary
Orlando, FL

Phonics Corner

The sentence used to help children form the letter **b,**

The **boy bounces** the **big ball.**

may also be used to work on sound-letter correspondence. Repeat the sentence and call on volunteers to tell you the words they hear that begin with /b/.

Teach (page 60)

Call attention to the picture at the top of the page. Have children:
- recognize that the children in the drawing are holding butterfly nets shaped like the letter **b;**
- trace the first and second **b** of each butterfly net;
- draw the last butterfly net **b** themselves.

Call attention to the lower half of the page. Have children:
- finger trace the boxed letter **b** as you read aloud the letter description;
- pencil trace the gray letters;
- write the letter **b** using the starting dots;
- trace the word *bag.*

Follow Up

Self-Evaluation Have children check their own work by asking themselves:
- Did I start at the starting dots?
- Do my **b's** slant down and around?

Additional Resources

Manuscript Alpha Touch letter **b**
D'Nealian® Handwriting Big Book letter **b**

Letter Description

Top start; slant down, around, up, and a tummy.

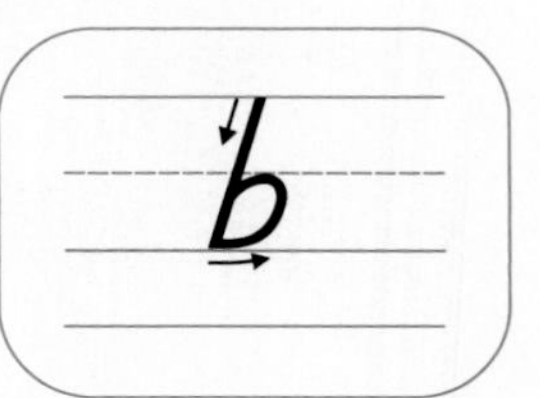

ACTIVITY BANK

Moving Write Along

Clothespin Game (Gross Motor, Letter Recognition) Provide a wide-mouthed bottle and clothespins. Write a letter on each clothespin and place the bottle on the floor in front of the first player. In small groups, the players name the letter on the clothespin and try to drop it from waist height into the bottle.

Practice Sheets (Letter Practice, Fine Motor) I first present a letter on the chalkboard. After doing a few correctly, I incorporate common errors for children to spot. Next, they are given a practice sheet of four rows. Letters in the first row are traced (I give oral directions). Remaining rows are done in a pattern of tracing and independent formation.

Linda Paavola
Star Center School
Lake Geneva, WI

Be a Listener (Letter Practice, Phonics) Ask children to write the letter **b** on index cards. Say several words, emphasizing the initial sound in each. Children raise their cards when they hear a word with the same initial sound as the one in *bag.*

Objectives

Learns the shape of **l** by finger tracing a large model letter.
Writes the lower-case letter **l** and traces a word with **l.**

Prepare

Sing a song of the letter **l** with the children, beginning with Ella Jenkins's "It's a Holiday." This cheery tune is easy to sing and includes a chorus that repeats the sound *la la la la la.* Other possibilities might be the well-known folk song "The Lion Sleeps Tonight" or "Hey Lolley Lolley Lo."

Be sure to display lots of **l's** around the room while you are singing its praises.

Use the *D'Nealian® Handwriting Big Book* to preview the page.

Teach (page 61)

Have children:
- identify the lower-case letter **l;**
- find the lion at the starting arrow;
- finger trace the path from the lion to the lake while you say the following mnemonic sentence:
  Lead the lion to the large lake.
- air trace the letter **l.**

ACTIVITY BANK

Time to Grow 

The Leprechaun's Present (Letter Practice, Fine Motor) When introducing lower-case letter **l,** talk about leprechauns. Cover the chalkboard with green chalk and have each child write **l** with a finger. The child's green fingertip is the leprechaun's present.

At the writing center have children use green markers to write **l** on unlined paper.

Mrs. Barbara Snowberger
Franklin Elementary
Lehighton, PA

Listen to Lion (Auditory, Kinesthetic) Have children play "Lion Says," in which they obey only commands with **l** in them, as:

Lion says leap (*they leap*).
Lion says sit (*they don't sit*).

Phonics Corner

The sentence used to help children form the letter **l,**

Lead the **lion** to the **large lake.**

may also be used to work on sound-letter correspondence. Repeat the sentence and call on volunteers to tell you the words they hear that begin with /l/.

Teach (page 62)

Call attention to the picture at the top of the page. Have children:

- identify the picture as a lion on the plain;
- trace the **l's** on the lion's head and mane;
- color the picture.

Call attention to the lower half of the page. Have children:

- finger trace the boxed letter **l** as you read aloud the letter description;
- pencil trace the gray letters;
- write the letter **l** using the starting dots;
- trace the word *leaf.*

Follow Up

Self-Evaluation Have children check their own work by asking themselves:

- Do my **l's** have their monkey tails?
- Do my **l's** slant the same way?

Additional Resources

Manuscript Alpha Touch letter **l**
D'Nealian® Handwriting Big Book letter **l**

Letter Description

Top start; slant down, and a monkey tail.

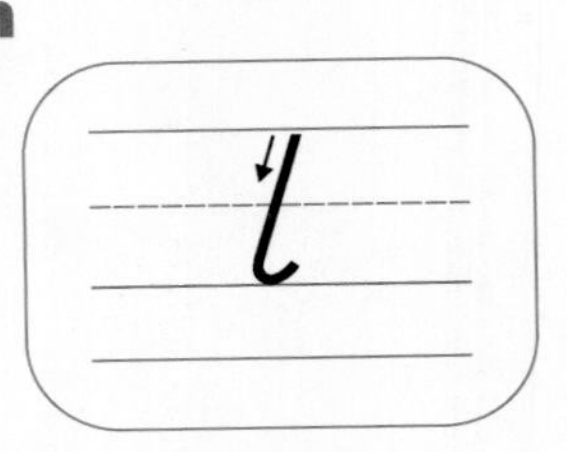

ACTIVITY BANK

Moving Write Along

Salt Trays (Letter Practice, Tactile) Fill a shallow box with salt. Make laminated cards—one for each lower-case letter. Punch a hole in a corner, and put cards on a curtain ring. Children look at cards and finger trace letters in the salt.

Diane Fioretti
Lake Garda School
Burlington, CT

Leaf Rubbing (Letter Practice, Fine Motor) Take a walk and collect various leaves. Have children place a leaf under a piece of white paper and gently rub a green crayon over the area covering the leaf. Have them write an **l** below the leaf that pops up on their papers.

Riddling with l (Oral Language, Critical Thinking) Write the letter **l** on writing lines on the chalkboard. Tell children you will ask some riddles. The answers begin with **l.** Volunteers will answer riddles and write **l's** on the board. Riddles begin, *I'm thinking of...*

something that is green and grows on trees.
something that roars and lives in a jungle.
the opposite of big.

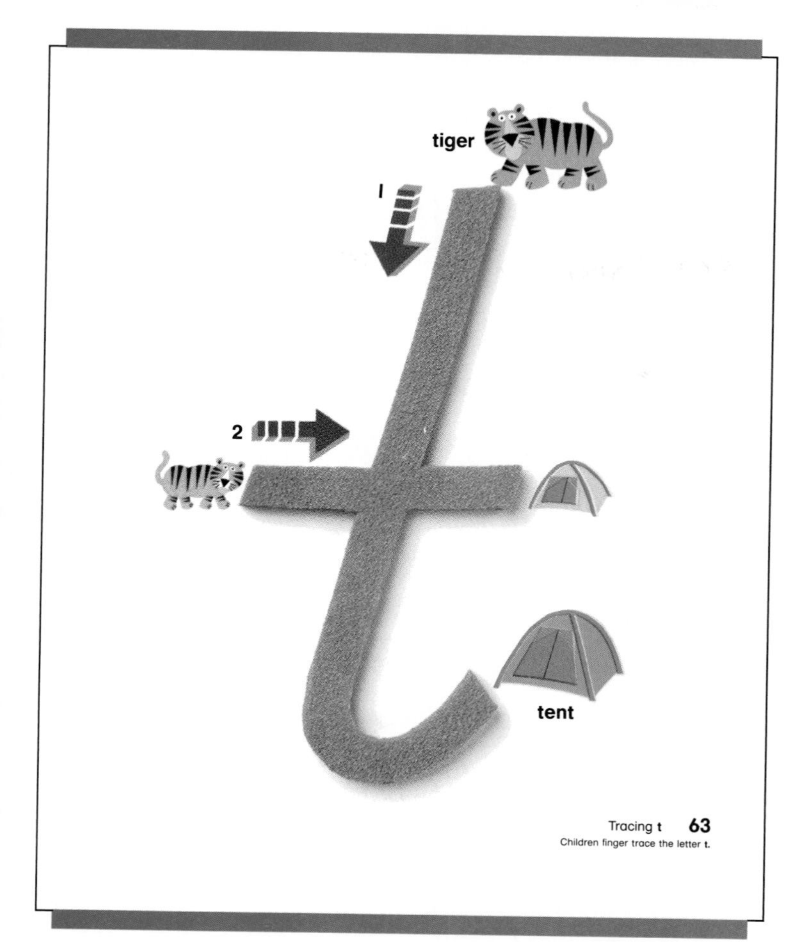

Objectives

Learns the shape of **t** by finger tracing a large model letter.
Writes the lower-case letter **t** and traces a word with **t**.

Prepare

Play "Taking a Trip to My Tent" with the children. The object of the game is to think of and remember as many **t** words as they can. Each child begins by saying, *I'm taking a trip to my tent, and I'm bringing a t_______*. Children must remember what each previous child said and add a **t** word of their own.

It might be fun to create a tentlike atmosphere with sheets and play the game *in* the tent.

Use the *D'Nealian® Handwriting Big Book* to preview the page.

Teach (page 63)

Have children:

- identify the lower-case letter **t;**
- find the large tiger at the starting arrow;
- finger trace the paths from each tiger to its tent while you say the following mnemonic sentence:
  Take the tall tiger down to its tent. Then, take the tiny tiger across to its tent.
- air trace the letter **t.**

ACTIVITY BANK

Time to Grow

Touch the t (Tactile, Letter Practice) Have children write **t** on tagboard at the writing center. Then ask them to glue materials such as glitter, yarn, or noodles over the letter to make it three-dimensional. This helps them "feel" the outline of the letter.

Sandra Pollock
East Prairie School
Skokie, IL

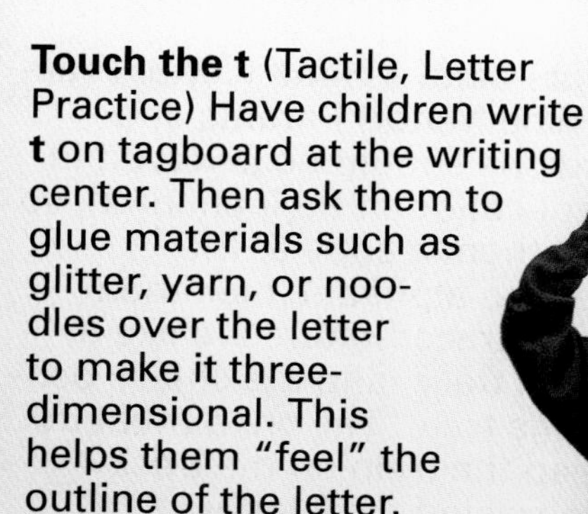

Hold That Tiger (Oral Language, Creative) Tell children to pretend they are on a tiger hunt. Have them describe the various animals and plants they see along the way. Ask them to illustrate their imaginary adventure. Hang their drawings around the room.

Phonics Corner

The sentence used to help children form the letter **t,**

Take the **tall tiger** down **to** its **tent**. Then, **take** the **tiny tiger** across to its **tent.**

may also be used to work on sound-letter correspondence. Repeat the sentence and call on volunteers to tell you the words they hear that begin with /t/.

Teach (page 64)

Call attention to the pictures at the top of the page. Have children:

- identify the letter **t** on each of the flags;
- identify the tent, the tiger, and the boot;
- listen as you read the words *tent, tiger,* and *boot;*
- circle each **t** in the three words.

Call attention to the lower half of the page. Have children:

- finger trace the boxed letter **t** as you read aloud the letter description;
- pencil trace the gray letters;
- write the letter **t** using the starting dots;
- trace the word *boot.*

Follow Up

Self-Evaluation Have children check their own work by asking themselves:

- Did I start at the starting dots?
- Did I cross all my **t's?**

Additional Resources

Manuscript Alpha Touch letter **t**
D'Nealian® Handwriting Big Book letter **t**

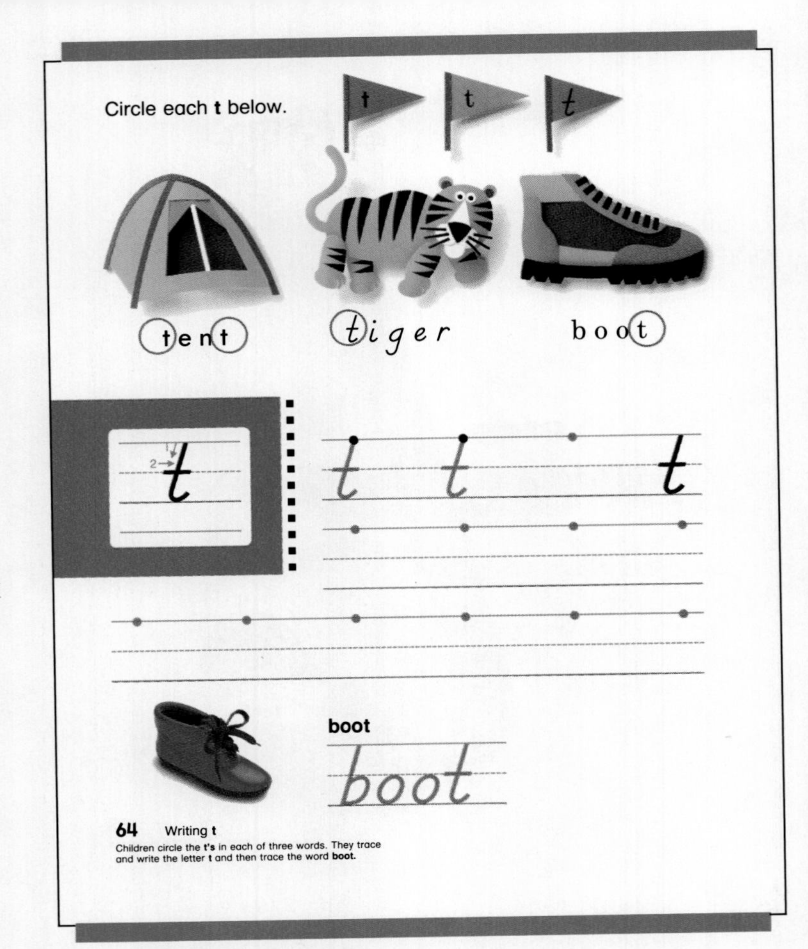

Children circle the **t's** in each of three words. They trace and write the letter **t** and then trace the word **boot.**

Letter Description

Top start; slant down, and a monkey tail. Cross.

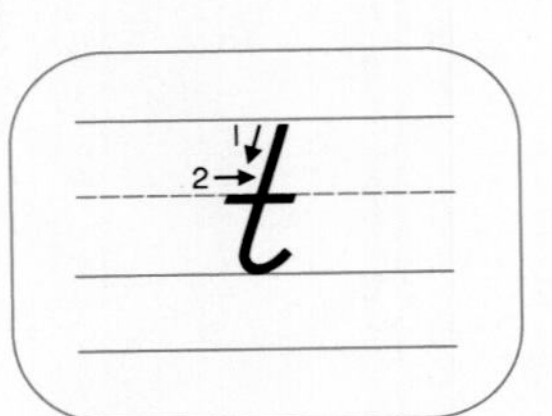

ACTIVITY BANK

Moving Write Along

A Pennant for t (Fine Motor, Letter Practice) Give each child a piece of paper shaped like a pennant and three white triangular shapes that will fit into the pennant. Have children color the triangles then paste them onto the pennant. Ask them to write a **t** on their pennants. Help them tape an ice-cream stick to the back. They can wave their pennants, chanting cheers for **t**.

Tracking Down t (Letter Practice, Print Awareness) Have children write the letter **t** at the top of a piece of heavy paper. Have them cut out examples of **t's** in words found in magazines and paste these onto their papers.

Parents Lend a Hand (Letter Practice, Fine Motor) Parents and guardians should be involved in the education of their children, so I send them a copy of the D'Nealian alphabet. I tell them that the tracer letters are like a railroad track, and the child's pencil is the train. The child must try to keep the train on the track while tracing each letter.

Elizabeth Luck
South Primary School
Disputanta, VA

Objectives

Learns the shape of **h** by finger tracing a large model letter.
Writes the lower-case letter **h** and traces a word with **h**.

Prepare

Have a "Hat Parade." First, read books about hats with the children, such as *The 500 Hats of Bartholomew Cubbins* and *Hats, Hats, Hats*, to get ideas. Have children describe the kind of hat they would wear in the hat parade. If there is time, let them create these hats. Then have them parade around the room wearing their real or imaginary hats. Finally, ask each child to describe the hat (real or imaginary) a friend is wearing.

Use the *D'Nealian® Handwriting Big Book* to preview the page.

Teach (page 65)

Have children:
- identify the lower-case letter **h**;
- find the horse at the starting arrow;
- finger trace the path from the horse to its hat while you say the following mnemonic sentence:
  The horse goes over the hill for its hat.
- air trace the letter **h**.

ACTIVITY BANK

Time to Grow 

h Is for Hat (Letter Practice, Fine Motor) Help children make hats out of newspapers. Have markers, feathers, glitter, and ribbon available at the writing center. Ask children to decorate their hats and to write a big **h** on the front.

An h Cityscape (Phonics, Letter Practice) Put large squares of paper on a bulletin board. Draw a large, curving shape to represent a city sidewalk. Help children think of words beginning with **h** to put in this city (*houses, hotel*). Ask children to draw or cut out these images, label them with an **h**, and paste them in the city.

Phonics Corner

The sentence used to help children form the letter **h**,

The **horse** goes over the **hill** for its **hat**.

may also be used to work on sound-letter correspondence. Repeat the sentence and call on volunteers to tell you the words they hear that begin with /h/.

Teach (page 66)

Call attention to the picture at the top of the page. Have children:

- describe the hats they see in the picture;
- trace the letter **h** in the feathered hat;
- color the picture.

Call attention to the lower half of the page. Have children:

- finger trace the boxed letter **h** as you read aloud the letter description;
- pencil trace the gray letters;
- write the letter **h** using the starting dots;
- trace the word *hat.*

Follow Up

Self-Evaluation Have children check their own work by asking themselves:

- Do my **h's** stretch to the top line?
- Do my **h's** slant the same way?

Additional Resources

Manuscript Alpha Touch letter **h**
D'Nealian® Handwriting Big Book letter **h**

Trace the **h.** Color the picture.

h h h h

hat

hat

66 Writing **h**

Children trace the **h** in the hat and then color the picture. They trace and write the letter **h** and then trace the word **hat.**

Letter Description

Top start; slant down; up over the hill, and a monkey tail.

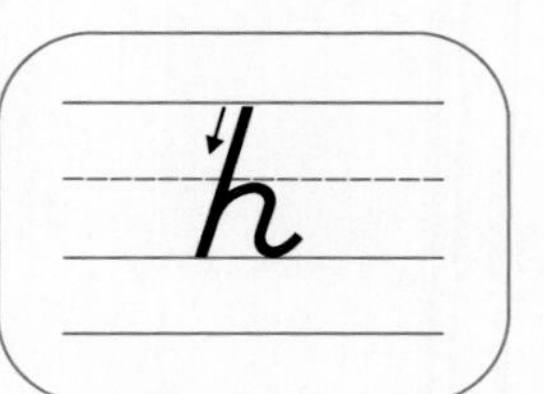

ACTIVITY BANK

Moving Write Along

Hat Day (Celebrating Cultural Diversity) Ask children to bring in a hat they really like. You should also bring in a few hats of your own, preferably from other countries. Discuss what the hats are used for and talk about the people around the world who wear them.

Pulling Letters from a Hat (Letter Recognition, Letter Practice) Distribute scraps of paper to each child. Have them write either **a, d, o, g, c, e, s, f, b, l, t,** or **h** on the paper. Put the papers in an unusual hat. Have one child at a time pick a letter from the hat, write the letter on the chalkboard, and call on another child in the class to identify it.

Monkey Tales (Fine Motor, Letter Practice) Students may forget to put the tails on their letters. A catchy way to remind them is to tell them they mustn't pull the tail off the monkey **h** because if they do, the monkey can't swing around the room. This helps them remember. A stuffed monkey and books about Curious George also help bring the point home.

Penny Huempfner
Cadott Elementary
Cadott, WI

Objectives

Learns the shape of **k** by finger tracing a large model letter.
Writes the lower-case letter **k** and traces a word with **k.**

Prepare

Play "The King Finds the **k**" with the children. Distribute pencils and 8 1/2" x 11" unlined paper. Designate one child as "the king." This child will hunt for the letter **k.** Ask all the other children in the class to write any letter of the alphabet they have learned so far (**a, d, o, g, c, e, s, f, b, l, t)** or any letter they feel comfortable writing on paper. You will write the letter **k.** Next, while the king's eyes are closed, everyone places his or her letter on the floor (in rows or in a large circle facing inward). The king must then find and pick up the **k** for all to see.

The game can continue with children writing different letters for a new king.

Use the *D'Nealian® Handwriting Big Book* to preview the page.

Teach (page 67)

Have children:
- identify the lower-case letter **k;**
- find the king at the starting arrow;
- finger trace the path from the king to the key while you say the following mnemonic sentence:
  The king is off to find the kitchen key.
- air trace the letter **k.**

ACTIVITY BANK

Time to Grow 

Kindergarten Kingdom (Letter Practice, Fine Motor) Duplicate a crown outline on paper, making it long enough to fit a child's head. At the writing center, have children write letter **k's** on their crowns, decorate them, cut them out, and paste the ends together. Have them crown one another.

Manipulating the Alphabet (Tactile, Fine Motor) I follow a color-coded process for letter writing. I make laminated alphabet cards with the first part of the letter in purple and the last part in green. Children apply clay over these for tactile learning.

Anne K. O'Brien
Valdez Elementary
Denver, CO

Phonics Corner

The sentence used to help children form the letter **k,**

The **king** is off to find the **kitchen key.**

may also be used to work on sound-letter correspondence. Repeat the sentence and call on volunteers to tell you the words they hear that begin with /k/.

Teach (page 68)

Call attention to the pictures at the top of the page. Have children:

- identify the letter **k** on each of the scrolls;
- identify the lock, key, and hook.
- listen as you read the words *lock, key,* and *hook.*
- circle each **k** in the three words.

Call attention to the lower half of the page. Have children:

- finger trace the boxed letter **k** as you read aloud the letter description;
- pencil trace the gray letters;
- write the letter **k** using the starting dots;
- trace the word *hook.*

Follow Up

Self-Evaluation Have children check their own work by asking themselves:

- Do my **k's** touch the top line?
- Do my **k's** have nice little tummies?

Additional Resources

Manuscript Alpha Touch letter **k**
D'Nealian® Handwriting Big Book letter **k**

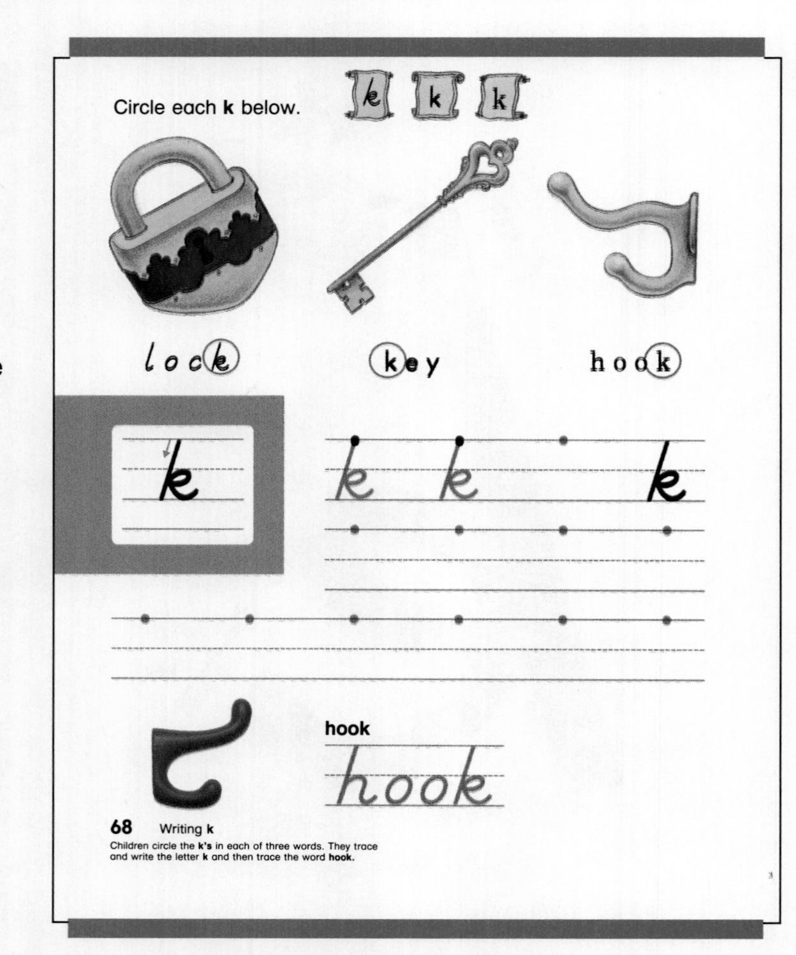

Letter Description

Top start; slant down, up into a little tummy, and a monkey tail.

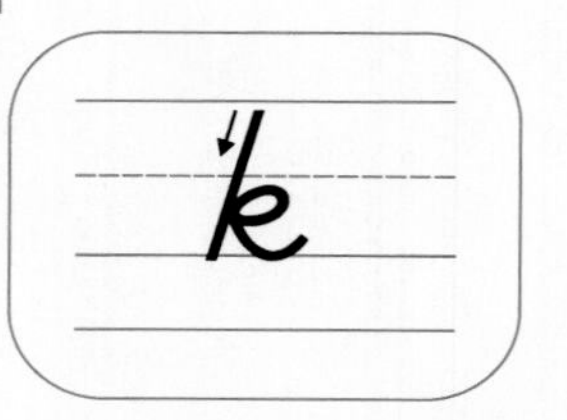

ACTIVITY BANK

Moving Write Along

Gel Bag Letters (Letter Practice, Tactile) When we study the sound of a letter, we also practice writing it. We like to write the letter on our "gel bags" (a zip-lock bag filled with colorful hair-styling gel). We use an index finger to write the letter on the bag, then we read the impression. Shake the bag to erase.

Ann Godorhazy
Asbury Elementary
Columbus, OH

Matching Shapes (Critical Thinking, Visual) Trace the shapes of some common objects, such as a key, a lock, a spoon, a watch, and so forth, on posterboard. Place the real objects in a sturdy bag. Have each child pull an object from the bag and match it to the shape.

Looking for k (Print Awareness, Letter Recognition) Give each child a page from a newspaper or magazine. Write the lower-case letter **k** at the top of the page using D'Nealian® Handwriting. Have children circle every **k** they can find on the page.

Practice

f f f

b b b

l l l

flag

flag

ball

ball

Practice 69

Children trace and write the letters f, b, and l and then trace the words **flag** and **ball**.

Objectives

Practices writing the lower-case letters **f, b,** and **l.** Traces the words *flag* and *ball.*

Prepare

Play variations of "Toss the Beanbag" with children using the letters **f, b,** and **l.** Secure masking tape on the floor in the shape of a tick-tack-toe grid or draw one with chalk. Put each of the letters in the spaces as shown below.

b	f	l
f	l	b
l	b	f

- Children throw the beanbags and identify the letters upon which they land.
- Children request a certain letter, and the thrower tries to land on that letter.

Teach (page 69)

Have children:
- identify the lower-case letters **f, b,** and **l;**
- pencil trace the gray letters;
- write each letter using the starting dots;
- trace the words *flag* and *ball.*

Follow Up

Self-Evaluation Have children check their own work by asking themselves:
- Did I start each letter at the starting dot?
- Do my **f's, b's,** and **l's** stretch to the top line?

Additional Resources

Manuscript Alpha Touch letters **f, b,** and **l**
D'Nealian® Handwriting Big Book letters **f, b,** and **l**

ACTIVITY BANK

Flag Day (Creative, Fine Motor) Ask children to identify the flag on page 69. Talk about how countries, cities, teams, and other groups have flags to represent them. Have children draw flags representing their family, school, or town. Have a parade.

Pick a Partner (Letter Recognition, Visual) Make two sets of cards—one marked in red and one in blue—with all the letters learned thus far on them. Distribute the cards and have children with red letters locate the children who have the matching blue letters.

Let Your Hands Do the Talking (Visual, Gifted) Extend the alphabet into a new language—sign language. As each letter is introduced, show children how it is signed. After reviewing all the letters learned, have volunteers sign a letter for the class to recognize and write.

You may wish to begin an ongoing "Sign Language Booklet" for the class to display in the classroom or in the school library.

Cheryl Stelter
Charleston Elementary
West Charleston, VT

Objectives
Practices writing the lower-case letters **t, h,** and **k.** Traces the words *basket* and *chalk.*

Prepare
Have children play "Alphabet Lotto" in groups of three, using the letters **f, b, l, t, h,** and **k.** Use index cards on which you or the children have written each of the target letters. Each letter should be written on two separate cards. Each group:
- shuffles the cards, places two of them face up, and deals the rest;
- takes turns matching one of the upturned cards to one in their hands or placing a card face up on the table;

The player with the most pairs at the end of the game wins.

If you have saved the lotto cards children made for the letters **a, d, o, g, c, e,** and **s,** you may want to mix these in and have them play the game using all the letters learned so far.

Teach (page 70)
Have children:
- identify the lower-case letters **t, h,** and **k;**
- pencil trace the gray letters;
- write each letter using the starting dots;
- trace the words *basket* and *chalk.*

Follow Up
Self-Evaluation Have children check their own work by asking themselves:
- Do all my letters slant the same way?
- Do my **t's, h's,** and **k's** stretch to the top line?

Additional Resources
Manuscript Alpha Touch letters **t, h,** and **k**
D'Nealian® Handwriting Big Book letters **t, h,** and **k**

ACTIVITY BANK

Special Needs (Kinesthetic Deficits) Children with a fine-motor deficit profit from multi-mode activities. Play "King's Tiger Hunt." The "king" wears a crown with a **k** on the front. Others sit in a circle wearing tiger-ear headbands with **f, b, l, t,** and **h** on the front. A "drum beater" beats as the king stalks around the circle.

When the beat stops, the king taps a shoulder to capture the nearest tiger. The king names and finger traces the tiger's letter, then crowns the tiger the new king. The game continues in this way.

Me and My Shadow (Letter Practice, Science) Tape together three or four lengths of shelf paper and place the paper on the floor. Have children take turns lying full-length on the paper while a classmate traces around them. Children label their body parts as follows:

h for head, hands, and hips
f for feet, fingers, and face
b for body
t for toes

Help children draw lines from these body parts to the margins of the paper. Ask them to write each corresponding letter at the end of a line. When they have done this, they may embellish their self-portraits.

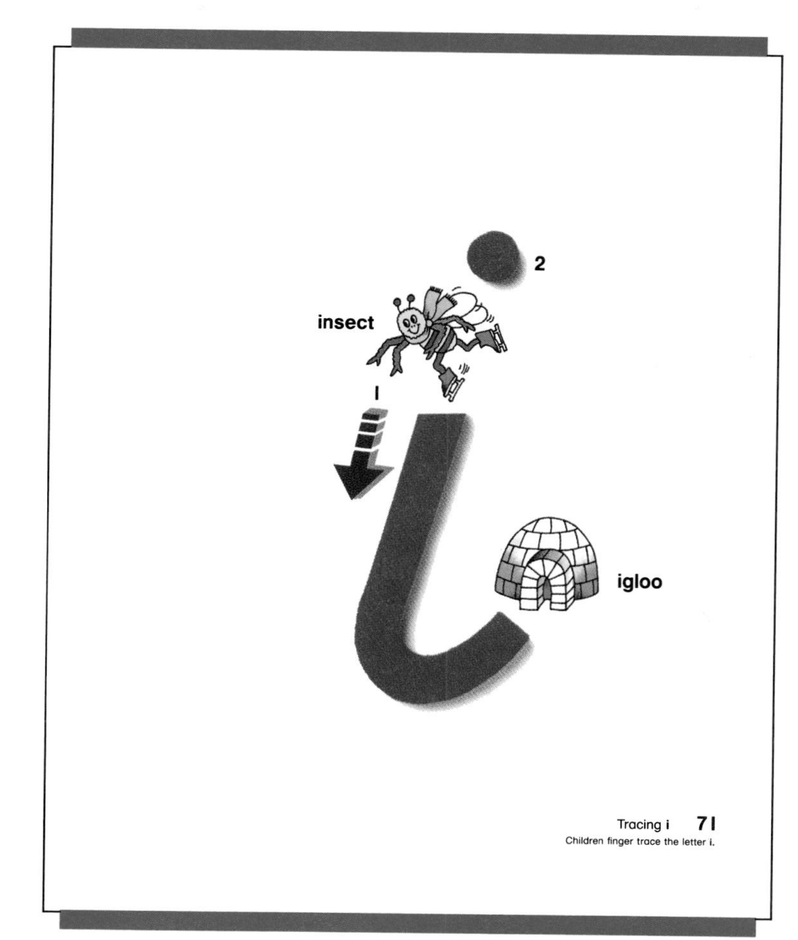

Objectives

Learns the shape of **i** by finger tracing a large model letter.
Writes the lower-case letter **i** and traces a word with **i.**

Prepare

Display a large photograph or drawing of an insect for the class. Point out that insects are divided into three parts: (head, thorax, abdomen) and that they have six legs and a pair of wings. Show pictures of flies, mosquitoes, butterflies, and bees as examples of insects. Draw the outline of an insect on the chalkboard without wings and with only three legs. Have children:

- identify what is missing;
- come to the board to draw in the wings;
- come to the board to draw in the missing legs;
- count together to be sure all the legs are there.

Repeat this activity, leaving off one wing and five legs, and so on. Then invite children to fly around the room like insects.

Use the *D'Nealian® Handwriting Big Book* to preview the page.

Teach (page 71)

Have children:

- identify the lower-case letter **i;**
- identify the insect at the starting arrow (allow children to comment on the difference between this fanciful insect and a real one);
- finger trace the path from the insect to the igloo then up to the dot while you say the following mnemonic sentence:

  The insect skates down to the igloo.
  Then it flies up to the dot.
- air trace the letter **i.**

ACTIVITY BANK

Time to Grow

Insect i (Letter Practice, Fine Motor) At the writing center, give each child three circles of paper. Children write lower-case **i** on each. They color the back of each circle yellow, blue, or orange, and glue these, colored-side up, to construction paper. Children add pipe cleaners for antennae and write another **i** below the insect.

The Sweet Smell of Letters (Letter Recognition, Tactile) Have children use scratch-and-sniff letters at home. Write a letter on an index card. Cover the letter with paste. Sprinkle flavored gelatin on it. When dry, it smells delightful as children run their fingers over it.

Cindy Renzelman
Graymont Elementary School
Graymont, IL

Phonics Corner

The sentence used to help children form the letter **i,**

The **insect** skates down to the **igloo.** Then **it** flies up to the dot.

may also be used to work on sound-letter correspondence. Repeat the sentence and call on volunteers to tell you the words they hear that begin with /i/.

Teach (page 72)

Call attention to the pictures at the top of the page. Have children:

- identify the images;
- listen as you read the words *igloo, skates,* and *insect;*
- circle the words that begin with **i.**

Call attention to the lower half of the page. Have children:

- finger trace the boxed letter **i** as you read aloud the letter description;
- pencil trace the gray letters;
- write the letter **i** using the starting dots;
- trace the word *igloo.*

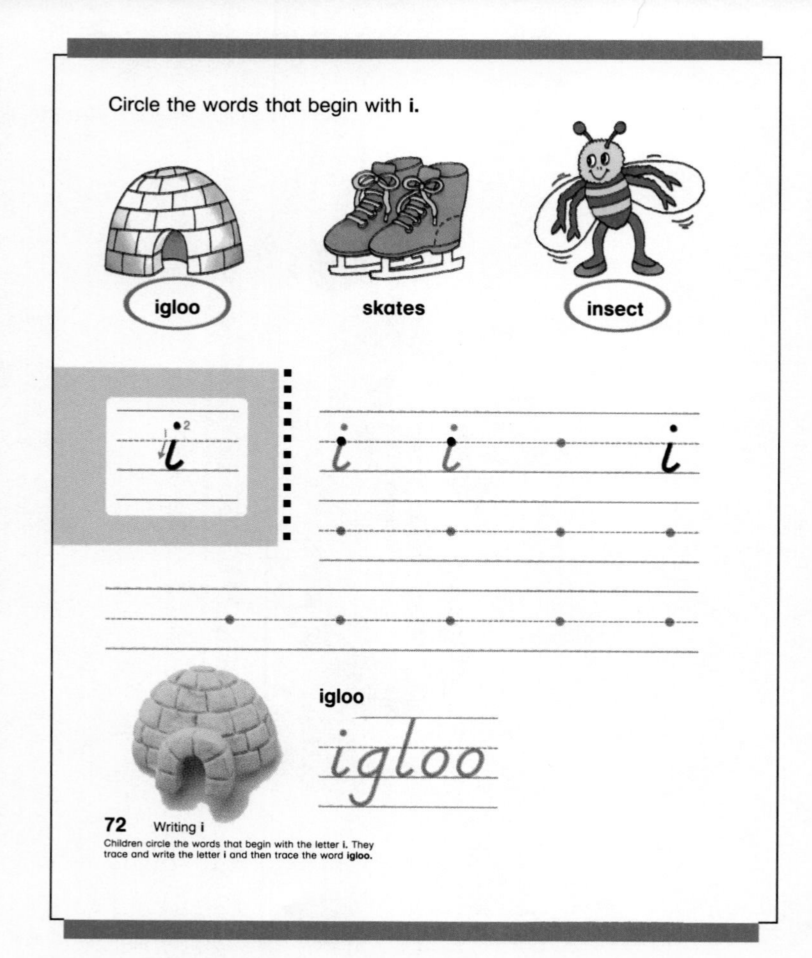

Circle the words that begin with **i.**

igloo skates insect

igloo

igloo

72 Writing i

Children circle the words that begin with the letter i. They trace and write the letter i and then trace the word **igloo.**

Follow Up

Self-Evaluation Have children check their own work by asking themselves:

- Do my **i's** have their monkey tails?
- Did I dot my **i's?**

Additional Resources

Manuscript Alpha Touch letter **i**
D'Nealian® Handwriting Big Book letter **i**

Letter Description

Middle start; slant down, and a monkey tail. Add a dot.

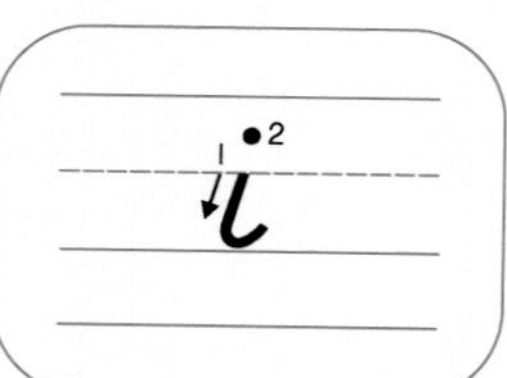

ACTIVITY BANK

Moving Write Along

i Domiciles (Letter Recognition, Social Studies) Write the word *igloo* on the chalkboard. Say the word and ask a volunteer to tell what an igloo is. Call on someone to come up and circle the **i.** Write the word *cabin* on the board and have someone define it. Ask a volunteer to circle the **i** in *cabin.* Write *wickiup* on the board, define it, and show a picture. Have a volunteer circle the **i's** in *wickiup.*

You Bug Me (Creative, Fine Motor) Provide paper bags, colored paper, yarn, and assorted materials for making insect costumes. Assist children in cutting the bag to allow for proper fit, sight, and ventilation.

Alphabet Artists (Gross Motor, Letter Practice) I have children dip clean paintbrushes in water and write large letters on the chalkboard. We do this one, two, or three people at a time. We do lower-case letters first, then capital letters, and finally all the letters.

Janice McCauley
Slate Run School
New Albany, IN

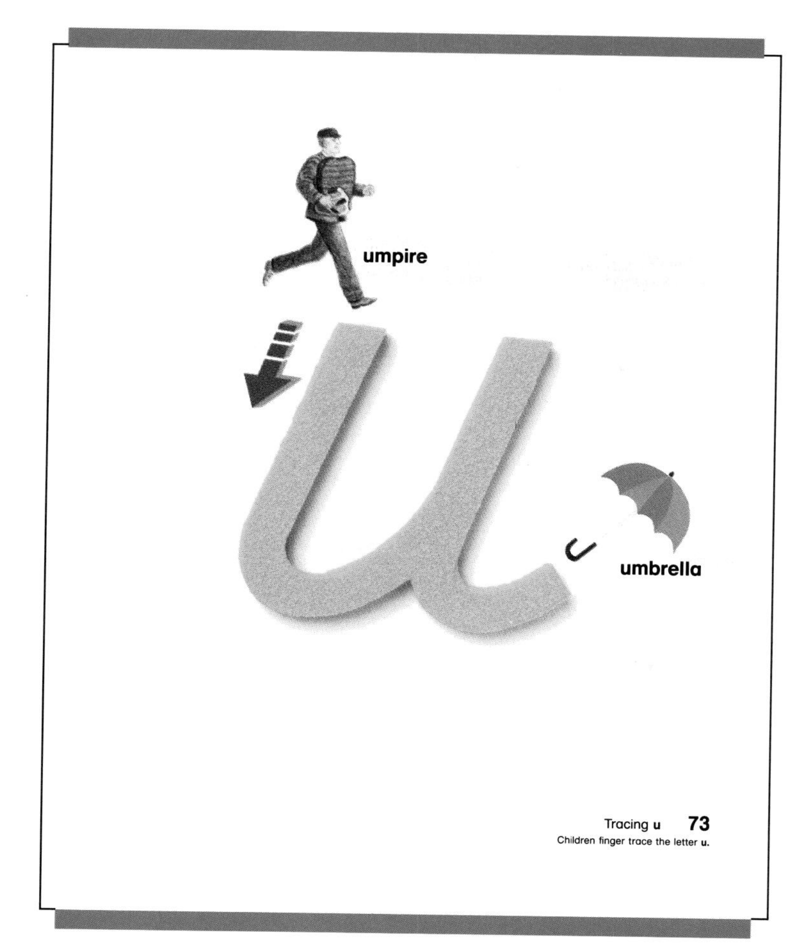

Objectives

Learns the shape of **u** by finger tracing a large model letter.
Writes the lower-case letter **u** and traces a word with **u**.

Prepare

Pass out imaginary umbrellas to the children. Tell them you will be going for a walk in the rain. Mime for them the way to open their umbrellas and hold them over their heads to shield against the rain. If possible, walk outdoors or into the halls with your imaginary umbrellas. Have children:

- describe the sound of the rain as it hits their umbrellas;
- tell what it feels like to step in a puddle;
- sing rainy day songs, such as "Rain, Rain Go Away."

You may want to recite for them Robert Louis Stevenson's poem "Rain," which reads:

The rain is raining all around,
It falls on field and tree,
It rains on the umbrellas here,
And on the ships at sea.

Use the *D'Nealian® Handwriting Big Book* to preview the page.

Teach (page 73)

Have children:

- identify the lower-case letter **u;**
- find the umpire at the starting arrow;
- finger trace the path from the umpire to the umbrella while you say the following mnemonic sentence:

  The umpire runs to get under his umbrella.
- air trace the letter **u.**

ACTIVITY BANK

Time to Grow 

Here's to u (Creative, Fine Motor) As a transitional step, children should write lower-case **u** on large pieces of unlined paper at the writing center. Have them turn their **u's** into a person or animal.

Alphabet Soup (Letter Recognition, Kinesthetic) Prepare three sets of cards for each letter, plus one "Alphabet Soup" card containing all the letters. Children sit in a circle. Give each child a card, being sure two are duplicates. Hold up a card. The two children with the same letter must exchange seats, saying the letter's name, before you sit in one of their chairs. The person without a chair now holds the letter. If the Alphabet Soup card is held up, everyone scurries to a new seat.

Phonics Corner

The sentence used to help children form the letter **u,**

The **umpire** runs to get **under** his **umbrella.**

may also be used to work on sound-letter correspondence. Repeat the sentence and call on volunteers to tell you the words they hear that begin with /u/.

Teach (page 74)

Call attention to the picture at the top of the page. Have children:

- describe the scene;
- find and circle each hidden **u**.

Call attention to the lower half of the page. Have children:

- finger trace the boxed letter **u** as you read aloud the letter description;
- pencil trace the gray letters;
- write the letter **u** using the starting dots;
- trace the word *bus.*

Follow Up

Self-Evaluation Have children check their own work by asking themselves:

- Do my **u's** slant the same way?
- Do my **u's** have their monkey tails?

Additional Resources

Manuscript Alpha Touch letter **u**
D'Nealian® Handwriting Big Book letter **u**

Letter Description

Middle start; down, around, up, down, and a monkey tail.

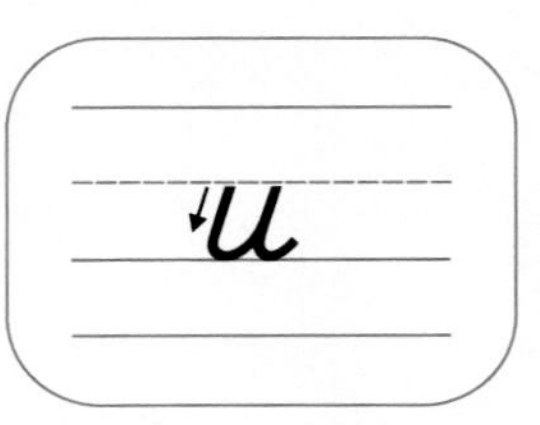

ACTIVITY BANK

Moving Write Along

Thumbprint Ball Game (Letter Practice, Fine Motor) Have children make thumbprint baseball players. Using ink pads, children make thumbprints on a square piece of paper where the catcher, first baseman, second baseman, and third baseman would stand. Children should top each thumbprint with a **u** to represent a baseball cap. Children may want to draw features on the thumbprint players also.

Primary Poets (Letter Practice, Rhymes) My students love poems! I have them help write a poem by filling in a letter in the last rhyming word in each line. Write the following on the chalkboard, for example:

Baseball

I leap off the bench and stand
at the p_ate.
The coaches warn me, ''Don't
swing _ate.''
I swing three times. "Strike!"
cries the _mp.
I crawl to the bench and
sit in a s _ump.

Below this write a word box with the rhyming words in it:

plate late ump slump

Read the poem to the children and then have them supply the last word as you read it again.

Amy Wolf
J. W. Reason School
Hilliard, OH

Objectives

Learns the shape of **w** by finger tracing a large model letter.
Writes the lower-case letter **w** and traces a word with **w.**

Prepare

Read Leo Lionni's book *The Alphabet Tree* to the children. Pay particular attention to the word-bug's advice: "I can teach you to make words. If you get together in threes and fours and even more, no wind will be strong enough to blow you away."

Give each child a blank card and tell them that without letters on the card, the wind will blow them away. Pretend to be the wind blowing the children around the classroom. Next, have them write a letter they have learned on the card as neatly as can be. Have them hold up their cards. Choose three or four children whose letters make a word. Let them stand before the class fortified against the wind with their letters. Let their classmates pretend to be the wind blowing, while the letter-holders stand fast with their letters held high. Help children read the word the letters spell.

Use the *D'Nealian® Handwriting Big Book* to preview the page.

Teach (page 75)

Have children:

- identify the lower-case letter **w;**
- find the wind at the starting arrow;
- finger trace the path from the wind to the web while you say the following mnemonic sentence:
  The wind blows the spider into its waiting web.
- air trace the letter **w.**

ACTIVITY BANK

Time to Grow 

The w Wiggle (Letter Practice, Kinesthetic) Play music with a variety of rhythms. Say action words beginning with **w,** such as *wave, walk, wiggle, wink,* and *weave.* Ask children to act out the words. Finally, have children walk, weave, or wiggle to the writing center to write wonderful **w's** on large, unlined paper.

Letter Boxes (Phonics, Letter Recognition) Label four boxes with the letters **w, h, l,** and **t.** Collect small objects and pictures of objects whose names begin with these letter sounds. Have children sort the items and put them into the corresponding boxes.

Phonics Corner

The sentence used to help children form the letter **w,**

The **wind** blows the spider into its **waiting web.**

may also be used to work on sound-letter correspondence. Repeat the sentence and call on volunteers to tell you the words they hear that begin with /w/.

■ Teach (page 76)

Call attention to the picture at the top of the page. Have children:
- describe what they see in the picture;
- trace each of the **w's** in the web;
- color the picture.

Call attention to the lower half of the page. Have children:
- finger trace the boxed letter **w** as you read aloud the letter description;
- pencil trace the gray letters;
- write the letter **w** using the starting dots;
- trace the word *web.*

■ Follow Up

Self-Evaluation Have children check their own work by asking themselves:
- Do my **w's** slant the same way?
- Do my **w's** sit on the bottom line?

■ Additional Resources

Manuscript Alpha Touch letter **w**
D'Nealian® Handwriting Big Book letter **w**

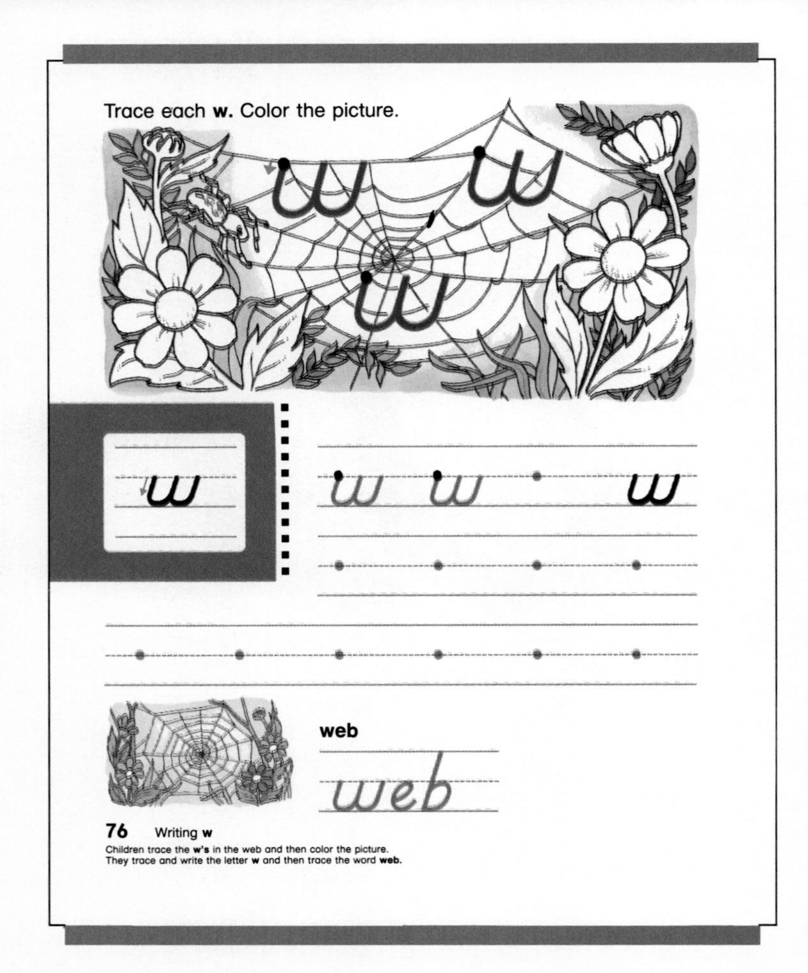
Trace each **w.** Color the picture.

web

76 Writing **w**

Children trace the **w's** in the web and then color the picture. They trace and write the letter **w** and then trace the word **web.**

■ Letter Description

Middle start; down, around, up, and down, around, up again.

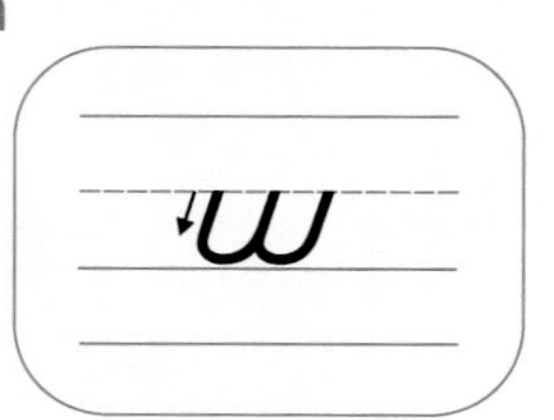

ACTIVITY BANK

Moving Write Along

Write and Draw (Letter Practice, Gifted) Prepare a worksheet with three rows containing four sections, the first three containing write-on lines, the last large enough to draw in. Write the word *web* on the board and say it aloud. Have children write each of the letters in *web* in the first three sections. Then have them draw a web in the last section. Continue with the words *owl* and *cow.*

Stencil Letters (Fine Motor, Small Groups) I make large D'Nealian stencils about 3/4" wide, so the children have room to trace inside the lines. We trace in small groups. The children choose their own colors and trace each letter several times. They enjoy it.

Teri Ingram
Shaner Elementary
Topeka, KS

The Spider's Web (Letter Recognition, Fine Motor) Make several worksheets using four letters in four rows. For example:

w x m p w
w w w w w
x m x p w
w x m p w

Tell children to look across and down to find and circle columns that contain all **w's.**

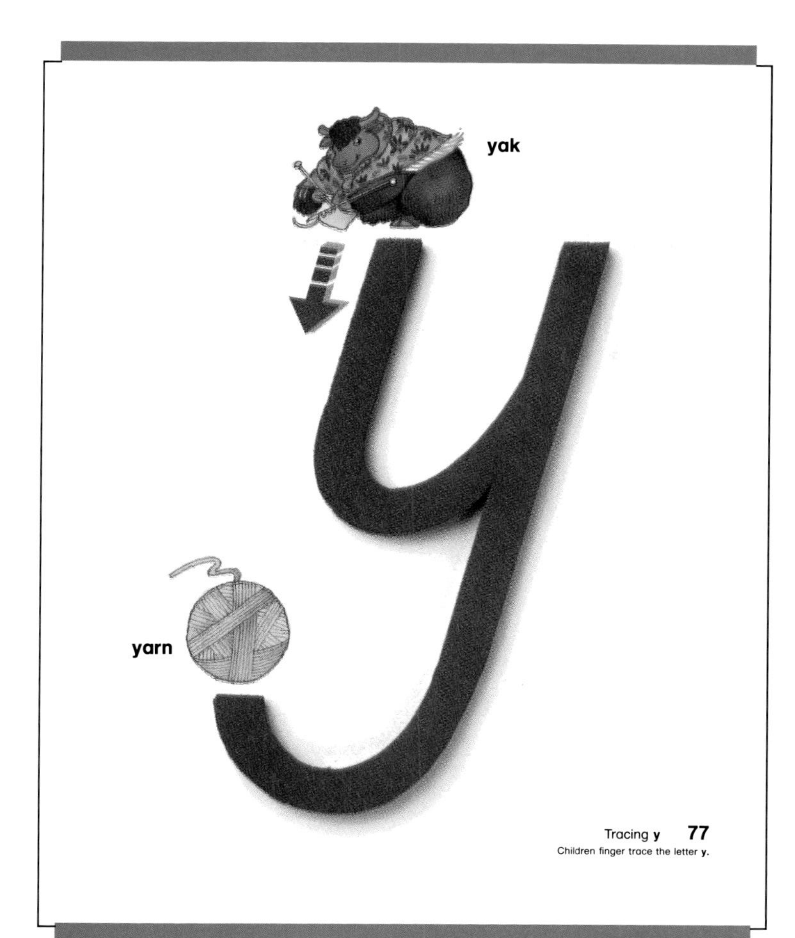

Objectives

Learns the shape of **y** by finger tracing a large model letter.
Writes the lower-case letter **y** and traces a word with **y.**

Prepare

Place a number of items in a covered basket or a shopping bag, including such things as a ball of yarn, a scarf, a tennis ball, and a comb. One by one, have children:

- reach into the bag and identify an object by touch;
- pull out the object and identify it;
- tell how the object might be used.

Use the *D'Nealian® Handwriting Big Book* to preview the page.

Teach (page 77)

Have children:

- identify the lower-case letter **y;**
- find the yak at the starting arrow;
- finger trace the path from the yak to the yarn while you say the following mnemonic sentence:
  Yes, you can help the yak find more yarn.
- air trace the letter **y.**

ACTIVITY BANK

Time to Grow

Writing y (Fine Motor, Letter Practice) As a transitional step, have children write lower-case **y** on unlined paper at the writing center. Have materials available for them to decorate their **y's.**

Sew and Sew (Eye-Hand Coordination, Tactile) Cut several large sewing cards from oaktag. Write the letter **y** on each card. Punch about 23 holes on cards to form the outline of the letter. Place a green dot around the first hole and a red dot around the last hole, indicating where to start and stop. Tie a knot in one end of a long piece of yarn and let children "sew" the **y's.**

Phonics Corner

The sentence used to help children form the letter **y,**

Yes, you can help the **yak** find more **yarn.**

may also be used to work on sound-letter correspondence. Repeat the sentence and call on volunteers to tell you the words they hear that begin with /y/.

Teach (page 78)

Call attention to the picture at the top of the page. Have children:

- identify the yak and the yarn;
- identify the letters **y, b,** and **g;**
- find each ball of yarn marked **y** and color it yellow;

Call attention to the lower half of the page. Have children:

- finger trace the boxed letter **y** as you read aloud the letter description;
- pencil trace the gray letters;
- write the letter **y** using the starting dots;
- trace the word *yak.*

Follow Up

Self-Evaluation Have children check their own work by asking themselves:

- Did I start at the starting dots?
- Do my **y's** have their fishhooks?

Additional Resources

Manuscript Alpha Touch letter **y**
D'Nealian® Handwriting Big Book letter **y**

Letter Description

Middle start; down, around, up, down under water, and a fishhook.

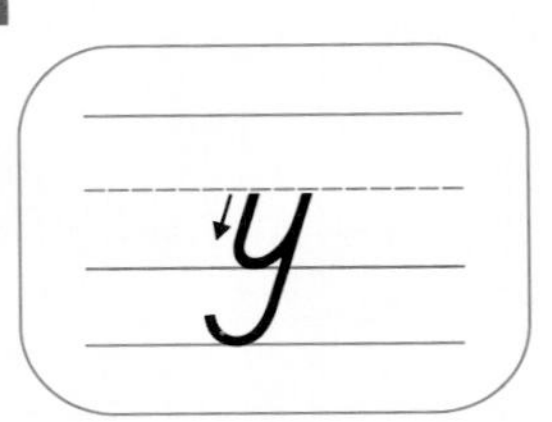

ACTIVITY BANK

Moving Write Along

Hidden Letters (Critical Thinking, Gross Motor) Draw simple pictures that contain the shape of the letter **y** on the chalkboard. Children come to the board and use colored chalk to trace the letter in the drawing. If children seem

able, invite them to draw a hidden **y** in a picture on the board for others to find.

Marly Glaw
Shreiner School and Academy
Marietta, GA

Color the Yarn (Fine Motor, Letter Recognition) Have children look again at the yarn they colored yellow for the yak on page 78. Ask them to read the letters on the remaining yarn. Have them guess what colors the letters **b** and **g** might stand for. Ask them to color the yarn using these colors.

Grid Writing (Letter Practice, Fine Motor) Cut several large squares from a piece of posterboard. Draw two vertical and two horizontal lines on each to form a tick-tack-toe grid. Laminate each board. Write a letter **y** with a directional arrow in the first space and a shaded letter **y** in the second space. Have children trace the letter and then practice writing seven additional **y's** in the remaining spaces. Clean and reuse the boards.

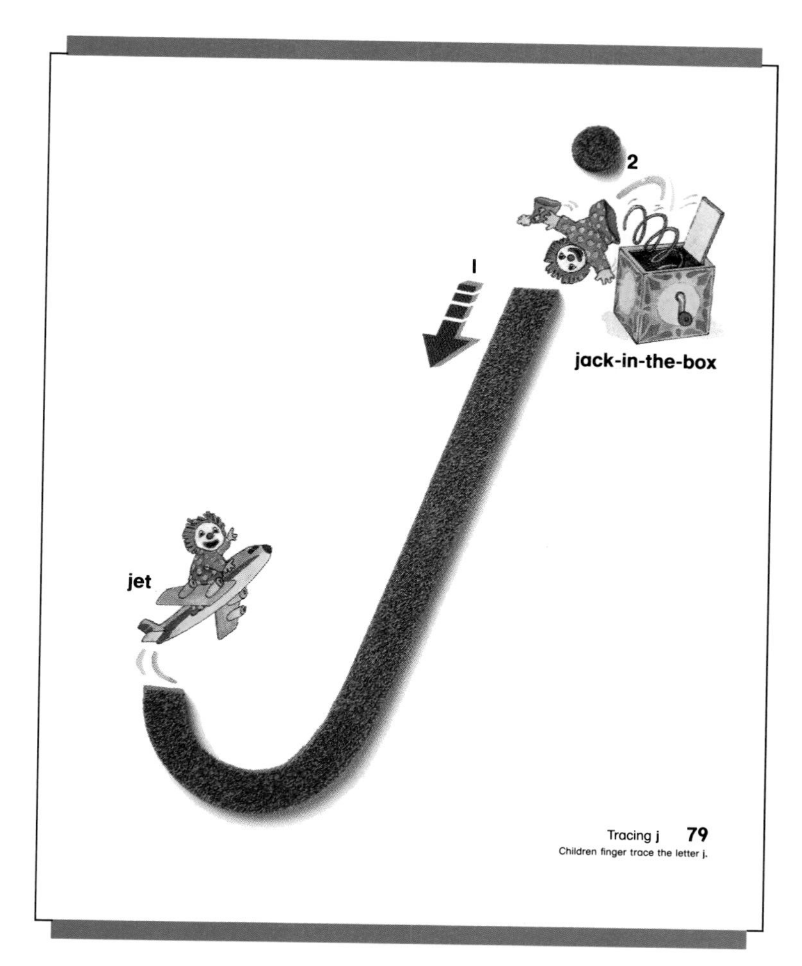

Objectives

Learns the shape of **j** by finger tracing a large model letter.
Writes the lower-case letter **j** and traces a word with **j.**

Prepare

Tell the children that they are going to pretend to be jack-in-the-boxes. Play lively music. When the music stops the children will spring up like the jack jumping up from the box. Have children:

- do a few jumping jacks to get into the mood;
- crouch down and sit on their haunches;
- listen for the music to stop;
- jump up high when the music stops.

Use the *D'Nealian® Handwriting Big Book* to preview the page.

Teach (page 79)

Have children:

- identify the lower-case letter **j;**
- find the jack-in-the-box at the starting arrow;
- finger trace the path from the jack to the jet then up to the dot while you say the following mnemonic sentence:

  The jack-in-the-box jumps down to the jet.
  Then he flies off to the dot.
- air trace the letter **j.**

ACTIVITY BANK

Time to Grow

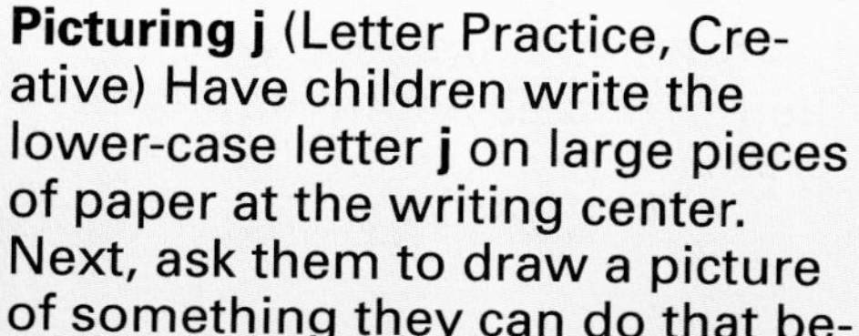

Picturing j (Letter Practice, Creative) Have children write the lower-case letter **j** on large pieces of paper at the writing center. Next, ask them to draw a picture of something they can do that begins with the letter **j.** (*Possibilities include jump, jog, and jiggle.*) Ask them to write **j** below the picture.

Jump for j (Kinesthetic, Auditory) Have children stand. Tell them to listen carefully as you read a list of words. Explain that each time they hear /j/, they should jump. Use words such as *job, chair, draw, jeep, tip, jeans, jet, goat, chest, joke, shell, chimp,* and *jacket.*

Phonics Corner

The sentence used to help children form the letter **j,**

The **jack-in-the-box jumps** down to the **jet.** Then he flies off to the dot.

may also be used to work on sound-letter correspondence. Repeat the sentence and call on volunteers to tell you the words they hear that begin with /j/.

Teach (page 80)

Call attention to the picture at the top of the page. Have children:
- identify the jack-in-the-box, the jet, and the jump rope;
- trace the **j** on the box;
- color the picture.

Call attention to the lower half of the page. Have children:
- finger trace the boxed letter **j** as you read aloud the letter description;
- pencil trace the gray letters;
- write the letter **j** using the starting dots;
- trace the word *jet.*

Follow Up

Self-Evaluation Have children check their own work by asking themselves:
- Do my **j's** have their fishhooks?
- Did I dot my **j's?**

Additional Resources

Manuscript Alpha Touch letter **j**
D'Nealian® Handwriting Big Book letter **j**

Trace the **j.** Color the picture.

jet

80 Writing j

Children trace the j on the box and then color the picture. They trace and write the letter j and then trace the word **jet.**

Letter Description

Middle start; slant down under water, and a fishhook. Add a dot.

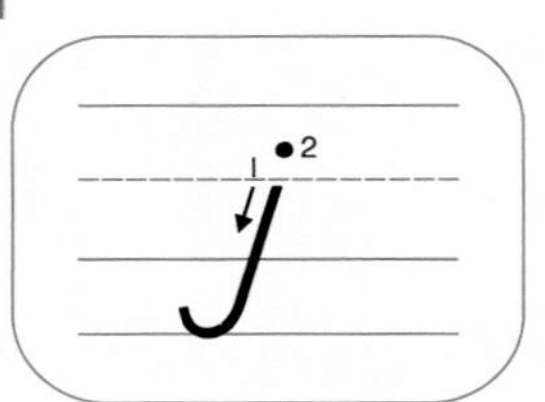

ACTIVITY BANK

Moving Write Along

Good Job! (Oral Language, Forms) Discuss the different kinds of jobs people have. You might suggest a judge or a jet pilot. Ask children to think of a job they perform at home, such as picking up their toys. Distribute job certificates with space for the child's name, the job to be performed, and an adult's signature. After children complete their jobs for a week, adults sign the certificates.

Go Fish (Letter Practice, Fine Motor) When teaching **g, j, y** and other fishhook letters, I explain that the fishing line must drop into the ocean (go under the baseline) and curve to the left to make a proper hook. Children then practice writing their letters as demonstrated.

Jane M. Iken
Koch Elementary
Milbank, SD

Jumping Jacks (Eye-Hand Coordination, Kinesthetic) Give each child a puppet and a box that is open on both ends. Play the song "Pop! Goes the Weasel." Children should have their puppets spring up from the box at the word *Pop.*

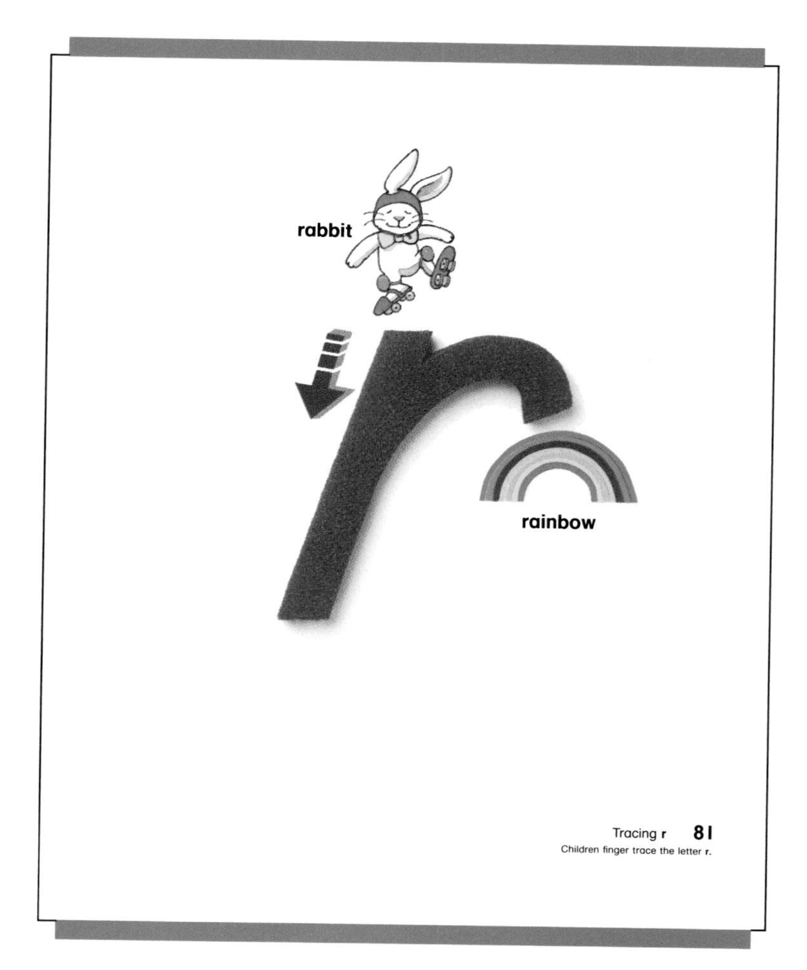
rabbit

rainbow

Tracing r 81

Children finger trace the letter r.

Objectives

Learns the shape of **r** by finger tracing a large model letter.
Writes the lower-case letter **r** and traces a word with **r.**

Prepare

On a tape recorder or record player let children listen to Ginni Clemmens's rendition of "Sing a Rainbow." The lyrics are written below. Give children cards that read: *red, yellow, pink, green, purple, orange,* or *blue* written in that color with an open square beneath each word. Have children color the square the color named on the card. As the song is sung and the colors are named, children holding the named colors should stand. Invite children to sing along.

Red and yellow and pink and green
Purple and orange and blue.
I can sing a rainbow, sing a rainbow,
sing a rainbow too.

Listen with your eyes, listen with your eyes,
And sing everything you see.
You can sing a rainbow, sing a rainbow.
Sing along with me.

Use the *D'Nealian® Handwriting Big Book* to preview the page.

Teach (page 81)

Have children:

- identify the lower-case letter **r;**
- find the rabbit at the starting arrow;
- finger trace the path from the rabbit to the rainbow while you say the following mnemonic sentence:
  A rabbit on roller skates races to the rainbow.
- air trace the letter **r.**

ACTIVITY BANK

Time to Grow

Rainbow r's (Letter Practice, Fine Motor) At the writing center, give children large pieces of paper shaped like a rainbow. Have them write letter **r** in different colors, curving them along the rainbow.

Rainbow Painting (Fine Motor, Creative) Supply brushes, black paint, and crayons. Ask children to use different crayons to color stripes across heavy paper. Have them paint their papers with black paint. Children then scrape a rainbow shape using a spoon and watch the colors peek through.

Pam Buffett
St. Athanasius School
Evanston, IL

Phonics Corner

The sentence used to help children form the letter **r,**

A **rabbit** on **roller** skates **races** to the **rainbow.**

may also be used to work on sound-letter correspondence. Repeat the sentence and call on volunteers to tell you the words they hear that begin with /r/.

Teach (page 82)

Call attention to the maze at the top of the page. Have children:
- identify the images on the page;
- identify the letters at the end of each path;
- finger trace the path from the rabbit to the **r**;
- draw a line from the rabbit to the **r**.

Call attention to the lower half of the page. Have children:
- finger trace the boxed letter **r** as you read aloud the letter description;
- pencil trace the gray letters;
- write the letter **r** using the starting dots;
- trace the word *rabbit*.

Follow Up

Self-Evaluation Have children check their own work by asking themselves:
- Did I start at the starting dots?
- Do my **r's** have a curved roof?

Additional Resources

Manuscript Alpha Touch letter **r**
D'Nealian® Handwriting Big Book letter **r**

Letter Description

Middle start; slant down, up, and a roof.

ACTIVITY BANK

Moving Write Along

Run, Run, Rabbit (Kinesthetic, Auditory) Play "Run, Run, Rabbit" with children. Whisper a different letter into each child's ear, and have the child write it on paper for you. Include all the letters learned thus far. Next ask children to sit in a large circle with a volunteer (the "rabbit") in the middle. The rabbit calls a letter and whoever was given that letter (a "hunter") must hold it up, call, *Run, run, rabbit!* and chase the rabbit around to the vacant spot in the circle. If no one has that letter, the rabbit calls a letter until someone does.

Letters, Letters Everywhere (Letter Practice, Fine Motor) Create copies of lower-case letter **r** on lightweight, white construction paper. Have children write this letter several times inside the large letter. When completed, have children cut out the letter and mount it on colored paper.

Marly Glaw
Shreiner School and Academy
Marietta, GA

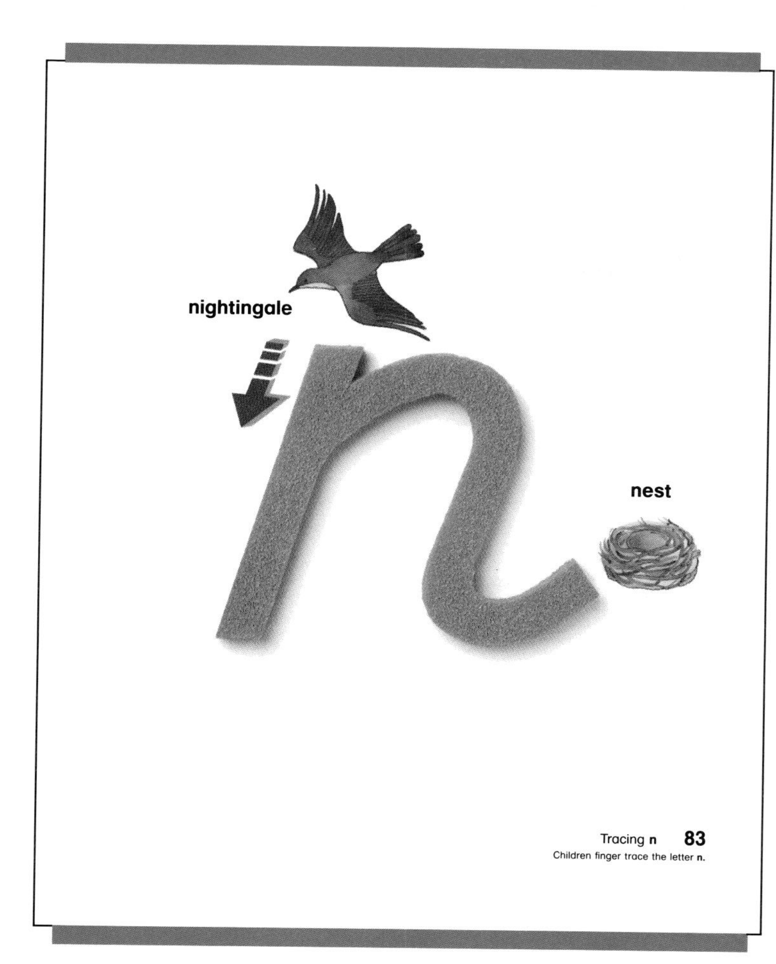

Objectives

Learns the shape of **n** by finger tracing a large model letter.
Writes the lower-case letter **n** and traces a word with **n**.

Prepare

Have children play "The Early Bird Catches the Worm." The object of the game is to be the first to recognize matching letters. Pass out laminated lower-case letter cards, one to each child, being sure that two children have matching cards. Write one of these letters on the chalkboard or place a large card containing the letter on the ledge. Children with matching letters should run up to the board and touch the letter. The first one to do so wins. Be sure to have both children identify the letters they hold.

Use the *D'Nealian® Handwriting Big Book* to preview the page.

Teach (page 83)

Have children:

- identify the lower-case letter **n;**
- find the nightingale at the starting arrow;
- finger trace the path from the nightingale to its nest while you say the following mnemonic sentence:
  Fly with the nightingale into its nest.
- air trace the letter **n.**

ACTIVITY BANK

Time to Grow

Nesting n (Fine Motor, Letter Practice) At the writing center, have children write **n** on unlined paper. Give them thin strips of paper in a variety of colors. Have them paste these strips together to form a nest. Next have them cut an egg shape around their **n's** and place these in the nest.

Answer with n (Phonics, Critical Thinking) Play "The **n** Game." Ask questions with answers that begin with the letter **n,** such as:
What is the opposite of day?
Where do birds lay their eggs?
What comes after eight?

Phonics Corner

The sentence used to help children form the letter **n,**

Fly with the **nightingale** into its **nest.**

may also be used to work on sound-letter correspondence. Repeat the sentence and call on volunteers to tell you the words they hear that begin with /n/.

Teach (page 84)

Call attention to the pictures at the top of the page. Have children:

- identify the images;
- listen as you read the words *nest, nut, moon,* and *tree;*
- circle the words that begin with **n**.

Call attention to the lower half of the page. Have children:

- finger trace the boxed letter **n** as you read aloud the letter description;
- pencil trace the gray letters;
- write the letter **n** using the starting dots;
- trace the word *nest.*

Follow Up

Self-Evaluation Have children check their own work by asking themselves:

- Do my **n's** slant the same way?
- Do my **n's** have their monkey tails?

Additional Resources

Manuscript Alpha Touch letter **n**
D'Nealian® Handwriting Big Book letter **n**

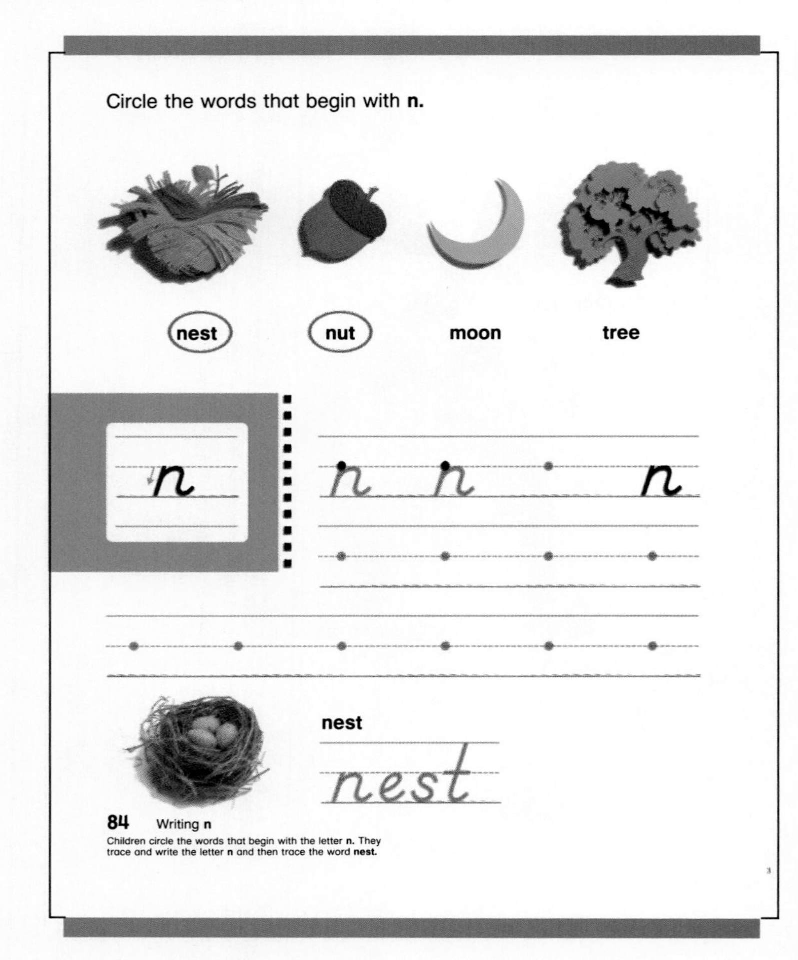
Circle the words that begin with **n**.

nest nut moon tree

nest

nest

84 Writing n

Children circle the words that begin with the letter **n**. They trace and write the letter **n** and then trace the word **nest**.

Letter Description

Middle start; slant down, up over the hill, and a monkey tail.

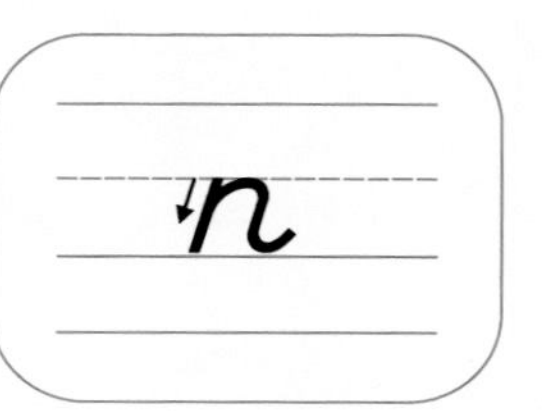

ACTIVITY BANK

Moving Write Along

Match-up (Critical Thinking, Small Groups) Draw five pairs of objects on separate index cards: a nut labeled **n,** a rabbit labeled **r,** a jar labeled **j,** a yoyo labeled **y,** and a whistle labeled **w.** One object of each pair should have detail and color, while the other should be a simple silhouette. Distribute the cards to groups of children and have them find a partner with the matching card.

Silly Strokes (Legibility, Visual) When I introduce a new letter, I model it on the board. Then I do some incorrect ("silly") letters, to show what not to do. The children tell me what's wrong with the silly letter I wrote. (*The monkey tail goes the wrong way!*) They laugh a lot! At the end of the year, they come up and do a silly letter themselves (after doing a correct one).

Melissa Leftwich
Crested Butte Elementary
Crested Butte, CO

Building a Nest (Fine Motor, Science) Set up a table of materials such as dry grass, twigs, and string. Talk to the class about birds and how they use these materials to build their nests. Have children work together to build their own nest.

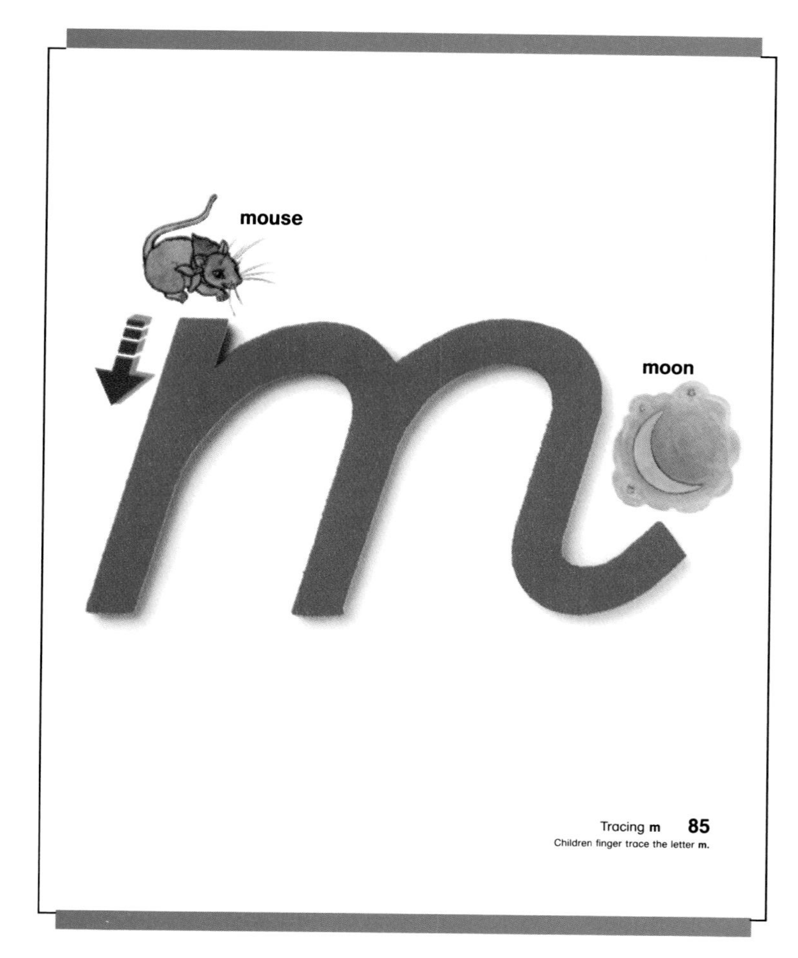

Objectives

Learns the shape of **m** by finger tracing a large model letter.
Writes the lower-case letter **m** and traces a word with **m.**

Prepare

- Talk to children about the moon. Draw full, half, and quarter moons on the board and invite the children to talk about what they see.
- Tell children that people used to say "the moon is made of green cheese." Ask them why they suppose people said that.
- Talk about silvery moons, new moons, crescent moons, waxing moons, and waning moons. Sing songs about the moon. Read *Goodnight Moon* by Margaret Wise Brown and *Harold and the Purple Crayon* by Crockett Johnson.
- Ask children to make up stories about the moon and tape-record them or write them in a special moon-shaped book.

Use the *D'Nealian® Handwriting Big Book* to preview the page.

Teach (page 85)

Have children:
- identify the lower-case letter **m;**
- find the mouse at the starting arrow;
- finger trace the path from the mouse to the moon while you say the following mnemonic sentence:
  The mouse moves over the mountains
  to see the moon.
- air trace the letter **m.**

ACTIVITY BANK

Time to Grow 

Manipulating m (Letter Practice, Creative)
Have children write an **m** or **m's** on unlined paper at the writing center. Ask them to turn their **m's** into a drawing. Before they begin drawing, show them an example on the board.

Carpet Tracing (Tactile, Fine Motor) I provide each child with his or her own small square of shaggy carpeting. This way, they can finger trace their letters whenever the mood hits. It's productive, stimulates motor memory, and is comforting all at the same time.

Pam Yeary
Pershing Elementary
Orlando, FL

Phonics Corner

The sentence used to help children form the letter **m,**

The **mouse moves** over the **mountains** to see the **moon.**

may also be used to work on sound-letter correspondence. Repeat the sentence and call on volunteers to tell you the words they hear that begin with /m/.

Teach (page 86)

Call attention to the picture at the top of the page. Have children:

- describe what they see in the picture;
- trace the letter **m** in the house;
- color the picture.

Call attention to the lower half of the page. Have children:

- finger trace the boxed letter **m** as you read aloud the letter description;
- pencil trace the gray letters;
- write the letter **m** using the starting dots;
- trace the word *mouse.*

Follow Up

Self-Evaluation Have children check their own work by asking themselves:

- Do each of my **m's** have two hills?
- Do my **m's** have their monkey tails?

Additional Resources

Manuscript Alpha Touch letter **m**
D'Nealian® Handwriting Big Book letter **m**

Letter Description

Middle start; slant down, up over the hill, up over the hill again, and a monkey tail.

ACTIVITY BANK

Moving Write Along

Bookmouse (Fine Motor, Creative) Tell the children they will make a mouse bookmark. Give them cutout shapes like the ones below and have them glue the shapes together so they look like this.

mouse/house (Creative, Letter Practice) Read the book *Mitten-Kitten* by Jerome Martin to children. Fold a piece of paper in half in such a way that it simulates the pages of this book. Write _*ouse* in D'Nealian® Handwriting on the bottom page and draw only a _ on the top page. Tell children to draw a house on the bottom page and a mouse on the top and to insert **h** and **m** on each page.

Sparkling Letters (Tactile, Letter Recognition) Draw write-on lines on pieces of cardboard. Have children write lower-case letters on these as they are introduced. Children trace the letters with glue, then sprinkle glitter over them. When letters are dry, children finger trace them to help memorize the pattern. Punch holes in each piece of cardboard and keep them all together on a 2" ring.

Joyce Brownsberger
Fairhope Elementary
Louisville, OH

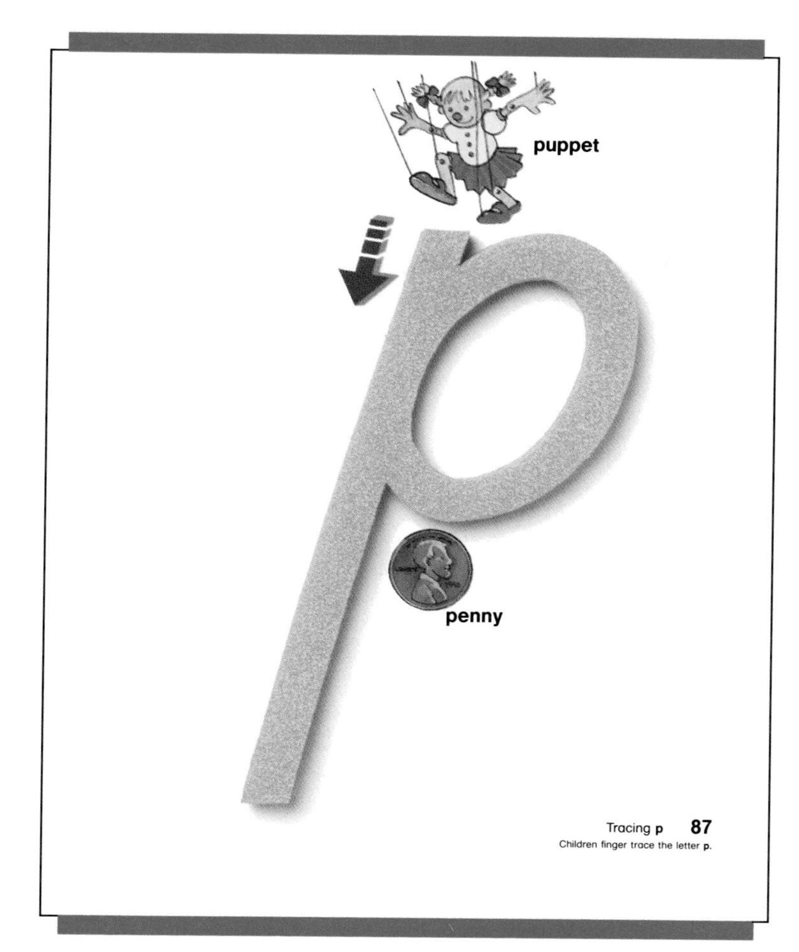

Objectives

Learns the shape of **p** by finger tracing a large model letter.
Writes the lower-case letter **p** and traces a word with **p**.

Prepare

Assign each child a partner and invite them to play "Puppet and Puppet Master." Ask a volunteer to help you demonstrate how to play. You will be the puppet master, who invents the movements that the puppet must mimic. Move your arms, hands, legs, and feet, and ask your volunteer puppet to do exactly the same. Ask the rest of the class to try it too. Then have the pairs of children:

- decide who will be master and who will be puppet;
- work together to create various movements;
- exchange roles and repeat the activity;
- volunteer to show classmates their movements.

Use the *D'Nealian® Handwriting Big Book* to preview the page.

Teach (page 87)

Have children:

- identify the lower-case letter **p;**
- find the puppet at the starting arrow;
- finger trace the path from the puppet to the penny while you say the following mnemonic sentence:
  The puppet finds a penny at the end of the path.
- air trace the letter **p.**

ACTIVITY BANK

Time to Grow 

Parade with p (Letter Practice, Kinesthetic) As a transitional step, children should write the lower-case letter **p** on large pieces of unlined paper at the writing center. Next, have them trace and cut out a large lower-case **p.** Play a John Philip Sousa march and let children parade around the room waving their **p's.**

Specialty of the House (Fine Motor, Tactile) Make pancakes in the shape of a letter **p.** Have children identify the letter. Tell them to eat their pancakes in the direction they would write the letter.

Phonics Corner

The sentence used to help children form the letter **p,**

The **puppet** finds a **penny** at the end of the **path.**

may also be used to work on sound-letter correspondence. Repeat the sentence and call on volunteers to tell you the words they hear that begin with /p/.

Teach (page 88)

Call attention to the pictures at the top of the page. Have children:

- identify the letter **p** on each of the sweaters;
- identify the puppy, puppet, and cup;
- listen as you read the words *puppy, puppet,* and *cup;*
- circle each **p** in the three words.

Call attention to the lower half of the page. Have children:

- finger trace the boxed letter **p** as you read aloud the letter description;
- pencil trace the gray letters;
- write the letter **p** using the starting dots;
- trace the word *puppet.*

Follow Up

Self-Evaluation Have children check their own work by asking themselves:

- Do my **p's** have nice round tummies?
- Do my **p's** slant down underwater?

Additional Resources

Manuscript Alpha Touch letter **p**
D'Nealian® Handwriting Big Book letter **p**

Letter Description

Middle start; slant down under water, up, around, and a tummy.

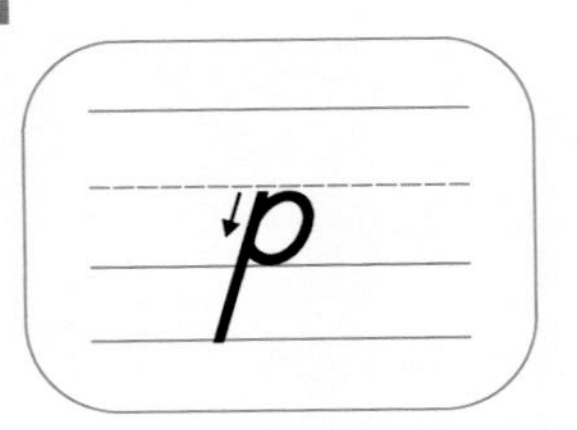

ACTIVITY BANK

Moving Write Along

Integrated Handwriting (Fine Motor, Phonics) In teaching handwriting, I utilize an integrated curriculum approach. I have children work on both the lower-case and capital letters. My students practice the letters in isolation first. When we practice the letter as part of words, we brainstorm words which contain that letter from our current unit of study. I also use this opportunity to reinforce grammar, phonics, spelling, and literary devices. Seize the moment!!

Kimberly Wachenheim
Erie Elementary
Chandler, AZ

Puppets Show Their Stuff (Fine Motor, Creative) Have groups of children make puppets from old socks. Help them draw eyes and a mouth with markers, or glue on buttons. Invite them to perform a puppet show. Ask the puppets to kindly write a few letter **p's** on the chalkboard.

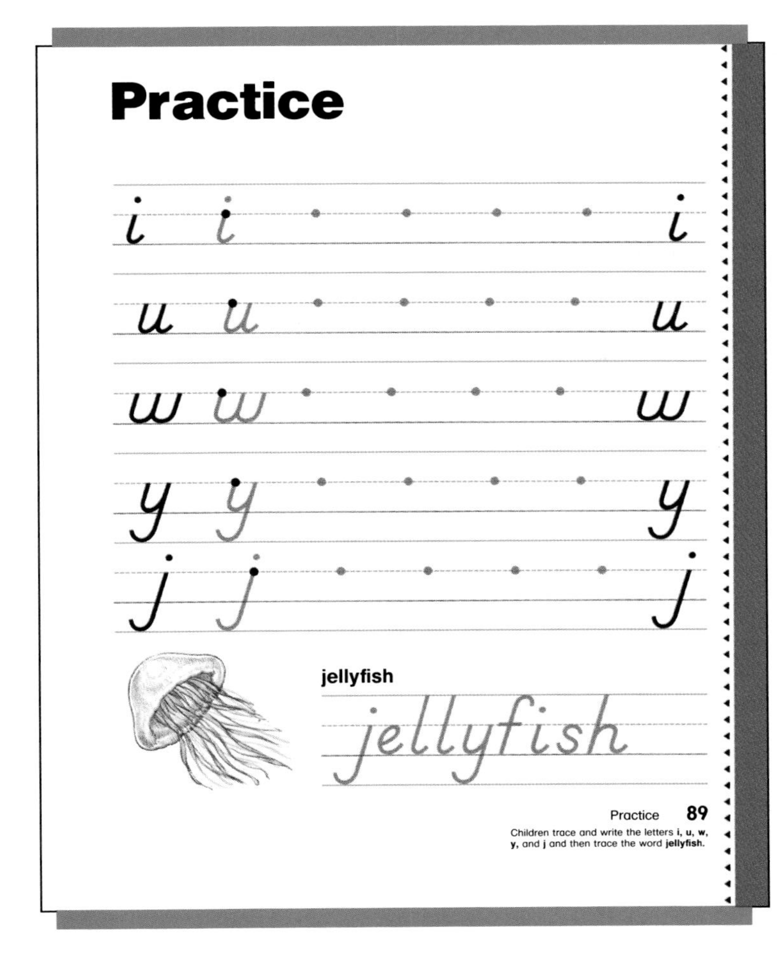

Practice

i i i

u u u

w w w

y y y

j j j

jellyfish

jellyfish

Practice 89

Children trace and write the letters **i, u, w, y,** and **j** and then trace the word **jellyfish**.

Objectives

Practices writing the lower-case letters **i, u, w, y,** and **j.**

Traces the word *jellyfish.*

Prepare

Play "Odd **u** Out" with groups of children using all the letters they have learned thus far **(a, d, o, g, c, e, s, f, b, l, t, h, k, i, u, w,** and **j)**. Use index cards on which you or the children have written all the target letters twice—except **u,** which is written only once. The game is played much like "Old Maid." Each group:

- shuffles the cards and deals them, in turn, to all players;
- takes turns asking others in the group if they have a certain letter, in order to make matches.

The player with the most matches at the end of the game wins, while the player holding the **u** loses.

Teach (page 89)

Have children:

- identify the lower-case letters **i, u, w, y,** and **j;**
- pencil trace the gray letters;
- write each letter using the starting dots;
- trace the word *jellyfish.*

Follow Up

Self-Evaluation Have children check their own work by asking themselves:

- Did I dot my **i's** and **j's?**
- Do all my letters slant the same way?

Additional Resources

Manuscript Alpha Touch letters **i, u, w, y,** and **j**

D'Nealian® Handwriting Big Book letters **i, u, w, y,** and **j**

ACTIVITY BANK

Fishhook Nibbles (Letter Practice, Fine Motor) Draw a fish eating a worm on the ends of **g, y, j,** and **q** to emphasize fishhooks when modeling for children. Have them write a few **j's** on the overhead projector. If fishhooks are too short, draw a hungry worm waiting for the hook.

Roxann Brown
Mullen Elementary
Mullen, NE

A School of Jellyfish (Fine Motor, Letter Practice) Give each child cardboard in the shape of a jellyfish body and lots of colorful ribbons. Have them color the body and write a **j** on the back. Ask them to glue on the ribbons to simulate tentacles.

Special Needs (Kinesthetic Deficits) Visually associating an object with a letter helps these children. Fill a fishbowl with water. The surface of the water represents the baseline. Write **j, y, u,** and **w** on tongue depressors, adding a rope of aluminum foil to fishhook strokes. Cut a slit in a red plastic lid and insert a tongue depressor, keeping the foil below the lid. Float the letters. Ask children to pick out those letters whose parts fall below the water line.

Objectives
Practices writing the lower-case letters **r, n, m,** and **p.**
Traces the word *pumpkin.*

Prepare
Play "What's My Letter?" with the entire class using only the letters **r, n, m,** and **p.** Have a volunteer write one of these letters on a piece of paper that the others cannot see. Help children:
- guess what the letter is by asking questions about how it is formed (*Does it have a fishhook? Is it a letter that has to be closed?* and so on).
- write the letter they think it is and compare it to the volunteer's letter.

The next person to write a letter should be one who guessed the previous letter correctly.

Teach (page 90)
Have children:
- identify the lower-case letters **r, n, m,** and **p;**
- pencil trace the gray letters;
- write each letter using the starting dots;
- trace the word *pumpkin.*

Follow Up
Self-Evaluation Have children check their own work by asking themselves:
- Do my **n's** and **m's** have their monkey tails?
- Are my **p's** closed at the top?

Additional Resources
Manuscript Alpha Touch letters **r, n, m,** and **p**
D'Nealian® Handwriting Big Book letters **r, n, m,** and **p**

Practice

r r r

n n n

m m m

p p p

pumpkin

pumpkin

90 Practice

Children trace and write the letters **r, n, m,** and **p** and then trace the word **pumpkin.**

ACTIVITY BANK

Pumpkin Prints (Fine Motor, Tactile) Bring a pumpkin to school and talk about how pumpkins grow. Display a pumpkin flower, if you can, and share some pumpkin seeds. Carve the pumpkin with children and cut out a few D'Nealian letters, including **p,** to use as stamps. Give them an ink pad and let them stamp away.

Thinking Books (Letter Practice, Journals) To get kindergartners into writing, have them keep a "thinking book" in which they record their thoughts and feelings each day. At first I simply put a date on their pictures. As the year progresses they use squiggly lines and eventually letters. Invented spellings are encouraged. It's easy to monitor letter formation while children are writing in their books.

Cam Miller
Black Hawk School
Black Hawk, SD

Pumpkin Patch (Fine Motor, Letter Practice) Reproduce a pumpkin shape like the one on page 90. Invite children to color it and cut it out. Ask them to write a large lower-case **p** on the back, then display the fruit of their labor.

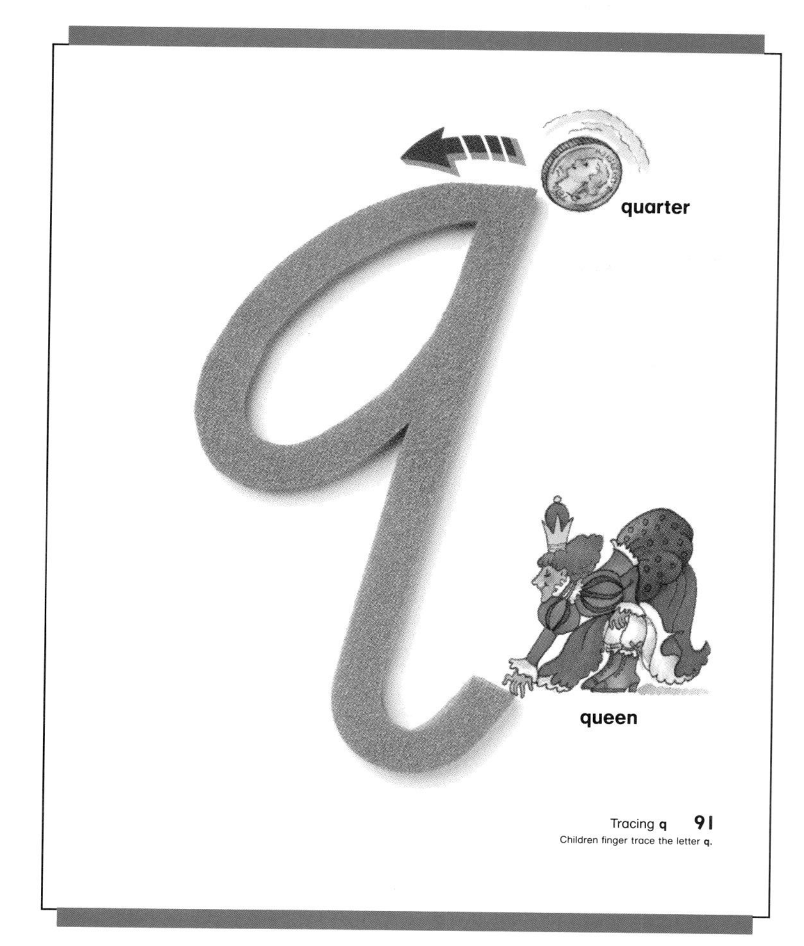

Objectives
Learns the shape of **q** by finger tracing a large model letter.
Writes the lower-case letter **q** and traces a word with **q.**

Prepare
Make a chart like the one below with headings that read **quarters, dimes, nickels,** and **pennies.** Put a pocket under each of the headings. Make a number of simulated coins out of cardboard with a D'Nealian **q, d, n,** or **p** on each. Post the chart and point out the various sizes of the coins. Match each coin to the appropriate heading on the chart. Have children close their eyes as you hide the coins around the classroom. Have children:
- hunt for the coins;
- put each coin they find in the pocket under the heading that starts with the matching letter;
- check the pocketed coins against the heading;
- count the coins in each pocket.

Use the *D'Nealian® Handwriting Big Book* to preview the page.

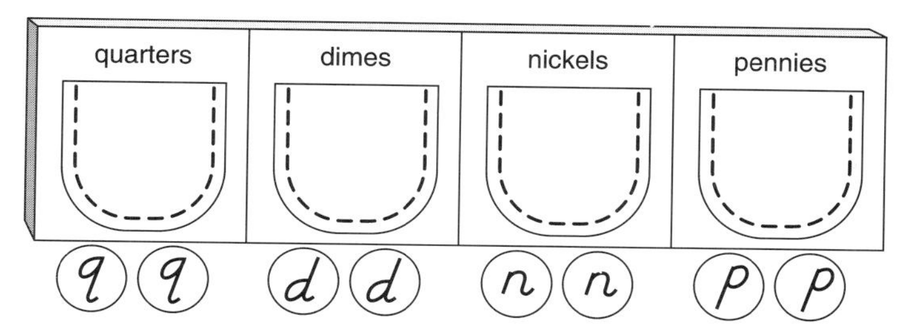

Teach (page 91)
Have children:
- identify the lower-case letter **q;**
- find the quarter at the starting arrow;
- finger trace the path from the quarter to the queen while you say the following mnemonic sentence:
  The quarter rolls quickly to the queen.
- air trace the letter **q.**

ACTIVITY BANK

Time to Grow 

Kindergarten Coronation (Letter Practice, Fine Motor) Duplicate a crown shape on paper, making it large enough to fit around a child's head.

At the writing center, have children decorate their crowns with letter **q's** written with colorful markers. Have them cut out the shape and paste the ends together. Children may crown one another.

All That Glitters (Tactile, Fine Motor) My classes enjoy producing letters using sand, glitter, rice, and so on. The children write the letter in glue and then add the material. When it dries, they can finger trace the letter on their own. Their favorite is the glitter.

Lynn Fortman
Lucas Elementary
Lucas, OH

Phonics Corner
The sentence used to help children form the letter **q,**

The **quarter** rolls **quickly** to the **queen.**

may also be used to work on sound-letter correspondence. Repeat the sentence and call on volunteers to tell you the words they hear that begin with /kw/.

Teach (page 92)

Call attention to the picture at the top of the page. Have children:
- describe what they see in the picture;
- trace each **q** in the quilt.

Call attention to the lower half of the page. Have children:
- finger trace the boxed letter **q** as you read aloud the letter description;
- pencil trace the gray letters;
- write the letter **q** using the starting dots;
- trace the word *queen.*

Follow Up

Self-Evaluation Have children check their own work by asking themselves:
- Are my **q's** closed at the top?
- Do my **q's** have their backward fishhooks?

Additional Resources

Manuscript Alpha Touch letter **q**
D'Nealian® Handwriting Big Book letter **q**

Trace each **q**.

queen

92 Writing **q**

Children trace the **q's** in the quilt. They trace and write the letter **q** and then trace the word **queen.**

Letter Description

Middle start; around down, close up, down under water, and a backward fishhook.

ACTIVITY BANK

Moving Write Along

Crown Jewels (Small Groups, Fine Motor) Divide the class into groups of four. On a large sheet of construction paper, draw the outline of a crown containing four jewels and four letter **q's.** Give this to each group. Have each child trace a letter and color a jewel.

Classroom Quilters (Fine Motor, Creative) Make a classroom quilt with children. Give them pieces of cloth about 4" square. Supply them with materials to decorate the squares. Have them choose one of the letters learned thus far cut from cloth. Help them sew or paste these onto squares, doing so in the direction they would write the letter. Sew the squares together and hang the quilt for all to see.

Delectable Letters (Letter Practice, Tactile) I often spread chocolate pudding or whipped cream on wax paper at tables. Children write a letter, wipe it off, then write another letter. They enjoy this activity.

Miriam Cyprus
Evans School
Colorado Springs, CO

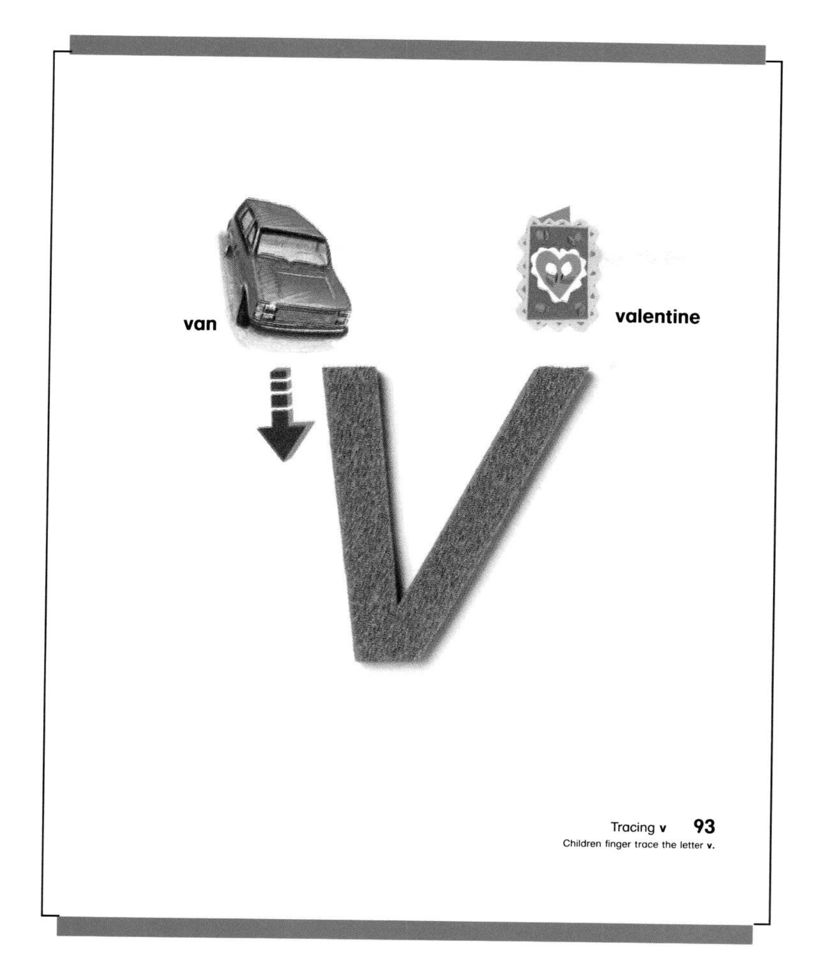

Objectives

Learns the shape of **v** by finger tracing a large model letter.
Writes the lower-case letter **v** and traces a word with **v.**

Prepare

Play "Pass the Valentine" with children. Make a large valentine with a white paper insert on which you have listed numbers from 1 to 26. Children pass the valentine to one another writing a letter that has *not yet* been written. Explain that if Sara writes **f** and Joe writes **n,** the people who are next in line cannot use those letters. Have children:

- write a letter next to each number;
- pass the valentine to the person next in line;
- look at the letters written and decide if any were duplicated.

Use the *D'Nealian® Handwriting Big Book* to preview the page.

Teach (page 93)

Have children:

- identify the lower-case letter **v;**
- find the van at the starting arrow;
- finger trace the path from the van to the valentine while you say the following mnemonic sentence:
  Drive the van to pick up the valentine.
- air trace the letter **v.**

ACTIVITY BANK

Time to Grow 

Writing—Plain and Simple (Letter Practice, Phonics) After we write a letter together on the chalkboard a few times, my class takes plain paper and writes the letter on their own. We often draw a picture of something that begins with that letter sound on the back of the letter we have written.

Pam Buffett
St. Athanasius School
Evanston, IL

Have a Heart (Letter Practice, Fine Motor) Have children write lower-case **v** on colorful unlined paper. Show them how to fold the paper to cut a heart shape around the letter. Help them add lace or a doily to their hearts.

Phonics Corner

The sentence used to help children form the letter **v,**

Drive the **van** to pick up the **valentine.**

may also be used to work on sound-letter correspondence. Repeat the sentence and call on volunteers to tell you the words they hear that begin with /v/.

Teach (page 94)

Call attention to the picture at the top of the page. Have children:

- describe the scene;
- find and circle each hidden **v**.

Call attention to the lower half of the page. Have children:

- finger trace the boxed letter **v** as you read aloud the letter description;
- pencil trace the gray letters;
- write the letter **v** using the starting dots;
- trace the word *van.*

Follow Up

Self-Evaluation Have children check their own work by asking themselves:

- Are my **v's** sitting on the bottom line?
- Do my **v's** slant the same way?

Additional Resources

Manuscript Alpha Touch letter **v**
D'Nealian® Handwriting Big Book letter **v**

Circle each hidden **v**.

van

94 Writing v

Children find and circle the **v's** hidden in the picture. They trace and write the letter **v** and then trace the word **van.**

Letter Description

Middle start; slant down right, and slant up right.

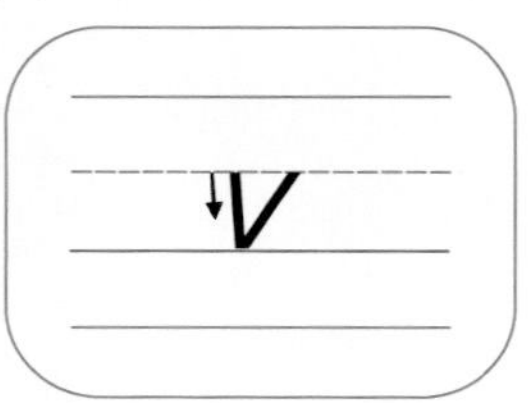

ACTIVITY BANK

Moving Write Along

Writing in a Coffee Can (Letter Practice, Creative) We make "Coffee-Can Learning Kits" to practice D'Nealian letters. We cover a three-pound can with pretty wallpaper or contact paper. We label it *D'Nealian® Handwriting.* Inside the can, we store our materials—a box of crayons, a piece of carpet used for erasing, and a set of 4" x 5" tagboard cards containing all the letters. Children place one card at a time under the clear plastic lid of the coffee can and practice each of the letters this way.

Lois R. Vogel
David Turnham Center
Dale, IN

Flying in v-Formation (Kinesthetic, Letter Recognition) Talk about the birds that fly south in winter. Ask children if they have ever seen geese flying in a v-formation. Choose a group leader and have children arrange themselves in a **v** shape. Ask them to "fly" across the room staying in formation.

v's to Touch (Tactile, Letter Practice) Provide macaroni, rice, lentils, and dried peas. Have children write several **v's** on a sheet of paper and glue a different material on each. Then have them finger trace their letters.

Objectives

Learns the shape of **z** by finger tracing a large model letter.
Writes the lower-case letter **z** and traces a word with **z**.

Prepare

Bring a number of stuffed animals or pictures of animals to class; among them a zebra, an elephant, a gorilla, a monkey, a lion, a tiger, and a bear; and place them around the room. Write the first letter of each animal's name on the chalkboard. Tell children you are going to take a trip to "the classroom zoo."
Have children:

- walk around the room, with you as their guide, visiting the various animals;
- identify the animals they encounter;
- volunteer to go to the chalkboard and circle the letter beginning the word for that animal;
- agree that this is, in fact, the correct letter;
- continue in this way until all the animals' letters are circled.

You may want to invite children to bring in stuffed animals of their own when you next play this game.
Use the *D'Nealian® Handwriting Big Book* to preview the page.

Teach (page 95)

Have children:

- identify the lower-case letter **z;**
- find the zebra at the starting arrow;
- finger trace the path from the zebra to the zoo while you say the following mnemonic sentence:
  Zigzag with the zebra to the zoo.
- air trace the letter **z.**

ACTIVITY BANK

Time to Grow 

zzzing Zebra (Letter Practice, Fine Motor) Have children write lower-case **z** on pieces of unlined paper at the writing center. Children should then tape these papers together in a long row. Draw a picture of a sleeping zebra on the bulletin board. Help children pin the **z's** all around this sleepyhead.

Transparent Tracers (Letter Practice, Visual) I reproduce D'Nealian letters for use as transparencies. I use them as an overhead activity so that the class can see me tracing the letters with them. Children learn to make letters step by step.

Audrey E. Kithcart
Meagher Elementary
Kingston, NY

Phonics Corner

The sentence used to help children form the letter **z,**

Zigzag with the **zebra** to the **zoo.**

may also be used to work on sound-letter correspondence. Repeat the sentence and call on volunteers to tell you the words they hear that begin with /z/.

Teach (page 96)

Call attention to the maze at the top of the page. Have children:

- identify the zebra and the zoo in the directions;
- find the zebra and then the pizza, the puzzle, and the zoo along the path;
- finger trace the path from the zebra to the zoo;
- draw a line from the zebra to the zoo.

Call attention to the lower half of the page. Have children:

- finger trace the boxed letter **z** as you read aloud the letter description;
- pencil trace the gray letters;
- write the letter **z** using the starting dots;
- trace the word *zoo.*

Follow Up

Self-Evaluation Have children check their own work by asking themselves:

- Do my **z's** slant the same way?
- Did I start at the starting dot?

Additional Resources

Manuscript Alpha Touch letter **z**
D'Nealian® Handwriting Big Book letter **z**

Letter Description

Middle start; over right, slant down left, and over right.

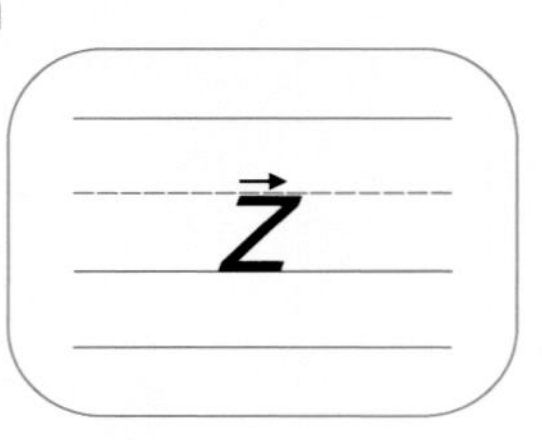

ACTIVITY BANK

Moving Write Along

Picturing z (Letter Practice, Visual) Distribute cards with pictures and their corresponding words. Include words with the letter **z** in them. Write **z** on the chalkboard. Children holding cards with **z** should come to the board. Write the letters in each word up to and after the **z**, then have children fill in the **z.** Say the word for children. Cards can be shuffled and passed out again.

Big on Letters (Gross Motor, Letter Practice) Tape pieces of poster-sized paper containing large writing lines to the floor. Have children stretch out on the floor facing the lines. As you say a letter, children write it using a pencil, crayon, or marker.

Evangelina Reyna De La Rosa
Lyford Junior High
Lyford, TX

The Zebra's Stripes (Letter Practice, Fine Motor) Give small groups of children the outline of a zebra and black markers. Tell them they are going to give the zebra its stripes. Children, in turn, will write a **z** on the outline until the zebra is covered with them. Have them add eyes and a mouth to complete the picture.

Objectives

Learns the shape of **x** by finger tracing a large model letter.
Writes the lower-case letter **x** and traces a word with **x.**

Prepare

- Talk to children about hospitals and how they help people. Read such books as *Emergency Room* by Anne and Harlow Rockwell and *Going to the Hospital* by Fred Rogers.
- Let children describe any hospital experiences they may have had.
- If possible, bring in an x ray for children to examine. Try to bring in a stethoscope, a tongue depressor, an ophthalmoscope, and any other medical instruments you feel the children would find interesting.

Use the *D'Nealian® Handwriting Big Book* to preview the page.

Teach (page 97)

Have children:

- identify the lower-case letter **x;**
- find the fox at the starting arrow;
- finger trace the path from the fox to the x ray and from the ox to the x ray while you say the following mnemonic sentence:

  Help the fox find its x ray. Then, help the ox find its x ray.
- air trace the letter **x.**

ACTIVITY BANK

Time to Grow

X-ray x (Letter Practice, Fine Motor) Have children write "x-ray **x's**" at the writing center. Give each child large pieces of black paper and a piece of white chalk. Tell them to write a large **x** on each piece of paper.

Good Clean Fun (Letter Practice, Tactile) We enjoy writing D'Nealian letters in shaving cream on our tables. Spray the foam in front of children and have them spread it out with their palms. Dictate the letters. They write and erase as many times as necessary. When done, children clean the tables with a sponge. The room smells fresh and clean!

Ann Stowell
Lake Elementary
Gunnison, CO

Phonics Corner

The sentence used to help children form the letter **x,**

Help the **fox** find its **x ray.** Then, help the **ox** find its **x ray.**

may also be used to work on sound-letter correspondence. Repeat the sentence and call on volunteers to tell you the words they hear with /ks/.

Teach (page 98)

Call attention to the scene at the top of the page. Have children:

- describe what they see in the picture;
- trace each **x** on the tick-tack-toe game;
- tell who won the game if the fox drew the **x's** and the ox drew the **o's** (*the fox*).

Call attention to the lower half of the page. Have children:

- finger trace the boxed letter **x** as you read aloud the letter description;
- pencil trace the gray letters;
- write the letter **x** using the starting dots;
- trace the word *fox.*

Follow Up

Self-Evaluation Have children check their own work by asking themselves:

- Do my **x's** have their monkey tails?
- Are all my **x's** the same size?

Additional Resources

Manuscript Alpha Touch letter **x**
D'Nealian® Handwriting Big Book letter **x**

Letter Description

Middle start; slant down right, and a monkey tail. Cross down left.

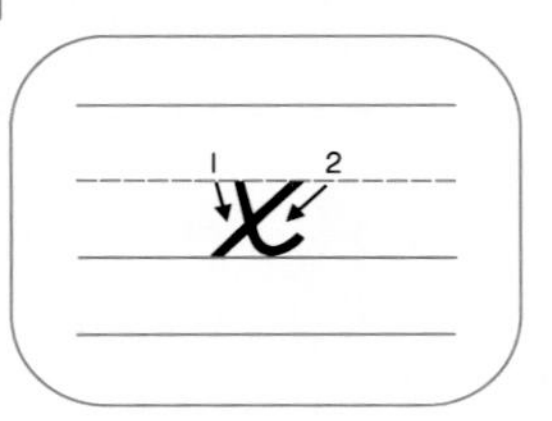

ACTIVITY BANK

Moving Write Along

Tick-tack-toe (Letter Practice, Critical Thinking) Give children a large grid and invite them to play their own game of tick-tack-toe using D'Nealian **o's** and **x's.** Demonstrate the game on the chalkboard before children play.

Illustrating Letters (Creative, Letter Practice) Read the book *Animalia* by Graeme Base to the class. Allow them time to look at the book. Assign each child a lower-case letter to illustrate. When they are done, they write that letter at the top of their page. The class can then assemble their pages and put together a volume from **a** through **z.**

Kathleen V. Sullivan
North Pembroke Elementary
Pembroke, MA

But I Know What I Like (Letter Practice, Fine Motor) Invite children to become "art critics." Give them copies of laminated pictures, including fine art, photographs, and amateur drawings. Have them use red wax pencils to write a D'Nealian lower-case **x** on the images they do not like and a check on the ones they do. Encourage them to discuss their choices.

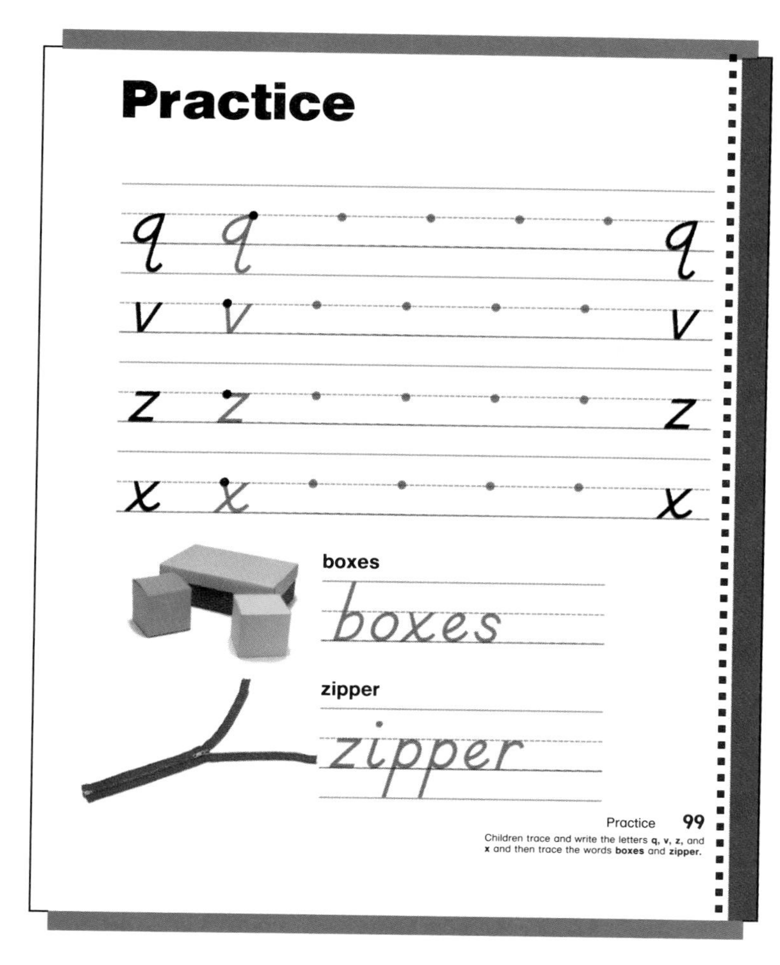

Practice

q q q

v v v

z z z

x x x

boxes

boxes

zipper

zipper

Practice 99

Children trace and write the letters **q, v, z,** and **x** and then trace the words **boxes** and **zipper.**

Objectives

Practices writing the lower-case letters **q, v, z,** and **x.**
Traces the words *boxes* and *zipper.*

Prepare

Call on any children in your class who have a **q, v, z,** or **x** in their names, such as Ale**x,** La**v**onne, Ro**z,** or Ja**q**ui, to come to the board. Do not tell them why you chose them. Ask them to write their names on the board in their best D'Nealian® Handwriting. Next ask other children to come to the board and circle the **q's, v's, z's,** and **x's** in the names written there. You may wish to repeat this activity with other letters children have learned.

Teach (page 99)

Have children:
- identify the lower-case letters **q, v, z,** and **x;**
- pencil trace the gray letters;
- write each letter using the starting dots;
- trace the words *boxes* and *zipper.*

Follow Up

Self-Evaluation Have children check their own work by asking themselves:
- Do my **q's** and **x's** have their monkey tails?
- Do all my letters start at the starting dot?

Additional Resources

Manuscript Alpha Touch letters **q, v, z,** and **x**
D'Nealian® Handwriting Big Book letters **q, v, z,** and **x**

ACTIVITY BANK

I Can Do It (Oral Language, Print Awareness) Give children an opportunity to talk about things they have learned to do that were once difficult for them, such as tying shoes, zipping jackets, getting dressed, and so forth.

Zip Down (Letter Practice, Phonics) Give each child a long, narrow piece of white paper. Have them write lower-case **z's** down the sheet to make a zipper. Encourage them to run their fingers down their zippers, making a sustained **z** sound as they do so.

Fun with Letters (Letter Practice, Alphabetical Order) I have large classes. We sit in a semicircle on the floor and practice D'Nealian letters on small slates. I model the letters and help those children who need help. We usually add phonics by having children draw something that begins with each particular letter sound.

Next, I might distribute one alphabet card per child and have them arrange themselves in alphabetical order.

Etta L. Davenport
Jefferson Street School
Old Town, ME

Objective
Writes the lower-case alphabet.

Prepare
Separate the class into four groups. Randomly assign each child a lower-case letter of the alphabet. (If there are fewer than 26 children, you may want to assign yourself the remaining letters.) Have children:
- write their letters on the chalkboard, large enough to be seen from across the room;
- stand a good distance from the board and line up in four rows;
- run, four at a time, to the letter on the board that you call out.

The child who reaches the letter first is the winner.

Keep track of team scores. Later, you may want to let a volunteer call the letters.

Teach (page 100)
Have children:
- identify all the lower-case letters;
- write each letter using the starting dots.

Follow Up
Self-Evaluation Have children check their own work by asking themselves:
- Do all my letters start at the starting dot?
- Do all my letters slant the same way?

Additional Resources
Manuscript Alpha Touch letters **a** through **z**
D'Nealian® Handwriting Big Book letters **a** through **z**

a b
c d e f
g h i j
k l m n
o p q r
s t u v
w x y z

100 Review
Children write the lower-case letters.

ACTIVITY BANK

Vanishing Alphabet (Letter Practice, Gross Motor) Handwriting practice needs variety. My students love to write the alphabet with water and a paintbrush on a sidewalk or the blackboard. They try to get to **z** before the **a** evaporates.

Mary Lee Vitton
Mockingbird School
Omaha, NE

Special Needs (Immature Learners) These children respond well to writing activities involving large-muscle work and a playlike atmosphere. Have them hunt for "dinosaur eggs." Set up a number of large easels. Hide plastic eggs with a different letter in each. Ask children to hunt for the eggs. When an egg is found, the child opens it up, identifies the letter, and writes it in fluorescent paint at the easel. The game continues until all hunters have found eggs. Eggs may be hidden again.

Gone Fishing (Eye-Hand Coordination, Letter Recognition) Tape a paper clip on index cards containing lower-case letters. Place cards facedown on the floor. Then tie a string around a magnet and invite children to "fish" for a card. When children catch a fish, they must identify it.

MEET:

Mimi Brodsky Chenfeld
Author, Teacher, Consultant

Unless children are taught to be cautious or to repress their feelings, their movement and play combine language, improvisation, problem solving, imagination, and physical coordination.

Daily doses of friendly reassurance are very important. I always begin by greeting and welcoming children into a safe, warm environment. We share simple welcome rituals using songs, poems, and gestures from many sources.

Warming up is an enjoyable, positive experience. As we shake our muscles, wiggle, jiggle, twist, clap, kick, and stretch, we practice listening skills, following directions, demonstrating comprehension, paying attention, expanding vocabularies, and learning cooperation.

I encourage children to add their own interpretations to every warm-up. My music is eclectic—from Bach to folk to pop to rock. If we're studying the circus, we use circusy music and do circus warm-ups like juggling, walking on tiptoes, and marching.

Movement is our first means of expression and communication.

Warm-ups or exercise times during the school day are healthy, pleasant breaks for you and the children. They're important ends in themselves, as well as steps on the way to more challenging activities. If we don't invite children to stretch and shake out their muscles for a few minutes as part of every day, then how can we expect them to be ready to participate in a major movement activity? They need to know that movement is part of their daily schedule, as natural as snack time or story time.

When you look for movement possibilities in whatever you're doing, you'll see how easy it is and how delighted children are to "show off" their ideas.

[Excerpted from the essay on pages T29-T31 of this teacher's edition.]

Teacher to Teacher

Q. *What do I do about pupils who transfer to my class after I have taught most of the letter forms?*

A. To a great extent, students learn and do what they see their peers doing. At the same time, it is important that the new pupil not feel that his or her handwriting is "wrong." Explain that D'Nealian® Handwriting is different, that learning D'Nealian manuscript will make cursive easier. Keep in mind that manuscript is reviewed thoroughly at the beginning of each year, so no child will be left behind, in any case.

Q. *My pupils are having trouble maintaining a consistent slant. What should I do?*

A. Be sure that children's papers are slanted comfortably on their desks. Putting a right-angle corner of masking tape on each desk will help with alignment.

Call attention to the slant of your own handwriting as you write on the chalkboard or charts.

Q. *Some of my pupils' parents are concerned because D'Nealian letters don't look like the manuscript they wrote. What can I say?*

A. Most parents respond favorably when they see that the connection between D'Nealian manuscript and cursive letter forms leads to an earlier and easier transition to cursive writing.

Activity Bank Guide Unit 4

An Activity Bank appears with each lesson. It offers suggestions that can enrich the lesson, tailor it to specific needs, or provide additional practice. In Unit 4, activities in the following categories appear on pages given in parentheses.

Early Literacy

Creative

Critical Thinking

Gifted and Talented

Learning Modalities: Auditory

Kinesthetic

Tactile

Visual

Legibility

Letter Practice

Multicultural/Multilingual

Practical Applications

Small Groups

Special Needs

Unit Overview

In this last unit, children are introduced to the capital D'Nealian alphabet, again in common stroke groups. As with the lower-case letters, they first finger trace a large image of the capital letter while listening to a mnemonic sentence. They then turn the page and complete a pencil activity involving the letter, trace and write the letter, then trace a name beginning with the letter. The name used relates to the activity children have completed on the page.

After each stroke group, two practice pages are provided, featuring names that contain the capitals learned. After completing all the capital letters, children write them in alphabetical order.

Bibliography

You may wish to obtain the following books to read aloud or provide for independent reading.

Chernoff, Goldie Taub. *Easy Costumes You Don't Have to Sew.* New York: Fair Winds Press, 1975.

Cousins, Lucy. *The Little Dog Laughed.* New York: E. P. Dutton, 1989.

Isadora, Rachel. *City Seen from A to Z.* New York: Greenwillow, 1983.

Schlein, Miriam. *Pandas.* New York: Atheneum, 1989.

Sherlock, Sir Philip. *The Iguana's Tail: Crick Crack Stories from the Caribbean.* New York: Crowell, 1969.

Siracusa, Catherine. *No Mail for Mitchell.* New York: Random House, 1990.

Extending Writing Through Activities

A "School/Neighborhood Seen from A to Z" book can be created, using *City Seen from A to Z* by Rachel Isadora as a model. Children generate words from A to Z naming things seen around them. As capital letters are introduced, children write each letter at the top of a page and design a full-page illustration to go with it. When children have finished all capital letters, they have a completed ABC book filled with things that are meaningful to them.

Related writing activities might include dictating a list of signs they see every day that use all capital letters.

Objective
Matches capital letters.

Prepare
On the chalkboard or on a large sheet of paper, write three capital letters, one of which matches the first letter. The letters below are an example.

- Call on a volunteer to tell what the first letter is.
- Have another child find the matching letter and circle it.

Repeat using other capital letters.

Teach (page 102)
Have children:

- identify the baseball caps and the letters on each;
- circle the letter in each box that matches the letter on the cap.

Follow Up
Self-Evaluation Have children check their own work by asking themselves:

- Did I circle a letter in each box?
- Does the letter I circled match the letter on the baseball cap?

Additional Resource
Manuscript Alpha Touch letters **A** through **Z**

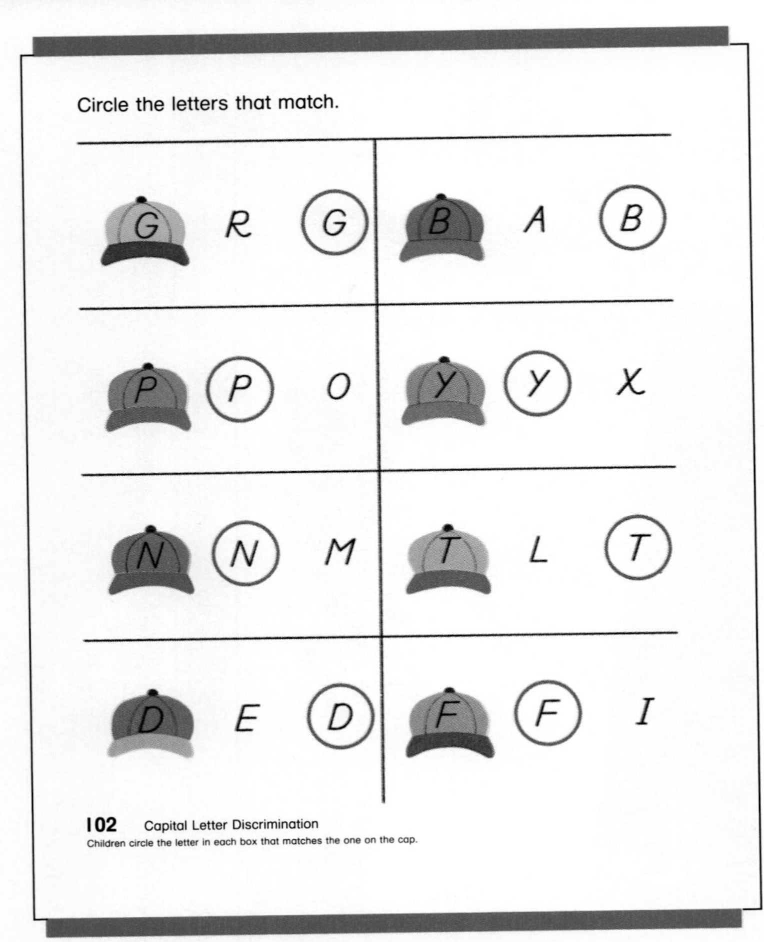
Circle the letters that match.

G R G | B A B
P P O | Y Y X
N N M | T L T
D E D | F F I

102 Capital Letter Discrimination

Children circle the letter in each box that matches the one on the cap.

ACTIVITY BANK

Name Dropping (Letter Recognition) Write each child's name in D'Nealian letters on writing lines, and attach this to rectangular cardboard. Laminate and punch a hole in all corners. Put yarn through the holes, and tie.

Children wear their names around their necks either upside down (which allows them to hold it out and read it) or right side up (which allows others to read it) by pulling the yarn.

Denise Downhour
Crestview Elementary
Cottage Grove, MN

Alphabet Books (Letter Practice, Phonics) Make worksheets with writing lines in one corner. Have children write a lower-case letter on the lines and draw a picture of a word beginning with that letter. As the pages are completed, staple them together to form a book. Have children write capital letters next to their lower-case counterparts as they learn them.

The ABC Game (Letter Recognition, Kinesthetic) Make a set of letter cards containing all the capital letters. Distribute one or more cards to children. Sing "The Alphabet Song." As each child's letter is identified, the child stands up and shows the card.

Objectives

Learns the shape of **C** by finger tracing a large model letter.

Writes the capital letter **C** and traces a name beginning with **C.**

Prepare

Write a capital **C** on the chalkboard. Ask children to try to form a **C** with their bodies. Next write the following names on the board, pronouncing them for children: *Calvin, Bart, Lisa, Conan, Corcoran,* and *Maggie.* Have children:

- come to the chalkboard and circle only the names beginning with capital **C;**
- circle the lower-case **c** in one of these names;
- draw a picture on the board representing each of these made-up names.

Use the *D'Nealian® Handwriting Big Book* to preview the page.

Teach (page 103)

Have children:

- identify the capital letter **C;**
- find Carlos at the starting arrow;
- finger trace the path from Carlos to the colt while you say the following mnemonic sentence:
  Carlos carries carrots to his colt.
- air trace the letter **C.**

ACTIVITY BANK

Time to Grow 

Picture This (Letter Practice, Fine Motor) Create a classroom picture gallery. As each capital letter is introduced, have those children whose first name begins with that letter write it on unlined paper at the writing center. Have them draw or bring in a picture of themselves to paste above the letter. Display pictures.

Chalkboard Capitals (Letter Practice, Fine Motor) I have individual chalkboards for each child. They write a large letter while I demonstrate it on the board. It's different from paper and pencil, and it's fun.

Sandy Szymkowiak
Meadowvale School
Toledo, OH

Phonics Corner

The sentence used to help children form the letter **C,**

Carlos carries carrots to his **colt.**

may also be used to work on sound-letter correspondence. Repeat the sentence and call on volunteers to tell you the words they hear that begin with /k/.

Teach (page 104)

Call attention to the scene at the top of the page. Have children:

- identify the people as contestants in a game;
- listen as you identify *Carlos, Alice,* and *Cory;*
- circle the names that begin with **C;**
- name the person with the most points (*Cory*).

Write a capital **C** on the chalkboard. Ask a volunteer to write a lower-case **c.** Compare them.

Call attention to the lower half of the page. Have children:

- finger trace the boxed letter **C** as you read aloud the letter description;
- pencil trace the gray letters;
- write the letters using the starting dots;
- trace the name *Cory.*

Follow Up

Self-Evaluation Have children check their own work by asking themselves:

- Do my **C's** slant the same way?
- Do my **C's** curve around and up?

Additional Resources

Manuscript Alpha Touch letter **C**
D'Nealian® Handwriting Big Book letter **C**

Circle the names that begin with **C.**

104 Writing C
Children circle the names that begin with **C**. They trace and write the letter **C** and then trace the name **Cory.**

Letter Description

Start below the top; curve up, around, down, up, and stop.

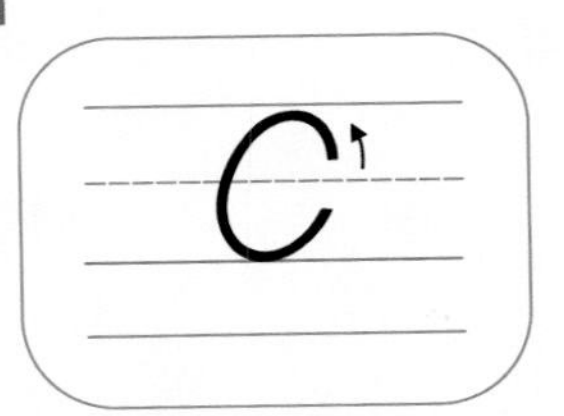

ACTIVITY BANK

Moving Write Along

Quiz Show (Phonics, Critical Thinking) Tell the class to pretend they are quiz-show contestants trying to think up words. Write a lower-case letter on the chalkboard and ask them to think of words beginning with that letter. Children score a point for each correct word. They keep their own scores.

Circle Pictures (Fine Motor, Letter Practice) Hand out sheets of paper with _ **is for circle** at the bottom. Have pupils trace and cut out circles of all colors, and paste them on the paper to create a design. They may add details using crayons. Ask children to fill in the blank with a capital **C**. Students show their pictures to the class and count the number of circles used.

C is for circle

Marly Glaw
Shreiner School and Academy
Marietta, GA

Cookie Tree (Fine Motor, Letter Practice) Provide colored construction paper, fabric scraps, and beads to use in making a cookie tree. Use a branch cut from a shrub to make the tree. Have children cut cookies from paper, decorate them, write capital **C** on each, and hang on the branch.

Objectives

Learns the shape of **G** by finger tracing a large model letter.
Writes the capital letter **G** and traces a name beginning with **G**.

Prepare

Have children play "A Garden of **G's**." Write the letter **G** on four separate index cards. Write several other capital letters on index cards also. Attach these cards to ice-cream sticks so that they may be inserted into a sand table or tub of sand. Lean the cards face up all around the classroom. Write a large **G** on the chalkboard and say its name with children. Have children:

- hunt for the cards with **G's** on them;
- stake these cards in the sand;
- trace the letter **G** in the sand below the cards.

Use the *D'Nealian® Handwriting Big Book* to preview the page.

Teach (page 105)

Have children:

- identify the capital letter **G;**
- find Gabby the Gorilla at the starting arrow;
- finger trace the path from Gabby to the garden while you say the following mnemonic sentence:
  Gabby is going to dig in her garden.
- air trace the letter **G**.

ACTIVITY BANK

Time to Grow

G Gardeners (Letter Practice, Fine Motor) Have large unlined paper, colored paper in the shape of a flower, and yellow circles made by a hole puncher available at the writing center. Have children write capital **G's** on their papers. When they have made a **G** they are happy with, tell them to turn it into a **G** garden by pasting flowers on it.

Stand for Your Letter (Letter Recognition, Kinesthetic) Give each child a different capital letter written on a large piece of cardboard. Project a capital letter onto a light surface. Children stand when they see their letter.

Phonics Corner

The sentence used to help children form the letter **G,**

Gabby is **going** to dig in her **garden**.

may also be used to work on sound-letter correspondence. Repeat the sentence and call on volunteers to tell you the words they hear that begin with /g/.

Teach (page 106)

Call attention to the maze at the top of the page. Have children:

- identify Gabby the Gorilla and the letters **C, O,** and **G** on the sweaters;
- finger trace the path from Gabby to the **G;**
- draw a line from Gabby to the **G.**

Write a capital **G** on the chalkboard. Ask a volunteer to write a lower-case **g.** Compare them.

Call attention to the lower half of the page. Have children:

- finger trace the boxed letter **G** as you read aloud the letter description;
- pencil trace the gray letters;
- write the letter **G** using the starting dots;
- trace the name *Gabby.*

Follow Up

Self-Evaluation Have children check their own work by asking themselves:

- Did I start at the starting dot?
- Do my **G's** slant the same way?

Additional Resources

Manuscript Alpha Touch letter **G**
D'Nealian® Handwriting Big Book letter **G**

Draw a line from [gorilla] to **G.**

Gabby

106 Writing G

Children draw a line to connect the gorilla to the letter **G.** They trace and write the letter **G** and then trace the name **Gabby.**

Letter Description

Start below the top; curve up, around, down, up, and over left.

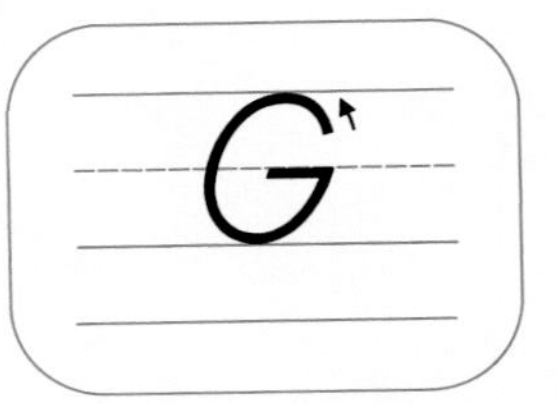

ACTIVITY BANK

Moving Write Along

Capital Meets Lower-case (Eye-Hand Coordination, Letter Recognition) Make two columns of letters, the first with capital **C, G, O, Q, S,** the second with the same letters in lower-case but in a different order. Have children connect matching letters.

Make a Maze (Letter Practice, Letter Recognition) Create a maze like the one on page 106, with objects at the end of three paths. Distribute these to children. Have children write a different letter on each object. Ask them to write one of these letters at the top of the maze and to trade papers with a friend. The friend draws a line to the letter indicated.

Writing Behind One's Back (Kinesthetic, Tactile) After we air trace a letter, we sit on the rug in two rows and pretend that the person in front of us has a chalkboard back. Our index finger is our magic chalk. Our other hand is our eraser. We gently write the letter on our "backboard," and then erase our writing. Then the whole row turns around, and we do it all over again.

Janice Kane
St. Helena Elementary
St. Helena, CA

Objectives

Learns the shape of **O** by finger tracing a large model letter.
Writes the capital letter **O** and traces a name beginning with **O**.

Prepare

Play "Find Ollie Now" with children. On individual pieces of cardboard write the names *Ollie, Holly, Mollie, Polly,* and *Dollie*. Write *Ollie* at least six times. You might also want to draw or paste a picture next to each name to help children associate the names with individuals (see the picture of Ollie on pages 107 and 108 of pupil book). Divide children into groups of five or six. Have children:

- close their eyes as you place the cards all around the room;
- seek and collect only the *Ollie* cards.

The team with the most *Ollies* wins the game and can then hide all the cards the next time around, sitting the game out while the others search.

Use the *D'Nealian® Handwriting Big Book* to preview the page.

Teach (page 107)

Have children:

- identify the capital letter **O;**
- find Ollie at the starting arrow;
- finger trace the path from Ollie to the olive while you say the following mnemonic sentence:

  Ollie runs around to find his olive.
- air trace the letter **O**.

ACTIVITY BANK

Time to Grow

A Can of O's (Letter Practice, Creative) At the writing center, give each child a cutout of a can made from posterboard. Ask children to write an **O** on the can and then decorate it. On the back, have them draw something beginning with **O** that the can could hold.

Observing O and o (Print Awareness, Kinesthetic) Hang posters, ads with large print, and words containing **O** or **o** about the room. Invite children to stroll around looking for these letters. As children spy an **O** or an **o** they should say, "I observe an **O**."

Phonics Corner

The sentence used to help children form the letter **O,**

Ollie runs around to find his **olive.**

may also be used to work on sound-letter correspondence. Repeat the sentence and call on volunteers to tell you the words they hear that begin with /o/.

Teach (page 108)

Call attention to the picture at the top of the page. Have children:

- describe the scene;
- find and circle each hidden **O**.

Write a capital **O** on the chalkboard. Ask a volunteer to write a lower-case **o**. Compare them.

Call attention to the lower half of the page. Have children:

- finger trace the boxed letter **O** as you read aloud the letter description;
- pencil trace the gray letters;
- write the letter **O** using the starting dots;
- trace the name *Ollie.*

Follow Up

Self-Evaluation Have children check their own work by asking themselves:

- Are my **O's** closed at the top?
- Are my **O's** the correct size?

Additional Resources

Manuscript Alpha Touch letter **O**
D'Nealian® Handwriting Big Book letter **O**

Letter Description

Top start; around down, and close up.

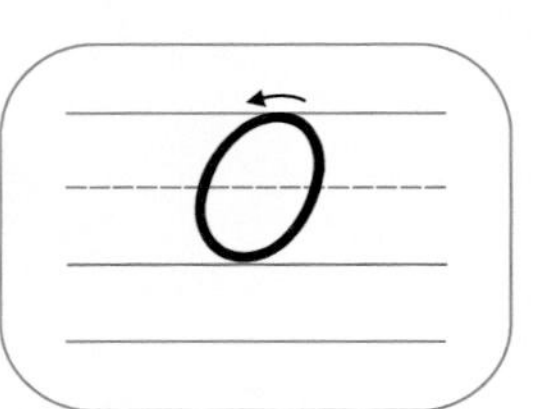

ACTIVITY BANK

Moving Write Along

Sing a Song of Ollie (Kinesthetic, Creative) Draw a large D'Nealian **O** on the floor. Have children stand on the outside of the **O**, with one child ("Ollie") in the center. Have them make up a song about Ollie (to the tune of "Mary Had a Little Lamb") as they move around the **O**. Have the child in the middle spin around slowly with eyes closed and point to a new Ollie when the music stops.

Magic Fingers (Gross Motor, Kinesthetic) We begin a lot of our handwriting activities in the air, using our "magic finger." The students enjoy erasing letters and doing them one more time.

Betty Collett
Beard Elementary
Fort Smith, AR

Transforming O (Fine Motor, Creative) Draw a capital **O** in the middle of a piece of unlined paper, reproduce it, and distribute it to children. Ask them to transform the **O** into something new, such as a sun or a hole in a tree. Encourage children to draw their own **O's** and to transform these also.

Objectives

Learns the shape of **Q** by finger tracing a large model letter.
Writes the capital letter **Q** and traces a name beginning with **Q**.

Prepare

Write the capital letters **C, G, O,** and **Q** on index cards, writing **Q** three times and all others twice. Shuffle the cards and invite children to play "Clap for **Q**." You will hold up each letter in turn, and when the **Q** is on display all children must clap heartily for **Q**. If the children seem ready, you may want to challenge them with additional variations, such as "Giggle for G" and "Click for C."

Use the *D'Nealian® Handwriting Big Book* to preview the page.

Teach (page 109)

Have children:
- identify the capital letter **Q;**
- find Quinn at the starting arrow;
- finger trace the path from Quinn around and across to the quilt while you say the following mnemonic sentence:

  Quinn quickly stitches around and across her quilt.
- air trace the letter **Q**.

ACTIVITY BANK

Time to Grow 

Letter Quilts (Letter Practice, Fine Motor) Help children make quilts by pasting squares of fabric, wallpaper, or colored paper on a large sheet of posterboard. Let children use markers at the writing center to write a **Q** on each patch before pasting.

Quinn Commands (Auditory, Kinesthetic) Play "Quinn Commands." Distribute letter cards for **C/c, G/g, O/o,** and **Q/q** among eight children. As you give commands, the child with the appropriate letter must follow them, as:

Quinn commands that capital **Q** stand up.
Quinn commands that lower-case **g** turn around.

Phonics Corner

The sentence used to help children form the letter **Q**,

Quinn quickly stitches around and across her **quilt.**

may also be used to work on sound-letter correspondence. Repeat the sentence and call on volunteers to tell you the words they hear that begin with /kw/.

Teach (page 110)

Call attention to the pictures at the top of the page. Have children:

- listen as you read the names *C.Q. Bach, Quinn Quilby,* and *Queen Bea;*
- describe each person named;
- circle each **Q** in the three names.

Write a capital **Q** on the chalkboard. Ask a volunteer to write a lower-case **q**. Compare them.

Call attention to the lower half of the page. Have children:

- finger trace the boxed letter **Q** as you read aloud the letter description;
- pencil trace the gray letters;
- write the letter **Q** using the starting dots;
- trace the name *Quinn.*

Follow Up

Self-Evaluation Have children check their own work by asking themselves:

- Are my **Q's** closed at the top?
- Do my **Q's** have their bottom curve?

Additional Resources

Manuscript Alpha Touch letter **Q**
D'Nealian® Handwriting Big Book letter **Q**

Circle each **Q.**

C.Q. Bach Quinn Quilby Queen Bea

Quinn

Quinn

110 Writing Q

Children circle the **Q's** in each of three names. They trace and write the letter **Q** and then trace the name **Quinn.**

Letter Description

Top start; around down, and close up. Cross with a curve down right.

ACTIVITY BANK

Moving Write Along

Going Mobile (Eye-Hand Coordination, Fine Motor) Have children use stencils to trace the first letter in their names or their initials. Have them cut these letters out and glue them onto a paper plate. Staple the plates to strings and create "letter mobiles."

Priscilla Miller
Beacon School
Harper Woods, MI

Take a Q from Us (Fine Motor, Tactile) Give each child the two strokes used in the D'Nealian **Q,** cut from colorful construction paper. Have children paste these two pieces in the correct position on a large piece of colorful cardboard. Encourage children to feel the **Q** with their fingers.

What's in a Name? (Celebrating Cultural Diversity) Ask children to tell the class something about their name. Why was this name chosen? Who gave them the name? Does it have a special meaning? Is it the name of someone else in the family or someone in history? Talk about why people have names.

Objectives

Learns the shape of **S** by finger tracing a large model letter.
Writes the capital letter **S** and traces a name beginning with **S.**

Prepare

Write the words *Sara sips soda* on the chalkboard. Tell children that you know a little girl named Sara who loves to say sentences with **s's** in them, like *Sara sips soda.* Ask children to repeat the sentence with you. Next, invite children to:

- think of a similar sentence, either using the name Sara or some other name;
- come to the front of the room and repeat their sentences for their classmates;
- act out their sentences for the class;

Use the *D'Nealian® Handwriting Big Book,* to preview the page.

Teach (page 111)

Have children:

- identify the capital letter **S;**
- find Sara at the starting arrow;
- finger trace the path from Sara to the soda while you say the following mnemonic sentence:

  Sara sips her soda.
- air trace the letter **S.**

ACTIVITY BANK

Time to Grow

The Name Game (Letter Practice, Phonics) My students love to write the names of their classmates on their capital letter practice sheets. Have them write **S** at the writing center on unlined paper, then encourage them to write names beginning with **S** on the back of their papers.

Karla Kensey
Britton Elementary
Hilliard, OH

S Sounds (Phonics, Oral Language) Give each child paper with a capital **S** on it. Tell them to look around the room and find something that begins with this sound. They then place the paper beside their choices. When everyone has done so, children describe their choices.

Phonics Corner

The sentence used to help children form the letter **S,**

Sara sips her **soda.**

may also be used to work on sound-letter correspondence. Repeat the sentence and call on volunteers to tell you the words they hear that begin with /s/.

Teach (page 112)

Call attention to Sara, collecting letters at the top of the page. Have children:

- listen as you read the names on the letters: *Sara, Judit,* and *Paco;*
- circle the name *Sara;*
- tell how many letters Sara received. (*three*)

Write a capital **S** on the chalkboard. Ask a volunteer to write a lower-case **s.** Compare them.

Call attention to the lower half of the page. Have children:

- finger trace the boxed letter **S** as you read aloud the letter description;
- pencil trace the gray letters;
- write the letters using the starting dots;
- trace the name *Sara.*

Follow Up

Self-Evaluation Have children check their own work by asking themselves:

- Did I start at the starting dot?
- Do my **S's** curve smoothly?

Additional Resources

Manuscript Alpha Touch letter **S**
D'Nealian® Handwriting Big Book letter **S**

112 Writing S
Children circle the name **Sara.** They trace and write **S** and then trace the name **Sara.**

Letter Description

Start below the top; curve up, around, down, and a snake tail.

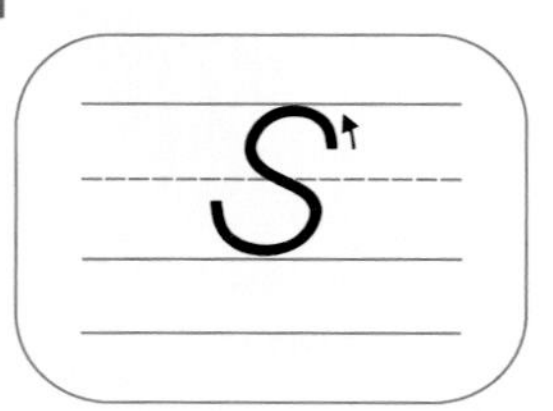

ACTIVITY BANK

Moving Write Along

Practice Mats (Fine Motor, Letter Practice) I use 8" x 11" colored construction paper to make practice mats. On the top are write-on lines with the child's first name written in D'Nealian letters. They trace this. On the bottom are write-on lines for independent writing. I decorate and laminate the mats. Children write in crayon and erase with a piece of carpet.

Lois R. Vogel
David Turnham Center
Dale, IN

Safety Shapes (Fine Motor, Health) Provide cardboard octagons, pentagons, and squares for children to trace. Have them create road signs using these symbols. Help them write *Stop, Slow,* and *School* on the appropriate shape. Encourage them to glue these shapes to heavy cardboard. Have children show their signs to the class and discuss what each one represents.

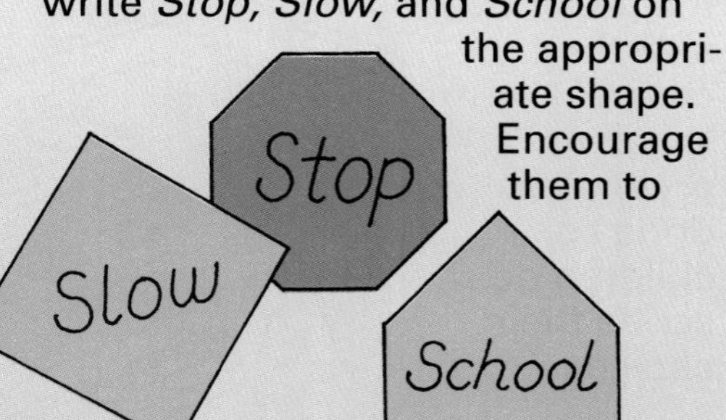

Friendly Letters (Letter Practice, Creative) Tell children they are going to write a letter to Sara Sonia Segundo. Give them sheets of colorful writing paper and ask them to write Sara a newsy letter or to draw her an action-packed picture. Have them fold their letters, place them in an envelope, and address them: **S S S.**

Objectives

Practices writing the capital letters **C, G,** and **O.** Traces the names *Canaries* and *Gulls.*

Prepare

Play "Canaries, Gulls, and Orioles," a throwing and catching game, with children. Allow each child to choose a letter: **C** for Canaries, **G** for Gulls, and **O** for Orioles. Write these three names on the chalkboard. Have children form a circle around you, and ask each one to identify his or her team name and team initial: Canaries/**C,** Gulls/**G,** or Orioles/**O.** Explain that as the ball is thrown into the air either the team name or initial will be called out. Only players on that team should try to catch the ball. The one who catches the ball gets to throw it and call another team name or initial.

Teach (page 113)

Have children:
- identify the capital letters **C, G,** and **O;**
- pencil trace the gray letters;
- write each letter using the starting dots;
- trace the names *Canaries* and *Gulls.*

Follow Up

Self-Evaluation Have children check their own work by asking themselves:
- Are all my letters rounded and smooth?
- Do all my letters start at the starting dot?

Additional Resources

Manuscript Alpha Touch letters **C, G,** and **O**
D'Nealian® Handwriting Big Book letters **C, G,** and **O**

ACTIVITY BANK

Overhead Letters (Letter Practice, Tactile) Cut a rectangle from the bottom of a cardboard box. Insert wax paper over the rectangle and up the sides. Reinforce with tape. Place two cups of sand into the carton and place on an overhead projector. Have students trace D'Nealian letters with their fingers. *Voilà!* Their letters appear on the screen. Children love writing this way.

Bonnie L. Gaynor
Franklin Elementary
Franklin, NJ

Sort It Out (Print Awareness, Letter Recognition) Cut out printed capital and lower-case letters **C, G,** and **O** and tape them on six sections of an egg carton. Write matching D'Nealian capital and lower-case letters on small squares of paper. Let children take turns sorting the written letters into the correct sections of the egg carton.

Bird Watching (Letter Practice, Visual) Hang a poster containing pictures of gulls and canaries and a write-on line below each. Title the poster **Gulls and Canaries.** Invite children to write a **C** under canaries and a **G** under gulls.

Objectives
Practices writing the capital letters **Q** and **S**.
Traces the names *Quails* and *Sandpipers.*

Prepare
Have children play "That's My Letter" using the capital letters **C, G, O, Q,** and **S**. Use large poster-board on which you or the children have written each of the target letters. Assign each child one of the five letters. Have children:
- watch as you hold up one of the letters;
- run to the board if their letter is displayed;
- write the letter if they are designated as the first to the board;
- say the name of the letter.

You may want to reassign the letters and play the game a few more times. You could also play "Canaries, Gulls, Orioles, Quails, and Sandpipers" (see page 113) with all the capital letters they have learned thus far.

Teach (page 114)
Have children:
- identify the capital letters **Q** and **S;**
- pencil trace the gray letters;
- write each letter using the starting dots;
- trace the names *Quails* and *Sandpipers.*

Follow Up
Self-Evaluation Have children check their own work by asking themselves:
- Do all my letters slant the same way?
- Do my **Q's** have their bottom curve?

Additional Resources
Manuscript Alpha Touch letters **Q** and **S**
D'Nealian® Handwriting Big Book letters **Q** and **S**

Practice

Q Q Q

S S S

Quails

Quails

Sandpipers

Sandpipers

114 Practice

Children trace and write the letters **Q** and **S** and then trace the names **Quails** and **Sandpipers.**

ACTIVITY BANK

Making Tracks (Critical Thinking, Visual) Let children play investigator. You'll need damp sand and objects for making tracks (a fork, ball, cookie cutters). Have children close their eyes while you press one of the objects into the sand a few times. Children decide which object left the "trail."

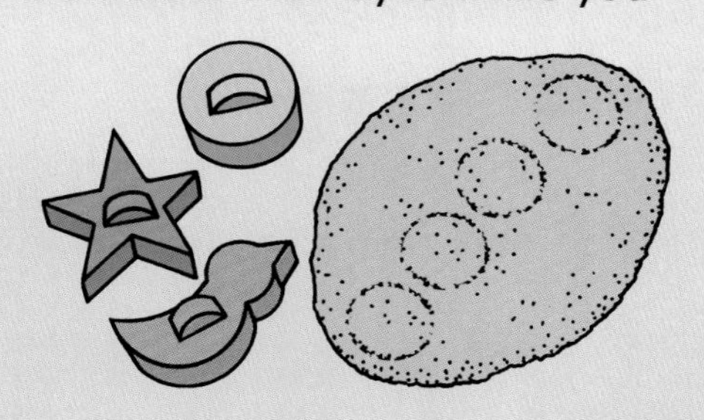

Beanbag Letters (Kinesthetic, Letter Practice) Write **C, G, O, Q,** and **S** on 9" x 12" cards. Tape the cards to the floor. Have children name one of the letters and toss the beanbag to the appropriate card. Children who hit the letter can write that letter on the board.

Special Needs (Visual Deficits) Motor-memory activities help these children. Let them warm up the large muscles by twirling a jump rope attached to a doorknob.

Write a large D'Nealian **Q** and **S** on the chalkboard for them to trace.

At their desks, have them place rolled clay on a D'Nealian **S** written on write-on lines. Children finger trace the **S** with eyes closed.

Have children use puffy paint to make textured **Q** cards and finger trace these also.

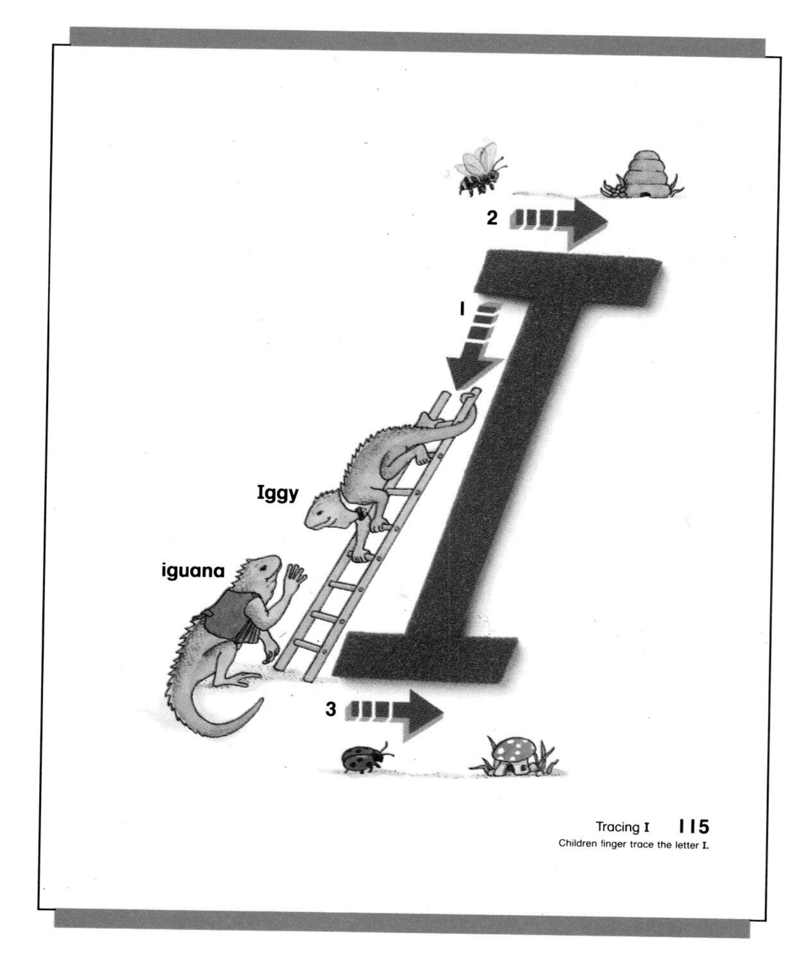

Objectives

Learns the shape of **I** by finger tracing a large model letter.
Writes the capital letter **I** and traces a name beginning with **I**.

Prepare

Write a capital **I** on the chalkboard. Ask children to determine how many of them it would take to form an **I** with their bodies. Have volunteers try it. Next ask children to play "Private **I**." Hide a capital **I** card out of view in the classroom. Children search for the card while you tell them whether they are close ("hot") or far away ("cold"). The child who finds the **I** gets to hide it and give the "hot" and "cold" clues.

Use the *D'Nealian® Handwriting Big Book* to preview the page.

Teach (page 115)

Have children:

- identify the capital letter **I**;
- find Iggy the Iguana at the starting arrow;
- finger trace the path from Iggy to his iguana friend, from the bee to the hive, and from the ladybug to the toadstool while you say the following mnemonic sentence:

  Iggy climbs down to his iguana friend.
  Then, each insect runs home.
- air trace the letter **I**.

ACTIVITY BANK

Time to Grow 

Tricolor I (Letter Practice, Eye-Hand Coordination) Have children write capital **I** on unlined paper at the writing center. Next have them cut three strips of different-colored paper to match the lengths of the strokes in **I**. Have them paste these on blue paper in the order they would write each stroke.

Letters with Style (Letter Practice, Tactile) We use hair-styling gel to practice letter writing. Put 1/2 cup of hair-styling gel in a sealable plastic bag. Add food coloring. Children write letters on the bag and erase by running their hand over it to smooth out the gel.

Cindy Renzelman
Graymont Elementary School
Graymont, IL

Phonics Corner

The sentence used to help children form the letter **I**,

> **Iggy** climbs down to his **iguana** friend. Then, each **insect** runs home.

may also be used to work on sound-letter correspondence. Repeat the sentence and call on volunteers to tell you the words they hear that begin with /i/.

■ Teach (page 116)

Call attention to the scene at the top of the page. Have children:

- identify the animals as iguanas;
- listen as you identify *Iggy, Tuffy,* and *Izzy;*
- circle the names that begin with **I;**

Write a capital **I** on the chalkboard. Ask a volunteer to write a lower-case **i.** Compare them.

Call attention to the lower half of the page. Have children:

- finger trace the boxed letter **I** as you read aloud the letter description;
- pencil trace the gray letters;
- write the letters using the starting dots;
- trace the name *Iggy.*

■ Follow Up

Self-Evaluation Have children check their own work by asking themselves:

- Did I start at the starting dots?
- Did I cross the top and bottom of each **I?**

■ Additional Resources

Manuscript Alpha Touch letter **I**
D'Nealian® Handwriting Big Book letter **I**

■ Letter Description

Top start; slant down. Cross the top and the bottom.

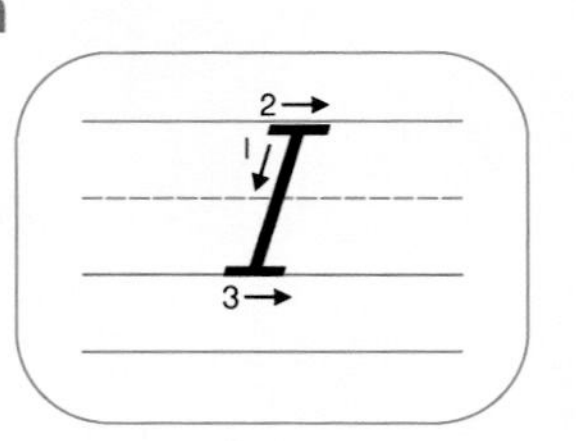

ACTIVITY BANK

Moving Write Along

Iguana Tales (Oral Language, Auditory) Read the book *The Iguana's Tail, Crick Crack Stories from the Caribbean* to children. Tell them that when people first told these stories, the teller would say, "Crick, crack" before beginning, and the listeners would reply, "Break my back." At story's end the call would be, "Wire bend," and the response, "Story end." As you read each tale, practice this call and response.

Capital Rubbings (Tactile, Fine Motor) Cut D'Nealian capital letters from heavy sandpaper. Encourage children to finger trace them. Provide drawing paper and unwrapped crayons. Have children make rubbings of the letters and then write the corresponding lower-case letters below.

Vickie Foreman
Travis School
San Angelo, TX

I Like... (Creative, Letter Recognition) Give children worksheets with **I like** written at the top in D'Nealian letters. Read the words to them, then have them trace the words. Ask them to complete the sentence by drawing or pasting in pictures of things they like. When they are finished, ask children to "read" their papers.

Objectives

Learns the shape of **L** by finger tracing a large model letter.
Writes the capital letter **L** and traces a name beginning with **L**.

Prepare

Talk to the children about libraries—school libraries, community libraries, and bookmobiles. Display a large stack of books at the front of the classroom that you have selected from a library. Be sure that many of these books have a capital **L** in the title. (Try to supply as many **L**-titled books as there are children in the class.) Invite the children to come to the table and look at the books. Next, ask the children to pick up only a book with an **L** on the cover—one book to a customer. (You may, however, want to have children do this in pairs.) Have children:

- return to their tables, desks, or the rug;
- describe, in turn, the cover of the books they have chosen;
- point out the **L** on the cover for all to see;
- choose *any* book from the pile that interests them and share it with a friend.

Use the *D'Nealian® Handwriting Big Book* to preview the page.

Teach (page 117)

Have children:

- identify the capital letter **L;**
- find Latoya at the starting arrow;
- finger trace the path from Latoya to the library while you say the following mnemonic sentence:
  Latoya likes the short walk to the library.
- air trace the letter **L.**

ACTIVITY BANK

Time to Grow 

L Pictures (Letter Practice, Creative) Have children write capital letter **L's** at the writing center on unlined paper. Next, have them write five **L's** on the bottom of a piece of plain paper and turn these into a picture of an animal. (Suggest that they use their **L's** as legs and feet.) Help them give their animals names beginning with **L**.

Susan Bell
Sharon School
Sharon, WI

Sightseeing (Letter Recognition, Kinesthetic) Take a walk around your community with your class. Have them find street names that begin with **L**. Write them on a worksheet for children to trace.

Phonics Corner

The sentence used to help children form the letter **L**,

Latoya likes the short walk to the **library**.

may also be used to work on sound-letter correspondence. Repeat the sentence and call on volunteers to tell you the words they hear that begin with /l/.

Teach (page 118)

Call attention to the scene at the top of the page. Have children:

- describe what they see in the picture (talk about perspective);
- connect the dots from 1 to 8 to complete the door;
- color the door.

Write a capital **L** on the chalkboard. Ask a volunteer to write a lower-case **l**. Compare them.

Call attention to the lower half of the page. Have children:

- finger trace the boxed letter **L** as you read aloud the letter description;
- pencil trace the gray letters;
- write the letter **L** using the starting dots;
- trace the name *Lake St.*

Follow Up

Self-Evaluation Have children check their own work by asking themselves:

- Are my **L's** slanted in the same direction?
- Do my **L's** sit nicely on the bottom line?

Additional Resources

Manuscript Alpha Touch letter **L**
D'Nealian® Handwriting Big Book letter **L**

Connect the dots. Color the door.

Lake St.

Lake St.

118 Writing L

Children connect the dots from 1 to 8 in the shape of an L and then color the door. They trace and write the letter L and then trace the name **Lake St.**

Letter Description

Top start; slant down, and over right.

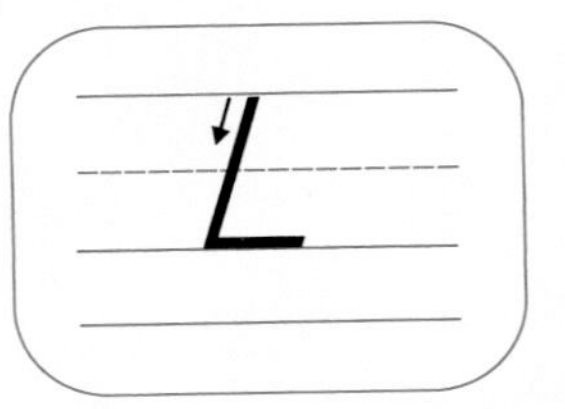

ACTIVITY BANK

Moving Write Along

Feeling Their Way (Tactile, Letter Practice) Cut the following letters from heavy sandpaper: **C, G, O, Q, S, I,** and **L.** Place them in a bag and have children close their eyes and pick a letter. Let children feel the letter thoroughly, then return it to the bag. Have them write their letter on the chalkboard.

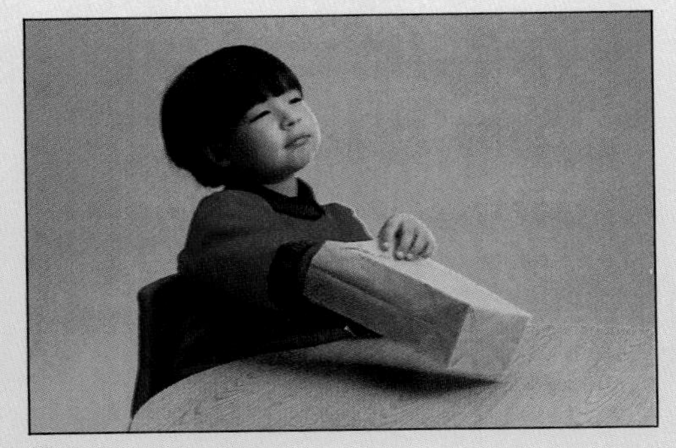

City and Country (Celebrating Cultural Diversity) Have children cut from magazines pictures of things they would see in the city or the country. When they have enough examples, have them hold up pictures and discuss where they would be seen. Have them paste these pictures on a poster under the headings **City** and **Country.**

Take Another Look (Visual, Oral Language) Place a teddy bear on a chair. Have groups of children lie on the floor so they are looking up at the bear. Next have them kneel just in front of it. Finally, hold their hands as they stand on a table, one by one, and view the bear from above. Talk about how the bear looks from each of these different perspectives.

Objectives

Learns the shape of **T** by finger tracing a large model letter.
Writes the capital letter **T** and traces a name beginning with **T**.

Prepare

Play "Take Time for **T**" with children. Have children sit at tables in groups of six. Supply each group with about 32 index cards, each card displaying either a **C, G, O, Q, S, I, L,** or **T**. Put five spoons in the middle of the table. Have children:

- shuffle and distribute the cards facedown around the table;
- quickly turn up their cards, one after the other;
- quietly pick up a spoon when a **T** is turned up.

The player without a spoon loses that round.

Use the *D'Nealian® Handwriting Big Book* to preview the page.

Teach (page 119)

Have children:

- identify the capital letter **T;**
- find Tim at the starting arrow;
- finger trace the path from Tim to the tub and from his twin to the right while you say the following mnemonic sentence:

    Tim tumbles toward the tub. Then Tom tiptoes across the tightrope.

- air trace the letter **T**.

ACTIVITY BANK

Time to Grow 

Done to a T (Letter Practice, Creative) Help children remember **T** as a telephone pole with birds sitting on top or as a tightrope holding Tom Tightrope-Walker. Ask children to write capital **T** at the writing center on large, unlined paper. Then have them draw Tom, the telephone birdies, or whatever strikes their fancy on the top of their **T's**.

Marilyn Knudson
Alice Terry Elementary
Englewood, CO

Dough T Dough (Tactile, Kinesthetic) Provide bread dough for children to use in shaping capital **T**. Show them how to roll out ropes of dough, break off two pieces, and make a **T**. Help children bake the letters. Have children eat them.

Phonics Corner

The sentence used to help children form the letter **T**,

Tim tumbles toward the **tub.** Then **Tom tiptoes** across the **tightrope.**

may also be used to work on sound-letter correspondence. Repeat the sentence and call on volunteers to tell you the words they hear that begin with /t/.

Teach (page 120)

Call attention to the picture at the top of the page. Have children:

- identify the various letters;
- find and color each **T** red and each **S** blue;
- identify the resulting picture as a circus tent;
- color the rest of the picture in other colors.

Write a capital **T** on the chalkboard. Ask a volunteer to write a lower-case **t.** Compare them.

Call attention to the lower half of the page. Have children:

- finger trace the boxed letter **T** as you read aloud the letter description;
- pencil trace the gray letters;
- write the letter **T** using the starting dots;
- trace the name *Tiptop.*

Follow Up

Self-Evaluation Have children check their own work by asking themselves:

- Did I cross the top of each **T?**
- Do my **T's** slant the same way?

Additional Resources

Manuscript Alpha Touch letter **T**
D'Nealian® Handwriting Big Book letter **T**

Color each T red. Color each S blue.

Tiptop Circus

Tiptop

120 Writing T

Children color spaces marked **T** red and spaces marked **S** blue to reveal the circus tent. They trace and write the letter **T** and then write the name **Tiptop**.

Letter Description

Top start; slant down.
Cross the top.

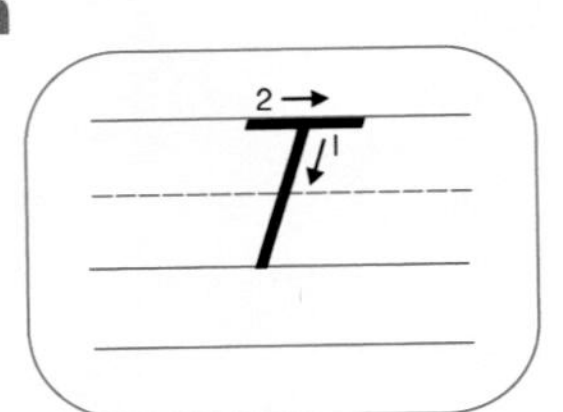

ACTIVITY BANK

Moving Write Along

Animal Match-up (Letter Recognition, Visual) Write these animals and names in two columns on the chalkboard: *tiger, snake, cat, otter; Carl, Susie, Ollie, Tom.* Have children match the name with the animal having the same letter at the beginning of its name. Children might then choose one of the animals to illustrate.

T Tower (Phonics, Fine Motor) Make a large cutout of capital **T** and pin it to the bulletin board. Provide magazines for children to look through in order to cut out pictures of things beginning with /t/. Help children pin their pictures around the **T**.

Letter Band (Kinesthetic, Letter Recognition) Give each child one of the capital letters learned so fa and a musical instrument such as rhythm sticks or bells. Explain that children are to play their instruments only when the card yo hold up is the lower-case letter of the capital they hold. After a few practice trials, hold up two or more letters at one time.

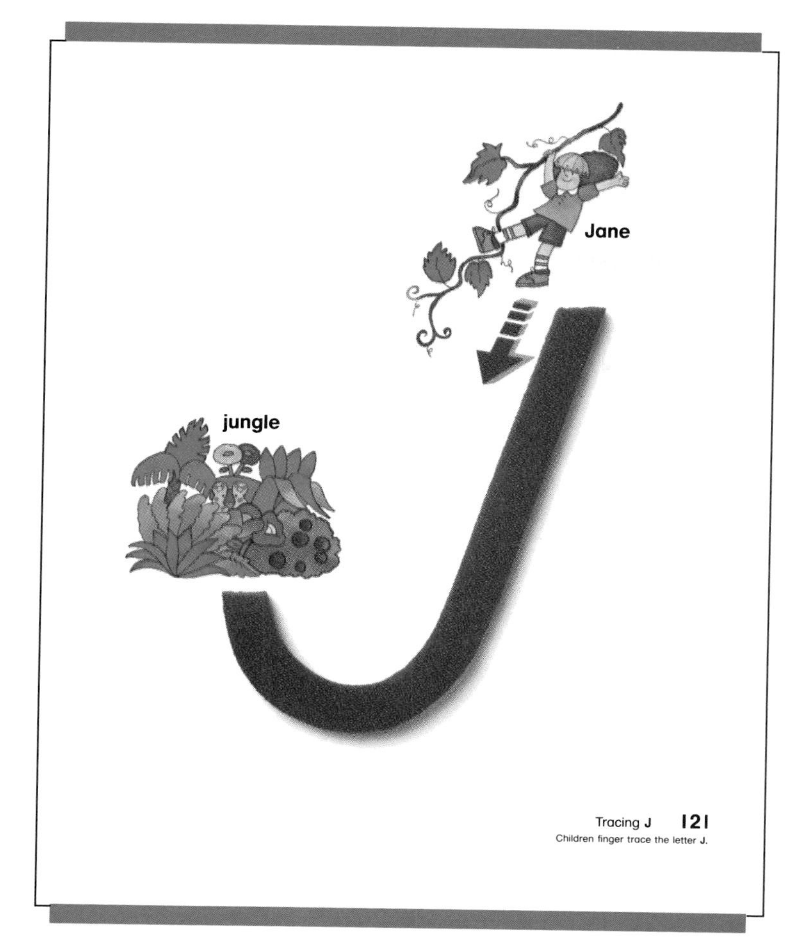

Objectives

Learns the shape of **J** by finger tracing a large model letter.
Writes the capital letter **J** and traces a name beginning with **J**.

Prepare

Play "Jump for Jane" with children. Tell them that you are going to read them a story, and every time they hear the name *Jane* they are to jump up from their seats and say, *Jump for Jane!* The story could begin something like the following:

> Once upon a time in the jungle, there lived a girl named *Jane.* She lived with a cat named Jake and a dog named Joker. Jake loved *Jane,* but Joker was always giving *Jane* a hard time. *Jane* loved to swing from the vines and jump into the jungle, but one day Joker put grease on the vines and *Jane* slipped and fell. . . .

Use the *D'Nealian® Handwriting Big Book* to preview the page.

Teach (page 121)

Have children:

- identify the capital letter **J;**
- find Jane at the starting arrow;
- finger trace the path from Jane to the jungle while you say the following mnemonic sentence:
  Jane jumps from the vine into the jungle.
- air trace the letter **J.**

ACTIVITY BANK

Time to Grow 

J Pictures (Letter Practice, Creative) At the writing center, have children write capital **J** on plain paper. Tell them to use the **J** as part of a picture, such as an umbrella handle, a person's nose, or a slide at the park. Display finished drawings.

Jungle Hunt (Letter Practice, Critical Thinking) Look at page 121 with children. Ask them to describe what Jane is doing. Tell them there is a jaguar hiding on the page and ask them to help find it (*amid the jungle*). Write _*aguar* and _*ane* on the chalkboard and ask a volunteer to come up and insert the lower-case **j** and capital **J** on the proper line.

Phonics Corner

The sentence used to help children form the letter **J,**

> **Jane jumps** from the vine into the **jungle.**

may also be used to work on sound-letter correspondence. Repeat the sentence and call on volunteers to tell you the words they hear that begin with /j/.

Teach (page 122)

Call attention to the books at the top of the page. Have children:

- identify the pictures and the **J's** on the books;
- listen as you read the titles: *Tarzan and Jane, Japan Today,* and *July;*
- circle each **J** in the three titles.

Write a capital **J** on the chalkboard. Ask a volunteer to write a lower-case **j**. Compare them.

Call attention to the lower half of the page. Have children:

- finger trace the boxed letter **J** as you read aloud the letter description;
- pencil trace the gray letters;
- write the letter **J** using the starting dots;
- trace the name *Japan.*

Follow Up

Self-Evaluation Have children check their own work by asking themselves:

- Do my **J's** curve up left?
- Do my **J's** slant the same way?

Additional Resources

Manuscript Alpha Touch letter **J**
D'Nealian® Handwriting Big Book letter **J**

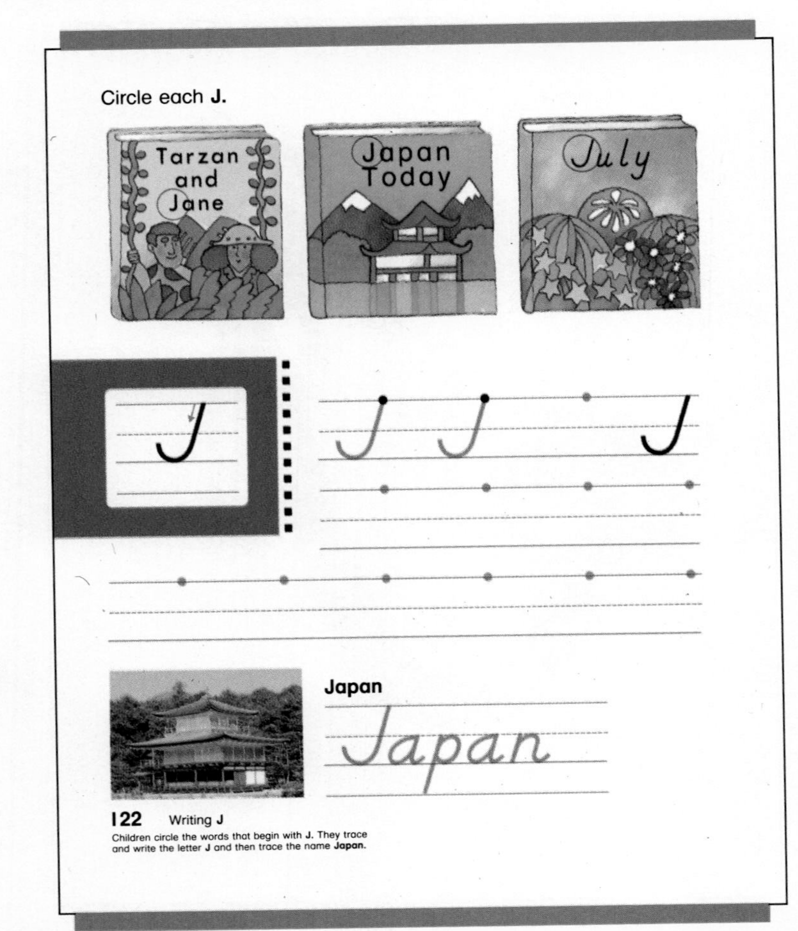

122 Writing J
Children circle the words that begin with J. They trace and write the letter J and then trace the name **Japan**.

Letter Description

Top start; slant down, and curve up left.

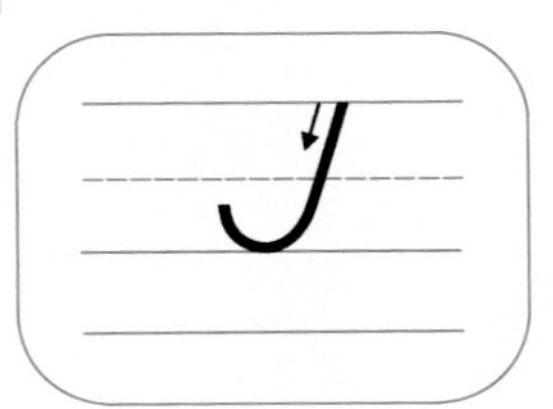

ACTIVITY BANK

Moving Write Along

A Bang of a Holiday (Celebrating Cultural Diversity) Talk about the Fourth of July. Discuss how most Americans spend this holiday (*watching a parade, going on a picnic, having a barbecue, watching fireworks*). Ask if anyone can tell about how other countries celebrate their national holidays.

Book Designers (Letter Practice, Creative) Distribute colored construction paper, yarn, glue, and crayons to children. Tell them they are book designers and must make a cover for the letter **J**. Have children write **J** and use the yarn to trace the letter. Children can decorate the cover using crayons.

Origami Artists (Fine Motor, Creative) Talk about the ancient Japanese art of origami. Bring in books on the subject and demonstrate a few simple projects to children. Give them origami paper and help them fold it into a **J**-like shape. Display their work.

Objectives

Learns the shape of **U** by finger tracing a large model letter.
Writes the capital letter **U** and traces a name beginning with **U**.

Prepare

Play "What's in the Box?" with children by drawing various shapes on the chalkboard and telling them that they contain special gifts—the letters of the alphabet from which we write the words that tell all the stories in the world. Below are a few shapes you might try:

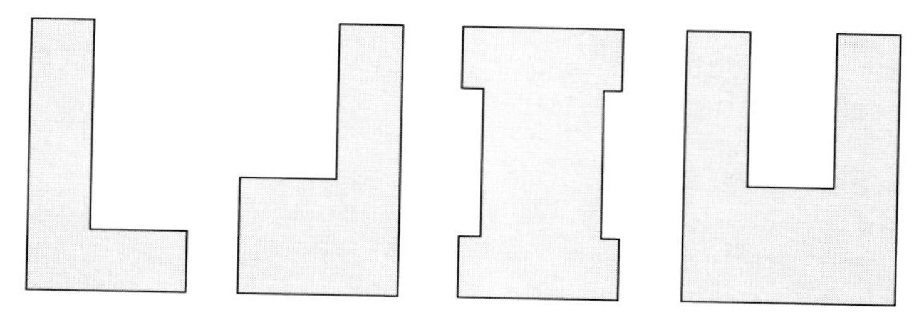

Have children:
- guess the names of the letters that would fit into the boxes;
- come to the chalkboard and write the letter that would fit in each box on or below the box;
- think of some other box shapes and draw them on the board for others to guess.

Use the *D'Nealian® Handwriting Big Book* to preview the page.

Teach (page 123)

Have children:
- identify the capital letter **U**;
- find Ulrika at the starting arrow;
- finger trace the path from Ulrika to her uncle while you say the following mnemonic sentence:
  Ulrika brings an unusual gift to her unhappy uncle.
- air trace the letter **U**.

ACTIVITY BANK

Time to Grow

Horseshoe U (Letter Practice, Fine Motor) Tell children to think of capital **U** as a horseshoe with an extra curve. Have them write a number of **U's** on unlined paper at the writing center. Display their **U's** as tracks leading to a horse.

Marilyn Knudson
Alice Terry Elementary
Englewood, CO

Musical Letter Chairs (Kinesthetic, Letter Recognition) Tape to chairs capital letters learned so far. Have children march around chairs and sit when the music stops. They name the letters on their chairs. The child without a chair may get back in the game by naming a letter someone else doesn't know. Remove a chair each round.

Phonics Corner

The sentence used to help children form the letter **U**,

Ulrika brings an **unusual** gift to her **unhappy uncle.**

may also be used to work on sound-letter correspondence. Repeat the sentence and call on volunteers to tell you the words they hear that begin with /u/.

Teach (page 124)

Call attention to the picture at the top of the page. Have children:
- describe what they see in the picture;
- find and circle the **U's** hidden in the picture.

Write a capital **U** on the chalkboard. Ask a volunteer to write a lower-case **u**. Compare them.

Call attention to the lower half of the page. Have children:
- finger trace the boxed letter **U** as you read aloud the letter description;
- pencil trace the gray letters;
- write the letter **U** using the starting dots;
- trace the name *Ulrika.*

Follow Up

Self-Evaluation Have children check their own work by asking themselves:
- Did I start at the starting dots?
- Do my **U's** slant the same way?

Additional Resources

Manuscript Alpha Touch letter **U**
D'Nealian® Handwriting Big Book letter **U**

Letter Description

Top start; down, around, up, down, and a monkey tail.

ACTIVITY BANK

Moving Write Along

U Words Tell Where (Creative, Letter Recognition) Duplicate a cutaway picture of a two-story house. Next to the house are the words *Upstairs, Up, Upon,* and *Under.* Children draw according to your directions:

Upstairs is a bed.
Upon the bed is a cat.
Up from the chimney comes smoke.
Under the bed is a mouse.

Have them circle the **U** each time a **U** word is used. Let them complete the picture.

UUUsing the Library (Letter Recognition, Creative) Take children to the picture book area of the school library. Have them find books whose titles begin with **U**. Help them read these titles. Back in the classroom, have them draw their own book covers.

We Want U (Letter Practice, Social Studies) Laminate maps with labels of countries that begin with **U**. Have children circle the **U** on each label. Discuss the various countries with children.

Pam Yeary
Pershing Elementary
Orlando, FL

Objectives

Learns the shape of **H** by finger tracing a large model letter.

Writes the capital letter **H** and traces a name beginning with **H**.

Prepare

Have children play "Letter Partners." Write each of the capital letters learned thus far **(C, G, O, Q, S, I, L, T, J, U,** and **H)** on pieces of note paper, then write a matching letter on another piece of note paper. You should have 22 letters in all. Pin one on the back of each child without the child seeing the letter. Have children:

- try to find their matching letter by asking one another questions about the letter they are wearing;
- line up at the front of the room with their partner;
- write their letters on the chalkboard.

Use the *D'Nealian® Handwriting Big Book* to preview the page.

Teach (page 125)

Have children:

- identify the capital letter **H;**
- find Hector the Hawk at the starting arrow;
- finger trace the path from Hector at 1 to the hay, from 2 to the henhouse, and from 3 to the hen while you say the following mnemonic sentence:

  Hector looks for the hen in the hay.
  He looks for the hen in her home.
  Then, he finds her on the hill.

- air trace the letter **H**.

ACTIVITY BANK

Time to Grow 

H Is for House (Letter Practice, Oral Language) Have children write capital **H** at the writing center on large pieces of unlined paper. Invite them to turn the **H** into the house of their dreams. Help them write *My House* at the top of their papers. Write down their descriptions of their houses.

Monkey-bar H (Letter Practice, Fine Motor) I teach capital **H** as the "monkey bar" letter. The first stroke is the left pole, the second is the right pole, and the third is the middle bar. When children write a nice **H,** I draw a monkey hanging from the bar saying, "Good job!"

Marilyn Knudson
Alice Terry Elementary
Englewood, CO

Phonics Corner

The sentence used to help children form the letter **H,**

Hector looks for the **hen** in the **hay. He** looks for the **hen** in her **home.** Then, **he** finds **her** on the **hill.**

may also be used to work on sound-letter correspondence. Repeat the sentence and call on volunteers to tell you the words that begin with /h/.

Teach (page 126)

Call attention to the animals at the top of the page. Have children:

- identify the animals as birds (*hawk, hen,* and *peacock*);
- listen as you read *Hector, Hilda,* and *Paul;*
- circle the names that begin with **H**.

Write a capital **H** on the chalkboard. Ask a volunteer to write a lower-case **h.** Compare them.

Call attention to the lower half of the page. Have children:

- finger trace the boxed letter **H** as you read aloud the letter description;
- pencil trace the gray letters;
- write the letters using the starting dots;
- trace the name *Hector.*

Follow Up

Self-Evaluation Have children check their own work by asking themselves:

- Do my **H's** have bars across the middle?
- Do my **H's** touch the top line?

Additional Resources

Manuscript Alpha Touch letter **H**
D'Nealian® Handwriting Big Book letter **H**

Letter Description

Top start; slant down. Another top start, to the right; slant down. Middle bar across.

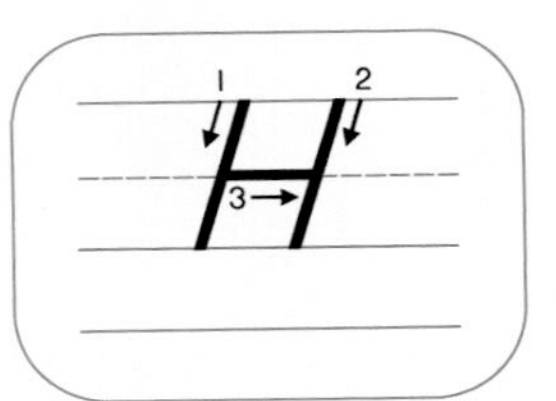

ACTIVITY BANK

Moving Write Along

Farming for H (Critical Thinking, Fine Motor) Make a letter farm using capital **H** and lower-case **h**.

Put squares of paper, a white paper fence, and a barn on the bulletin board to create a farm scene. Help children think of animals beginning with /h/. Let them draw or cut out pictures to put on the farm. Next, have them decide on proper names beginning with **H** for each animal. Write each animal's entire name on a "sign" and let children trace the name. Hang the names on the bulletin board.

H Strips (Tactile, Fine Motor) Cut out two strips 4" long and one strip 3" long for each child. Have children paste these three strips on a large piece of paper to make the letter **H,** pasting in the same order they would write the letter.

Clapping for H (Auditory, Small Groups) Give small groups of children paper with capital **H** written on it in colored glue that has dried. Children take turns finger tracing as you clap your hands for each stroke. Children can also air trace as you clap.

Objectives

Learns the shape of **K** by finger tracing a large model letter.
Writes the capital letter **K** and traces a name beginning with **K**.

Prepare

Write the name *Kim* on the chalkboard. Say the name for the children then ask them to say it with you. Erase the **K** and ask a volunteer to come up to the board and write a capital **J.** Now say the name *Jim* with the children. Have a volunteer erase the **J.** Call on another child to come up and write a capital **T.** Say the name *Tim* with the children. Give each child a card containing either *Kim, Jim,* or *Tim.* Have children:

- stand up as you read the name on their card;
- volunteer to read their own cards and have those with similar cards sit down;
- exchange cards and read the name they have been given.

Use the *D'Nealian® Handwriting Big Book* to preview the page.

Teach (page 127)

Have children:

- identify the capital letter **K;**
- find Kim at the starting arrow;
- finger trace the path from Kim to the kite and his kitten to the kitchen while you say the following mnemonic sentence:

  Kim hurries to find his kite. Kim's kitten kicks the kite string into the kitchen.
- air trace the letter **K.**

ACTIVITY BANK

Time to Grow 

Finding K and k (Letter Practice, Fine Motor) Use a chalkboard at the writing center to write names that include capital **K** and lowercase **k** (*Kent Lisker* and *Tanyka King,* for example). Read them aloud and ask a volunteer to erase both **K** and **k.** Let another child put the letters back. Continue with other names.

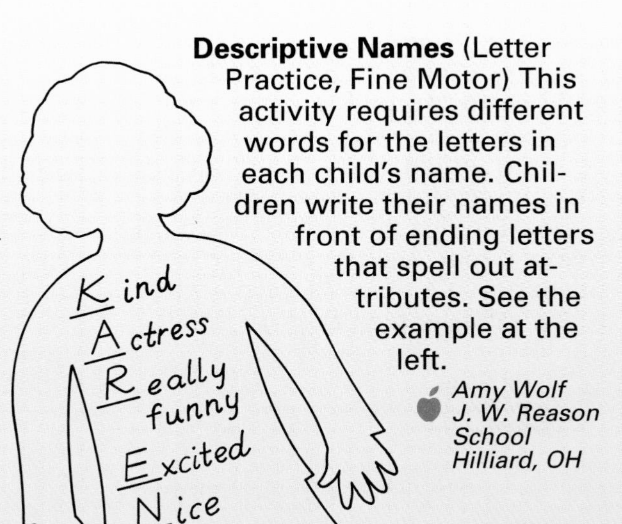

Descriptive Names (Letter Practice, Fine Motor) This activity requires different words for the letters in each child's name. Children write their names in front of ending letters that spell out attributes. See the example at the left.

Amy Wolf
J. W. Reason School
Hilliard, OH

Phonics Corner

The sentence used to help children form the letter **K,**

Kim hurries to find his **kite. Kim's kitten kicks** the **kite** string into the **kitchen.**

may also be used to work on sound-letter correspondence. Repeat the sentence and call on volunteers to tell you the words they hear that begin with /k/.

Teach (page 128)

Call attention to the picture at the top of the page. Have children:

- describe what they see in the picture;
- trace the **K** on the kite;
- color the kite.

Write a capital **K** on the chalkboard. Ask a volunteer to write a lower-case **k.** Compare them.

Call attention to the lower half of the page. Have children:

- finger trace the boxed letter **K** as you read aloud the letter description;
- pencil trace the gray letters;
- write the letter **K** using the starting dots;
- trace the name *Kim.*

Follow Up

Self-Evaluation Have children check their own work by asking themselves:

- Did I start at the starting dots?
- Do my **K's** have their monkey tails?

Additional Resources

Manuscript Alpha Touch letter **K**
D'Nealian® Handwriting Big Book letter **K**

Letter Description

Top start; slant down. Another top start, to the right; slant down left, touch, slant down right, and a monkey tail.

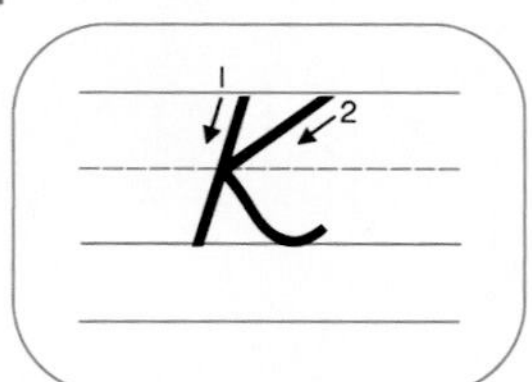

ACTIVITY BANK

Moving Write Along

Kite Creations (Eye-Hand Coordination, Letter Practice) Duplicate four large triangles and six small triangles on paper. Have each child write capital **K** on the large triangles and lower-case **k** on the small triangles. Have them cut out the shapes, form a kite with the large triangles, and paste them on heavy paper. Next have them paste down a piece of yarn and the small triangles to form a tail and bows.

Marly Glaw
Shreiner School and Academy
Marietta, GA

Go Fly a Kite (Creative, Kinesthetic) Help children make kites from construction paper. Have them write capital **K** on the kites and decorate them with paper cutouts, glitter, or poster paint. Let children take their kites outside and "fly" them.

Katie Kitten (Fine Motor, Letter Practice) Distribute an outline of a kitten made from construction paper. Have children write capital **K** on their kittens and decorate the tails and ears with pieces of cotton.

Objectives

Practices writing the capital letters **I, L, T,** and **J.**
Traces the names *Tiny* and *Jojo.*

Prepare

Draw a slanted line like the first stroke in **I, L, T,** and **J** on the chalkboard, making it fairly large. Tell children they are going to be "alpha-magicians" who can change this single line into capital letters. Have children, in turn:

- come to the board and draw the top stroke that will change the line into a **T;**
- erase the top stroke and add the bottom stroke that will turn the line into an **L;**
- erase the bottom stroke and add the two strokes that will turn the line into an **I;**
- erase these two strokes and add the curve that will turn the line into a **J.**

Repeat the process until all children have had a chance to be alpha-magicians.

Teach (page 129)

Have children:

- identify the capital letters **I, L, T,** and **J;**
- pencil trace the gray letters;
- write each letter using the starting dots;
- trace the names *Tiny* and *Jojo.*

Follow Up

Self-Evaluation Have children check their own work by asking themselves:

- Do my **I's** and **T's** have cross strokes?
- Does my **J** curve left?

Additional Resources

Manuscript Alpha Touch letters **I, L, T,** and **J**
D'Nealian® Handwriting Big Book letters **I, L, T,** and **J**

ACTIVITY BANK

Streetcar Capitals (Letter Practice, Gross Motor) Have children play "Streetcar." One child, the "conductor," stands behind the chair of the first child in the group. The conductor holds up a lower-case letter associated with one of the capital letters learned so far. If the seated child writes the capital letter correctly on the chalkboard, the conductor moves behind the next chair. If the child cannot write the letter correctly, the conductor may try. After a time, call for a new conductor.

Rain Forest Alert (Science, Phonics) The rain forest is a current topic, and students are learning about the many animals that live there. Talk about the three-toed sloth, the tapir, toucan, tamarin, and tarantula. Show the children the animals' pictures. Ask them to think of personal names that begin with **T** for these animals. Write them on the board.

Karla Kensey
Britton Elementary
Hilliard, OH

Animal Parade (Kinesthetic, Letter Recognition) Tape a large **I, L T,** and **J** on the floor. One at a time, children will pretend to be either Iggy Iguana, Liz Lion, Tom Turtle, or Jack Jaguar. They must tell their animal name and move like that animal to the letter that starts the name.

Objectives
Practices writing the capital letters **U, H,** and **K.**
Traces the names *Hubie* and *Koko.*

Prepare
Write the capital letters learned thus far in block print on different pieces of large cardboard. Place them in different locations around the classroom. Give each child an index card with one of these letters written in D'Nealian® Handwriting on it. Have children:
- hold their card facedown until you tell them to look at it;
- stand together in the center of the room;
- look at their card and search for the large matching letter displayed in the classroom;
- line up beside that letter holding up the match.

Teach (page 130)
Have children:
- identify the capital letters **U, H,** and **K;**
- pencil trace the gray letters;
- write each letter using the starting dots;
- trace the names *Hubie* and *Koko.*

Follow Up
Self-Evaluation Have children check their own work by asking themselves:
- Do my **H's** have their middle bars?
- Do my **K's** have their monkey tails?

Additional Resources
Manuscript Alpha Touch letters **U, H,** and **K**
D'Nealian® Handwriting Big Book letters **U, H,** and **K**

Practice

U U U
H H H
K K K

Hubie
Hubie

Koko
Koko

130 Practice

Children trace and write the letters **U, H,** and **K** and then trace the names **Hubie** and **Koko.**

ACTIVITY BANK

Special Needs (Auditory Deficits) For these children, brilliant fluorescent colors help implant a strong mental image of letter form and size. On a black plastic kite, write a very large **K** in fluorescent paint. Invite children to take turns finger tracing the **K.** Give each child plain white paper on which to write the same letter. Have children highlight the letters with a fluorescent marker. Cut them out and attach them to the tail of the kite. If possible, fly the kite on a windy day.

Evaluating Letters (Letter Form, Visual) In order to encourage self-evaluation, I ask my class to analyze letter formation. They circle the letter in each row of the lesson that they feel is closest to the model. I also select a letter.

Sometimes the choice is the same, but sometimes it is not. I find this to be a positive way to share evaluation.

Diann Bates
Roeland Park Elementary
Roeland Park, KS

Show and Tell (Oral Language, Letter Recognition) Have children bring in their favorite stuffed animals or dolls and name them or give them names. Write these names on the chalkboard. Let children tell about their dolls and animals in front of the class.

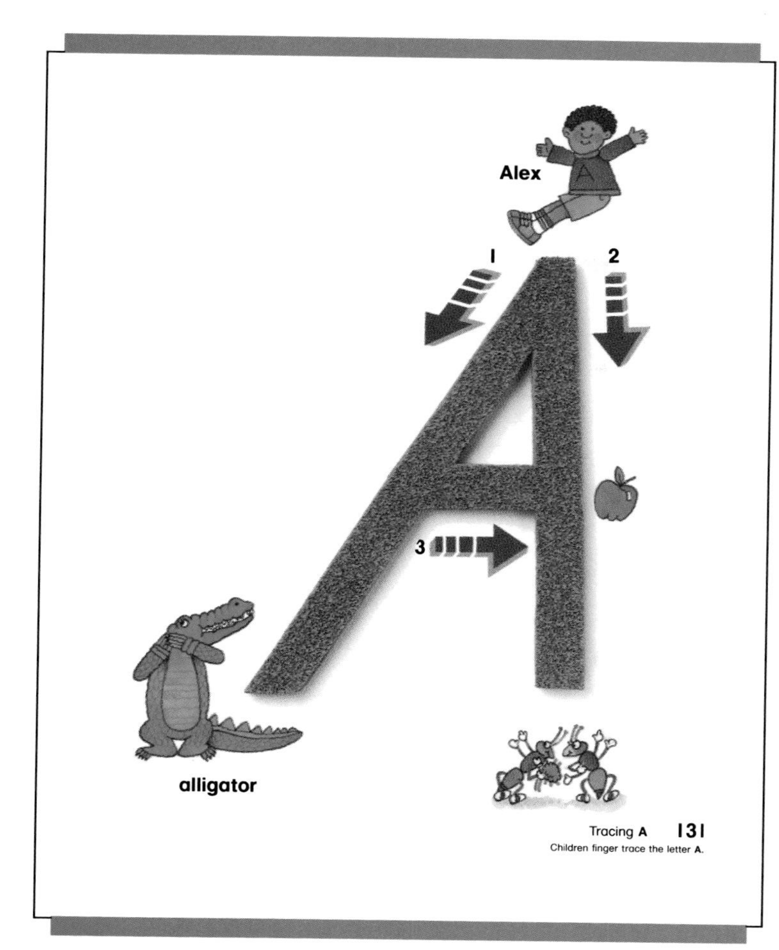

Objectives

Learns the shape of **A** by finger tracing a large model letter.
Writes the capital letter **A** and traces a name beginning with **A.**

Prepare

Play "My Name Is Alex" with children. Write a capital **A** on the chalkboard and say this sentence: *My name is Alex, and my dog's name is Annie, and we come from Alaska, and we sell apples.* Ask for volunteers to think of other **A** words they could use in the sentence, such as *Allen, Alberta, Alabama,* and *artichokes.* Continue playing until children run out of **A** words.

Use the *D'Nealian® Handwriting Big Book* to preview the page.

Teach (page 131)

Have children:
- identify the capital letter **A;**
- find Alex at the starting arrow;
- finger trace the path from Alex to the alligator, the ants, and the apple while you say the following mnemonic sentence:

  Alex visits the alligator. Alex visits the ants. Then, Alex eats an apple.
- air trace the letter **A.**

ACTIVITY BANK

Time to Grow

The A's Have It (Phonics, Letter Practice) In small groups at the writing center, have children listen as you read. Tell them that each time they hear a name that begins with **A,** they should write **A** on their unlined papers. Read these names: *Alex, Jack, Ann, Oscar, Alice, Tom, Hal, Albert,* and *Kathy.* Have them count the number of **A's** they have written and write the number on their papers (*4*).

Alpha People (Kinesthetic, Critical Thinking) As a part of handwriting, the children decide how many people would be needed to make each letter using their bodies. They then demonstrate.

Jo Ann M. Spear
Clark Community School
Weldon, IA

Phonics Corner

The sentence used to help children form the letter **A,**

Alex visits the **alligator. Alex** visits the **ants**. Then, **Alex** eats **an apple.**

may also be used to work on sound-letter correspondence. Repeat the sentence and call on volunteers to tell you the words that begin with /a/.

Teach (page 132)

Call attention to the scene at the top of the page. Have children:

- describe the scene;
- find and circle each hidden **A**.

Write a capital **A** on the chalkboard. Ask a volunteer to write a lower-case **a.** Compare them.

Call attention to the lower half of the page. Have children:

- finger trace the boxed letter **A** as you read aloud the letter description;
- pencil trace the gray letters;
- write the letters using the starting dots;
- trace the name *Alex.*

Follow Up

Self-Evaluation Have children check their own work by asking themselves:

- Do my **A's** have bars across the middle?
- Do my **A's** touch the top line?

Additional Resources

Manuscript Alpha Touch letter **A**
D'Nealian® Handwriting Big Book letter **A**

Letter Description

Top start; slant down left. Same start; slant down right. Middle bar across.

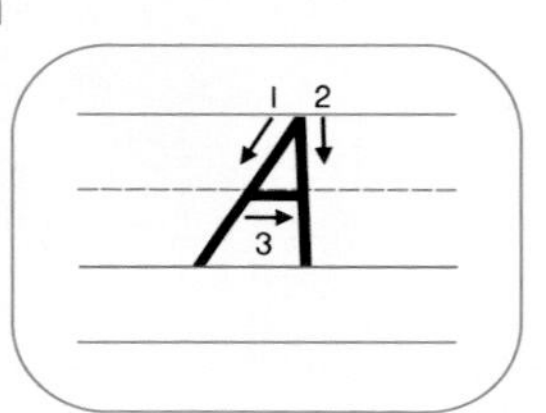

ACTIVITY BANK

Moving Write Along

Practice Makes Perfect (Letter Practice, Fine Motor) I make dittos like the one below for the children to use before working in their books or at the writing center. I do this for all letters.

On the back we write a word several times. Perhaps children could also draw a picture.

Vonda Lichtenfelt
Salk Elementary
Fraser, MI

I Spy A (Kinesthetic, Letter Recognition) Tell children to close their eyes as you hide a capital **A** and a lower-case **a** around the room. Ask them to look for the letters and, when they spot them, to sit down immediately and say, *Capital* ***A,*** *little* ***a,*** *I spied both today.* Play the game until all children have spied **a** and **A.**

Bake an A (Tactile, Kinesthetic) Make bread dough and distribute a small amount of it to each child. Have children tear off pieces of dough, roll them into strips, and form the strips into capital **A's.** Bake the letters and invite children to eat them.

Objectives

Learns the shape of **B** by finger tracing a large model letter.
Writes the capital letter **B** and traces a name beginning with **B.**

Prepare

Have children play "Bicycling to **B.**" Place four large cards, each containing the letter **B,** across the room. Arrange the class into four lines. Tell children they are going to pretend to ride a bicycle to the **B** and back again. (Use real tricycles if they are available.) Upon returning, each bicyclist must tap the hand of his or her waiting teammate to start that person racing. The line of children who finish racing to **B** and back first wins.

Use the *D'Nealian® Handwriting Big Book* to preview the page.

Teach (page 133)

Have children:
- identify the capital letter **B;**
- find Beth at the starting arrow;
- finger trace the path from Beth past the butterfly and bees to the bench while you say the following mnemonic sentence:

  Beth bicycles by a butterfly and two bees before resting on a bench.
- air trace the letter **B.**

ACTIVITY BANK

Time to Grow 

Writing B (Letter Practice, Tactile)
Children should write capital letter **B** on large pieces of unlined paper at the writing center. Have materials available for them to make their **B's** tactile.

Butterfly B (Creative, Fine Motor)
Draw a large **B** on the outside of a folded piece of plain paper. Have children trace the **B** and cut along the curves of the letter. (Caution them not to cut on the fold.)

When children open the paper, a butterfly shape appears. Have glitter, bits of paper, paint, and so on available for decorating. Help children tape pipe-cleaner antennae to their butterflies.

Phonics Corner

The sentence used to help children form the letter **B,**

Beth bicycles by a **butterfly** and two **bees before** resting on a **bench.**

may also be used to work on sound-letter correspondence. Repeat the sentence and call on volunteers to tell you the words they hear that begin with /b/.

Teach (page 134)

Call attention to the picture at the top of the page. Have children:

- describe what they see in the picture;
- trace each **B** on the insects' bodies;
- color the picture.

Write a capital **B** on the chalkboard. Ask a volunteer to write a lower-case **b.** Compare them.

Call attention to the lower half of the page. Have children:

- finger trace the boxed letter **B** as you read aloud the letter description;
- pencil trace the gray letters;
- write the letter **B** using the starting dots;
- trace the name *Betty.*

Follow Up

Self-Evaluation Have children check their own work by asking themselves:

- Are my **B's** closed at the top and bottom?
- Are my **B's** the correct size?

Additional Resources

Manuscript Alpha Touch letter **B**
D'Nealian® Handwriting Big Book letter **B**

Trace each **B.** Color the picture.

Presenting: Betty Butterfly and Bob Bee

B B B B

Betty

Betty

134 Writing **B**

Children trace the **B** in the butterfly and the bee and then color the picture. They trace and write the letter **B** and then trace the name **Betty.**

Letter Description

Top start; slant down, up, around halfway, close, around again, and close.

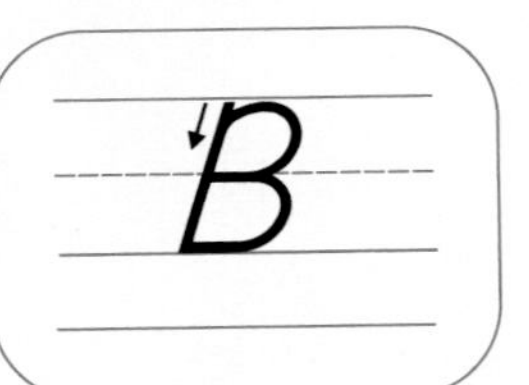

ACTIVITY BANK

Moving Write Along

Bob Bee and the Stingers (Oral Language, Kinesthetic) Write *Presenting: Betty Butterfly and Bob Bee* on the chalkboard. Invite volunteers to come up and pretend to be this famous singing duo. Suggest that they make up songs such as "Bee, You Are Such a Honey," "Flutter By, Butterfly," and equally silly titles. Write the titles they suggest on the board.

Foamy Writing (Letter Practice, Tactile) I put a small blob of shaving cream on each student's desk. They smear it around and practice their letters. They love it!

Lea Rae Porta
Lakeland Elementary
Lowry City, MO

Buzzing B (Phonics, Auditory) Read the names of baseball players to children, telling them to make a buzzing sound when they hear a name beginning with the same sound they hear in *Beth* and *bench.* Use such names as *Fisk, Boggs, Gooden, Butler, Sandberg, Boddicker, Baker, Ryan, Bonds,* and *Bell.*

Objectives

Learns the shape of **D** by finger tracing a large model letter.
Writes the capital letter **D** and traces a name beginning with **D**.

Prepare

Play "Dance to **D**" with children. Call four children to the chalkboard. These children will, in turn, write a **D, S, B,** or **T,** whichever they choose. Instruct the rest of the class to stand and respond to the letter written in these ways: Dance to the **D.** Shake to the **S.** Bounce to the **B.** Turn to the **T.** Children must remember which activity corresponds to each of the four letters, and react accordingly. After a time, call four different children to the board.

Use the *D'Nealian® Handwriting Big Book* to preview the page.

Teach (page 135)

Have children:
- identify the capital letter **D;**
- find Daisy at the starting arrow;
- finger trace the path from Daisy to the door while you say the following mnemonic sentence:
  Daisy dances down and around to the door.
- air trace the letter **D.**

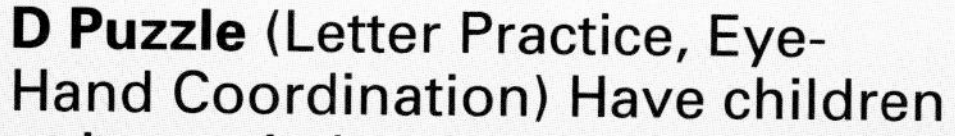

Time to Grow

D Puzzle (Letter Practice, Eye-Hand Coordination) Have children write capital **D** on sheets of construction paper at the writing center. Ask them to pick their best **D** and draw a picture of Daisy Doe, Davy Duck, or Diggy Dog below it.

Next, have them cut their papers into puzzle pieces and exchange them. Have children put the puzzles back together.

D Is for Dinosaur (Visual, Letter Recognition) Read the story *Danny and the Dinosaur* by Syd Hoff with children. Before you begin, show the class the cover and have volunteers point to each capital **D** in the title.

Phonics Corner

The sentence used to help children form the letter **D,**

Daisy dances down and around to the **door.**

may also be used to work on sound-letter correspondence. Repeat the sentence and call on volunteers to tell you the words they hear that begin with /d/.

Teach (page 136)

Call attention to the picture at the top of the page. Have children:
- describe what they see in the picture;
- listen as you read *Daisy Doe's Dance Studio;*
- circle each **D** in the title.

Write a capital **D** on the chalkboard. Ask a volunteer to write a lower-case **d.** Compare them.

Call attention to the lower half of the page. Have children:
- finger trace the boxed letter **D** as you read aloud the letter description;
- pencil trace the gray letters;
- write the letter **D** using the starting dots;
- trace the name *Daisy.*

Follow Up

Self-Evaluation Have children check their own work by asking themselves:
- Do my **D's** start at the dot?
- Are my **D's** closed at the bottom?

Additional Resources

Manuscript Alpha Touch letter **D**
D'Nealian® Handwriting Big Book letter **D**

Letter Description

Top start; slant down, up, around, and close.

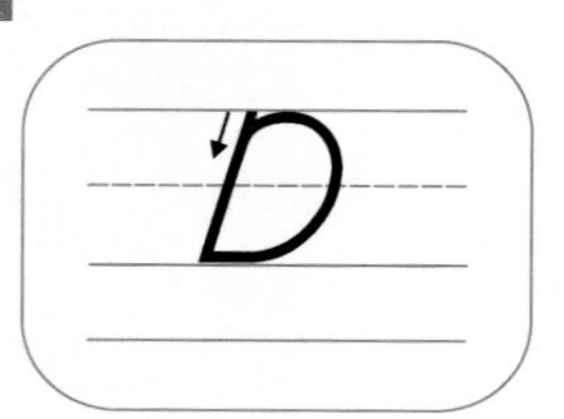

ACTIVITY BANK

Moving Write Along

Dr. Doctor (Letter Recognition, Letter Practice) Print the name *Dr. Doctor* on a headband and appoint one child to be the "eye doctor." Make an "eye chart," using the following capital letters: **C, G, O, Q, S, I, L, T, J, U, H, K, A, B,** and **D.** As the doctor points with a yard-stick to each capital letter, children, in turn, write the corresponding lower-case letter on the chalkboard.

Letters in a Name (Letter Recognition, Visual) On the chalkboard, list the names of all the children. Have a child come to the board, point to a name that contains a capital **D,** and underline the letter. Continue with other letters.

Dandy D (Letter Practice, Visual) Take a walk and pick dandelions that have gone to seed. Have children brush white glue onto dark paper in the shape of a **D.** Have them gently blow the dandelions at the paper. Enjoy the fluffy **D's.**

Objectives

Learns the shape of **M** by finger tracing a large model letter.
Writes the capital letter **M** and traces a name beginning with **M.**

Prepare

Play "What's in the Mailbag?" with children. Write each child's first initial on two envelopes. Place all envelopes in a bag or sack. Let one child be the mail carrier, who dumps all the letters onto a table or rug. Children sort through and find their two "letters." Next, put the envelopes back in the bag and have children, in turn, pick an envelope, read the letter, and give it to a child with that initial.

Use the *D'Nealian® Handwriting Big Book* to preview the page.

Teach (page 137)

Have children:

- identify the capital letter **M;**
- find Mary at the starting arrow;
- finger trace the path from Mary to the mail and then to the mailbox while you say the following mnemonic sentence:

  Mary picks up the mail.
  Then, Mary puts the mail in the mailbox.
- air trace the letter **M.**

ACTIVITY BANK

Time to Grow

Cards for MOM (Letter Practice, Fine Motor) Tint white glue with food coloring. Have children squeeze the letters **MOM** onto a piece of 11" x 8" construction paper at the writing center. Let the letters dry. Have children fold the card, sign it, and put it into an envelope addressed *MOM.*

Joyce Morrison
Martinsville School
Martinsville, TX

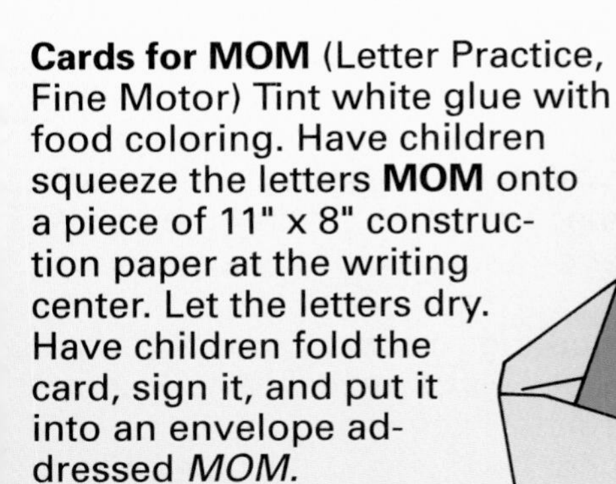

A Tale of Mail (Letter Recognition, Creative) Read *No Mail for Mitchell* by Catherine Siracusa to children. Ask volunteers to point to the **M's** on the cover. Have children draw pictures and write letters to Mitchell, a mailman for whom ". . . the mail must go through . . ." despite wind, rain, or storm.

Phonics Corner

The sentence used to help children form the letter **M,**

Mary picks up the **mail.**
Then, **Mary** puts the **mail** in the **mailbox.**

may also be used to work on sound-letter correspondence. Repeat the sentence and call on volunteers to tell you the words they hear that begin with /m/.

Teach (page 138)

Call attention to the scene at the top of the page. Have children:

- recite the numbers from 1 through 8 with you;
- connect the dots from 1 through 8;
- find the **M** shape they have created;
- color Mary's journal.

Write a capital **M** on the chalkboard. Ask a volunteer to write a lower-case **m.** Compare them.

Call attention to the lower half of the page. Have children:

- finger trace the boxed letter **M** as you read aloud the letter description;
- pencil trace the gray letters;
- write the letter **M** using the starting dots;
- trace the name *Mary.*

Follow Up

Self-Evaluation Have children check their own work by asking themselves:

- Do my **M's** touch the top line?
- Do my **M's** slant the same way?

Additional Resources

Manuscript Alpha Touch letter **M**
D'Nealian® Handwriting Big Book letter **M**

Connect the dots. Color the book.

138 Writing **M**

Children connect the dots from 1 to 8 in the shape of an **M** and then color the book. They trace and write the letter **M** and then trace the name **Mary.**

Letter Description

Top start; slant down. Same start; slant down right halfway, slant up right, and slant down.

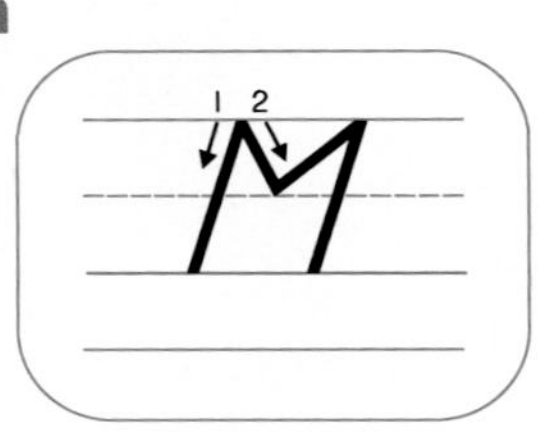

ACTIVITY BANK

Moving Write Along

Journals (Letter Practice, Creative) Put lined paper in booklets so that each child can keep a journal. They practice letters using a finger for spacing. Have them decide upon an animal or insect that begins with the letter and then draw a picture of it or write a sentence about it. As students progress, they write more sentences, and finally stories. The kids love their journals, which reflect their writing progress.

Melody Searle
Olathe Elementary
Olathe, CO

M Is for Mail (Letter Practice, Fine Motor) Give children envelopes of all sizes and colors. Have them write capital **M's** on the envelopes. Give each child colored squares of paper to serve as stamps, assigning each a different number. Children paste that number of stamps on their envelopes. Then they count each other's stamps, writing the number on the back of the envelopes.

Noodling Around (Fine Motor, Tactile) Have available dark construction paper and thick, uncooked spaghetti. Have children glue the pasta to the paper to make capital **M's.**

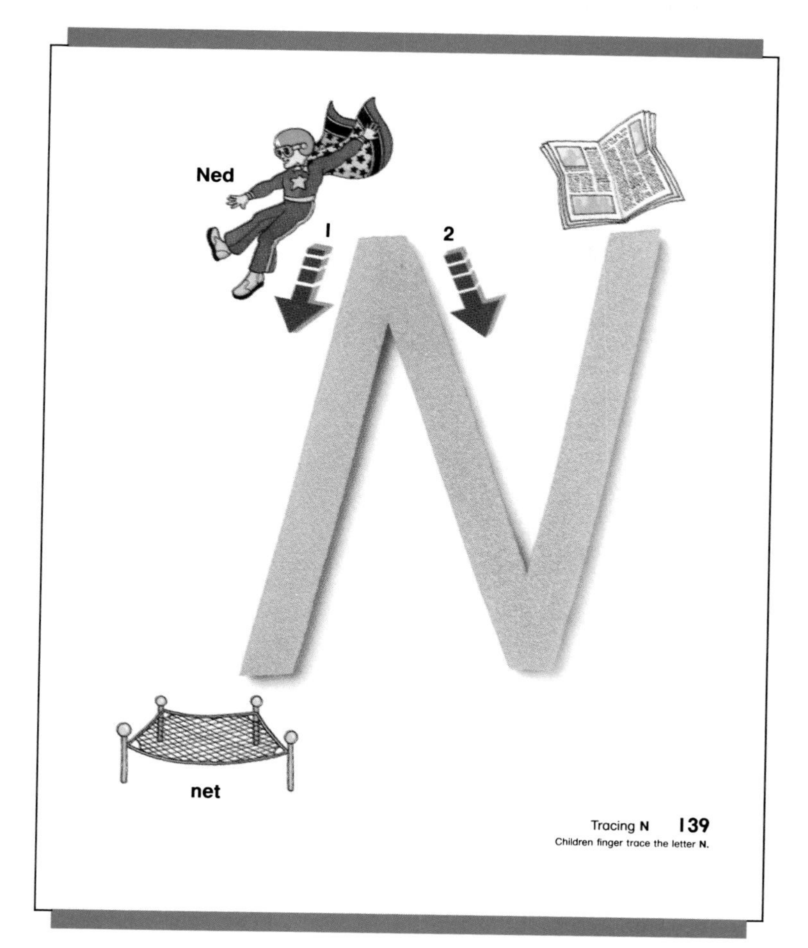

Objectives

Learns the shape of **N** by finger tracing a large model letter.
Writes the capital letter **N** and traces a name beginning with **N.**

Prepare

Have children describe their favorite superhero. What does the superhero wear? What makes a superhero super? Challenge children to pretend to be a superhero, then have them draw pictures of themselves as superheroes.

Use the *D'Nealian® Handwriting Big Book* to preview the page.

Teach (page 139)

Have children:

- identify the capital letter **N;**
- find Ned at the starting arrow;
- finger trace the path from Ned to the net and then to the newspaper while you say the following mnemonic sentence:

    Ned jumps into the net.
    Then, Ned reads the newspaper.
- air trace the letter **N.**

ACTIVITY BANK

Time to Grow

Sparkling N (Letter Practice, Tactile) Have children go to the writing center and write capital **N** on plain paper. Then have them trace the letter with glue and sprinkle it with glitter. When dry, children finger trace the letter.

Joyce Brownsberger
Fairhope Elementary
Louisville, OH

Jumping Ned (Kinesthetic, Letter Recognition) Tape a grid on the floor with capital letters in three rows of four each. Reproduce these in lower-case on index cards. In small groups, children draw cards and "jump like Ned" to the corresponding capitals. They draw and jump until they cannot reach the letter specified.

Phonics Corner

The sentence used to help children form the letter **N,**

Ned jumps into the **net**.
Then, **Ned** reads the **newspaper**.

may also be used to work on sound-letter correspondence. Repeat the sentence and call on volunteers to tell you the words they hear that begin with /n/.

Teach (page 140)

Call attention to the picture at the top of the page. Have children:

- identify the newspaper;
- listen as you read the words *News, Ned,* and *Nevada;*
- circle the word that matches *News.*

Write a capital **N** on the chalkboard. Ask a volunteer to write a lower-case **n.** Compare them.

Call attention to the lower half of the page. Have children:

- finger trace the boxed letter **N** as you read aloud the letter description;
- pencil trace the gray letters;
- write the letter **N** using the starting dots;
- trace the word *News.*

Follow Up

Self-Evaluation Have children check their own work by asking themselves:

- Do my **N's** start at the dot?
- Are my **N's** the correct size?

Additional Resources

Manuscript Alpha Touch letter **N**
D'Nealian® Handwriting Big Book letter **N**

Circle the matching word.

140 Writing N

Children circle the word at the right that matches the word **News.** They trace and write the letter **N** and then trace the word **News.**

Letter Description

Top start; slant down. Same start; slant down right, and slant up.

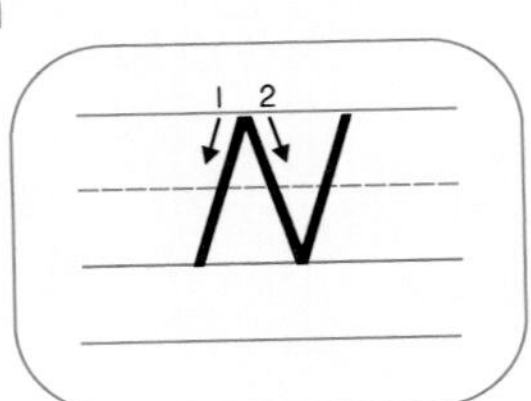

ACTIVITY BANK

Moving Write Along

Names in Categories (Letter Practice, Critical Thinking) On the chalkboard, draw a grid made of twenty-four squares. Ask the class to suggest categories to write in at the top, such as **States, Cars,** and **Books.** Volunteers write capital **C, O, T, D,** and **N** along the side. Children offer names that would fit into these categories. Write them under their headings. Children may write the capitals.

	States	Cars	Books
C	Colorado		Cat in the Hat
O			
T	Texas	Toyota	
D		Dodge	

Joanna Ransom
Smallwood Drive School
Amherst, NY

The Name's the Game (Letter Recognition, Oral Language) On separate cards, write each child's first name. Have the children show and read their cards to the class. Collect all the cards, display them, and invite children to come up and read someone else's name.

News of the Day (Oral Language, Letter Recognition) Bring in newspapers for children to look at with you. Talk about what a newspaper does, its format, and type style. Ask why they think some words are larger than others. Write a capital **N** on the chalkboard and ask children to find an **N** in their papers. Have them search for other letters in their newspapers.

Objectives

Learns the shape of **P** by finger tracing a large model letter.
Writes the capital letter **P** and traces a name beginning with **P**.

Prepare

Talk to children about pandas. Tell them that pandas come from China and love to eat bamboo stalks and leaves. People used to call them panda bears, but some scientists now believe pandas are not bears at all, but are actually related to raccoons. Bring in pictures of a panda, a raccoon, and a bear. Have children:

- compare and contrast the animals;
- draw a picture of a panda and a picture of the animal they think it most closely resembles.

Count the results of your survey and make a graph. Post the graph on the bulletin board.

Use the *D'Nealian® Handwriting Big Book* to preview the page.

Teach (page 141)

Have children:

- identify the capital letter **P;**
- find Pat at the starting arrow;
- finger trace the path from Pat to the park while you say the following mnemonic sentence:

  Pat picks a pear and a peach on the way to the park.
- air trace the letter **P.**

ACTIVITY BANK

Time to Grow

Popcorn P's (Tactile, Fine Motor) Bring a popcorn popper to class and make popcorn. Have the popped corn and large pieces of dark construction paper available to children at the writing center. Have children write capital **P** on the paper in white chalk or crayon, then glue popcorn over it. When they are finished, children can eat the remaining popcorn while finger tracing their letters.

Bright Writing (Letter Practice, Tactile) I put bright tempera paint into a heavy freezer bag and seal. Children then lay the bag on black paper and use a finger to write their letters on the bag.

Janis A. Giblin
Meadowview School
Oak Creek, WI

Phonics Corner

The sentence used to help children form the letter **P,**

Pat picks a **pear** and a **peach** on the way to the **park.**

may also be used to work on sound-letter correspondence. Repeat the sentence and call on volunteers to tell you the words they hear that begin with /p/.

Teach (page 142)

Call attention to the picture at the top of the page. Have children:

- describe what they see in the picture;
- trace the **P** on Pat's cap;
- color the cap.

Write a capital **P** on the chalkboard. Ask a volunteer to write a lower-case **p**. Compare them.

Call attention to the lower half of the page. Have children:

- finger trace the boxed letter **P** as you read aloud the letter description;
- pencil trace the gray letters;
- write the letter **P** using the starting dots;
- trace the name *Pat.*

Follow Up

Self-Evaluation Have children check their own work by asking themselves:

- Are my **P's** closed at the top?
- Do my **P's** slant the same way?

Additional Resources

Manuscript Alpha Touch letter **P**
D'Nealian® Handwriting Big Book letter **P**

Letter Description

Top start; slant down, up, around halfway, and close

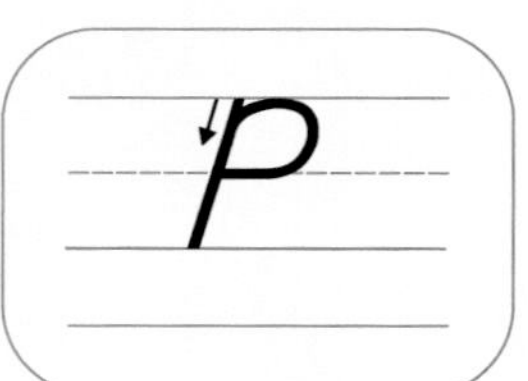

ACTIVITY BANK

Moving Write Along

Pat's Hat (Letter Practice, Kinesthetic) Draw a picture of Pat the Panda and put it on the bulletin board. Pass out baseball caps cut from paper. Have each child write a different capital letter on the cap. Children then exchange caps. As you call out letters, they place the appropriate cap on Pat's head.

Pat's Pear (Phonics, Creative) Ask children to name foods that begin with /p/, such as pears, pizza, and pasta. Write them on the chalkboard. Next ask for animal names, such as Pat Panda and Paul Pig, that begin with /p/. Write these on the board. Have children choose a food and an animal from those listed and draw them, writing a big **P** underneath.

Towering Letters (Letter Recognition, Tactile) I use an overhead projector to make D'Nealian letters about 24" high on posterboard. When cut out and hung up, children can attach pictures to them and finger trace them to help with letter recognition and formation.

Vickie Foreman
Travis School
San Angelo, TX

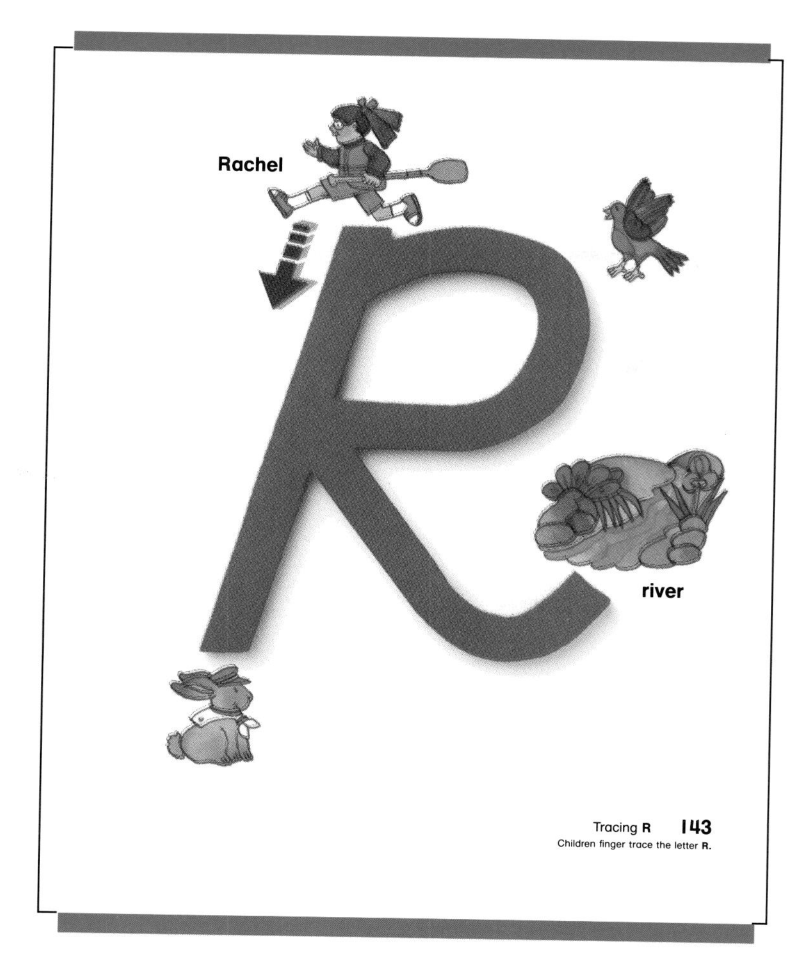

Objectives

Learns the shape of **R** by finger tracing a large model letter.
Writes the capital letter **R** and traces a name beginning with **R.**

Prepare

Write the names of various rivers that flow through the United States on the chalkboard, including the Rio Grande and the Red River. Now play "Rush to the River" with children. Have them each write on an index card a capital letter they have learned thus far. (Be sure **R** is included.) Shuffle and pass out cards facedown. Have children:

- line up in a row across the room from the board;
- look at their cards;
- run to the board if they have a capital **R.**

The first one to get to the board circles all the **R's.**

Use the *D'Nealian® Handwriting Big Book* to preview the page.

Teach (page 143)

Have children:

- identify the capital letter **R;**
- find Rachel at the starting arrow;
- finger trace the path from Rachel to the river while you say the following mnemonic sentence:
  Rachel runs by a rabbit and a robin on her race to the river.
- air trace the letter **R.**

ACTIVITY BANK

Time to Grow 

River of R's (Letter Practice, Fine Motor) Create a river on the bulletin board using blue paper. At the writing center, give children unlined paper cut in the shape of a canoe. Have them write capital **R** on their canoes and color them. Help children arrange their canoes in the river.

Pasta and Penmanship (Small Groups, Letter Practice) Have children work in pairs using alphabet macaroni. They take turns setting out a pasta letter that the other writes using D'Nealian letters.

Pam Herrmann
Boyd Elementary
Alamosa, CO

Phonics Corner

The sentence used to help children form the letter **R,**

Rachel runs by a **rabbit** and a **robin** on her **race** to the **river.**

may also be used to work on sound-letter correspondence. Repeat the sentence and call on volunteers to tell you the words they hear that begin with /r/.

Teach (page 144)

Call attention to the picture at the top of the page. Have children:

- identify the letters **R, G,** and **B;**
- find and color each **R** red, each **G** green, and each **B** blue;
- identify the red **R** on Rachel's canoe.

Write a capital **R** on the chalkboard. Ask a volunteer to write a lower-case **r.** Compare them.

Call attention to the lower half of the page. Have children:

- finger trace the boxed letter **R** as you read aloud the letter description;
- pencil trace the gray letters;
- write the letter **R** using the starting dots;
- trace the name *Rock River.*

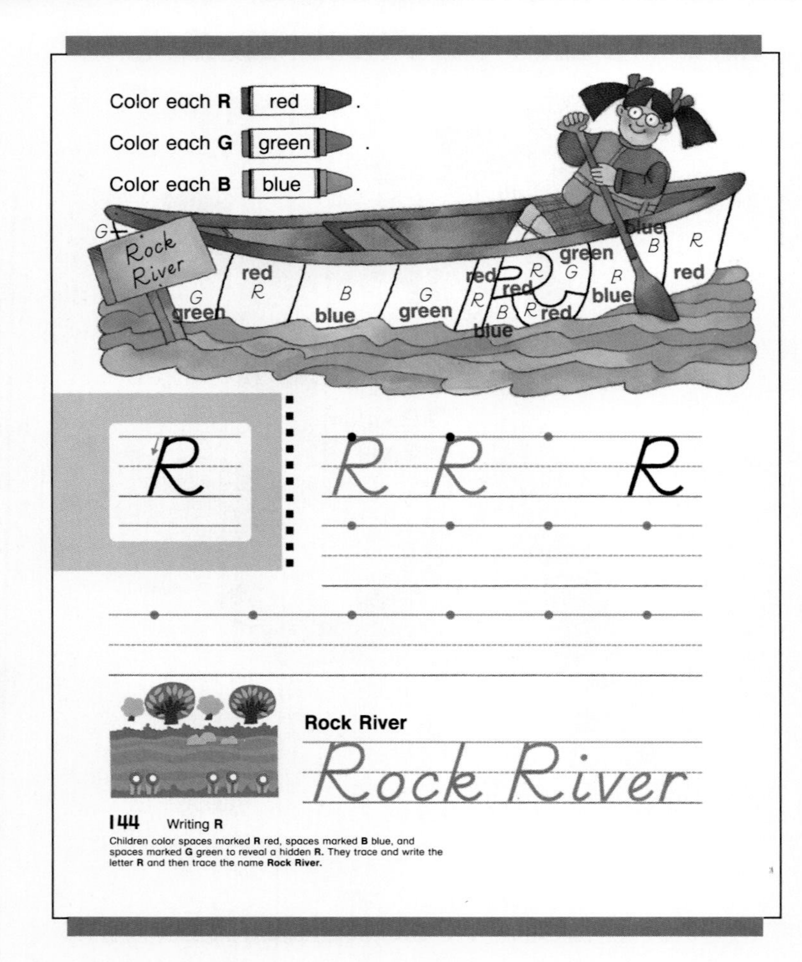

Color each **R** red.

Color each **G** green.

Color each **B** blue.

Rock River

144 Writing R

Children color spaces marked **R** red, spaces marked **B** blue, and spaces marked **G** green to reveal a hidden **R**. They trace and write the letter **R** and then trace the name **Rock River.**

Follow Up

Self-Evaluation Have children check their own work by asking themselves:

- Do my **R's** start at the dot?
- Are my **R's** closed at the top?

Additional Resources

Manuscript Alpha Touch letter **R**
D'Nealian® Handwriting Big Book letter **R**

Letter Description

Top start; slant down, up, around halfway, close, slant down right, and a monkey tail.

ACTIVITY BANK

Moving Write Along

Leaving Their Mark (Tactile, Letter Practice) My kindergarten children enjoy using their fingers to write in a variety of materials. We have used shaving cream on tables, windows, and mirrors. We have written in chocolate pudding and finger paint on wax paper. We have also written in corn meal, sand, salt, steam, and chalk dust.

Lois R. Vogel
David Turnham Center
Dale, IN

R Cities (Letter Recognition, Gross Motor) Write the following place names on the chalkboard and read them to the class: *Reno, Austin, Rockford, Newark, Casper, Richmond, Chicago, Rochester,* and *Raleigh.*

Have children come up and circle the cities whose names begin with capital **R.**

If children can think of more cities beginning with **R,** write them on the board.

Rock River Slap (Letter Recognition, Small Groups) Invite children to play "Rock River Slap" in small groups. Write capital letters on index cards (adding a few extra **R's**) and place them face-down. Children turn up cards one at a time and slap only **R's**. The one with the most **R's** wins.

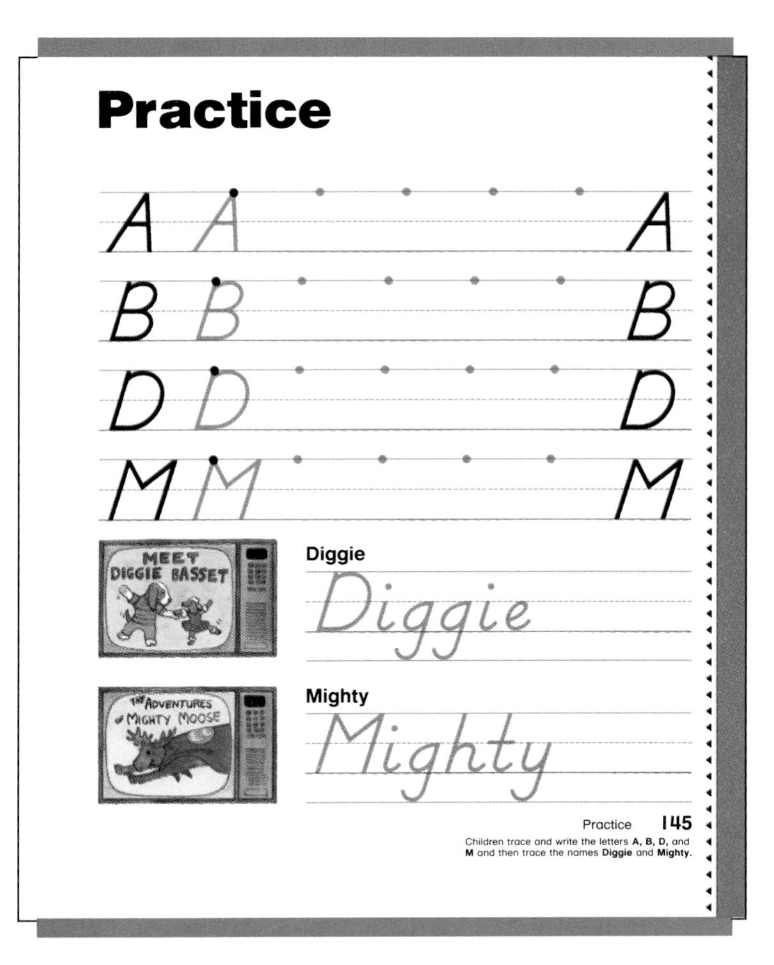

Practice

A A A

B B B

D D D

M M M

MEET DIGGIE BASSET

Diggie

Diggie

THE ADVENTURES of MIGHTY MOOSE

Mighty

Mighty

Practice 145

Children trace and write the letters **A, B, D,** and **M** and then trace the names **Diggie** and **Mighty.**

Objectives

Practices writing the capital letters **A, B, D,** and **M.** Traces the names *Diggie* and *Mighty.*

Prepare

Invite children to perform in "The D'Nealian® Handwriting Show." Make a large cardboard television like the one shown below. Each child writes either capital **A, B, D,** or **M** on a piece of paper. Have children:

- hold the mock television so that it frames the face, and describe the letter they have written without telling its name;
- guess the performer's letter by going to the chalkboard and writing it there.

Continue until all children have performed.

Teach (page 145)

Have children:

- identify the capital letters **A, B, D,** and **M;**
- pencil trace the gray letters;
- write each letter using the starting dots;
- trace the names *Diggie* and *Mighty.*

Follow Up

Self-Evaluation Have children check their own work by asking themselves:

- Do all my letters start at the dot?
- Are my **B's** and **D's** curved and closed?

Additional Resources

Manuscript Alpha Touch letters **A, B, D,** and **M**
D'Nealian® Handwriting Big Book letters **A, B, D,** and **M**

ACTIVITY BANK

Diggie and Mighty (Oral Language, Gross Motor) Write *Diggie Basset* and *Mighty Moose* on the chalkboard. Have children get together in groups and think up a story about either of these characters. Invite groups to tell their stories to the class.

Missing Letters (Letter Practice, Phonics) Write several names on the chalkboard, but do not supply the first letter of each name. Tell children they must supply the missing capital letter **A, B, D,** or **M.** Have children come to the board and write the letter they think the name begins with. The following are possibilities:

_avid _etty _ndy _ary

Kid Alphabet (Kinesthetic, Critical Thinking) Make the letters of the alphabet with the children on the floor. They have to figure out how many children they'll need to make the letter; then call on classmates to try it.

Roxann Brown
Mullen Elementary
Mullen, NE

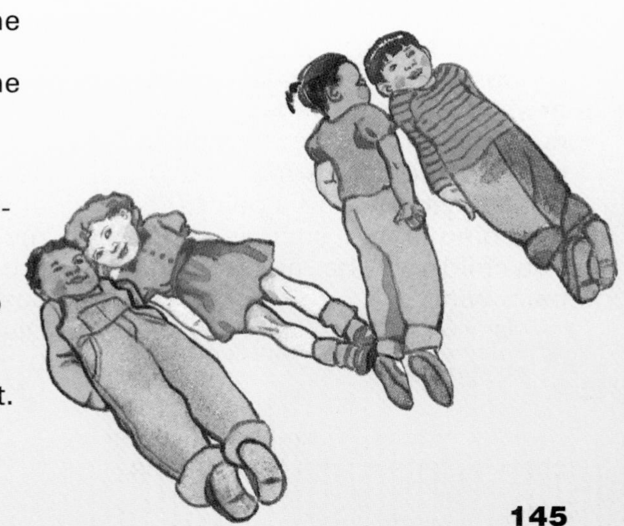

Objectives
Practices writing the capital letters **N, P,** and **R**. Traces the names *Natalie* and *Rainbow.*

Prepare
Write the capital letters **N, P,** and **R** about two feet apart on the chalkboard. Have children:
- line up across the room from the board;
- listen as you read a name beginning with **N, P,** or **R;**
- stand, one at a time, in front of the letter that begins the name you read.

Continue until all children have had a turn.

Teach (page 146)
Have children:
- identify the capital letters **N, P,** and **R;**
- pencil trace the gray letters;
- write each letter using the starting dots;
- trace the names *Natalie* and *Rainbow.*

Follow Up
Self-Evaluation Have children check their own work by asking themselves:
- Do my letters sit nicely on the bottom line?
- Are my **P's** and **R's** curved and closed?

Additional Resources
Manuscript Alpha Touch letters **N, P,** and **R**
D'Nealian® Handwriting Big Book letters **N, P,** and **R**

ACTIVITY BANK

Letter Concentration (Letter Practice, Fine Motor) Students play in groups of four or five, using five or six lower-case and capital letters made from 3" x 5" cards cut in half. Students turn over two cards, trying to find a pair of matching letters, such as **r** and **R.** The child with the most matching pairs wins.

Marly Glaw
Shreiner School and Academy
Marietta, GA

Special Needs (Visual Deficits) By shaping letters with their hands, children with visual problems strengthen motor memory. Provide children with pizza cardboard that has a writing line and a model **N, P,** or **R** under clear acetate. Distribute bread dough. Children roll dough into a rope and align it on top of the letter. Then they stroke tomato sauce along the dough with a pastry brush. Bake the letters on a pizza pan and have a party.

Row to R, Pedal to P (Letter Recognition, Gross Motor) Play "Row, Pedal, or Nap" with children. Explain that they should pretend to row when you hold up an **R,** pretend to pedal when you hold up a **P,** and pretend to nap when you hold up an **N.**

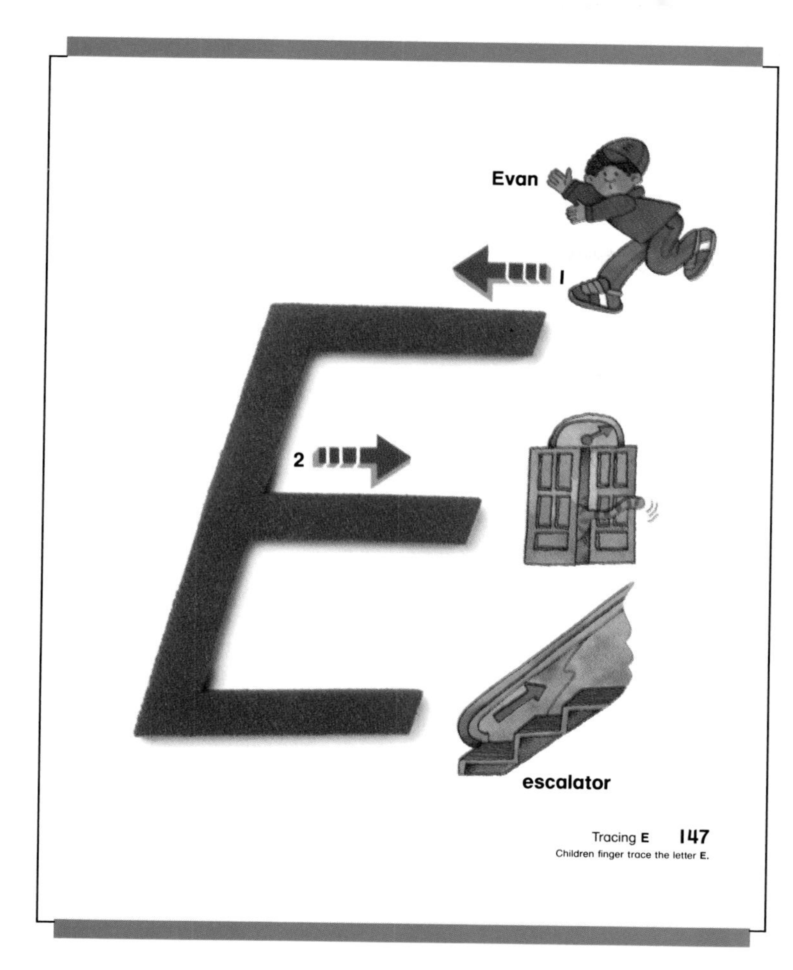

Objectives

Learns the shape of **E** by finger tracing a large model letter.
Writes the capital letter **E** and traces a name beginning with **E.**

Prepare

Play "Who's in the Elevator?" with children. Draw an elevator like the one on page 147 on the chalkboard or on a large piece of cardboard with a slit where the doors meet. One at a time, draw (or insert) portions of various animals sticking out through the doors.
Have children:

- guess the animal that belongs to the part drawn;
- give the animal a proper name beginning with the letter that starts its name—*Tony Tiger,* for example;
- come up and draw an animal part for others to guess.

Use the *D'Nealian® Handwriting Big Book* to preview the page.

Teach (page 147)

Have children:

- identify the capital letter **E;**
- find Evan at the starting arrow;
- finger trace the path from Evan to the escalator and then to the elevator while you say the following mnemonic sentence:

    Evan chased his pet down the escalator.
    He found it in the elevator.

- air trace the letter **E.**

ACTIVITY BANK

Time to Grow

I See an E (Letter Recognition, Kinesthetic) At the writing center, label a number of objects, including *Eraser* and *Egg.* Tell children that when they see a label beginning with **E,** they should copy this capital letter on unlined paper. They then name the object and spell it.

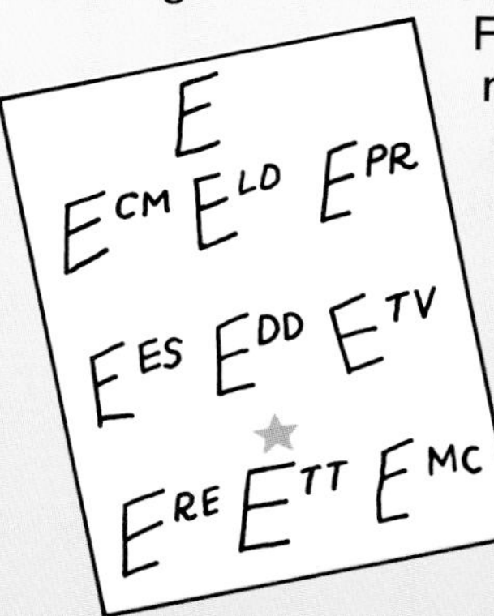

Penmanship Stars (Letter Form, Fine Motor) One student in each row writes a capital letter on paper using D'Nealian letters. Papers are then passed along, as each student writes the letter and initials it. This continues until the paper returns to the originator, who puts a star next to the best writing.

Sheridan Pierson
Onamia Elementary
Onamia, MN

Phonics Corner

The sentence used to help children form the letter **E,**

Evan chased his pet down the **escalator.** He found it in the **elevator.**

may also be used to work on sound-letter correspondence. Repeat the sentence and call on volunteers to tell you the words they hear that begin with /e/.

Teach (page 148)

Read the sentences at the top of the page with children. Help them finger trace the paths before using a pencil. Have children:

- draw a line from Evan to the door marked 8E;
- draw a line from the elevator to 11E;
- tell what capital letter the path resembles.

Write a capital **E** on the chalkboard. Ask a volunteer to write a lower-case **e.** Compare them.

Call attention to the lower half of the page. Have children:

- finger trace the boxed letter **E** as you read aloud the letter description;
- pencil trace the gray letters;
- write the letter **E** using the starting dots;
- trace the name *Evan.*

Follow Up

Self-Evaluation Have children check their own work by asking themselves:

- Do my **E's** have bars across the middle?
- Do my **E's** slant the same way?

Additional Resources

Manuscript Alpha Touch letter **E**
D'Nealian® Handwriting Big Book letter **E**

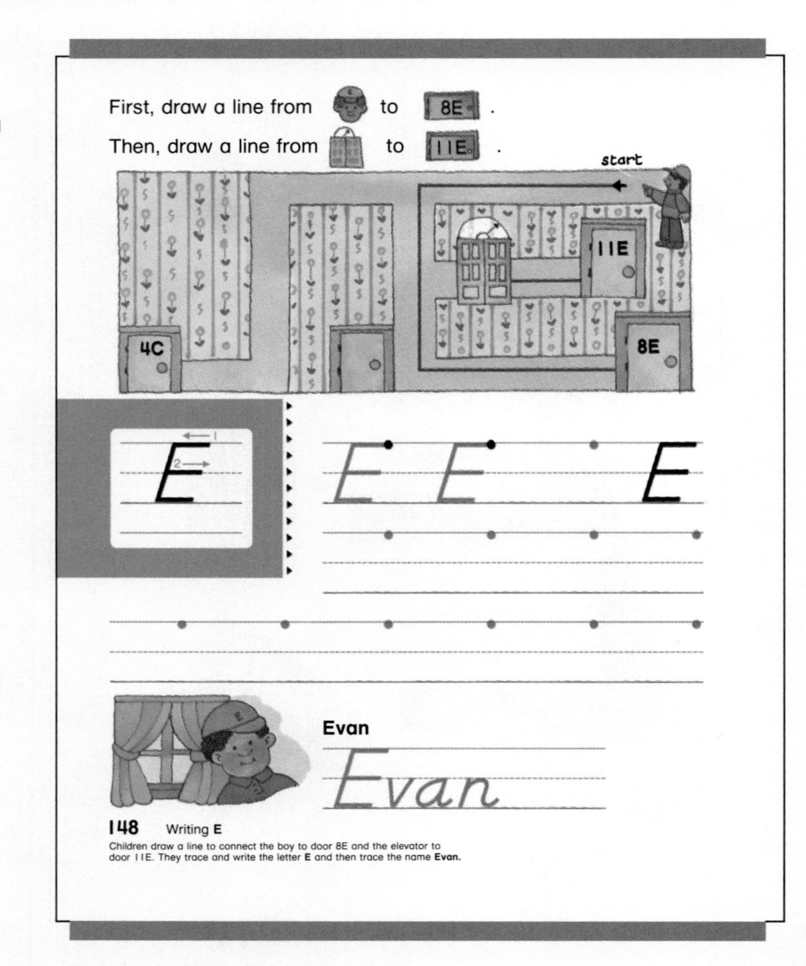

Letter Description

Top start; over left, slant down, and over right. Middle bar across.

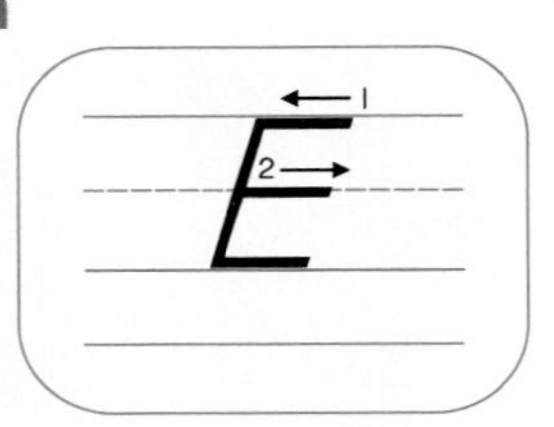

ACTIVITY BANK

Moving Write Along

Auto Graphs (Letter Practice, Fine Motor) During the first weeks of school we practice writing our names on 1" graph paper. The kinders enjoy filling in the spaces. Then each child cuts the paper to the "size" of his or her name.

Janie Walters
Sublette Grade School
Sublette, KS

Eyes or Ears (Fine Motor, Critical Thinking) Give each child a worksheet headed **Eyes** and **Ears,** with pictures of eyes and ears arranged vertically under the headings. Talk about the five senses, and tell children they will circle either the eyes or the ears as you hold up a painting, play a record, write a letter on the chalkboard, and so on.

Elevator Up (Kinesthetic, Letter Recognition) Have children do a bit of playacting. Write *Elevator, Stairs, Up,* and *Down* in D'Nealian letters on index cards, and read them all with children. Place the first two words in one pile and the second two in another. Ask children, in turn, to pick one card from each pile and act out what the cards say. The class then guesses what the child is doing.

Objectives

Learns the shape of **F** by finger tracing a large model letter.
Writes the capital letter **F** and traces a name beginning with **F**.

Prepare

Write a capital **F** on the board. Ask children how many people they think it would take to form an **F** with their bodies. Ask for three volunteers to try it for the class. Have children:

- raise their hands if they know someone whose name begins with an **F;**
- have the other children guess what that name could be. The one who guesses correctly then takes a turn.

Use the *D'Nealian® Handwriting Big Book* to preview the page.

Teach (page 149)

Have children:

- identify the capital letter **F;**
- find Felicia at the starting arrow;
- finger trace the path from Felicia to the fern and then to the forest while you say the following mnemonic sentence:

  First, Felicia finds the fern.
  Then, Felicia finds the forest.
- air trace the letter **F.**

ACTIVITY BANK

Time to Grow

Stamp Your Best (Fine Motor, Letter Form) Have children write capital **F** on pieces of large unlined paper at the writing center. As they work, wander around with a stamp bearing the image of something beginning with /f/, such as a fairy. Have them point to their "best" letter, and stamp the image next to it.

Ruth Van Matre
Hillcrest Elementary
Delphi, IN

Felicia's Favorites (Phonics, Kinesthetic) Explain that Felicia Fairy loves things that begin with the same sound as her name. Read the following list of items and have children raise their hands when they hear the name of an item Felicia might like: *fern, sunlight, bee, feathers, vine, forest, fig.*

Phonics Corner

The sentence used to help children form the letter **F,**

First, Felicia finds the **fern.**
Then, **Felicia finds** the **forest.**

may also be used to work on sound-letter correspondence. Repeat the sentence and call on volunteers to tell you the words they hear that begin with /f/.

Teach (page 150)

Call attention to the picture at the top of the page. Have children:

- describe what they see in the picture;
- circle each **F** in the letter;
- read the message from Fuzzy Wuzzy, with your help. (*For Felicia, I love you.*)

Write a capital **F** on the chalkboard. Ask a volunteer to write a lower-case **f.** Compare them.

Call attention to the lower half of the page. Have children:

- finger trace the boxed letter **F** as you read aloud the letter description;
- pencil trace the gray letters;
- write the letter **F** using the starting dots;
- trace the name *Fuzzy.*

Follow Up

Self-Evaluation Have children check their own work by asking themselves:

- Do my **F's** have bars across the middle?
- Do my **F's** start at the dot?

Additional Resources

Manuscript Alpha Touch letter **F**
D'Nealian® Handwriting Big Book letter **F**

Circle each **F.** Read the letter.

Friday
4
u
Fuzzy

Fuzzy

150 Writing **F**

Children circle the **F's** in a friendly letter. They trace and write the letter **F** and then trace the name **Fuzzy.**

Letter Description

Top start; over left, and slant down. Middle bar across.

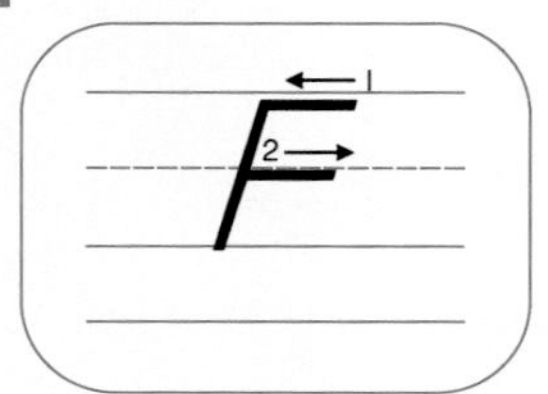

ACTIVITY BANK

Moving Write Along

F Wishes (Letter Recognition, Fine Motor) Distribute toy catalogs and scissors to groups of children. Let them find headings with names of toys that begin with **F,** and have them circle each one. Children should then cut out the pictures and paste them on paper on which they have written capital **F.** Hang these papers on the bulletin board under the heading **Our F Wishes.**

A Forest Walk (Kinesthetic, Phonics) Go on an imaginary hike in the forest with the class. As you walk around the room, pretend to be on a path, near a lake, and climbing a hill. Call out things you might see beginning with /f/.

Fuzzy's Rebus (Critical Thinking, Letter Recognition) Read the letter from Fuzzy on page 150 with children once again. Then write the following rebus on the board and invite children to read what it says: **U R A BU T. I NV U.** *(You are a beauty. I envy you.)* Think up more rebuses together.

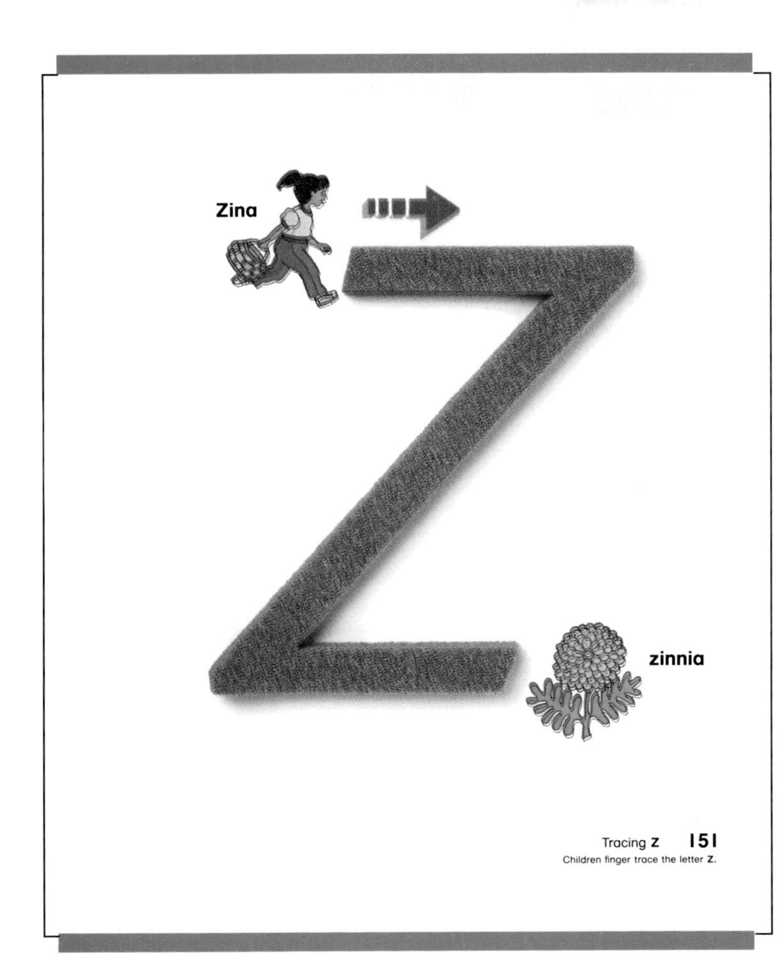

Objectives

Learns the shape of **Z** by finger tracing a large model letter.
Writes the capital letter **Z** and traces a name beginning with **Z.**

Prepare

Play "Zip to the Zinnias" with children. Using white tape, create a large D'Nealian **Z** on the classroom floor. If possible, place a pot of zinnias at the end of the letter. Have children:

- listen as you read sentences with names in them, some of which start with a **Z;**
- take turns zipping from the start to the end of the **Z** when they hear /z/;
- sit down next to the **Z** if they do not hear /z/.

Following are a few sentences you might use: *Mary makes her way to the market. Zina zigzags to pick her zinnia. Waldo walks with Wayne. Zoe zips to the zoo. Jane jumps into the jeep. Zippy tugs on his zipper. Bob bathes in bubbles.*

Use the *D'Nealian® Handwriting Big Book* to preview the page.

Teach (page 151)

Have children:

- identify the capital letter **Z;**
- find Zina at the starting arrow;
- finger trace the path from Zina to the zinnia while you say the following mnemonic sentence:
  Zina zigzags to pick her zinnia.
- air trace the letter **Z.**

ACTIVITY BANK

Time to Grow 

Flowering Z's (Letter Practice, Tactile) Bring in a bag of flower petals, preferably zinnias. Have children write capital letter **Z** on large pieces of unlined paper at the writing center. Have them glue the petals along the stroke of the **Z** in the proper direction.

Zinnia Graph (Critical Thinking, Charts) Distribute a paper cup, some soil, and zinnia seeds to each child. Have them write their name and a capital **Z** on the cup. Help them plant their seeds in the soil and water the soil. Prepare a graph showing each child's name and the number of weeks each plant takes to blossom.

Phonics Corner

The sentence used to help children form the letter **Z,**

Zina zigzags to pick her **zinnia.**

may also be used to work on sound-letter correspondence. Repeat the sentence and call on volunteers to tell you the words they hear that begin with /z/.

Teach (page 152)

Call attention to the picture at the top of the page. Have children:

- describe what they see in the picture;
- trace the **Z** on Zina's shirt;
- color the picture.

Write a capital **Z** on the chalkboard. Ask a volunteer to write a lower-case **z.** Compare them.

Call attention to the lower half of the page. Have children:

- finger trace the boxed letter **Z** as you read aloud the letter description;
- pencil trace the gray letters;
- write the letter **Z** using the starting dots;
- trace the name *Zina.*

Follow Up

Self-Evaluation Have children check their own work by asking themselves:

- Do my **Z's** touch the top line?
- Do my **Z's** sit nicely on the bottom line?

Additional Resources

Manuscript Alpha Touch letter **Z**
D'Nealian® Handwriting Big Book letter **Z**

Trace the **Z**. Color the picture.

Zina

152 Writing Z

Children trace the **Z** on the shirt. They trace and write the letter **Z** and then trace the name **Zina.**

Letter Description

Top start; over right, slant down left, and over right.

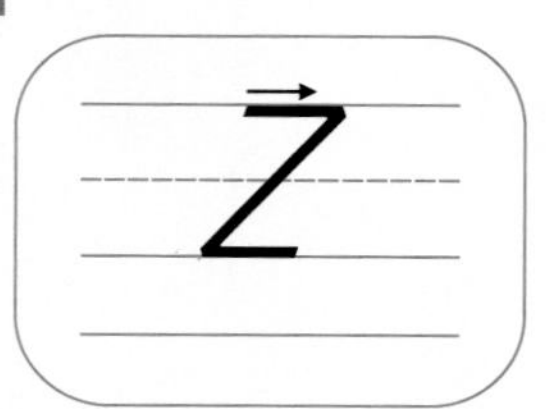

ACTIVITY BANK

Moving Write Along

Z Bouquet (Letter Practice, Eye-Hand Coordination) Use a template to trace flower petals on different-colored pieces of construction paper. Have children cut out petals and paste them around the edge of a small paper plate. Have them write a capital **Z** in the center.

Petal Power (Letter Practice, Small Groups) Give each child an envelope containing six colored petal shapes. Write one of the D'Nealian capitals they have learned on the envelope. Ask them to write that letter on each petal. Have children sit in groups of four and place their petals in a shuffled pile facedown. Children try to collect all of their own petals. When they have done so, they paste them on paper, drawing a center, stem, and leaves.

We're a Z! (Kinesthetic, Letter Recognition) Play "Ring Around the Rosy" with children. Instead of singing *We all fall down,* however, have children sing, *We all form* __, singing the name of either **G, O, S, L, T, U, H, A, M, N, E, F,** or **Z.** As they do so, they arrange themselves into the shape of each of these capital letters.

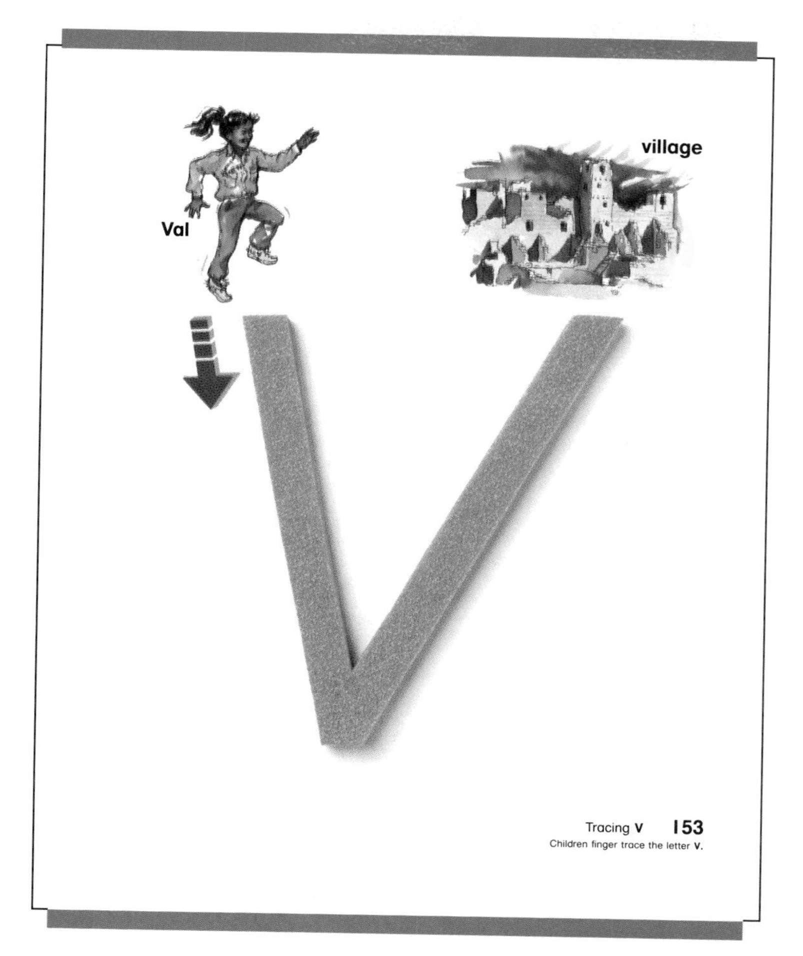

Objectives
Learns the shape of **V** by finger tracing a large model letter.
Writes the capital letter **V** and traces a name beginning with **V.**

Prepare
Invite children to play "Val in the Valley." Have children:
- line up, then arrange themselves into a **V** shape;
- turn the person at the start of the **V** (whose eyes are closed), passing him or her along, while saying *Val goes into the valley;*
- continue passing the person to the bottom of the **V,** then saying *Val goes out of the valley,* as they pass the person up the **V** and to the end.

The game continues in this way with a new person "going into the valley" each time.

Use the *D'Nealian® Handwriting Big Book* to preview the page.

Teach (page 153)
Have children:
- identify the capital letter **V;**
- find Val at the starting arrow;
- finger trace the path from Val to the village while you say the following mnemonic sentence:
  Val runs into the valley to view the village.
- air trace the letter **V.**

ACTIVITY BANK

Time to Grow 

V Is for Valentine (Letter Practice, Fine Motor) Capital **V** is the valentine letter. At the writing center, have children write **V's** on large unlined paper. Help them turn their **V's** into valentines by adding two hills on top. Let them cut out the valentines, adding rickrack and glitter.

Marilyn Knudson
Alice Terry Elementary
Englewood, CO

Drive the V Road (Fine Motor, Kinesthetic) Place strips of adhesive tape on tables in the shape of a capital **V.** Put a green dot at the start of the letter and a red dot at the end. Children "drive" toy cars down and up the road from green dot to red dot.

Phonics Corner
The sentence used to help children form the letter **V,**

Val runs into the **valley** to **view** the **village.**

may also be used to work on sound-letter correspondence. Repeat the sentence and call on volunteers to tell you the words they hear that begin with /v/.

Teach (page 154)

Call attention to the pictures at the top of the page. Have children:
- describe what they see in each picture;
- listen as you read the names *Val, Mesa Verde,* and *Monument Valley;*
- circle the **V** in each name.

Write a capital **V** on the chalkboard. Ask a volunteer to write a lower-case **v.** Compare them.

Call attention to the lower half of the page. Have children:
- finger trace the boxed letter **V** as you read aloud the letter description;
- pencil trace the gray letters;
- write the letter **V** using the starting dots;
- trace the name *Val.*

Follow Up

Self-Evaluation Have children check their own work by asking themselves:
- Do my **V's** start at the dot?
- Do my **V's** slant the same way?

Additional Resources

Manuscript Alpha Touch letter **V**
D'Nealian® Handwriting Big Book letter **V**

Letter Description

Top start; slant down right, and slant up right.

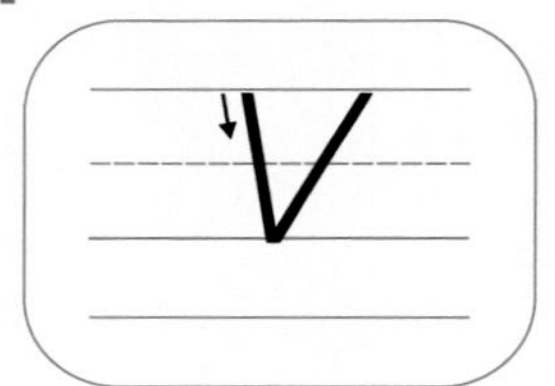

ACTIVITY BANK

Moving Write Along

Native American Literature (Celebrating Cultural Diversity) Monument Valley and Mesa Verde are both awe-inspiring treasures of the American West. This is a good opportunity to acquaint children with the history and culture of the people who first settled this region. Read origin stories and folk tales of the Navajo, Apache, Zuñi, and other Native Americans, and discuss them with children.

Paper Vests (Eye-Hand Coordination, Creative) Give each child a large brown shopping bag. Have children cut one hole in the bottom for their heads and two holes in the sides for their arms. Cut a slit along the length of the front of the bag to make a vest. Have children cut along the bottom to create fringe, decorate with yarn, paint, add buttons, and write a capital **V** on the back.

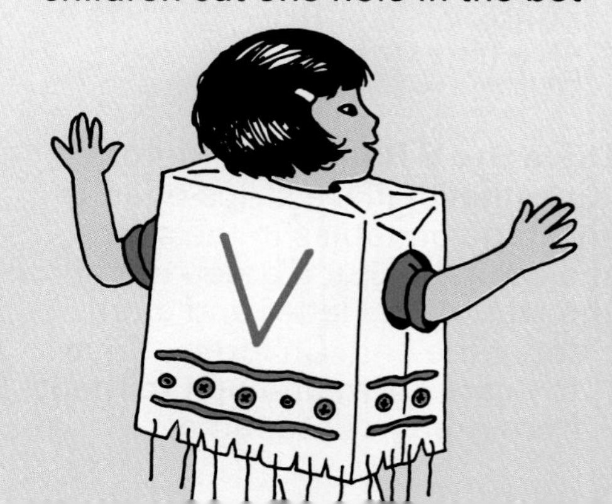

V Sticks (Tactile, Fine Motor) Distribute two ice-cream sticks, glue, and glitter to children. Let them glue the sticks together to form a **V,** and add glitter. Children can finger trace the **V.**

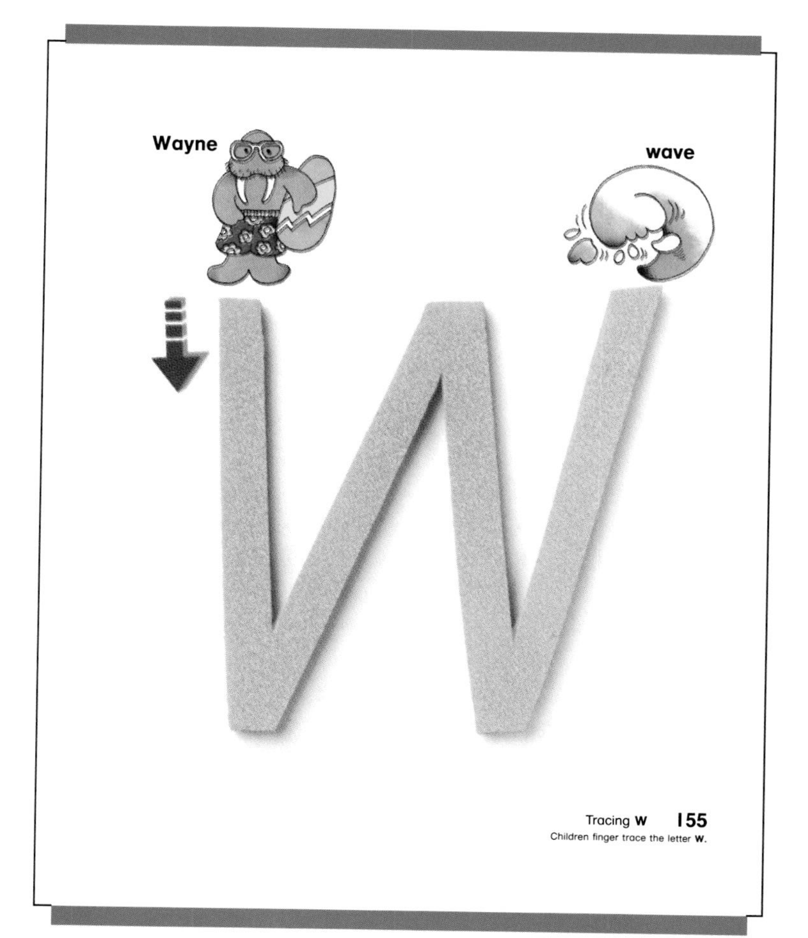

Objectives

Learns the shape of **W** by finger tracing a large model letter.
Writes the capital letter **W** and traces a name beginning with **W**.

Prepare

Invite a group of children to the chalkboard. Have them write a capital **V,** and then return to their seats. Next invite a new group to come to the board and write a second set of **V's** that are attached to the left side of the first set. (You may want to demonstrate.) Ask this group to be seated. Have children:

- determine what these double **V's** have become;
- come to the board yet again and write **W's**.

Use the *D'Nealian® Handwriting Big Book* to preview the page.

Teach (page 155)

Have children:

- identify the capital letter **W;**
- find Wayne at the starting arrow;
- finger trace the path from Wayne to the wave while you say the following mnemonic sentence:
  Wayne wants to ride the wave.
- air trace the letter **W.**

ACTIVITY BANK

Time to Grow 

W Waves (Letter Practice, Fine Motor) As a transitional step, children should write a row of capital **W's** on large pieces of unlined paper at the writing center. Tell them to then pretend that their **W's** are waves, and to draw something that would float on the top.

Wee Will (Letter Recognition, Visual) Write *Wee Willie Winkie* on the board. Have children circle the three **W's.** Then read the poem:

Wee Willie Winkie
Runs through the town,
Upstairs and downstairs,
In his nightgown;
Rapping at the window,
Crying through the lock,
"Are the children in their beds?
For now it's eight o'clock."

Phonics Corner

The sentence used to help children form the letter **W,**

Wayne wants to ride the **wave.**

may also be used to work on sound-letter correspondence. Repeat the sentence and call on volunteers to tell you the words they hear that begin with /w/.

Teach (page 156)

Call attention to the scene at the top of the page. Have children:

- describe what is happening in the picture;
- connect the dots from 1 through 5;
- find the **W** shape they have created;
- color the picture.

Write a capital **W** on the chalkboard. Ask a volunteer to write a lower-case **w.** Compare them.

Call attention to the lower half of the page. Have children:

- finger trace the boxed letter **W** as you read aloud the letter description;
- pencil trace the gray letters;
- write the letter **W** using the starting dots;
- trace the name *Wayne.*

Follow Up

Self-Evaluation Have children check their own work by asking themselves:

- Do my **W's** touch the top line?
- Do my **W's** slant the same way?

Additional Resources

Manuscript Alpha Touch letter **W**
D'Nealian® Handwriting Big Book letter **W**

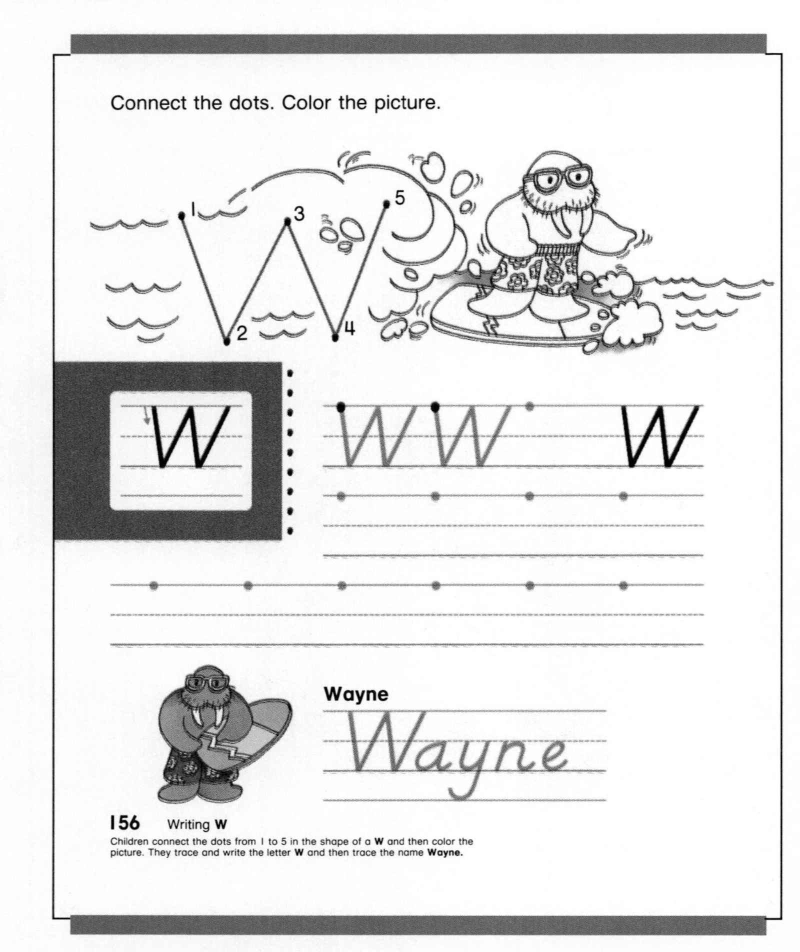

Letter Description

Top start; slant down right, slant up right, slant down right, and slant up right again.

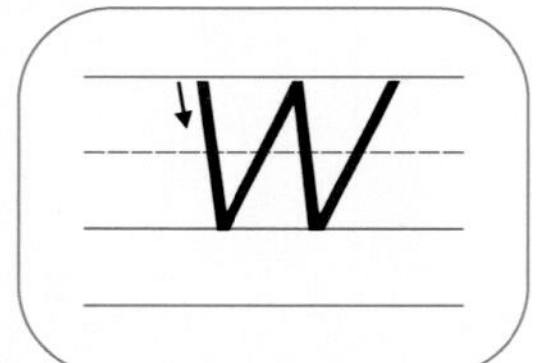

ACTIVITY BANK

Moving Write Along

Jump the Waves (Kinesthetic, Letter Recognition) Cut out surfboards from construction paper about 11" x 18" in size. Have children write one capital letter they have already learned on each. Tape them to the floor. Let the children take turns jumping from surfboard to surfboard, naming each letter they land on.

Work with W (Auditory, Gross Motor) Read the names of various professions to children, including several that begin with /w/. Include waiter, waitress, and welder. Children should raise their hands when they hear this sound, and then act out the job.

W Love (Letter Practice, Fine Motor) Help children remember capital **W** by teaching it as double **V,** meaning double love. Have them practice double-love **W** on writing paper.

Marilyn Knudson
Alice Terry Elementary
Englewood, CO

Objectives

Learns the shape of **X** by finger tracing a large model letter.
Writes the capital letter **X** and traces a name beginning with **X**.

Prepare

Have children help you draw an imaginary creature on the chalkboard. Have children:

- decide whether the creature should be furry, feathery, hairless, round, square, fat, thin, and so on;
- take turns coming to the board to draw what the creature would need in order to fly, to swim, to walk, to see, to eat, and to hear;
- imitate the sound the creature would make;
- give their imaginary creature a name.

Use the *D'Nealian® Handwriting Big Book* to preview the page.

Teach (page 157)

Have children:

- identify the capital letter **X;**
- find **X. J.** at the starting arrow;
- finger trace the path from **X. J.** to the **x** and his friend to the second **x** while you say the following mnemonic sentence:

  X. J. goes down to the red **x.**
  His friend goes down to the green **x.**
- air trace the letter **X.**

ACTIVITY BANK

Time to Grow 

Let's Play (Letter Practice, Critical Thinking) At the writing center, have large tick-tack-toe grids available. Have children pair off to play the game, using capital **X's** and **O's**. Watch how they form their **X's**. Have them play again, with the person who was writing **O** now writing **X**.

X Marks the Spot (Kinesthetic, Letter Recognition) Hide a capital letter **X** somewhere in the classroom. Duplicate a map that leads to this **X**. Give groups of children the map, and help them read it in order to find the treasure.

Phonics Corner

The sentence used to help children form the letter **X,**

X.J. goes down to the red **x.**
His friend goes down to the green **x.**

may also be used to work on sound-letter correspondence. Repeat the sentence and call on volunteers to tell you the words they hear with /eks/.

Teach (page 158)

Call attention to the picture at the top of the page. Have children:

- describe X. J., the creature they see in the picture;
- trace the **X** on the lid of the chest;
- draw a gift in the chest for X. J.

Write a capital **X** on the chalkboard. Ask a volunteer to write a lower-case **x**. Compare them.

Call attention to the lower half of the page. Have children:

- finger trace the boxed letter **X** as you read aloud the letter description;
- pencil trace the gray letters;
- write the letter **X** using the starting dots;
- trace the name *X. J.*

Follow Up

Self-Evaluation Have children check their own work by asking themselves:

- Do my **X's** cross at the middle?
- Do my **X's** have their monkey tails?

Additional Resources

Manuscript Alpha Touch letter **X**
D'Nealian® Handwriting Big Book letter **X**

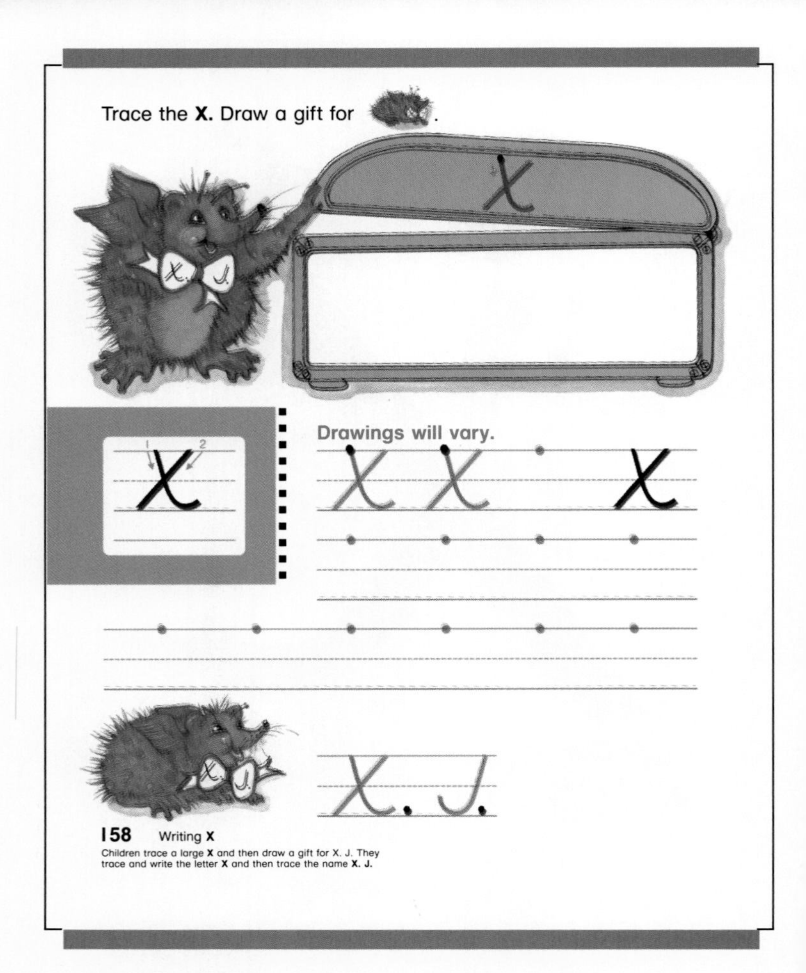

Letter Description

Top start; slant down right, and a monkey tail. Cross down left.

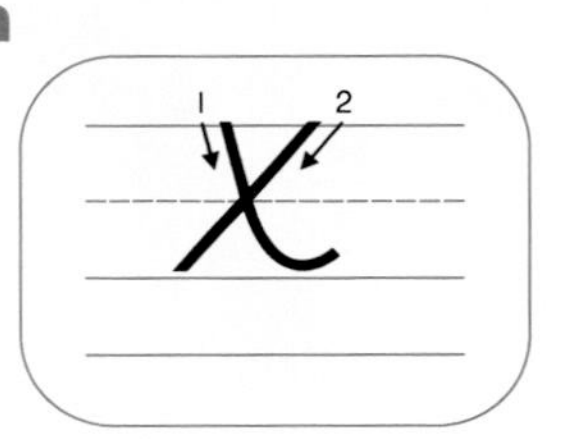

ACTIVITY BANK

Moving Write Along

X. J. Up Close (Oral Language, Creative) Talk to children about X. J., the imaginary animal in their books. Ask them to describe its nose and feet. Ask how X. J might get from place to place and what it might feel like to pet X. J.

Matching Caps (Letter Practice, Letter Recognition) Draw six rows of writing lines on the chalkboard. Write these lower-case letters vertically on the board: **e, z, f, x, v,** and **w.** Invite children to come to the board and write the capital letters next to their lower-case counterparts.

Pam Yeary
Pershing Elementary
Orlando, FL

Cross Out Danger (Letter Practice, Critical Thinking) Pass out dittos that show four scenes involving children:

a family at dinner
a child riding a tricycle on a busy street
a child in a classroom
a child playing with matches

Discuss the scenes with children and have them write a large capital **X** on those that involve dangerous activities.

Objectives

Learns the shape of **Y** by finger tracing a large model letter.
Writes the capital letter **Y** and traces a name beginning with **Y.**

Prepare

Play "Yea for Y," a game of letter recognition, with children. Fill a paper bag with the capital letters learned so far, including a few extra **Y's.** Have children:

- pass the bag around, each child pulling out one letter at a time;
- look at letter and say its name;
- say *Yea* if it is a **Y;**
- put the letter back.

Points are given to children who say *Yea.* If a child who pulls a **Y** forgets to say *Yea* and another child remembers, the child who says it gets the point.

Use the *D'Nealian® Handwriting Big Book* to preview the page.

Teach (page 159)

Have children:

- identify the capital letter **Y;**
- find Yoshio at the starting arrow;
- finger trace the path from Yoshio to the yard and from **2** to the other yard while you say the following mnemonic sentence:

  Yoshio slides into his yard.
  Then, Yolanda slides into her yard.
- air trace the letter **Y.**

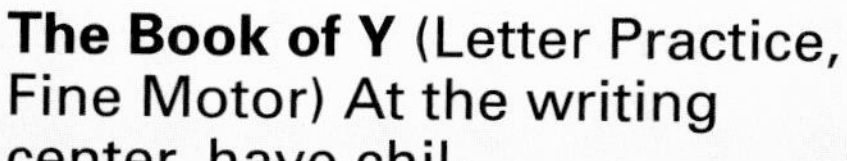

Time to Grow

The Book of Y (Letter Practice, Fine Motor) At the writing center, have children write capital **Y** on large pieces of unlined paper. Give them construction paper, crayons, colorful wrapping paper, and glue, and invite them to make a cover for their **Y** pages. Help them staple their covers.

Yawn for Yoshio (Auditory, Phonics) Tell children Yoshio is tired after practicing baseball and that they can help him sleep by yawning, as yawns are catching. Tell them to yawn each time they hear a word that begins with the same sound as Yoshio. Say words such as *bird, yard, yellow, tree, nest, yoyo, apple, yell, insect, young,* and *yak.*

Phonics Corner

The sentence used to help children form the letter **Y,**

Yoshio slides into his **yard.**
Then, **Yolanda** slides into her **yard.**

may also be used to work on sound-letter correspondence. Repeat the sentence and call on volunteers to tell you the words they hear that begin with /y/.

Teach (page 160)

Call attention to the pictures at the top of the page, and read the directions. Have children:

- identify the letters **Y** and **R** on the baseball shirts;
- find and color each shirt marked **Y** yellow and each shirt marked **R** red;
- tell the number of shirts colored red and yellow.

Write a capital **Y** on the chalkboard. Ask a volunteer to write a lower-case **y.** Compare them.

Call attention to the lower half of the page. Have children:

- finger trace the boxed letter **Y** as you read aloud the letter description;
- pencil trace the gray letters;
- write the letter **Y** using the starting dots;
- trace the name *Yankees.*

Follow Up

Self-Evaluation Have children check their own work by asking themselves:

- Do my **Y's** start at the dot?
- Do my **Y's** slant the same way?

Additional Resources

Manuscript Alpha Touch letter **Y**
D'Nealian® Handwriting Big Book letter **Y**

Color Y yellow
Color R red

Yankees
Yankees

160 Writing Y
Children color the uniforms marked **Y** yellow and those marked **R** red. They trace and write the letter **Y** and then trace the name **Yankees.**

Letter Description

Top start; slant down right halfway. Another top start to the right; slant down left, and touch on the way.

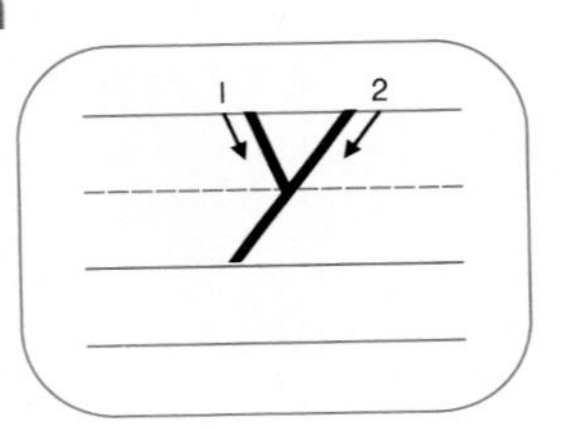

ACTIVITY BANK

Moving Write Along

Tissue Paper Letters (Fine Motor, Eye-Hand Coordination) Have 5" x 7" rectangles of colored tissue paper available to the children. Have them write capital letter **Y** on the paper. Help them carefully tear around the letter and use white glue to put the letter on colorful construction paper, gently smoothing it out.

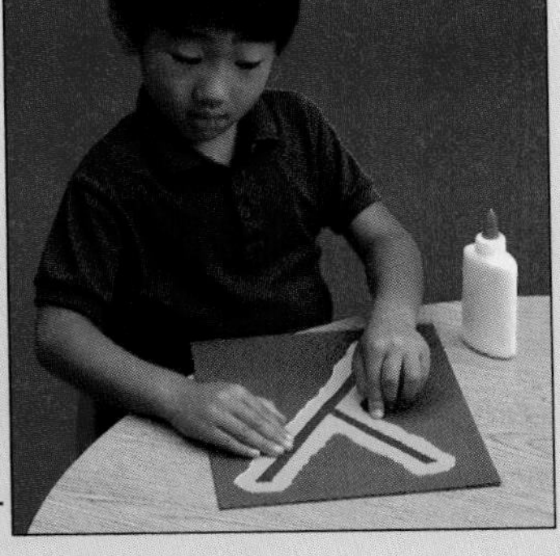

Marly Glaw
Shreiner School and Academy
Marietta, GA

My Book of Colors (Letter Practice, Fine Motor) Make a book of colors. Use capital letters learned so far to write a color name at the top of each page. Possibilities include **Red, Green, Blue,** and **Yellow.** Have children trace the name using a marker of the same color, and cut out and paste pictures containing that color below each word.

Capital Baseball (Letter Practice, Visual) Divide the class into two teams and draw a baseball diamond on the floor, numbering each base. Place cards with the 26 lower-case letters facedown. Children draw a card and move to a base by writing on the board the capital letter that matches the lower-case letter on the card.

Practice

E E E
F F F
Z Z Z
V V V

Eggs
Eggs

Zipper
Zipper

Practice 161

Children trace and write the letters **E, F, Z,** and **V** and then trace the nicknames **Eggs** and **Zipper.**

Objectives

Practices writing the capital letters **E, F, Z,** and **V**. Traces the nicknames *Eggs* and *Zipper.*

Prepare

Talk to the children about nicknames. Discuss the fact that nicknames are often shortened forms of a given name, as when Beth Claire is called B. C. Observe that in some cultures, letters are sometimes added to loved one's names to make them more endearing, as when Carlos is called Carlito. Ask for volunteers to tell about their nicknames or the nicknames of family members or friends. Ask volunteers to write their nicknames on the chalkboard.

Teach (page 161)

Have children:

- identify the capital letters **E, F, Z,** and **V;**
- pencil trace the gray letters;
- write each letter using the starting dots;
- trace the names *Eggs* and *Zipper;*
- tell why they think these people have these nicknames.

Follow Up

Self-Evaluation Have children check their own work by asking themselves:

- Do my **E's** and **F's** have bars across the middle?
- Do all my letters slant the same way?

Additional Resources

Manuscript Alpha Touch letters **E, F, Z,** and **V**
D'Nealian® Handwriting Big Book letters **E, F, Z,** and **V**

ACTIVITY BANK

Collage Egg (Fine Motor, Letter Practice) Have children cut small squares, triangles, and circles out of construction paper in a variety of colors. Have children practice writing **E, F, Z,** and **V** on these shapes. Give them a sheet of heavy paper shaped like an egg. Then have them make collages by pasting the various shapes onto the egg.

Before and After (Letter Recognition, Letter Practice) Have children play "Before and After." Invite a volunteer to come to the board and write his or her name. The next child to come to the board would be one whose name begins with the last letter of the previous name. So, if Zippe**r** wrote her name, **R**andy could come up and write his. If no one has a name beginning with the last letter, call another volunteer.

Pass the Slate (Letter Practice, Small Groups) Have children practice writing **E, F, Z** and **V** on slates. Tell them to write their best letters and then pass the slate to their partner. The partner circles the letter that he or she thinks is best and returns it. Children then erase their slates and write another letter.

Objectives

Practices writing the capital letters **W, X,** and **Y.** Traces the names *Willa X.* and *Yetta X.*

Prepare

Play "Exercise with **X**" with children. Ask them to show you how they would form an **X** with their bodies while standing. Ask them to also form a **Y,** a **T,** an **M,** and an **A.** Use the pictures below to help them get the idea. Now play rousing music and call out letters for them to imitate. If you think they are ready, ask volunteers to spell out words such as *ax, tax, may, mat,* and *yam.*

Teach (page 162)

Have children:

- identify the capital letters **W, X,** and **Y;**
- pencil trace the gray letters;
- write each letter using the starting dots;
- trace the names *Willa X.* and *Yetta X.*

Follow Up

Self-Evaluation Have children check their own work by asking themselves:

- Do all my letters start at the dot?
- Do all my letters sit nicely on the bottom line?

Additional Resources

Manuscript Alpha Touch letters **W, X,** and **Y**
D'Nealian® Handwriting Big Book letters **W, X,** and **Y**

ACTIVITY BANK

Dot-to-Dot (Fine Motor, Letter Practice) Make several different dot-to-dot worksheets using the capital letters **L, V, W,** and **Z.** Include a writing line at the bottom. Children connect the dots, write the letter, and then color each picture.

A New Look (Critical Thinking, Gross Motor) Write a large capital **W, X,** and **Y** on the chalkboard. Demonstrate how to turn one of the letters into a picture (the **Y** into a tree, for instance). Call on volunteers to come up and use colored chalk to turn the remaining letters into pictures.

Marly Glaw
Shreiner School and Academy
Marietta, GA

Special Needs (Visual Deficits) Tactile stimulation helps children with a visual deficit. Pair children and ask them to play "Palm Reading" at the chalkboard. One child closes his or her eyes while the other child traces a letter on the partner's palm. The child tries to identify, air trace, and write the letter on the board. Partners check the written letter for accuracy and then reverse roles. The game continues in this manner.

blocks blocks blocks

Circle each **a**.

clay

crayon

aquarium

Print Awareness **163**

Children compare the same letters in different type styles. They circle the **a** in three different words.

Objectives

Demonstrates print awareness.
Finds and circles different **a's.**

Prepare

Have children bring their favorite books from home or choose books from the classroom library. Ask them to break up into groups of four and compare their books. Have them compare one specific letter in each book. Ask them to report to the class as to whether their letters looked exactly alike or were different in some way.

Teach (page 163)

Have children:

- identify the letters **b, l, o, c,** and **k;**
- listen as you read the word *block;*
- listen as you read the words *clay, crayon,* and *aquarium;*
- circle each **a** in the three words;
- tell how many **a's** they have circled (*four*).

Follow Up

Self-Evaluation Have children check their own work by asking themselves:

- Did I circle an **a** in each word?
- Did I circle four **a's?**

Additional Resources

Manuscript Alpha Touch capital and lower-case letters

D'Nealian® Handwriting Big Book capital and lower-case letters

ACTIVITY BANK

Schoolhouse Stories (Letter Practice, Visual) Make a book by cutting two schoolhouses from red paper. Staple writing paper cut into quarters between the two schoolhouses. On the front write **Classroom Words.** Prior to this, label items in the classroom. Students walk around the room and copy the labels. They draw a picture of each so they can read it at home.

Sandy Rissler
Reelsville Elementary School
Reelsville, IN

Greetings (Print Awareness, Letter Practice) Give children a pile of old greeting and thank-you cards. Ask them to find a particular lower-case or capital letter in three different cards and circle that letter. Have them compare the type in each. Ask them to write that letter on the back of one of the cards using D'Nealian® Handwriting. Continue with other letters.

Letter Match (Print Awareness, Kinesthetic) Prepare sets of letter cards in different kinds of type. Divide the cards equally among the children. Tell children they must compare their cards in order to find a matching pair. Ask children to show their matches to the rest of the class.

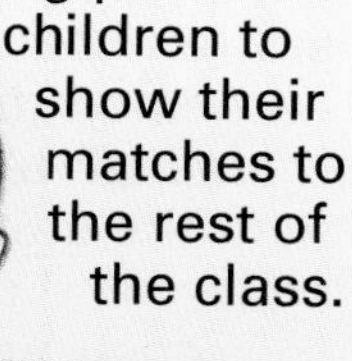

Objectives

Demonstrates print awareness.
Finds and circles different **i's.**

Prepare

Have children cut out large letters from print ads, posters, and so on, and paste them to pieces of posterboard, one per board. Keep this pile near the chalkboard. Hold up one of the letters and ask children to identify it. Next, ask if any children have this letter in their name. Have a volunteer come to the board and write this letter using D'Nealian® Handwriting.

Teach (page 164)

Have children:

- identify the letters **T, e, d, d,** and **y;**
- listen as you read the name *Teddy;*
- listen as you read the names *Ali, Slinkie,* and *Rip;*
- circle each **i** in the three names;
- tell how many **i's** they have circled (*four*).

Follow Up

Self-Evaluation Have children check their own work by asking themselves:

- Did I circle an **i** in each word?
- Did I circle four **i's?**

Additional Resources

Manuscript Alpha Touch capital and lower-case letters

D'Nealian® Handwriting Big Book capital and lower-case letters

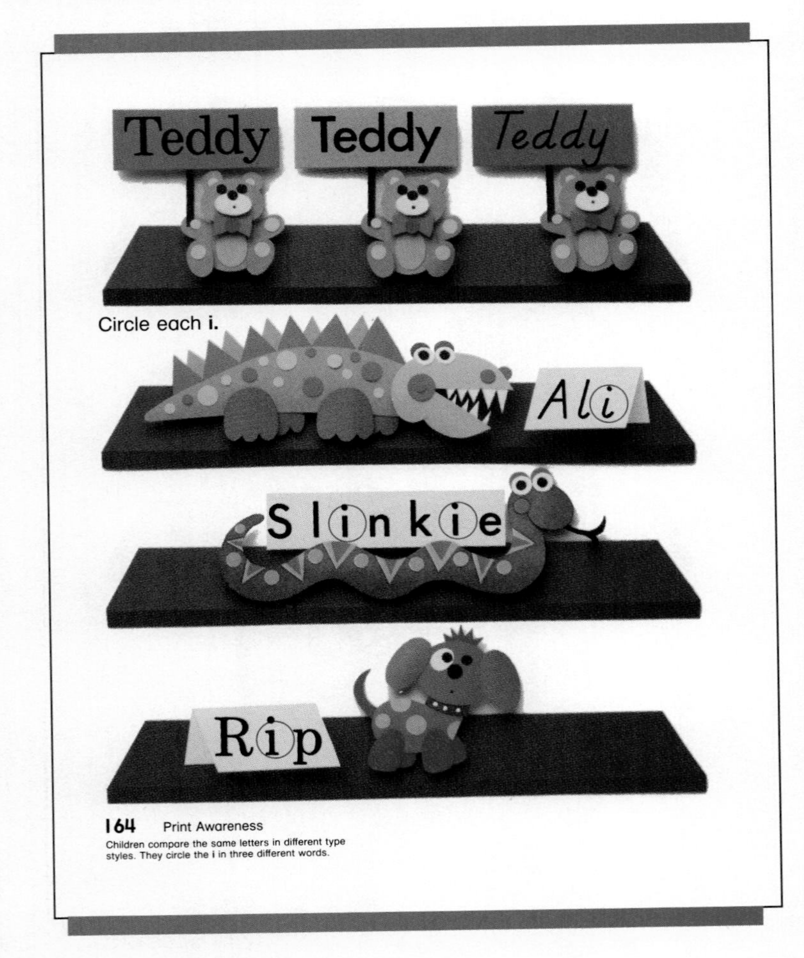

ACTIVITY BANK

AKA Ted (Phonics, Letter Recognition) Have children look at page 164 of their books. Ask them to think of other names beginning with capital **T** they could call the stuffed bear. Write these new names on the chalkboard using D'Nealian letters. Do the same with the stuffed rhinoceros, snake, and dog. Call on children to come to the board and circle particular letters in the names they have suggested.

Special Needs (Auditory Deficits) Play a visual game to help children who have trouble listening to explanations about differing print styles. Ask for the names of their pets. Type the pet names on a computer in three different type fonts, using the largest size possible. If you don't have a computer, use newspaper headlines containing the same names in different fonts. Paste these names onto cards and have children match the same three names.

Favorite Stories (Print Awareness, Oral Language) Ask children to bring in their favorite storybook, and tell why this is a favorite. Ask children if there is a capital **T** in their title, and if so, have them compare the type. Let them suggest other letters to compare.

A B C D E F G H I J K L M

Review 165

Children write the capital letters.

Objective

Writes the capital alphabet from **A** through **M**.

Prepare

Bring to class the book *Easy Costumes You Don't Have to Sew* by Goldie Taub Chernoff and invite children to make their own hats. (See, particularly, pages 34 through 38.) Supply paper, buttons, braid, glitter, feathers, yarn, and so on. When children have finished making their hats, ask them to write their names on them. One at a time, have children:

- place hats on a large table;
- pick up the hat with a distinguishing feature;
- pick up the hat with particular letters on it;
- pick up the hat that is a particular color.

Continue in this way until all hats have been picked up. Then let children claim their own hats.

Teach (page 165)

Have children:

- take turns reading the capital letters aloud;
- write each capital letter from **A** through **M**.

Follow Up

Self-Evaluation Have children check their own work by asking themselves:

- Do all my letters start at the dot?
- Did I write a capital letter on each line?

Additional Resources

Manuscript Alpha Touch letters **A** through **M**
D'Nealian® Handwriting Big Book letters **A** through **M**

ACTIVITY BANK

A to M Order (Alphabetical Order, Kinesthetic) Distribute large cards containing capital **A** through **M** to thirteen children. Have them arrange themselves in alphabetical order at the front of the room. Be sure classmates agree that the letters are in alphabetical order.

It's a Match! (Letter Recognition, Critical Thinking) Make a set of 26 cards that include capital and lower-case D'Nealian letters from **a/A** through **m/M.** Shuffle them and place them facedown on the floor. Children turn over two cards, trying to make a match. If they do, they keep the pair. If they do not, the cards are turned facedown again, and the next player takes a turn.

Chalk It Up (Letter Practice, Kinesthetic) Write the capital letters **A** through **M** on the chalkboard with writing lines next to each one. Print the same letters in lowercase on index cards. Pass out a card to thirteen children, who write on the lines, in turn, the capital letter corresponding to the lowercase letter he or she is holding.

Objective
Writes the capital alphabet from **N** through **Z**.

Prepare
Have children write a capital letter from **N** through **Z** on a piece of heavy paper. Ask thirteen children to come to the front of the room with their letters **N** through **Z**. Have these children:
- line up in alphabetical order;
- step forward if they are holding **N** and **O** and say, *Read me.* (Help children read the word *NO.*)
- step forward again, this time if they are holding **N, O,** and **T,** and again say, *Read me.* (Help children read the word *NOT.*)

Then let seated children come up and take the letter cards and repeat the activity. This time you may want to rearrange them so they spell *TOP* or *STOP.*

Teach (page 166)
Have children:
- take turns reading the capital letters on the page aloud;
- write each capital letter from **N** through **Z.**

Follow Up
Self-Evaluation Have children check their own work by asking themselves:
- Do all my letters start at the dot?
- Did I write a capital letter on each line?

Additional Resources
Manuscript Alpha Touch letters **N** through **Z**
D'Nealian® Handwriting Big Book letters **N** through **Z**

N O
P Q R
S T U
V W X
Y Z

166 Review
Children write the capital letters.

ACTIVITY BANK

My Name Is Alice (Alphabetical Order, Gifted) Have children play "A—My Name Is Alice," an alphabet game in which they must name four things that begin with a particular capital and lower-case letter. Examples might be:

A—My name is Alice, and my husband's name is Al. We come from Alabama, and we sell apricots.

B—My name is Bob, and my wife's name is Betty. We come from Baltimore, and we sell banjos.

Encourage children to help one another when playing.

What's My Name? (Phonics, Letter Practice) Bring to class large, colorful pictures of various literary or television characters that children would easily recognize. Have children volunteer the names of the characters, then let them write the letter the characters' names begin with on the overhead projector. For example, children would write **J** after recognizing Jack and Jill.

Fran Moore
Lake Forest Country Day School
Lake Forest, IL

Alphagame (Auditory Letter Practice) Have children line up in two rows. One row writes capital letters and one writes lower-case letters. Call out letters and have pairs race to the chalkboard and neatly write their respective letters. The first row finished wins.

Objective
Reviews capital and lower-case letters by tracing sentences.

Prepare
One by one, have each child come to the chalkboard and write his or her first name. Then ask all children to brainstorm an action word that would be most appropriate for this child. An example might be: *Mary dances.* You write the action word next to the child's name and have the child trace the action word you have written. If possible, ask the child to demonstrate the sentence for the class.

Teach (page 167)
Have children:
- listen as you read each sentence;
- trace the letters.

Follow Up
Self-Evaluation Have children check their own work by asking themselves:
- Did I trace all the words?

Additional Resources
Manuscript Alpha Touch capital and lower-case letters

D'Nealian® Handwriting Big Book capital and lower-case letters

ACTIVITY BANK

Lights, Camera, Action (Kinesthetic, Language Arts) Talk about action words, giving examples. Ask children to take turns coming to the front of the room and acting out an action word. Write a sentence on the chalkboard about the action, using the child's name, such as *Juan skates* or *Abby golfs.* Children can then trace their own sentences.

Action Animals (Letter Practice, Creative) As an ongoing project, make an alphabet book with children, focusing on things animals do. Start by writing on the chalkboard: *Ants work.* Have children come up and trace this sentence. Ask them to suggest a sentence for bats, such as *Bats fly.* Duplicate these sentences when you have covered **A** through **Z** (make up one for **X**). Have children draw pictures beneath each sentence. Help them make covers.

How's the Weather? (Letter Practice, Science) Talk about weather words: *sunny, rainy, cloudy, cold, warm,* and so on. Make a weather report each day and write a simple sentence on the chalkboard. Children may draw a picture and write sentences based on your weather report.

Index

Dear Family,

Your child, like all of us, must learn to write legibly—clearly enough for another person to read what has been written. We will be teaching this important basic skill in our classroom this year with the D'Nealian® Handwriting Program. The D'Nealian system was developed in the late 1960s by an experienced teacher, Donald Neal Thurber, and its title was coined from his name.

One of the hallmarks of the D'Nealian philosophy of handwriting is respect for individuality: if it is readable, it is acceptable, as long as size, form, slant, and spacing are consistent.

The D'Nealian® Handwriting Program introduces letters in groups that are formed by similar writing strokes. Children immediately write words that are presented in a meaningful context. This encourages children to write to communicate rather than to try to copy machine-made models of letters.

The D'Nealian method has been successfully used for many years; thousands of enthusiastic teachers report a dramatic increase in children's ability to write legibly, especially as they begin cursive handwriting.

Please join us in helping your child learn another important skill for success in school and beyond.

Sincerely,

Estimada familia:

Su hijo o hija, como todos nosotros, tiene que aprender a escribir legiblemente—lo suficientemente claro para que otra persona pueda leer lo que ha sido escrito. Este año escolar enseñaremos en nuestra clase esta importante destreza de base utilizando el Programa de Escritura D'Nealian®. El sistema D'Nealian fue creado en los últimos años de la década de 1960 por un maestro de experiencia, Donald Neal Thurber, y el nombre del sistema fue acuñado a partir de su nombre.

Una de las constantes de la filosofía de la escritura D'Nealian es el respeto a la individualidad: tomamos en cuenta si lo escrito se puede leer, y si es aceptable siempre y cuando el tamaño, la forma, la inclinación y el espacio sean uniformes.

El Programa de Escritura D'Nealian® introduce las letras por grupos que se forman por medio de similares trazados de escritura. Si tienen confianza en las letras que han aprendido previamente, los niños y niñas inmediatamente escriben palabras que se les presentan en contextos que tienen sentido. Esto hace que los niños y niñas deseen escribir para comunicar en vez de solamente escribir tratando de copiar modelos de letras hechos a máquina.

El método D'Nealian ha sido utilizado con éxito durante muchos años; millares de entusiásticos maestros relatan un incremento dramático en cuanto a la habilidad de sus estudiantes para escribir legiblemente, especialmente cuando comienzan la escritura cursiva.

Por favor, únanse a nosotros en ayudar a su niño o niña a aprender otra destreza importante para su éxito en la escuela y la vida.

Atentamente,

Dear Family,

Your child is now learning a number of skills needed for good handwriting. Our class will soon start to write numbers, using the D'Nealian® Handwriting Program.

Meanwhile, you can help your child achieve success in school. You and your child can do some enjoyable activities that will help develop the discrimination and coordination necessary for success, not only in handwriting but in other subjects as well.

Make up games using common household items such as buttons, bottle caps, jar lids, coins, magnets, and small toys. Your child can count the items and tell which are alike and which are different. Let your child cut out pictures from newspapers, magazines, and catalogs and group similar ones. Use words like *top, middle, bottom, up, down, over,* and *under* when you ask your child to get something for you or to put something away. Encourage your child to talk about what goes on in class.

Thank you for your help. You will be receiving another letter when the class starts learning to write numbers.

Sincerely,

Estimada familia:

Su hijo (hija) está aprendiendo varias técnicas necesarias para escribir bien. Muy pronto los niños y niñas van a aprender a escribir números usando el Programa de Escritura D'Nealian®.

Mientras tanto, ustedes pueden ayudarlo a lograr el éxito deseado en la escuela. Pueden realizar actividades entretenidas que le permitirán a su hijo (hija) desarrollar la diferenciación y la coordinación necesarias para la labor escolar.

Organicen actividades usando diversos artículos tales como botones, tapas, monedas, imánes y pequeños juguetes. Su hijo (hija) puede contar los artículos, decir cuáles son iguales y cuáles son diferentes. Permítanle que recorte y agrupe ilustraciones de periódicos, revistas y catálogos. Usen palabras como sobre, abajo, entre, arriba, abajo, sobre y debajo cuando le pidan que les dé o les guarde algo. Pídanle a su hijo (hija) que les cuente lo que está haciendo en la escuela.

Les agradecemos su cooperación. Recibirán otra carta cuando los niños y niñas empiecen a escribir números.

Atentamente,

Dear Family,

Your child is now learning to write numbers: first **1**, then **2** and **3**, **4** and **5, 6** and **7, 8** and **9,** and finally **10,** using the D'Nealian® Handwriting method. Writing numbers is, in part, a preparation for learning to write manuscript letters, the next step in the program.

During this period, you can help make your child more conscious of numbers and their uses. Draw attention to a number on a license plate or sign and let your child find a matching number on another license plate or sign. Make sure your child knows and can dial your phone number. Each day put a different number of buttons, marbles, or other small objects in a jar or other container. Your child can take the objects out and count them or arrange the objects in sets of two, three, or four and tell how many sets there are. Number ten sheets of paper from **1** to **10.** From magazines, newspapers, and catalogs, let your child cut out pictures of, say, one car, two dogs, three cats, and so on up to ten, and paste or tape each set of pictures on the appropriate page.

Children enjoy counting. Giving your child opportunities to identify numbers and count objects at home will reinforce school learning. Thank you for your cooperation and interest in helping your child learn to write.

Sincerely,

Estimada familia:

Su hijo (hija) está aprendiendo a escribir los números usando el método de Escritura D'Nealian®. Los niños y niñas comienzan con 1, después siguen con 2 y 3, 4 y 5, 6 y 7, 8 y 9, y finalmente 10. Escribir los números es parte de la preparación para aprender a escribir cartas a mano, que es el siguiente paso del programa.

Durante este período, ustedes pueden ayudar a que su hijo (hija) esté más consciente de los números y de sus usos. Traten de que se fije en el número de alguna placa de carro, o en una señal, y que más tarde busque el mismo número en otra placa u otra señal. Asegúrense de que su hijo (hija) sepa marcar su número de teléfono. Todos los días, coloquen en un recipiente una cantidad diferente de botones, canicas u otros objectos. Su hijo (hija) puede colocarlos en grupos de dos, tres o cuatro, y decir cuántos grupos hay. Numeren diez hojas del 1 al 10. Pídanle a su hijo (hija) que recorte ilustraciones de revistas, periódicos y catálogos. Estos recortes pueden ser de un carro, dos perros, tres gatos y así sucesivamente, hasta llegar a diez. Luego díganle que pegue cada grupo de figuras en la página correspondiente.

A los niños les gusta mucho contar. Al ofrecerle a su hijo (hija) la oportunidad de contar objetos en su casa reforzarán lo que ha aprendido en la escuela. Les agradecemos su cooperación e interés en ayudar a su hijo (hija) a aprender a escribir.

Atentamente,

Dear Family,

Your child is now learning to form letters, using the D'Nealian® Handwriting method. The class is learning manuscript handwriting (printing) in which letters are formed separately. The letters of the D'Nealian® Handwriting manuscript alphabet are probably somewhat different from those you learned to print. The letters slant, and some have ending strokes. The ending strokes make it easy to join letters when children later learn cursive handwriting.

The class will first learn lower-case (small) letters. Then the class will learn to form the upper-case (capital) letters. Letters are taught in groups of letters that are formed with similar writing strokes. (Alphabetical order comes later.) By tracing and writing letters and tracing words, your child will get a feel for consistent form, size, slant, and spacing—all important in producing readable handwriting.

Your child may want to try writing letters and words at home. Please keep pencils and lined paper on hand as practice materials for your child.

Thank you for your help. If you would like to learn more about the D'Nealian® Handwriting Program, feel free to get in touch with me.

Sincerely,

Estimada familia:

Su hijo (hija) está aprendiendo a formar letras usando el método de Escritura D'Nealian®. Los niños y niñas están aprendiendo a escribir con letra de molde, formando cada letra por separado. Las letras de molde del alfabeto del método de la Escritura D'Nealian son un poco diferentes a las que ustedes conocen. Son letras inclinadas y algunas tienen trazos finales. Estos trazos ayudan a unir las letras cuando los niños aprenden la escritura cursiva.

Los niños y niñas aprenderán primero las letras minúsculas y después las mayúsculas. Las letras se enseñan en grupos formados por letras que se escriben con trazos similares. (El orden alfabético se enseña más adelante.) Trazando y escribiendo letras, y trazando palabras, su hijo (hija) podrá captar la uniformidad en forma, tamaño, inclinación y espacio entre las letras. Todos estos son aspectos importantes cuando se trata de lograr una escritura legible.

Es posible que su hijo (hija) quiera tratar de escribir letras y palabras en su casa. Por favor facilítenle lápiz y papel rayado para que practique.

Les agradecemos su cooperación. Si necesitan más información sobre el Programa de Escritura D'Nealian®, les ruego que se comuniquen conmigo.

Atentamente,

Dear Family,

Your child is now learning to form manuscript capital, or upper-case, letters using the D'Nealian® Handwriting method. As with lower-case letters, capital letters are taught in groups of letters formed by similar writing strokes. Once again, tracing and writing the capital letters and tracing words that begin with capital letters will help give your child a feel for the consistency in form, size, slant, and spacing so important to readable handwriting.

Please continue to encourage your child to be conscious of letters. Play games of letter searches in books, newspapers, magazines, and catalogs, as well as on signs in stores and along the street. Draw attention to both capital and lower-case letters. Feature a letter of the day, such as **cC** or **gG,** and with your child find the letter in as many places as you can. Write a letter at the top of a sheet of paper and let your child find and cut out or draw a picture of something that begins with that letter: an apple for **a,** for example, or a dog for **d.** For capital letters your child can draw a picture of someone whose name begins with the letter.

Thank you for your help in making the learning of handwriting an enjoyable and successful experience for your child.

Sincerely,

Estimada familia:

Su hijo (hija) está ahora aprendiendo a formar letras mayúsculas a mano, usando el método de Escritura D'Nealian®. Al igual que las minúsculas, las mayúsculas se enseñan en grupos formados por letras que se escriben con trazos similares. Trazando y escribiendo mayúsculas y palabras que comienzan con estas letras, su hijo (hija) podrá captar la uniformidad en forma, tamaño, inclinación y espacio entre las letras. Todos éstos son aspectos muy importantes para lograr una escritura legible.

Les rogamos que continúen pidiendo a su hijo (hija) que preste atención a las letras. Jueguen buscando, letras en libros, periódicos, revistas y catálogos, así también como en carteles de tiendas y en la calle. Traten de que su hijo (hija) se fije tanto en las mayúsculas como en las minúsculas. Elijan una letra por día, por ejemplo la c C o la g G, y ayúdenle a encontrar esa letra en tantos lugares como pueda. Escriban una letra en la parte superior de una hoja y pídanle a su hijo (hija) que busque y recorte una figura o que haga un dibujo de algo que comienza con esa letra. Puede ser un gato para la g o un perro para la p. Para las mayúsculas, su hijo (hija) puede hacer un dibujo de alguien cuyo nombre comience con esa letra.

Les agradecemos por ayudarnos a hacer del aprendizaje de la escritura una experiencia amena y exitosa para su hijo (hija).

Atentamente,

nombre

ardilla

autobús

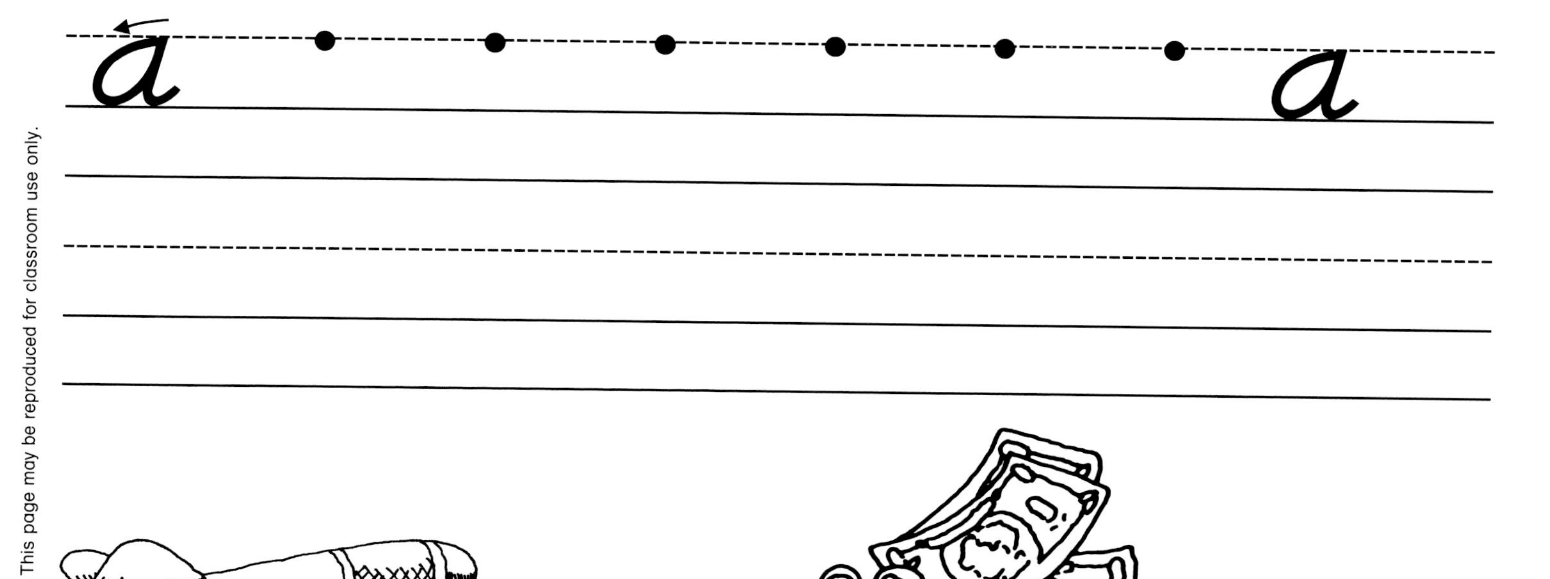

a a

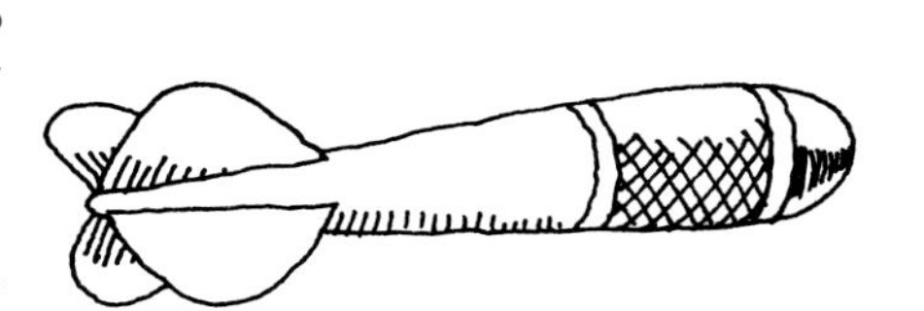

dardo

dinero

d d

nombre

oveja

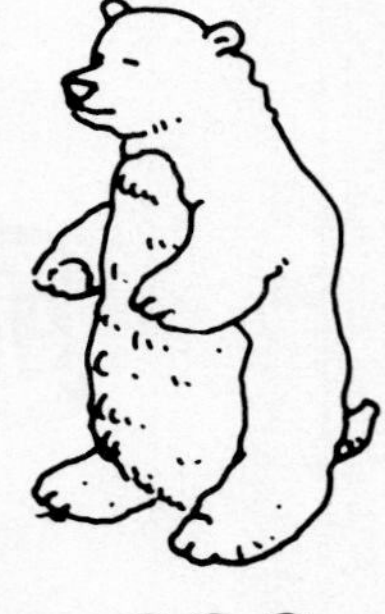

oso

o

gato

globo

g g

nombre

caballo

casa

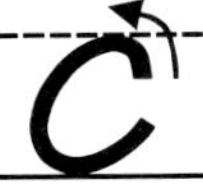

c • • • • • • • c

estatua

estrella

e • • • • • • • e

nombre

silbato

sombrero

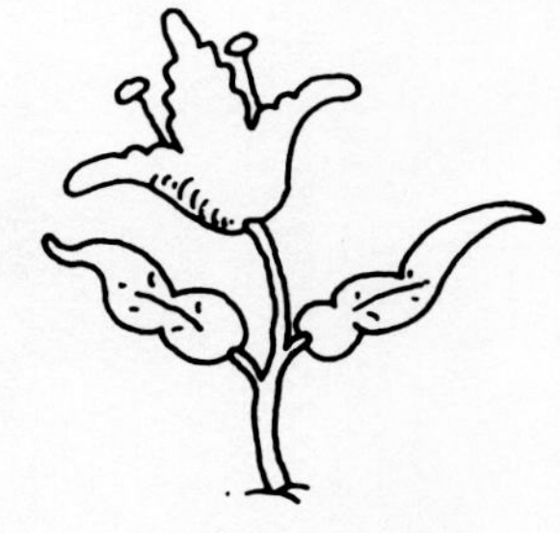

flor

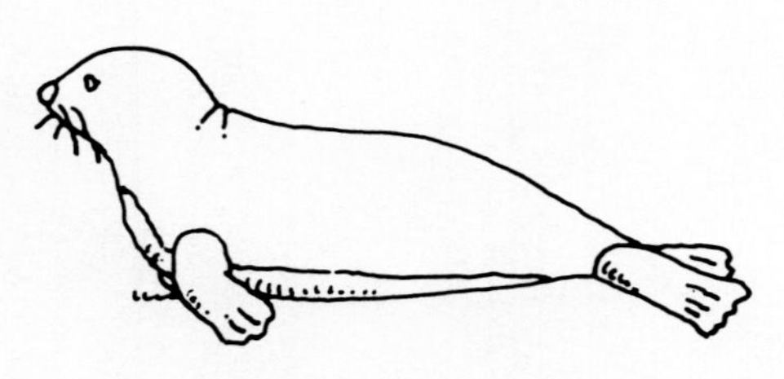

foca

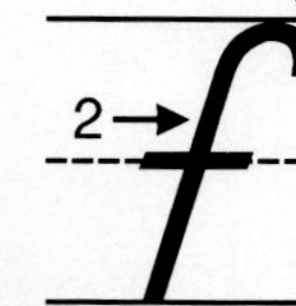

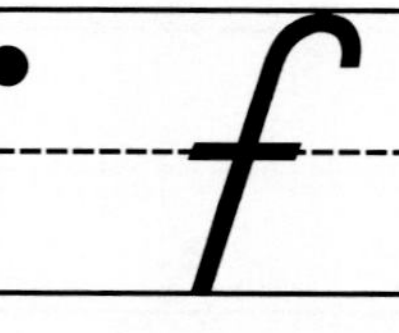

nombre

bañera

bebé

b b

lápiz

limón

l l

nombre

llama

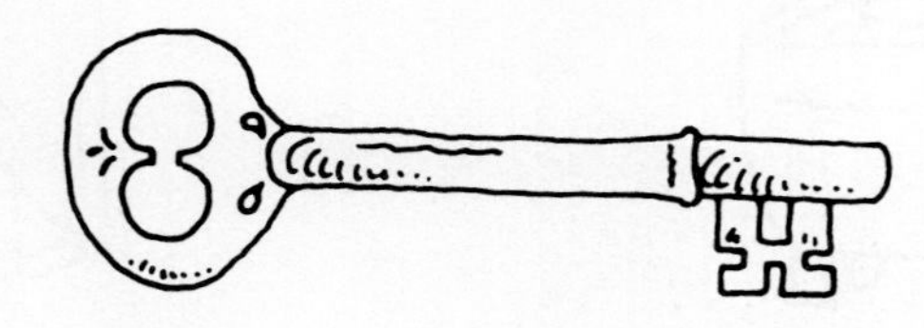

llave

ll

ll

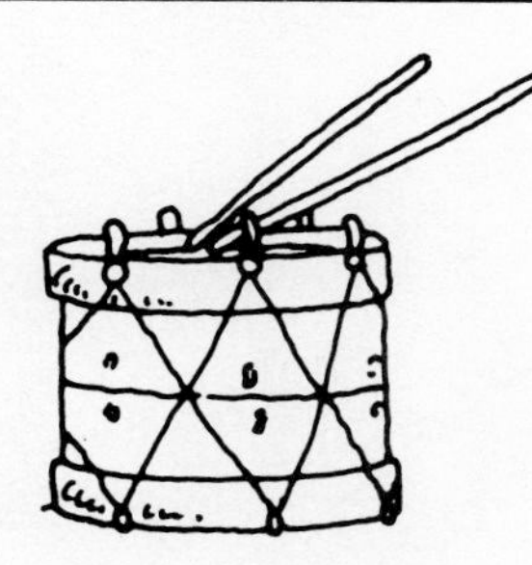

tambor

toro

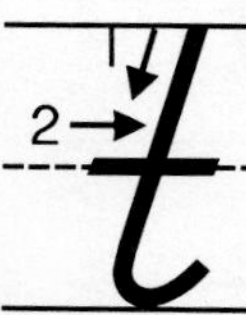

t

nombre

hoja

huevo

h h

chaqueta

chimpancé

ch ch

nombre

kiosko

koala

k k

isla

iguana

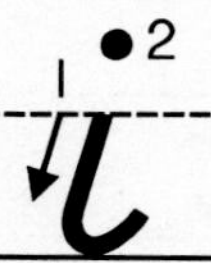

i

nombre

uvas

uno

u u

wafle

walabi

w w

nombre

yogurt

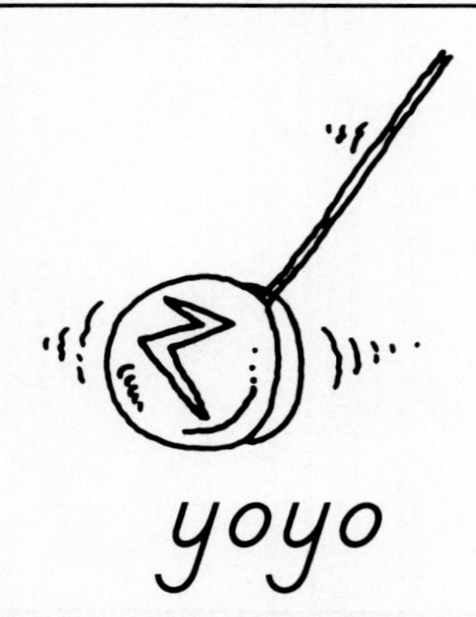

yoyo

y y

jabón

juguetes

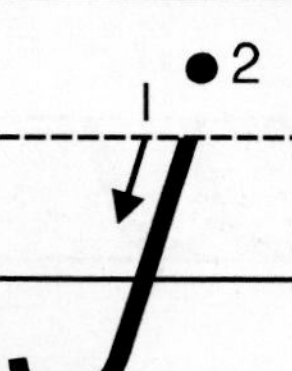

j

nombre

rana

rosa

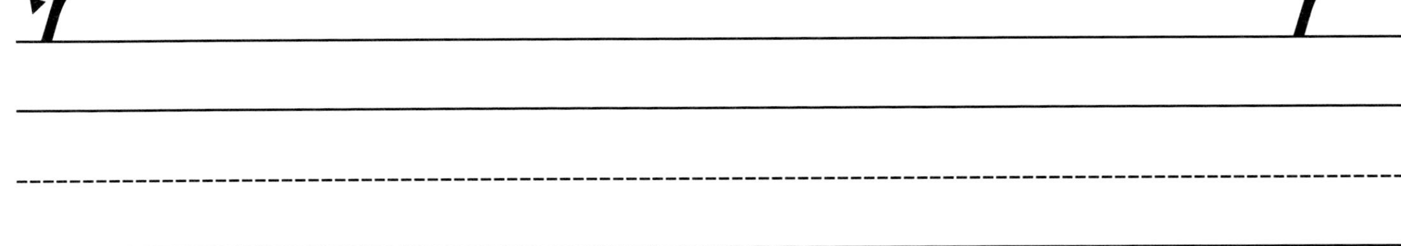

burro

jarro

rr rr

nombre

nube

nave

n • • • • • • n

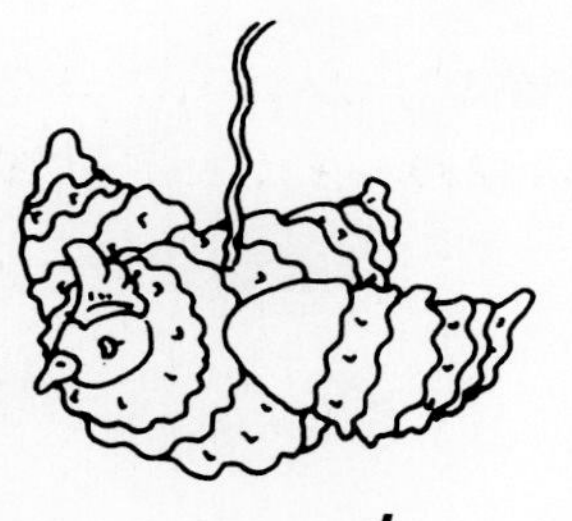

piñata

niña

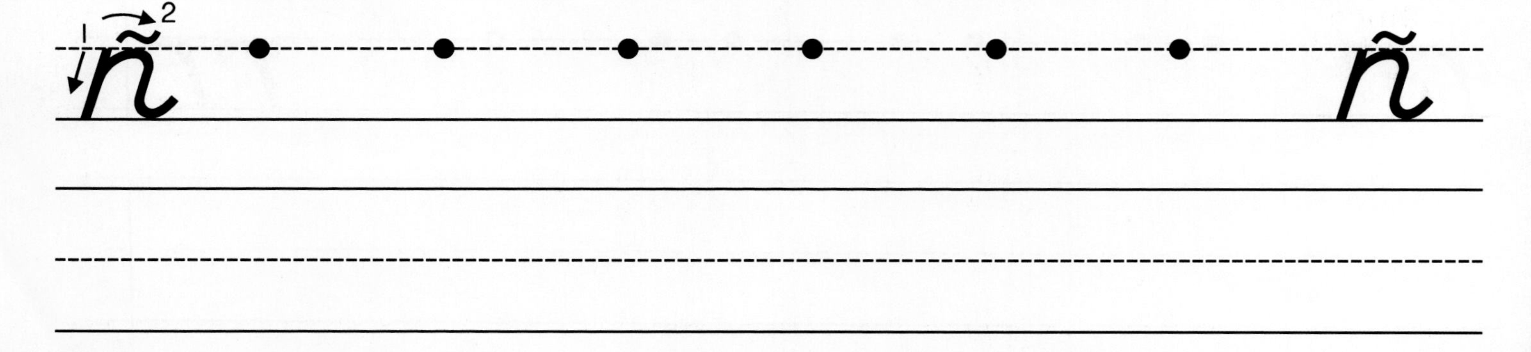

ñ • • • • • • ñ

nombre

maleta

mesa

perro

pato

nombre

queso

equipo

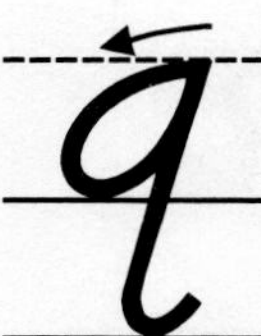

q

ventana

vaso

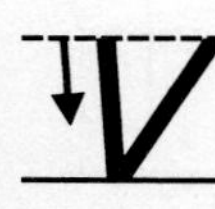

v

nombre

xilófono

boxeador

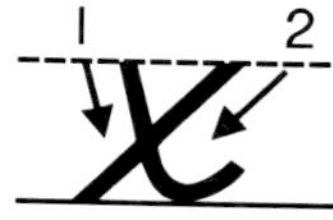

zapato

zanahoria

Z Z

nombre

0 1 2 3 4 5 6 7 8 9 10

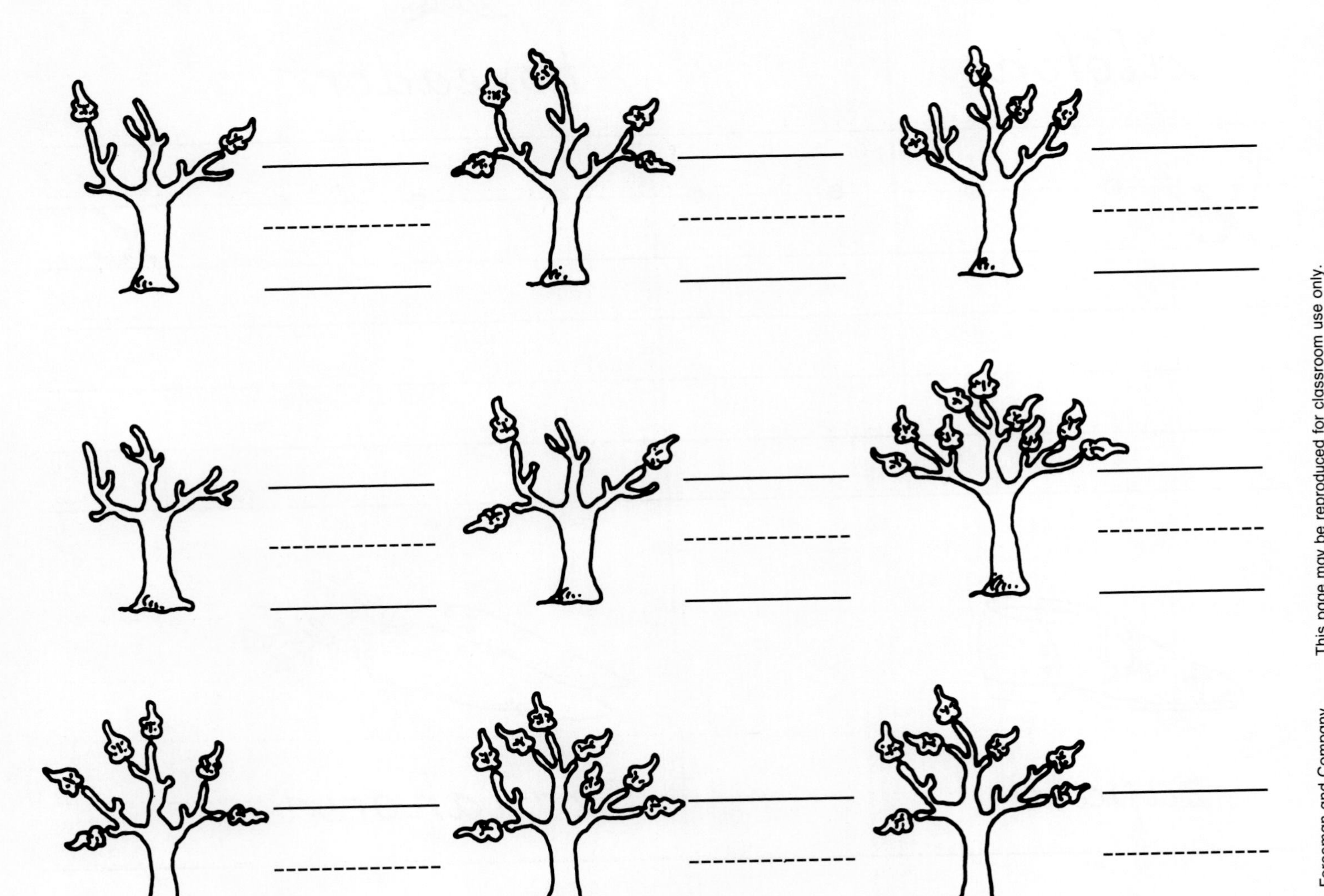

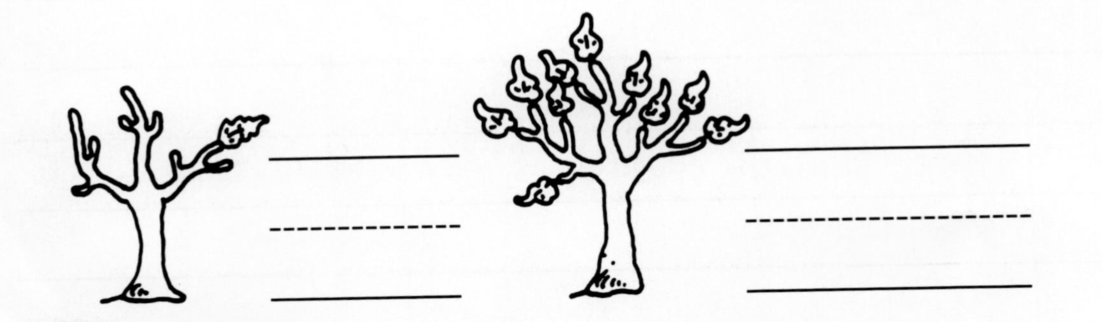

Index